Violent Death

ROUTLEDGE PSYCHOSOCIAL STRESS SERIES
Charles R. Figley, Ph.D., Series Editor

1. *Stress Disorders among Vietnam Veterans,* Edited by Charles R. Figley, Ph.D.
2. *Stress and the Family Vol. 1: Coping with Normative Transitions,* Edited by Hamilton I. McCubbin, Ph.D. and Charles R. Figley, Ph.D.
3. *Stress and the Family Vol. 2: Coping with Catastrophe,* Edited by Charles R. Figley, Ph.D., and Hamilton I. McCubbin, Ph.D.
4. *Trauma and Its Wake: The Study and Treatment of Post-Traumatic Stress Disorder,* Edited by Charles R. Figley, Ph.D.
5. *Post-Traumatic Stress Disorder and the War Veteran Patient,* Edited by William E. Kelly, M.D.
6. *The Crime Victim's Book, Second Edition,* By Morton Bard, Ph.D., and Dawn Sangrey.
7. *Stress and Coping in Time of War: Generalizations from the Israeli Experience,* Edited by Norman A. Milgram, Ph.D.
8. *Trauma and Its Wake Vol. 2: Traumatic Stress Theory, Research, and Intervention,* Edited by Charles R. Figley, Ph.D.
9. *Stress and Addiction,* Edited by Edward Gottheil, M.D., Ph.D., Keith A. Druley, Ph.D., Steven Pashko, Ph.D., and Stephen P. Weinsteinn, Ph.D.
10. *Vietnam: A Casebook,* by Jacob D. Lindy, M.D., in collaboration with Bonnie L. Green, Ph.D., Mary C. Grace, M.Ed., M.S., John A. MacLeod, M.D., and Louis Spitz, M.D.
11. *Post-Traumatic Therapy and Victims of Violence,* Edited by Frank M. Ochberg, M.D.
12. *Mental Health Response to Mass Emergencies:* Theory and Practice, Edited by Mary Lystad, Ph.D.
13. *Treating Stress in Families,* Edited by Charles R. Figley, Ph.D.
14. *Trauma, Transformation, and Healing: An Integrative Approach to Theory, Research, and Post-Traumatic Therapy,* By John P. Wilson, Ph.D.
15. *Systemic Treatment of Incest: A Therapeutic Handbook,* By Terry Trepper, Ph.D., and Mary Jo Barrett, M.S.W.
16. *The Crisis of Competence: Transitional Stress and the Displaced Worker,* Edited by Carl A. Maida, Ph.D., Norma S. Gordon, M.A., and Norman L. Farberow, Ph.D.
17. *Stress Management: An Integrated Approach to Therapy,* by Dorothy H. G. Cotton, Ph.D.
18. *Trauma and the Vietnam War Generation: Report of the Findings from the National Vietnam Veterans Readjustment Study,* By Richard A. Kulka, Ph.D., William E. Schlenger, Ph.D., John A. Fairbank, Ph.D., Richard L. Hough, Ph.D., Kathleen Jordan, Ph.D., Charles R. Marmar, M.D., Daniel S. Weiss, Ph.D., and David A. Grady, Psy.D.
19. *Strangers at Home: Vietnam Veterans Since the War,* Edited by Charles R. Figley, Ph.D., and Seymour Leventman, Ph.D.
20. *The National Vietnam Veterans Readjustment Study: Tables of Findings and Technical Appendices,* By Richard A. Kulka, Ph.D., Kathleen Jordan, Ph.D., Charles R. Marmar, M.D., and Daniel S. Weiss, Ph.D.
21. *Psychological Trauma and the Adult Survivor: Theory, Therapy, and Transformation,* By I. Lisa McCann, Ph.D., and Laurie Anne Pearlman, Ph.D.
22. *Coping with Infant or Fetal Loss: The Couple's Healing Process,* By Kathleen R. Gilbert, Ph.D., and Laura S. Smart, Ph.D.
23. *Compassion Fatigue: Coping with Secondary Traumatic Stress Disorder in Those Who Treat the Traumatized,* Edited by Charles R. Figley, Ph.D.
24. *Treating Compassion Fatigue,* Edited by Charles R. Figley, Ph.D.
25. *Handbook of Stress, Trauma and the Family,* Edited by Don R. Catherall, Ph.D.
26. *The Pain of Helping: Psychological Injury of Helping Professionals,* by Patrick J. Morrissette, Ph.D., RMFT, NCC, CCC.
27. *Disaster Mental Health Services: A Primer for Practitioners,* by Diane Myers, R.N., M.S.N, and David Wee, M.S.S.W.
28. *Empathy in the Treatment of Trauma and PTSD,* by John P. Wilson, Ph.D. and Rhiannon B. Thomas, Ph.D.
29. *Family Stressors: Interventions for Stress and Trauma,* Edited by Don. R. Catherall, Ph. D.
30. *Handbook of Women, Stress and Trauma,* Edited by Kathleen Kendall-Tackett, Ph.D.
31. *Mapping Trauma and Its Wake,* Edited by Charles R. Figley, Ph.D.
32. *The Posttraumatic Self: Restoring Meaning and Wholeness to Personality,* Edited by John P. Wilson, Ph.D.

Violent Death

Resilience and Intervention
Beyond the Crisis

Edited by Edward K. Rynearson

Routledge
Taylor & Francis Group
New York   London

Routledge is an imprint of the
Taylor & Francis Group, an informa business

Routledge
Taylor & Francis Group
270 Madison Avenue
New York, NY 10016

Routledge
Taylor & Francis Group
2 Park Square
Milton Park, Abingdon
Oxon OX14 4RN

© 2006 by Taylor & Francis Group, LLC
Routledge is an imprint of Taylor & Francis Group, an Informa business

Printed in the United States of America on acid-free paper
10 9 8 7 6 5 4 3 2 1

International Standard Book Number-10: 0-415-95323-5 (Hardcover)
International Standard Book Number-13: 978-0-415-95323-8 (Hardcover)

Visit the Taylor & Francis Web site at
http://www.taylorandfrancis.com

and the Routledge Web site at
http://www.routledgementalhealth.com

Contents

About the Editor   ix

Contributors   xi

Series Editor's Foreword   xxi

Introduction   xxiii

Editor's Note: Suggestions for Utilizing the Companion DVD   xxxiii

PART I   RESTORATIVE AND CLINICAL ESSENTIALS

Chapter 1   Clinical Theories of Loss and Grief   3
              Beverley Raphael, Garry Stevens, and, Julie Dunsmore

Chapter 2   Grief, Trauma, and Resilience   31
              George A. Bonanno

Chapter 3   Family Resilience After Violent Death   47
              Alison Salloum and Edward K. Rynearson

Chapter 4   Spiritual Essentials   65
              Janice Harris Lord

Chapter 5   Fragmented Stories: The Narrative Integration of
              Violent Loss   85
              Joseph M. Currier and Robert A. Neimeyer

Chapter 6   Meaning Making for Survivors of Violent Death   101
              Marilyn Peterson Armour

Chapter 7   Considering Medication Use in the Wake of Traumatic
              Experience: Neurobiology, Affect Dysregulation, and the
              Psychiatrist as a Witness Who May Also Prescribe   123
              Richard A. Chefetz

PART II   RESTORATIVE AND CLINICAL INTERVENTIONS

Chapter 8   Exorcising Ghosts: The Counting Method and
             Traumatic Death Imagery   145
             Frank M. Ochberg

Chapter 9   Treatment of Complicated Grief Following
             Violent Death   157
             Katherine Shear, Bonnie Gorscak, and Naomi Simon

Chapter 10   Evidence-Based Interventions for Parents Following
             Their Children's Violent Deaths   175
             Shirley A. Murphy

Chapter 11   Restorative Retelling After Violent Dying   195
             *Edward K. Rynearson, Fanny Correa, Jennifer Favell,
             Connie Saindon, and Holly Prigerson*

Chapter 12   Intervention Continuity in Posttraffic Fatality:
             From Notifying Families of the Loss to
             Establishing a Self-Help Group   217
             Ruth Malkinson and Yael Geron

Chapter 13   What about the Very Young Child?   233
             Sharon Gancarz Davies and Alison Salloum

Chapter 14   Treating Childhood Traumatic Grief   255
             Judith A. Cohen and Anthony P. Mannarino

Chapter 15   Restorative Retelling with Incarcerated Juveniles   275
             *Edward K. Rynearson, Jennifer Favell, Vicki Belluomini,
             Richard Gold, and Holly Prigerson*

PART III   COMMUNITY OUTREACH AND
              INTERVENTION AFTER DISASTER
              AND WARFARE

Chapter 16   Mass Violent Death and Military Communities:
             Domains of Response in Military Operations,
             Disaster, and Terrorism   295
             David M. Benedek and Robert J. Ursano

Chapter 17   Community Outreach Following a Terrorist Act:
              Violent Death and the Oklahoma City Experience   311
              James R. Allen, Phebe Tucker, and Betty Pfefferbaum

Chapter 18   Healing After September 11: Short-Term Group
              Intervention with 9/11 Families   335
              Priya J. Shahani and Heather M. Trish

Chapter 19   Group Therapy for Palestinian Family Members
              After Violent Death   357
              Khader Rasras, Suad Mitwalli, and Mahmud Sehwail

Closing Thoughts   371
Edward K. Rynearson

Index   379

About the Editor

Edward K. (Ted) Rynearson, M.D., is a semiretired clinical psychiatrist from Seattle, WA, where he founded the section of psychiatry at Virginia Mason Medical Center in the early 1970s. In addition to full-time clinical practice, he has served on the clinical faculty of the University of Washington as a clinical professor of psychiatry.

For more than 20 years Dr. Rynearson has maintained a particular clinical and research focus on the effects of violent death on family members, published in clinical papers, book chapters, and a book entitled *Retelling Violent Death*. Since his retirement from full-time practice, he has conducted numerous national and international trainings on the management of clinical effects of violent death and, with grant support, has founded a nonprofit organization (the Violent Death Bereavement Society) with its own Internet site (http://www.vdbs.org) to establish an informative network for service providers, teachers, and researchers of violent death.

Dr. Rynearson lives on Puget Sound where he rows each dawn in his rowing scull (weather and tide permitting) and almost always sees a seal or an eagle.

Contributors

James Allen, M.D., is a member of the Department of Psychiatry at the University of Oklahoma Health Sciences Center, Oklahoma City. At the time of the Oklahoma City bombing, he was involved in a variety of capacities in the aftermath, including direct treatment, research, and in organizational response.

Marilyn Peterson Armour, Ph.D., is an assistant professor at the University of Texas at Austin. She, herself, is a survivor of spousal suicide. Additionally, she has over 30 years' experience as a psychotherapist with survivors of violent death. Dr. Armour has written extensively on topics such as meaning making, the impact of negative social responses, and forgiveness with a special focus on the lived experience of homicide survivors. She is currently involved in studying the effectiveness of clinical interventions for survivors including restorative justice dialog.

David M. Benedek, M.D., is associate professor of psychiatry and assistant chairman for student education in the Uniformed Services University's Department of Psychiatry. He is also a senior scientist at the University's Center for the Study of Traumatic Stress. He is a past president of the Society of Uniformed Service Psychiatrists — the Military District Branch of the American Psychiatric Association. He is a Distinguished Fellow of the American Psychiatric Association. In addition to his operational experience in Bosnia and Croatia, Dr. Benedek has deployed to Cuba, Iraq, and Kuwait in conjunction with the global war on terrorism. In 2004 he was appointed consultant to the U.S. Army Surgeon General for forensic psychiatry.

George A. Bonanno, Ph.D., is an associate professor of clinical psychology in the Department of Counseling and Clinical Psychology, Teachers College, Columbia University. He received his Ph.D. from Yale University in 1991. His research and scholarly interests since the mid-1990s have centered on the question of how human beings cope with extreme adversity, as well as the role in coping played by self-deception, emotion, and emotion regulatory processes. More recently, Professor Bonanno has focused his empirical and theoretical work on the topic of adult resilience in the context of loss or potential traumatic events, including a study of resilience and adjustment among individuals in or near the World Trade Center during the 9/11 terrorist attack (funded by the National Science Foundation). He has also been exploring the salutary role of laughter in coping and is coeditor of the book, *Emotion: Current Issues and Future Directions*, published in 2001 by Guilford Press.

Richard A. Chefetz, M.D., is a psychiatrist in private practice in Washington, DC. Dr. Chefetz is a diplomate of the American Boards of Psychiatry and Neurology, Medical Hypnosis, and Family Practice (1979–1998). He specializes in the treatment of complex posttraumatic and dissociative disorders in adults. He is a past president of the International Society for the Study of Dissociation (2002–2003), and codirector of their Dissociative Disorders Psychotherapy Training Program. Dr. Chefetz is a distinguished visiting lecturer at the William Alanson White Institute of Psychiatry, Psychoanalysis, and Psychology. He is on the faculties of the Advanced Institute of Contemporary Psychotherapy and Psychoanalysis, and New Directions in Psychoanalysis at the Washington Psychoanalytic Society where he is an interdisciplinary member. Dr. Chefetz is also a certified consultant in hypnosis of the American Society of Clinical Hypnosis.

Judith A. Cohen, M.D., is a board certified child and adolescent psychiatrist, medical director of the Center for Traumatic Stress in Children and Adolescents at Allegheny General Hospital in Pittsburgh, PA, and professor of psychiatry at Drexel University College of Medicine. With Tony Mannarino, Ph.D., and Esther Deblinger, Ph.D., she has developed and tested Trauma-Focused Cognitive Behavioral Therapy (TF-CBT) for sexually abused and multiply traumatized children and their nonoffending parents since the early 1980s. Since 1983, Dr. Cohen has been funded by more than a dozen federally supported grants to conduct research related to the assessment and treatment of traumatized children. She has served on the board of directors of the International Society for Traumatic Stress Studies, and is associate editor of its *Journal of Traumatic Stress* as well as the first author of its published guidelines for treating childhood PTSD. Dr. Cohen is the principal author of "Practice Parameters for the Assessment and Treatment of Childhood PTSD" published by the American Academy of Child & Adolescent Psychiatry.

Fanny Correa, M.S.W., C.T., clinical director, Separation and Loss Services in Seattle, WA, works with families after sudden, violent death, and facilitates debriefing sessions and training workshops. As clinical affiliate to the Dart Center for Journalism and Trauma at the University of Washington, she teaches journalism students the impact of violent death. She recently served as chair of the Washington Coalition for Crime Victim Advocates.

Joseph M. Currier, M.A., LCPC, is a doctoral student in clinical psychology at the University of Memphis. He worked previously as a therapist and clinical supervisor at Family Care of Illinois in Chicago, where he initially became interested in trauma and loss. He has authored several empirical and theoretical papers in this area, all of which utilize narrative and constuctivist concepts to elucidate the mechanisms underlying the grieving process for those persons recovering from the experience of traumatic loss.

Julie Dunsmore, Ph.D., is a psychologist with 25 years experience in the area of loss, grief, and trauma. She is the president of the National Association of Loss and Grief and currently provides outreach and support to survivors, the bereaved, and others involved with or witness to the Bali bombing. Dr. Dunsmore has worked closely with a range of support agencies including the Coroners Court and the Australian Federal Police. She is the director of health promotion in Northern Sydney Health and has made a number of award-winning documentaries on loss and grief, particularly related to cancer and neonatal death.

Jennifer L. Favell, Ph.D., a graduate of Stanford University and of the University of Washington, was the clinical director of Separation and Loss Services at Virginia Mason Medical Center, Seattle, and was clinical director on several national-level research and training grants offering clinical services to families after the violent loss of loved ones. She has worked with prosecuting attorneys, medical examiners, victims' assistance workers, psychiatric residents, and incarcerated adolescents. Currently, in her position with the Lawyers Assistance Program, Washington State Bar Association, Dr. Favell specializes in treating trauma, stress, grief, eating disorders, depression, and life transition issues. She provides training to local, state, and national organizations. She maintains a private psychotherapy practice in Seattle.

Sharon M. Gancarz-Davies, MSW, is a clinical social worker at Children's Bureau of New Orleans where she developed the Infant Mental Health Component to Project LAST, a program which provides counseling and support to child survivors of homicide victims and their families. Ms. Gancarz-Davies graduated from Tulane University School of Social Work. She was a Harris Fellow and received her certification in infant mental health from Louisiana State University Health Sciences Center.

Yael Geron, Ph.D., School of Social Work, Tel Aviv University, Israel, specializes in research and clinical work in family and couple therapy, group work, and bereavement. She published and presented in Israel and internationally, and has served as president of the Israeli Association of Family Therapy and for the last 10 years has been the head of the expert committee of the Israeli Council of Social Work. She is a member of the Judicial Appeal Committee on adoption.

Richard Gold founded and runs the Pongo Publishing Teen Writing Project, a 10-year-old nonprofit organization that offers writing therapy to adolescents who are homeless, in jail, or in other ways leading difficult lives. Pongo volunteers go inside detention centers, shelters, and other sites to work with youth over the course of six-month writing projects. At the culmination of a project, Pongo publishes the young people's writing in chapbook collections. One thousand copies of these chapbooks are given away each year to incarcerated youth, and also to agencies, judges, libraries, and therapists. The Pongo Publishing Web site is http://www.pongopublishing.org.

Bonnie Gorscak, Ph.D., Psychology, is in private practice in Pittsburgh, PA.

Janice Harris Lord, MSSW, LMSW, LPC, received her MSSW degree from University of Texas at Arlington and is a licensed social worker (LMSW) and professional counselor (LPC). She is a fellow in thanatology with the Association of Death Education and Counseling and is a member of the International Society of Traumatic Stress Studies. Janice has worked in the crime victims' movement since 1976 and was national director of victim services for Mothers Against Drunk Driving for 14 years. Janice has written two books for the popular market, *No Time for Goodbyes: Coping with Sorrow, Anger, and Injustice After a Tragic Death* and *Beyond Sympathy: How to Help Another Through Injury, Illness, or Loss*. She has recently coauthored a book on multifaith perspectives of spiritually sensitive victim services which is in publication with the Office for Victims of Crime, U.S. Department of Justice, and a book on death notification which is also awaiting publication. Janice received the U.S. Presidential Award for "Outstanding Service on Behalf of Victims of Crime" from President Bill Clinton and U.S. Attorney General Janet Reno in 1994.

Ruth Malkinson, Ph.D., School of Social Work, Tel Aviv University, specializes in research and clinical work in bereavement, family, and couple therapy from the CBT perspective. She is a past president of the Israeli Association for Family and Marital Therapy. She is the author of numerous articles on loss, bereavement, trauma, and cognitive grief therapy. She is the coeditor of two books on loss and bereavement. Her book, *Cognitive Grief Therapy: Constructing a Rational Meaning to Life Following Loss*, will be published by W.W. Norton.

Anthony P. Mannarino, Ph.D., is currently chairman, Department of Psychiatry, and director of the Center for Traumatic Stress in Children and Adolescents at Allegheny General Hospital, Pittsburgh, PA. He is also professor of psychiatry at the Drexel University College of Medicine. Dr. Mannarino has been a leader in the field of child traumatic stress since 1980. He has been awarded numerous federal grants from the National Center on Child Abuse and Neglect and the National Institute of Mental Health to investigate the clinical course of traumatic stress symptoms in children and to develop effective treatment approaches for traumatized children and their families. Dr. Mannarino is currently serving a two-year term as the president of APSAC and is president-elect of the Section on Child Maltreatment,

Division of Child, Youth, and Family Services, American Psychological Association.

Suad Mitwalli, M.A., clinical psychologist, is a staff psychologist at the Treatment and Rehabilitation Center for Victims of Torture in Ramallah, Palestine. For the last two years, Dr. Mitwalli has served as coleader of a community-based support program at the trauma center that includes a time-limited group intervention for adult family members after violent death.

Shirley A. Murphy, R.N., Ph.D., FAAN, is professor emeritus of the Department of Psychosocial and Community Health in the School of Nursing at the University of Washington in Seattle. Dr. Murphy began studying violent death bereavement in 1980 following the Mount. St. Helens disaster. In the 1990s, Dr. Murphy conducted a randomized clinical trial involving parents whose adolescent and young adult children died by accident, homicide, or suicide. Since 1988, Dr. Murphy has been a coinvestigator on studies of occupational stress and coping funded by CDC. Dr. Murphy's study results have been published widely in peer-reviewed journals. She is a peer reviewer for several multidisciplinary journals and is associate editor of two nursing journals. She has served as peer-reviewer for NIH and currently serves as an expert witness on behalf of bereaved parents. In 2004, Dr. Murphy was the recipient of the Research Recognition Award of the Association of Death Education and Counseling (ADEC). She is a member of the American Academy of Nursing, the International Society for Traumatic Stress Studies and ADEC.

Robert A. Neimeyer, Ph.D., is professor and director of psychotherapy in the Department of Psychology, University of Memphis, where he also maintains an active clinical practice. Since completing his doctoral training at the University of Nebraska in 1982, he has published 20 books, including *Meaning Reconstruction and the Experience of Loss*, and *Lessons of Loss: A Guide to Coping*, and serves as editor of the journal *Death Studies*. The author of over 200 articles and book chapters, he is currently working to advance a more adequate theory of grieving as a meaning-making process, both in his published work and through his frequent professional workshops for national and international audiences. Neimeyer served as a member of the American Psychological Association's Task Force on End-of-Life Issues, and chair of the International Work Group for Death, Dying and Bereavement. In recognition of his scholarly contributions, he has been granted the Eminent Faculty Award by the University of Memphis, made a fellow of the Clinical Psychology Division of the American Psychological Association, and given the Research Recognition Award by the Association for Death Education and Counseling.

Frank Ochberg, M.D., is founding board member of the International Society for Traumatic Stress Studies and recipient of its highest honor, the Lifetime

Achievement Award. He edited the first text on treatment of posttraumatic stress disorder (PTSD) and served on the committee that defined PTSD. He was associate director of the National Institute of Mental Health and director of the Michigan Mental Health Department. At Michigan State University, he is a clinical professor of psychiatry, formerly adjunct professor of Criminal Justice and adjunct professor of journalism. Ochberg founded and secured the funding for the Dart Center on Journalism and Trauma, served as its first chairman, and now is chairman emeritus of the Center. He helps journalists understand traumatic stress, and he helps traumatic stress experts understand journalists.

Betty Pfefferbaum, M.D., is in the Department of Psychiatry at the University of Oklahoma Health Sciences Center, Oklahoma City. She was involved in a variety of capacities in the aftermath of the Oklahoma City bombing, in direct treatment, research, and organizational response. Dr. Pfefferbaum was a member of the Surgeon General's Task Force to Nairobi and Dar es Salaam after the American embassy bombings and is now director of the University of Oklahoma Terrorism and Disaster Center of the National Child Trauma Stress Network funded by SAMSA.

Holly G. Prigerson, Ph.D., has studied psychosocial factors that influence the quality of life and care received by terminally ill patients and factors influencing caregiver adjustment both before and after the death of a loved one since her dissertation work at Stanford in the late 1980s. She completed a postdoctoral fellowship in the epidemiology of aging at Yale University and then was funded by NIMH for a K-award to study psychosocial factors in bereavement-related depression while an assistant professor of psychiatry at Western Psychiatric Institute and Clinic in Pittsburgh. She then returned to Yale in 1997 to conduct a DSM field trial of consensus criteria for complicated grief, a psychiatric epidemiologic longitudinal prospective study of advanced cancer patients and the caregivers who survived them, and a study of psychosocial factors influencing ethnic disparities in end-of-life care and bereavement adjustment. She then moved to Dana-Farber Cancer Institute to assume leadership of the Center of Psycho-oncology and Palliative Care Research, with an academic appointment as associate professor of Psychiatry at Brigham and Women's Hospital, Harvard Medical School. She is now involved with a wide variety of research projects including intervention studies of complicated grief, a study to improve the cardiovascular health of recently bereaved cancer patient caregivers, and the factors influencing equanimity in the acknowledgment of terminal illness.

Beverley Raphael, A.M., MBBS, M.D., FRANZCP, FRCPsych., FASSA, Hon, is emeritus professor of psychiatry at the University of Queensland, professor of population mental health and disasters at the University of Western Sydney, and professor of psychological medicine at the Australian National University. She is known internationally for her expertise in trauma, grief, and disasters, having published and researched widely in this field. She has been involved in disaster response to a broad range of natural and man-made disasters, including response to the Bali bombing and the Indian Ocean tsunami. Her long-term interests include prevention in mental health, women's mental health, family issues, and issues affecting consumers in mental health care systems. She has also been involved in the development of Aboriginal mental health policy.

Khader Rasras, M.A., clinical psychologist, is a staff psychologist for the Treatment and Rehabilitation Center for Victims of Torture in Ramallah, Palestine. Since 2004, Dr. Rasras has served as a coleader of a community-based support program at the trauma center that includes a time-limited group intervention for adult family members after violent death.

Alison Salloum, Ph.D., LCSW specializes in working with children and families affected by violence, trauma, grief, and loss. Dr. Salloum received her MSW and Ph.D. from Tulane University School of Social Work. She is a visiting assistant professor at the University of South Florida, School of Social Work. Dr. Salloum is the author of *Group Work With Adolescents after Violent Death: A Manual for Practitioners,* (Brunner-Routledge, 2004), which focuses on ways adults can help adolescents in the aftermath of violent death. Her clinical and research interests focus on effective interventions for traumatized children.

Mahmud Sehwail, M.D., is the director of the Treatment and Rehabilitation Center for Victims of Torture in Ramallah, Palestine. He is a psychiatrist, teacher, author, and founding director of a community-based trauma center in Ramallah, Palestine that has provided emotional support for tortured and traumatized community members, including the trauma of violent death.

Priya Shahani, MSW, LCSW, received her master's degree in social work from New York University and is board certified as a licensed clinical social worker in the state of New York. Her focus in trauma developed while working for UCSF at the Trauma Recovery and Rape Treatment Center at San Francisco General Hospital, where she provided psychotherapy to victims of violence. Following the events of September 11, 2001, she returned to her hometown of New York City where she created and directed Safe Horizon's 9/11 mental health program at the Family Assistance Center. She worked as the senior counselor at Safe Horizon for three years providing clinical supervision to staff and counseling services to those impacted by the events of September 11. She facilitated several violent death bereavement groups for those who lost loved ones at the World Trade Center. Currently she is residing in the San Francisco Bay Area.

Connie Saindon, M.A., LMFT, is a licensed marital and family therapist. She is the founder and clinical director of the Survivors of Violent Loss Program in San Diego County and editor of the Survivors of Violent Loss Network Web site. She has been coauthor of a three-year pilot project and has presented at both local and national conferences on the topic.

Katherine Shear, M.D., Marion Kenworthy Professor of Psychiatry, Columbia University School of Social Work, is a distinguished clinician, teacher, and researcher who has written extensively on her studies of patients with enduring and complicated grief. Before her recent move to Columbia University, Dr. Shear was the lead investigator in seminal clinical studies conducted at the University of Pittsburgh School of Medicine on the clarification of complicated grief and development of specific, time-limited interventions with empirically demonstrated effectiveness.

Naomi Simon, M.D., M.Sc., is the associate director of the Center for Anxiety and Traumatic Stress Disorders at Massachusetts General Hospital.

Garry Stevens B.Sc. (Hons), M.Clin.Psych., MAPS, is a senior clinical psychologist with extensive experience in the field of child and adolescent mental health. He has previously researched and developed brief risk assessment and therapy models in child and adolescent clinical services. He has been involved more recently in the field of disaster mental health, including the response to the Indian Ocean tsunami and the Bali bombing. He is the current senior research fellow at the MH-DAT Unit (Mental Health Aspects of Disaster and Terrorism), University of Western Sydney, where he coordinates research programs.

Heather Trish, Ed.M., M.A., holds an Ed.M. in psychological counseling and a master's in organizational psychology from Teachers College, Columbia University, as well as a certificate in conflict resolution. Her experience in trauma work has included crisis counseling at domestic violence and sexual assault agencies and with downsized employees in a corporate setting. Since 2002, she has worked as a counselor and now as the assistant director of Safe Horizon's 9/11 Mental Health Programs, providing clinical supervision to staff as well as counseling services to family members, evacuees, witnesses, the injured, downtown residents, displaced workers, and rescue and recovery workers affected by 9/11. She is a national certified counselor with the National Board of Certified Counselors and a licensed professional counselor in the state of Colorado.

Phebe Tucker, M.D., is in the Department of Psychiatry at the University of Oklahoma Health Sciences Center, Oklahoma City. At the time of the Oklahoma City bombing, she was involved in a variety of capacities in the aftermath, both in direct treatment, research and in organizational response.

Robert J. Ursano, M.D., is a professor of psychiatry and neuroscience and chairman of the Department of Psychiatry at the Uniformed Services University of the Health Sciences, Bethesda, MD. He is director of the Center for the Study of Traumatic Stress. In addition, Dr. Ursano is editor of *Psychiatry,* the distinguished journal of interpersonal and biological processes founded by Harry Stack Sullivan.

Series Editor's Foreword

As a well-spent day brings happy sleep, so life well used brings happy death.

— *Leonardo da Vinci*

If only all deaths were so predictable and joyous. The numbing shock of discovering someone you loved is dead and has died violently can last a long time. The survivors seek answers to questions about the circumstances of the death. The fundamental differences between da Vinci's conception of death and violent death are among the topics in this book, the latest addition to the Routledge Psychosocial Stress Book Series. As series editor I am delighted to welcome this groundbreaking book to the series of groundbreaking books.

The first book in the Series, *Stress Disorders among Vietnam Veterans* (1978), ushered in the modern era of traumatology. Dr. Rynearson's book is also expected to make a significant contribution to both traumatology and thanatology fields because it brings into sharp focus the aftermath of violent death and an optimistic orientation to promoting resiliency.

It is important to note that the editor is an internationally renowned pioneer in the study and treatment of violent death. E. K. (Ted) Rynearson, M.D., is a semiretired psychiatrist. In 1972 he established the Section of Psychiatry at the Virginia Mason Medical Center in Seattle. He has had considerable clinical experience in managing over 2,000 cases of highly distressed family members after violent death. He published the first report of the specifics of bereavement after homicide that appeared in the *American Journal of Psychiatry* in 1984. Although his career has largely revolved around his role as a clinician, he is a clinical professor of psychiatry at the University of Washington Medical School and has conducted numerous national and international trainings describing clinical interventions for nonaccommodation following violent death.

Throughout his career and especially in his innovative work in the last several years he has emphasized the clinical importance of restoration and resilience rather than searching for pathology and diagnosis. He places far more stock in the crucial role of creative and imaginative approaches to grief and trauma interventions that include spirituality, art, and the power of family relationships. He has written a book on the topic that summarizes his recommendations entitled *Retelling Violent Death* (Brunner-Routledge, 2001).

The book closes with the latest focus of Dr. Rynearson's training. He has become active in promoting international collaborative training in the Middle East between Israeli and Palestinian clinicians, encouraging them to collaborate on ways of supporting one another in the wake of trauma and grief from violent death in both their countries. Throughout his writings, including this book, he emphasizes the importance of self-care and practices what he preaches: most early mornings on Puget Sound, weather permitting, he sculls with seals and eagles.

Professor Rynearson has assembled an extraordinary group of scholars and practitioners from nursing, ministry, psychology, psychiatry, and social work. For example, Beverley Raphael was recently included in a book of essays by pioneer traumatologists and is recognized for her work in trauma and death. George Bonanno, Columbia University psychology professor, has written some of the most groundbreaking work that challenges grief work and emphasizes the importance of denial and resilience. Robert Neimeyer, Shirley Murphy, Kathy Shear, and Holly Prigerson, though from different fields, are leaders in understanding violent death bereavement.

Violent death is the end of life from unnatural causes that could have been prevented. Although accidents, suicides, homicides, and warfare can be prevented, natural disasters cannot. However, as illustrated by Hurricane Katrina in September 2005, the thousands of deaths in New Orleans were caused by human failures of preparedness, protection, and rescue. All the chapters in this book address directly the consequences of preventable trauma and death.

The 19 chapters of the book are divided among three parts: "Restorative and Clinical Essentials," "Restorative and Clinical Interventions," and "Community Outreach and Interventions after Disaster and Warfare." Of special importance, among many in this book, is the nature of resilience and the "restorative" paradigm. Both represent the notion that a complete understanding of violent death bereavement flows from both trauma and grief. Moreover, the book not only recognizes contributions of grief and trauma but also emphasizes that the prognosis for violent death bereavement — despite assertions in the literature to the contrary — is good. Resilience is the norm. The general consensus is that interventions for the violently grieved should not only include the expectation of recovery, but they should be brief and focus on generating social support.

Grieving the death of a loved one is a natural and predictable part of life. Grieving the violent death of a loved one requires far greater emotional, intellectual, and social resources. Until now practitioners had no single source for guidance in helping clients grieving from such losses.

Charles Figley, Ph.D.
Series Editor

Introduction

An accurate indicator of the global distribution and incidence of violent death (from suicide, homicide, or warfare) appeared in an epidemiological study derived from the Global Burden of Disease Series and the U.S. National Center for Health Statistics (Reza & Mercy, 2001). The study estimated that 1,851,000 people die from violence (35.3 per 100,000), representing 3.7% of annual deaths occurring in the world. Suicide was the most frequent form of violent death (786,000 or 15.5 per 100,000) followed by homicide (563,000 or 10.5 per 100,000), and then war-related deaths (502,000 or 9.3 per 100,000). Suicide rates were highest in China and former socialist economies, homicide rates were highest in sub-Saharan Africa and Latin America/Caribbean, and war-related death rates were highest in sub-Saharan Africa and the Middle Eastern crescent. Over 90% of the war-related deaths involved innocent civilians, and over half of those victims were children.

Accidental dying (another form of violent dying) is the most common mode, but the most difficult to document. Had instances of accidental death been verifiable, the reported incidence of worldwide violent death would have at least doubled.

While this contemporary study cites its relatively low incidence, the rate of violent dying was presumably much higher during earlier stages of human history when violence was more prevalent. Violent death and its emotional aftermath have persistently threatened human life, and more particularly the lives of the young, since it is the most common cause of death from birth to young adulthood. This skewed occurrence means children and young adults are more vulnerable to its effects, not only directly as victims, but in terms of experiencing bereavement during a phase of intense attachment and dependency.

Since the mid-1990s, the literature on violent dying has produced too much on crisis response to violent death after a disaster or attack with many casualties, and not enough on the long-term support, outreach, and intervention for individuals and families after violent death from any cause. Despite the relative rarity of disaster or attack, the plentitude of recent papers, monographs, and books has become numbing, with flow charts of responsible agencies, instructions for organizing a family crisis center, and printed manuals describing strategies and techniques for crisis intervention. However, crisis response planning does not prepare the community for supporting vulnerable loved ones who fail to adapt to the trauma and loss months after the tragedy.

This book's purpose is to gather the written work of contemporary experts and their guiding theory and practice of spiritual and emotional support after violent dying, beyond the crisis. The authors comprise an impressive list of national and international clinicians and researchers who work within variable sociocultural contexts. Though several of the chapters deal specifically with instances of mass violent dying (the Oklahoma City bombing and the 9/11 terrorist attack), the majority describe community-based support programs for children and adults through community outreach and long-term support and intervention after violent death from suicide, homicide, or warfare.

Community-based support and intervention after violent dying appear to have a decided advantage over office-based treatments that passively await consultation and referral. Engaging a wide spectrum of community service providers (including clergy, first responders, media, police, and court victims' assistance workers, and clinicians) ensures the participation of providers already serving natural restorative tendencies (spiritual support, bereavement passage, restorative retelling, meaning making).

Community-based programs may also encourage a centralized service to organize a registry and an active outreach service that follows families and coordinates screening and intervention services for those who remain highly distressed. Home visits for traumatized and frightened families are particularly important and associated with increased participation.

Violent death presents a more complex synergism of distress than the natural death of a loved one. After violent death, accommodation includes the processing of trauma distress regarding the violent dying while at the same time processing separation distress regarding the irrevocable absence of the loved one. This dynamic appears more complex than the internalized dynamic of a solitary, traumatic experience (i.e., an assault or rape by a stranger) that is narrowly aversive. Instead, accommodation to violent dying may be challenged by waves of disparate memories — or the memory of the life of the deceased may have been all but eclipsed by the death. An early explanation of the dynamic difference of being "pulled" by loving and "pushed" by dying memories, and the early treatment objective of recovering the loving and living memories before reconstructing the dying, is intuitively reinforced in the early phases of most of the interventions.

The treatments described in this book have agendas, are time-limited, focused, and may include outcome data suggesting their effectiveness. However, none of the various interventions has undergone randomized, controlled trials or systematic comparison. Though treatments vary in therapeutic concepts and techniques, there is no documentation of a specific, corrective "mechanism." Instead, the agendas of various treatments follow a "passage" pattern of phases of identity transformation common to time-limited trauma or grief treatments in the staging and application of at least three common techniques:

1. The moderation of distress (through a confiding relationship, a safe setting, and stress reduction strategies — including medication — the subject partially surrenders his or her traumatized identity).

2. Exposure and *reconstructive* processing of the stressor (clarification of a rational scheme that explains symptoms, and an active procedure of "reliving" the stressor that restores health and meaningful reengagement) through a strategy of instruction and self-inquiry that revises identity.
   - Perhaps it is the counterbalancing of stress moderation and reconstructive exposure that forms the therapeutic ingredient of a given trauma or grief treatment.
   - Probably it is the trusting relationship and the encouragement of "externalizing" (through verbal and nonverbal retelling) that allow a reframing (paradigmatic shift via restorative retelling) of the traumatic memory through which participant(s) revitalizes and widens his or her identity in the reenactment story from immersion and helpless victim or witness to transcendence and survival.
3. Meaningful reengagement with valued, vital activities and relationships within the family and community in an altered identity that honors the transformation.

The explanation of treatment effect with each of the interventions cited in this book is most probably nonspecific; that is, various treatments are successful not so much from their unique model or technique(s), but because various agendas and interventions are based upon common principles of stress moderation, reconstructive exposure, and meaningful reengagement.

STRUCTURE OF THE BOOK

A book authored by a single writer may promise more coherence and consistency as themes are addressed, revised, and intertwined by one rather than many minds. As editor of a volume that contains 19 separate chapters from nearly as many authors, I have tried to avoid the disharmony inherent in loosely gathering separately authored chapters, disconnected and sometimes divergent from one another. Instead, I have organized chapters into three functional groupings corresponding to the paradigms developed in the introduction: (1) restorative and clinical essentials; (2) restorative and clinical interventions; and (3) community outreach and intervention after disaster and warfare.

The first seven chapters on *restorative and clinical essentials* after violent death clarify concepts fundamental to an understanding of grief and violent death: a revised theory of complicated grief, resources of resilience, spirituality, family support, narrative revision, meaning making, and the neurobiological substrate of trauma and death. Though these chapters include clinical formulations and case illustrations, their focus is more didactic than those that follow. Opening the book with these chapters provides a conceptual clarification and foundation for readers and prepares them for the intervention chapters that follow.

The next eight chapters on *restorative and clinical interventions* after violent death present evidence-based recommendations for community outreach, case identification, and time-limited/agenda-based treatments for adults and children after violent death from accident, suicide, or homicide. In this middle section of the book the authors more narrowly attend to clinical goals and techniques specific to managing the refractory responses of intense distress following the violent death of a loved one. Abundant case illustrations bring the reader an experiential and pragmatic appreciation of group and individual strategies of support and intervention.

The closing four chapters on *community outreach and intervention after disaster and warfare* describe long-term support and intervention strategies for entire communities suffering a natural disaster, terrorist attack, or warfare with mass casualties, including violent death. Providing outreach, case identification, and long-term support and interventions to a community traumatized by a highly lethal event are distinct from assisting a solitary family traumatized by an incidental homicide, suicide, or accident. These authors have planned and organized programs of long-term emotional support in the tumultuous aftermath of community despair and confusion.

Each chapter is introduced by an editorial précis, not to critique or analyze, but to establish a thematic connection and resonance between chapters.

FIRST PRINCIPLES OF VIOLENT DYING BEREAVEMENT

To better prepare the reader in understanding the chapters that follow, several fundamental human responses to violent death need to be considered:

The Constancy and Dread of Violent Dying

When humans developed an awareness of dying and death, the fear of death and particularly of violent dying, presumably became adaptive in enhancing survival. As a corollary, its emotional aftermath was so painful and driven that adaptive avoidance dictated preventive social norms within the society as well as religious proscriptions within texts and rituals — and the most basic of legal punishments demanding retaliation, retribution, and justice for relatives and community. Despite the universality of its dread, preventive norms, proscriptions, and laws, violent dying persists and so does the distress of loved ones haunted by the imaginary replay of the terror and helplessness their loved one suffered.

"Haunted" is an accurate descriptor. Those fortunate to die from natural causes at the end of a long life surrounded by a loving and respectful family may be more accepting and unperturbed while dying — but those who die violently are more likely to experience despair and impotence in the last moments of their living. Earliest accounts of human history record a common spiritual aftermath — the "soul" of the victim makes a spectral return to demand retribution and revenge. The ghost "haunts" the family because the soul of the deceased cannot rest until his or her honor has been restored, not because of death, but because of the violence of the victim's dying.

Ghosts are no longer a major part of contemporary belief systems — and certainly not by many contemporary clinical practitioners. Instead, we might theorize that a ghost is the product of a psychological projection, the externalization of an unfinished attachment with the memory of the deceased. Such a paradigm holds that after the violent dying of a loved one, the family member is not haunted but possessed by an internal dilemma; how to accept and be at peace with the reality of an abhorrent dying, admixed with the surrealistic replay (a narrative that ends in meaningless chaos) of what the loved one suffered. In the immediate aftermath of violent death family members and loved ones cannot keep their mind from an obsessive rumination and recounting of the dying action. Fortunately, in the vast majority of survivors the obsession subsides within days or weeks.

Another factor that reinforces its external or haunting quality is that violent dying is a spectacle. After all, violent dying is an external event or human act, differentiating it from natural dying from an internal disease. Because it is such a public event there is little respect for privacy or decorum. From the moment the dying is discovered, the surrounding community joins in an inquest to define the who, what, when, where, and why of the violent dying. This sort of dying must be explained if it is to be resolved. The family of the victim is not accorded "ownership" of the dying story. The media, police, and court construct their own explanatory recounting. This very public and stark replay of the events of the dying clashes with the private narrative of the family. The story of the family contains the nuanced story of the victim's life and his or her role within the matrix of the family; however, recounting the external drama of violent dying may be difficult to blend into that vital narrative.

To add outrage to violent death is the reality that this dying should not have happened. Someone was at fault for this killing if committed willfully — or dying from negligence if at fault: Was there a perpetrator? Is there someone to find and punish, someone from whom to exact a retribution or retaliation, to restore a sense of honor and justice to the victim's family? The demand for retaliatory justice has been enacted for thousands of years, directly accomplished by the family through their extended clan against the family and clan of the perpetrator — though in Western law retaliation and retribution have been deliberated and administered by courts since the advent of the jury system in the 12th century. However muted, this retaliatory ritual may still be considered compensatory, to quiet and honor the soul of the deceased.

Restorative Paradigms

Consistent with the broadening focus of this book, we need to look beyond dysfunction and familiar theories. There are "natural" restorative resources within the family unit and surrounding community to clarify and reinforce. A clarification of what is calming and enabling after violent dying is pivotal to fuller understanding. Appreciating restorative resources provides a direction toward a positive reengagement with life and hope for the future — outside the image of the violent death where a faith in life and the future cannot be found.

The paradigm of *spirituality,* or eternal transcendence over mortality, is a reassuring belief that counters the nihilism of violent death. Spiritual and religious beliefs hold an animating conviction that finite life is connected with God, or a transcendent and ultimate life force. That belief brings a restorative reframing because whatever we momentarily experience in mortal life is joined in a transcendent life energy or cycle. Religious liturgies and rituals provide a communal context for retelling the narrative of dying and death. The pain and disillusionment of violent dying can be counterbalanced by beliefs that the victim's spirit or soul is transcendent and no longer connected with the momentary terror and mortal despair of his or her violent dying.

Since the majority of people are sustained by a strong belief in God or in some transcendent life principle, it is not surprising that religious organizations and clergy and faith-based counselors play a supportive role for many loved ones and family members after violent dying. Clergy often accompany police and medical examiner investigators at the time of notification because of the intuitive role they can assume in softening the horror of the message. Within days of the death clergy not only offer emotional support, but also are instrumental in helping to plan and officiate at the memorial service and burial. Because of their ministerial and pastoral commitment, they may have continuous, long-term contact with families after violent death. This is different from professionals whose obligation ends after the notification, investigation, and trial. While joined in a network of the spiritual community, the clergy or pastoral counselor actively reaches out to loved ones and family members for months or years after a violent death to monitor their progress. Clergy and faith-based counselors are "natural" representatives within any community, already providing intermediate and long-term bereavement services.

The paradigm of *passage* describes a prototypical action that is self-transforming. Through a series of structured activities (rites of baptism, initiation, purification, marriage, funeral, to name a few) the subject willingly undergoes a transition of identity. The timeless rites of passage for adolescent boys and girls, preparatory to assuming roles as warriors and mothers, have been elaborate and time consuming, still demanding physical isolation and physical mutilation in some parts of the world. More contemporary passage rites are less dramatic and intense, but retain a fundamental ordering that follows three separable phases:

- Discontinuity of identity — in anticipation of increased stability and strength, the subject partially surrenders his or her attachment to his or her former identity.
- Revision of identity — through a strategy of instruction and self-inquiry, the subject revises his or her identity.
- Affirmation of identity — in an altered role, the subject commits to rejoining the community that honors and reinforces the transformation.

This paradigm of passage accompanies many psychological and social role transitions. With any change aversive enough to alter an individual's view of self and world, including traumatic events and bereavement, the availability of a passage "rite" provides a time and space for consolidating identity transition.

Over the ages the *narrative* paradigm — establishing a restorative story after a violent death — encourages coherence and meaning in the emotional aftermath. Stories serve a restorative psychological function by reframing the chaotic synergism of loss and trauma to include vital imagery.

In searching for texts of violent dying with themes of mastery, an obvious source comes from the oldest of stories — myths. The central purpose of myth is to provide meaningful explanations of life and guidance for dealing with the most basic existential dilemma of all: our helplessness in confronting our own dying. While many myths contain some mention of violent dying, the myth of Theseus includes not only the basic narrative ingredients of violent dying — love, violent dying, and vivid reenactment — but the dying is enacted in a labyrinth. It ends in heroic mastery, with a metaphorical theme of release and transformation. Telling and interpreting this myth highlights a reconstructive theme that has restorative utility for family members lost in the self-created labyrinth of retelling.

The Greek myth of Theseus, Adriadne, and the Minotaur contains not only the narrative horror and helplessness of violent dying, but a counterbalancing theme of mastery. Before Theseus enters the labyrinth to confront and slaughter the Minotaur, Adriadne gives him a golden cord that he unwinds as he descends into the confusion and chaos. Theseus kills the Minotaur; however, triumph over violent dying for Theseus could not serve as an ending, for recounting that dying story would leave him (and we as listeners) stranded in the dark limbo of violent death.

By following and rewinding the golden cord, Theseus is able to retrace his steps and return to the world of the living. The restorative theme that closes the myth suggests that surviving and redefining the self after violent dying requires a reconnection with a nurturing and meaningful life.

The mastery of violent dying for this mythic hero is only roughly analogous to the dilemma of a grieving family member. Theseus fought and triumphed over violent dying (symbolized by the Minotaur), but the family member can only imagine and helplessly recount the loved one's violent dying. Ariadne remained alive and waiting for Theseus, but for the family member, the loved one is forever absent. By rewinding the golden cord, Theseus separated himself from the horror of the labyrinth of violent dying that he escaped, but the family member cannot be released from his or her imaginary connection with a loved one's entrapment — a "golden cord" to enter or exit the labyrinth of violent death was never available.

Despite these limitations, this paradigm kindles a vector and agency for family members (particularly dependent children and mothers) who remain fixated on recounting the dying. It is common for highly distressed subjects to search for an "answer" in an obsessive retelling of violent dying reenactment, remorse, or retaliation where no meaningful answer or ending can be found. Metaphorically stranded in the limbo of the violent death story, trapped in their own imaginary identification with the violent dying (more than the living) of their loved one, this myth encourages a narrative reframing — by reconnecting with the store of vital memories of interactions with the deceased before the violent dying — an implicit "golden cord" is reestablished that leads to a restorative retelling and a recommitment to restorative activities beyond the dying.

The *dialectic* paradigm, the simultaneous opposition of contradictory concepts or forces and their resolution, is highly applicable to the aftermath of violent dying. The paradoxical legacy of violent death is based upon the incommensurable opposites of love (for the victim) and violence (of the act). When the victim is emotionally treasured (particularly the young, innocent child), the memory of the child is idealized and faultless, and when the dying is vicious, ruthless, and cruel (when the perpetrator is a brutal sociopath), the dying is associated with an absolute evil. How is one to reconcile such divergent experiences of goodness and evil when they could not coexist in the life of the victim, when the evil dying annihilated the goodness of a treasured life?

Over time, the surviving family member resolves the dialectic paradox by moderating his or her ideas, allowing the mind to rest from the quest for establishing an absolute meaning in the action of the dying. The bereaved keeps from overanalyzing what cannot be reasoned or reconciled through retaliation or retribution, thinks more about the victim's living and less about his or her dying. The loved one does not become lost in the mindless search for certainty or justice. This sort of dialectic resolution does not create a new "truth" but a protective detachment from what cannot be reconciled.

Clinical Paradigms

There are several restorative clinical paradigms which can be introduced because of their practical utility in identifying and easing the disabling effects of bereavement after violent dying.

Resilience is a clinical paradigm that is descriptive of the capacity to accommodate to trauma, including grief. It is a psychological function, innate and acquired, that is more evident when absent than present. When resilience is operative, the individual shows little internal or observable change to an adverse event; when resilience is defective, the individual may become highly distressed and dysfunctional.

Resilience is a psychological "offense" of great utility after violent dying, which allows a sense of calmness, self-control, detachment, and hope. Resilience performs the crucial function of psychological stabilization so the individual can effectively process and respond to the challenge(s) of trauma and grief. It is a capacity that needs more study and clarification so strategies and techniques for its reinforcement may be more widely applied.

The narrower clinical paradigm of disease considers the disability secondary to violent death of a loved one as a neurobiological vulnerability. Only a small minority of those who experience the violent death of a loved one become disabled, and this disease-oriented paradigm would observe the timing, course, and clustering of signs and symptoms consistent with criteria for a mental disorder. Mental disorders are presumably related to central nervous system deregulation (unfortunately there are no specific diagnostic tests or procedures to objectively document the pathophysiology) and are responsive to medications.

The mental disorders most commonly associated with trauma and grief include posttraumatic stress disorder, panic disorder, major depressive disorder, and substance abuse. Since each of these disorders is associated with a relatively specific treatment strategy with documented effectiveness, including medications, it is important to screen for their occurrence.

The broadest clinical paradigm views the disability secondary to the violent death of a loved one as a public health risk. While there are long-term health effects in vulnerable family members, and an enormous expenditure of energy and community resources in the investigation, trial, and punishment of violent death, there are no widely applied *public health* measures preventing violent dying before it happens (primary prevention); identifying community members at risk for disabling effects for early treatment (secondary prevention); or providing rehabilitation and education for community members in the aftermath (tertiary prevention). Ideally, a public health model of applied prevention of, intervention, and rehabilitation in the case of a violent death could diminish its immediate and long-term threats to public health. Applying this public health paradigm to the factors responsible for violent dying and its effects is productive, not because violent dying can be prevented through primary prevention (though regulation of firearms would undoubtedly help), but by viewing violent dying as one of a series of interconnected events, we can better understand when and how to intervene. Secondary prevention through active community outreach within three to six months of the violent death, followed by case identification and targeted support and intervention for those disabled, is a tangible clinical goal. Tertiary prevention to support and rehabilitate those who remain disabled, and educate the community about the acute, intermediate, and long-term effects of violent dying is also feasible.

REFERENCE

Reza, A., and Mercy, J. (2001). Epidemiology of violent deaths in the world. *Injury Prevention,* 7, 104–111.

Editor's Note: Suggestions for Utilizing the Companion DVD

I recommend that readers watch the enclosed DVD of two clinical interviews before reading the text to "ground" themselves in the experiential and dynamic interplay of the retelling of the violent death of a loved one. Understanding the process of narrative retelling is basic in caring for someone after violent death and for a fuller appreciation of the chapters that follow.

I interviewed patients whom I had not seen for a number of years following treatment for a reason. Adaptation to violent death changes over time regardless of therapy, and while therapy plays an important restorative theme in these interviews, it is only one of many. Adaptive resources of resilience and restoration, exclusive of therapy, are crucial to reinforce and need to be assessed before and throughout treatment.

Both interviews are filled with references to supportive family, friends, and co-workers, but particularly highlight the prominence of spiritual beliefs as restorative. I have no personal belief in a divine or supernatural promise of eternal life, but I am impressed with the clinical importance of spiritual beliefs in working with those bereaved by violent death — beliefs that reframe dying as "releasing" the deceased from the horrific dying narrative to a time and space of transcendence.

My focus during these interviews was dynamic rather than diagnostic. This is not to dismiss the importance of considering a co-morbid diagnosis during treatment. One of the patients interviewed met DSM criteria for Major Depression, and the other for Anxiety Disorder, for which I prescribed pharmacotherapy at the time of treatment. However, the primary intervention for their grief focused on unresolved feelings, memories, and images of the violent dying and the death of the loved one reprocessed through retelling, moderation, and revision.

During the interviews you will note that I specifically inquire about the change in memory residuals related to the dying event and recollections of the deceased — as an indirect indicator of internal accommodation to the combination of trauma and loss.

PRELIMINARY CONCEPTS

Preparatory to watching the DVD, there are several fundamental dynamic concepts you might consider while synthesizing your observations:

These interviews teach us that a retelling of bereavement after violent dying contains at least two separable "stories" — of a dying and a death — challenged by a *narrative dilemma:* how to retell the horrific story of the external spectacle of the dying while retelling the internal, nurturing story of the loved one's life. The traumatic story of their dying is repelling, the nurturing story of their living is attractive, and the teller is pushed and pulled in the dialectic of their contradiction.

As the narratives are retold, we can delineate at least three separable phases of accommodation that progressively unfold, but may appear in combination and recur:

Phase One is a period of *intense distress*, both trauma distress (intrusion, avoidance, autonomic arousal) to the dying, and separation distress (pining, longing, searching) to the death. Intense distress spontaneously diminishes within weeks in those who remain resilient, but a vulnerable minority of loved ones (particularly mothers and children of the deceased) remain highly distressed, like the mothers in the interviews.

Phase Two is a period of *imagery revision*, revising imagery of the dying combined with imagery of the living. Imagery related to the violent dying (reenactment, retaliation, remorse, dread of recurrence) alternates with imagery related to the nurturing attachment with the deceased (reunion, rescue, relinquishment, respect).

Phase Three is a period of *meaningful reengagement*, reconnecting with life beyond the violent dying by reestablishing life affirming activities and relationships — outside of the therapeutic relationship — that provide a sense of purpose and hope in the future.

The mastery of intense distress, imagery revision, and meaningful reengagement follows a rough staging in spontaneous progress or treatment — mastering intense distress is foundational to imagery revision, and mastering aberrant imagery is foundational to meaningful reengagement — for it is difficult to have requisite focus and energy for external activities and relationships when overwhelmed by intense distress, avoidance, and/or intrusive imagery.

Part I

Restorative and Clinical Essentials

1

Clinical Theories of Loss and Grief

BEVERLEY RAPHAEL, GARRY STEVENS, AND JULIE DUNSMORE

REVISION OF THEORY

The introductory chapter is remarkably comprehensive, covering themes of restoration, intervention, and community support after violent death, and is detailed in clarifying the development of contemporary grief theories — beginning with attachment, normal bereavement, pathologic grief, complicated grief, traumatic bereavement, and finally, violent death and grief. The authors also introduce the dynamic interplay of trauma and separation distress following violent death amplified by authors in later chapters on intervention. The chapter cites sources of vulnerability and resources of resilience after violent death, and closes by developing a clinical protocol brimming with relevant, clinical recommendations, a rich smorgasbord of clinical substance and wisdom.

The loss of a loved one following a violent death is a shocking experience. The loss may be an individual one — for instance when a family member is killed in a violent accident, or a sudden event of nature that takes the lives of many. The latter may not reflect violent intent, but the sudden, unexpected, untimely death, particularly of a young person, may be experienced as "violent." Such events have the power to shock, disrupt, and violently affect the lives of those left behind, of those bereaved. Other deaths may be readily seen through the prism of violence. Homicide is an obvious form

3

of individual and violent death, profoundly affecting the families of those who have died, and indeed, everyone touched by this event. Suicide deaths are also frequently violent, both in their suddenness, but also in the nature of the self-destroying act. With deaths such as these, the most profound bereavement may be experienced by those with intimate attachments, be they partner, spouse, parent, or child, but also across range of other intimate bonds.

Mass violence, involving multiple violent deaths, constitutes another overwhelming loss. The grief and bereavement that follow affect not only surviving family members of those who have died, but also their social networks and wider communities. While this may occur to some degree with the individual incidents noted above, when large numbers die violently the impact is profound, both emotionally and in the breaking up of social networks vital to the community and its recovery. Again, mass deaths may occur through violent natural events, such as the Armenian earthquakes, or the extraordinary circumstances of the Southeast Asian tsunami in 2004. They may take place as a result of mass technological accidents such as a plane crash or building collapse, where elements of human failure or specific negligence may come into question. History has seen mass death through conflict, war, or even genocide and through recent acts of terrorism such as September 11, the bombings in Madrid and London, or the Beslan, Chechnya school siege. These multiple scenarios concerning violent death have implications for the bereavement, for the reactive processes of grieving, and for outcomes. They are also contexts that require careful consideration in terms of the nature of care provided to those bereaved.

There is now burgeoning literature on bereavement with a wide range of theoretical constructs to inform understanding and practice. Given these diverse methodologies, the focus on bereavement through the lens of PTSD, and seminal events such as September 11, it is important to determine some key principles and guidelines that can inform interventions. There is also a need to further explore the opportunities that may exist to prevent adverse mental health and other outcomes associated with such losses.

It is widely acknowledged that grief and bereavement are a normal part of life experience. In Engel's (1961) influential model, for example, grief is not a "disease." Nevertheless the need to delineate and understand these normal phenomena is critical because such phenomena, and their psychophysiological correlates, can provide a baseline against which changed patterns can be assessed and measured. Key variations, for instance, may indicate pathological processes or be predictive of poorer outcomes. With regard to the specific clinical theories and orientations, Middleton, Moylan, Raphael, Burnett, and Martinek (1993) surveyed the theoretical constructs that informed bereavement research to that time, and found that attachment theory predominated as a conceptual basis. Other models included cognitive, assumptive models, and traumatic stress frameworks. For instance Horowitz (1976) described bereavement as a stressor that could lead to a traumatic stress syndrome.

Social structures and roles are profoundly impacted by bereavement, particularly in the aftermath of violent death, and clinical theories must be informed by these social and systemic dimensions. These events and processes affect the social identities involved, such as moving from identity of wife to that of widow; the possible changes in socioeconomic status; ongoing social and stressor impact of the consequences of the loss of the person; the presence, absence, perceived helpfulness or unhelpfulness of those attempting to comfort, console, or support the bereaved. All of these factors may significantly affect ongoing adaptation. Furthermore, the practices of ritual behaviors prescribed by culture, religion, or society contribute additional processes to be recognized in any systems of response and understanding. Broader community recognition of the loss may also provide a level of support. Alternatively, its absence, its specific form, may constitute a further stressor impact.

NORMAL BEREAVEMENT

What is considered "normal" may be defined not only in psychological, but also in sociocultural terms. For instance although weeping and distress were once considered "unmanly" in some Western cultures, these are psychologically normal processes. Work such as that of Bowlby (1980), Byrne and Raphael (1994), Jacobs (1993), Parkes and Markus (1998), and Middleton,Burnett, Raphael, and Martinek (1996), have shown that common sets of phenomena occur. These include shock, numbness, and disbelief as frequent initial responses; yearning, longing, protest, and searching behaviors; psychological mourning processes that involve preoccupation with images of the deceased and review of the lost relationship; and progressive relinquishment of bonds to the deceased. Associated affects include sadness, anger, guilt, and longing as it is increasingly accepted that the person will not return, that life, which involved this person, is permanently changed. Measures such as the Core Bereavement Items Measure (Burnett, Middleton, Raphael, & Martinek, 1997) and those of Middleton, Burnett, et al. (1996), attempt to identify and track such normal bereavement over time. Numerous other scales and measures have evolved for such purposes. The importance of measures such as the CBI, and also those such as Jacobs, Kasl, Ostfeld, et al. (1986), is that they can be used to track the phenomena as expressed by the bereaved person, rather than the risk factors or pathological items per se, which are also useful factors in themselves. Studies using these measures have shown the progressive attenuation of the acute grieving process in the early months, which occurs for the majority of those bereaved. A similar pattern is also observed regarding ongoing grief during the first year.

PATHOLOGICAL GRIEF

The review by Middleton, Moylan, Raphael, Burnett, and Martinek (1993) showed that, at that time, there was little conceptual agreement amongst researchers about the definition or nature of pathological grief, which was also variously called "absent grief" and "delayed grief." There was agreement to a greater degree about longer-term or "chronic grief." Many workers had commented about the overlap of grief and depression, while others had focused on factors that might correlate with poorer health outcomes, as measured a year or more following bereavement. Importantly, researchers began to define diagnostic criteria for pathological, complicated, or other anomalies of grieving. Prigerson et al. (1999) identified important patterns in a model of "complicated grief" for which a specific measure has now come into common use. These phenomena reflect a pattern of heightened anxiety, including separation anxiety, which follows the loss of a highly dependent relationship. These reflected phenomena are similar to those identified by Raphael (1977) and Parkes and Weiss (1983), and which these latter authors found to be predictive of poorer bereavement outcomes. Prigerson's work has been particularly valuable in furthering understanding within the field, notably through her empirically sound studies, use of tools to provide a basis for research, and for the subsequent improvement in the quality of intervention (Gray, Prigerson, & Litz, 2004). This work was somewhat complicated by the fact that for a period of time it was called "traumatic grief," and overlapped with different constructs that will be discussed below. Nevertheless complicated grief is now a central construct guiding work in this field.

Horowitz et al. (1997) developed a similar conceptual framework for complicated grief, which similarly reflected the findings of Prigerson's group, that complicated grief was distinct from depression (Prigerson & Jacobs, 2001; Prigerson, Maciejewski, et al., 1995). Many of the phenomena described as elevated or prolonged with complicated grief were similar to those that were found to persist as potential chronic grief in the work of Byrne and Raphael (1994) and Middleton et al. (1996). These latter studies involving two separate, well-selected community samples both found that approximately 9% had persisting levels of such grief when assessed at follow-up (Raphael & Minkov, 1999).

TRAUMATIC BEREAVEMENTS

Although the term *traumatic bereavements* has been widely applied, including to the complicated grief model noted above, it will be used in this chapter to denote the complex interaction that may occur between traumatic stress phenomena and bereavement phenomena. This may particularly arise where the circumstances of the death also evoke personal life threat and confrontation with death in gruesome, mutilating, and horrific forms, as with violent death (Raphael & Martinek, 1997; Raphael, Martinek, & Wooding, 2004; Raphael & Wooding, 2004). The distinct cognitive, affective, and psychophysiological aspects of bereavement and posttraumatic phenomena are outlined in Table 1.1. The former are characterized by distress, yearning, and an orientation "toward" the absent person; the latter by heightened fear and arousal, vigilance and a reactive orientation "away from" the feared event or its reminders. This delineation provides a useful basis for clinical assessment and intervention.

TABLE 1.1
Phenomenology of bereavement and traumatic stress reactions

	Bereavement	**Posttraumatic stress**
Cognition	Focus on lost person and images of person	Focus on death and images of horror
Affect	Yearning for lost person	Longing for security/safety
	Separation anxiety	Anxiety about threat
	Anger (protest)	Anger, irritability, and reminders of threat
	Sadness	Numbing
Arousal	Arousal to scan for lost person	Arousal focused on potential further threat
	Response to cues of that person	Response to stimuli with startle reactions

More recently there has been work such as that of Katherine Shear, which has emphasized the importance of intervention tailored to meet these specific needs (Shear , Frank, Houck, & Reynolds, 2005). These interventions will be discussed further below.

Pynoos also highlighted these separate phenomena and their potential interactions in his work with children (Pynoos, Nader, Frederick, Gonda, & Studer, 1987). He demonstrated traumatic stress reactions following death-threatening exposures, grief reactions following loss, and specific reactions to caregiver separation in children affected by a school sniper attack. More recently Judith Cohen has extended these concepts in her studies of traumatic grief in children (e.g., Cohen, 2004). All these studies highlight that the traumatic circumstances of these deaths is a critical factor affecting outcomes.

VIOLENT DEATHS AND GRIEF

An increasing number of studies have tried to conceptualize what happens after violent deaths, even though the impact of violence per se is not consistently and specifically addressed. An exception to this has been Rynearson's work with those bereaved by homicide deaths. His early reports (e.g., Rynearson, 1987; Rynearson & McCreery, 1993) and later therapy models (Rynearson, 2005; Rynearson & Sinnema, 1999) highlighted the particular significance of the violent intent of perpetrators as well as the distressing images of the circumstances of death. As noted above, violence may be associated with both natural events and accidental circumstances. These may lead to traumatic stress as well as bereavement reactions. However, when there is malevolent intent, as with homicide or the mass violence of terrorism, then there are additional stressor impacts to be addressed: those of coming to terms with what others have done to loved ones; that survivors themselves may have felt directly threatened; and that the threat itself may be ongoing or uncertain. These all add an extra dimension of distress. In these

circumstances, as Rynearson has discussed, there may also be legal impera-
tives shaping the environment in which the bereavement continues, and
which will bring their own concerns and uncertainties. These may include
the Disaster Victim Identification (DVI) process, the medical examiner's
requirements, crime scene demands, ongoing investigations, security, and
other constraints.

Vulnerabilities and Resilience in Those Bereaved

To deal with grief, to grieve for a loved one, may require certain conditions.
Some environmental factors, personal experience, and individual characteristics will make some people vulnerable to difficulties. Other factors in
these same domains may contribute to more positive grieving trajectories
and outcomes. As noted previously, both practical and emotional support
from others through this process may be helpful. For both psychological
trauma and grief processes, *perceptions* of the available support as helpful
is associated with better coping and outcomes (Maddison & Walker, 1967;
Stroebe, Hansson, Stroebe, & Schut, 2001). Past losses may leave some people
vulnerable, particularly if the overall impact of disadvantage or loss has
left little in the way of family or social networks. Earlier losses, for instance
of a parent in childhood, may in some circumstances make attachments
less secure, thus making the bereavement more complicated. Specific past
trauma, such as child abuse, has also been associated with vulnerabilities
affecting the course of bereavement (Silverman, Johnson, & Prigerson,
2001). However, grief and trauma in early life or previously may also have
been associated with personal growth (Tedeschi & Calhoun, 1995, 2004;
Vaillant, 1988) such that the individual may have developed strengths to
deal with the circumstances of the death and loss. A preexisting psychiatric
disorder may also influence the capacity to handle these major stressors, particularly when they are multiple and combined. Nevertheless, as Bonnano
(2004) and others have highlighted, many show great personal strengths
in the face of major losses. Other disabilities, such as physical illness and
incapacity and other life changes at the time of the death may add substantial
stressors that place an extra demand on those attempting to move on from
this experience.

Rituals around the traumatic or violent death may significantly affect
adjustment. The bereaved may be "blamed" or suffer survivor guilt, blaming
themselves. There may be an inability to meet religious requirements, which
are important to the bereaved in bidding farewell and paying tribute to the
deceased. Social disadvantages, both as an inherent stressor and as a con-
straint to the expression of grief, may add to vulnerability. Vulnerabilities
also exist for children and young people because of the demands of development. Events such as these may, in and of themselves, impact substantially
on the trajectory of the bereaved person's emotional, social, and cognitive
development.

The nature of the relationship with the deceased, including the broader
attachment dynamics within their family of origin and present family, may

significantly influence the way in which the bereaved adjust to this violence and loss. Relationships that had been highly ambivalent, perhaps even with violent, intense forms of attachment, are likely to make the grieving process more complex and protracted (van Doorn, Kasl, Beery, Jacobs, & Prigerson, 1998). Those bereaved in this relationship context may be more vulnerable to developing depressive constellations (Prigerson et al., 1995). In addition, there is the difficulty of dealing with what might be perceived as a consequence of violent fantasies, previously held toward the deceased person. This person may have been, at times, "wished dead" and now is dead, by violence, even if this was not perpetrated by the bereaved.

Survival: Psychological and Physical

When violent deaths occur and the circumstances of the death are particularly traumatic, survivors experience not only the psychological impact of such ways of dying but quite often threats to or fears concerning their own mortality. Where violent deaths occur through a terrorist attack such as a bombing there may be prolonged uncertainty regarding the likelihood of further attacks. In the violent deaths of mass disasters, such as the Southeast Asian tsunami and Hurricane Katrina, physical survival may be both an acute and ongoing concern for those affected. The early days, weeks, and even months may be taken up dealing with these realities as well as ongoing fear. The psychological commitment to survival may leave little room to work through the psychological trauma or to grieve — there may be no time for what has often been called the "luxury of grief." It is very important to recognize these forces, to support those affected in their survival strategies, and to be prepared to assist them with the physical and psychological processes they define as necessary for them to be able to move on with their lives. Issues to do with ongoing family survival will be prominent: for instance the woman who survives the violent death of a husband, child, or even both may be taken up with the needs of several other children. Their physical and psychological security may necessarily be her first priority. There is a balance between supporting survival and engaging those affected to confront and deal with the experiences and losses which have so devastated their existence. This relates to the issue of personal *timelines of readiness* to deal with what has happened, in terms of both trauma and grief. Experiences of providing counseling for Australians bereaved by the Bali bombings have shown that there may be a prolonged period of time before people can talk of the depth of the traumatic experience and the pain of grief (Raphael, Dunsmore, & Wooding, 2004; see also Danieli, 1993).

Survival strategies will often include a range of psychological defenses, activities, and behaviors (Valent, 1998). Denial, dissociation, numbness, running on "automatic," vicarious identification with the needs of others, withdrawal, and overactivity, are all common responses. So too is intense preoccupation with tasks which will contribute to safety and a basis for the future. Survivor guilt is a common response where personal survival is viewed against the deaths of others: the relief at finding one is still alive; the guilt at feeling the elation of survival; the sense that others should have survived instead of the self, for instance children; preoccupation with what one should or could have done to prevent the death or deaths; and for a few, awareness of their own violent fantasy or reality. As noted, guilt also often features where there has been a preexisting, intensely ambivalent relationship with those who have died. Recognition of these survival issues in assessments or interventions will be important for those so bereaved.

The Acute Situation

Responding to violent death commences from the moment of the death — determinations are made as to what is known and which structures of response need to be enlisted, including medical, legal, and social systems. Those bereaved may have been present, for instance, when someone was murdered. Not only would they experience the horror of being there, but also the personal life threat. Acute medical response will likely involve emergency services, police, and crime scene requirements. Those who were present may be subject to investigation as potential perpetrators. Black's work has highlighted the horror of such circumstances for children; for example, when a father kills a mother (Black & Kaplan, 1988; Harris-Hendriks, Black, & Kaplan, 2000). In mass casualty situations there is the need to establish the death and its cause through medical systems and the medical examiner's office, ultimately to determine whether blame can be apportioned and to whom. There are a number of key themes that are relevant to the acute response which relate to medical, legal, and societal requirements.

Notification of the Death

This may be clear-cut or complex: for instance, in a single circumstance, police notification; in circumstances where no body is found a prolonged period of "missing" dynamics may ensue; and the variable requirements for formal identification from viewing the deceased to specific victim identification protocols. The ways in which each of these requirements is handled may have significant implications for the person's ongoing mental health. It is particularly important that such processes are psychologically sound and supportive, while meeting legal requirements, so that they do not further traumatize those so bereaved (Mowll, 2005). Police, medical examiners, doctors, and all those likely to be involved should have protocols and training to support them in this process, not only for the practical tasks, but also for the psychological and emotional aspects.

Disaster Victim Identification

Experience of mass violence such as with Lockerbie, September 11, and the Bali bombings, have shown that bodies may be beyond recognition, disfigured or dismembered, burned, disintegrated, or indeed, not able to be found at all. Formal Disaster Victim Identification (DVI) will involve forensic processes which may be prolonged; for instance, dental and medical records and DNA analysis. Families bereaved in this way may have to provide descriptions, and even DNA samples, whilst they are trying to process the enormity of the destruction that took their loved one's life. Of concern for all the bereaved is whether the person who died suffered greatly. This concern is profound when they also have to confront horrific circumstances of this kind. Support through the whole process requires skilled workers, for instance counseling teams who deal with sudden and violent deaths, including those in mass disasters. A team such as this is attached to the city morgue in Sydney, Australia. It was initially set up after a major rail disaster but has continued these services, and defined its role and training since that time (Mowll, 2005). Protocols, skill, empathy, and experience all inform the important work of returning the remains of the deceased to the family for burial (see Table 1.2). This complex and sensitive work requires training, supervision, and support so that the circle of impact of the violent death does not adversely affect the well-being of such workers.

Saying Goodbye to the Deceased

Research has shown that people may benefit from the opportunity to see the body of a loved one, particularly one who has died suddenly and unexpectedly through circumstances such as a disaster (Hodgkinson, Joseph, Yule, & Williams, 1993). In fact one study indicated that following such events, a decision not to view was later regretted by 50% of participants (Singh & Raphael, 1981). Knowing the deceased was one's own loved one, that the person who died was *that* person, is part of the reality. The bereaved may have this opportunity with support at a morgue or funeral home, or may say their farewells in many other ways: for instance through visits to the graveyard or memorial; or during personal reminiscence or with subsequent counseling/therapy. Release of the remains, support for funeral processes, both practical and emotional, and protecting those bereaved from further traumatization will all be important early processes to mitigate the risk of ongoing problems.

Nevertheless, saying goodbye is additionally stressful when the remains are unable to be found, when the body is damaged beyond any physical recognition, or when the body is not whole. Support for those bereaved who wish to view a body that is severely mutilated will require compassionate, sensitive provision of information, choice for the bereaved, support through their decisions and what they actually do, as well as the period that follows. This is one component of the level of acute support and positive/preventive interventions that should be provided at this early stage, linked to concepts of psychological first aid for those bereaved in such circumstances.

Throughout this acute period, reliable sources of information are essential components of psychological support

TABLE 1.2
Viewing after multiple deaths: Benefits and process (Mowll, 2005)

Professional role	Key issues & processes
Forensic counselors / social work	Provide open discussion Sensitive exploration & description Viewing in safe context Hospital, etc., as different to finding at scene Advocacy of family needs Choice

Local disasters:
Thredbo avalanche/
  mining disaster/air crash
	Family sense of making own decision
	  with support
	Bureaucratic process necessary — but may
	  prevent access to choices

Overseas disasters:
Bali bombings (2002, 2005) &
  Southeast Asian tsunami
	Chaotic environments:
	  Survivors: trauma from visuals, guilt
	
	Missing loved ones/remains
	Variable support for families
	Difficult to limit family searches for bodies
	Dual bureaucracies
	Disfigured remains — unrecognizable by photograph
	Limited viewing access

	Options:
	Prior verbal descriptions, partial viewing,
	  closed casket viewing, viewing by photographs,
	  verbal descriptions only
	Family-appointed spokesperson: Advice on key
	  choices, may limit access, especially children
	Advocate for and work with family liaison officers
	Family counseling & referral to specialist
	  counseling & mental health services

Information/Communication

Information may range from that provided initially when it is uncertain whether a missing person is dead, to processes that are underway to establish their whereabouts and to information on DVI and other forensic requirements. Further information will pertain to legal/investigative requirements and to the personal and community supports that are available. A clearly identified, formal information point and process is a required strategy. Those providing control of responses and the media should have training and protocols about what is helpful, and how to support those concerned while providing accurate, consistent, and updated information. It is important that when information is limited (as frequently occurs with mass violence) that this is acknowledged but contextualized. Similarly, the same provisions apply when communicating actions that are being taken to provide further facts. A reliable, respected source for public information through the media enhances its acceptability. Such sources should be well informed on the needs of bereaved persons.

Community Context and Resources in Response

Social networks and wider structures form both a context in which bereavements occur and are defined but are also key resources that may be enlisted to help. These may be the institutions involved in formal response; the reactions of local and community "leaders"; religious or pastoral care providers; media reporting of violent death; stigmatized social construction of some violent deaths, such as some circumstances of suicide deaths; health care providers; schools, workplaces; and with mass death, the likelihood of state or national reaction. Each of these may be helpful to those bereaved, or inadvertently unhelpful. The *recognition* of the death, of the dead person's value, and of the trauma, loss, and suffering of those bereaved may be critical issues that enhance their capacity to adapt. Negative or controversial characterizations of the deceased, the circumstances of their death, or other associations risk further complicating recovery from what has happened.

Expectations about entitlements may form the basis of a prolonged "victim" status. While this may represent the only way that some bereaved feel they can be acknowledged, such roles may ultimately reinforce helplessness. The way in which the bereaved are supported in their acute phase is important. This could include protection from situations, convergence, or specific intrusions, which may add to negative impacts. Educating social networks and institutions on what is appropriate is thus part of an effective response. Self-help organizations may develop from individual or group experiences of such trauma and loss. The outreach and support from others who "have been through the same thing" and "know what it feels like" may be of great value. Sudden infant death syndrome (SIDS) groups have provided such support in the early stage, with those providing outreach having had such experiences themselves. Members are able to provide needed support as well as a message of hope that it is possible to survive when those acutely affected may feel it is impossible to go on with life.

A suicide survivors outreach service, local outreach to suicide survivors (LOSS; Campbell, Cataldie, McIntosh, & Millet, 2004) is another valuable model of such support for circumstances of sudden death, as are homicide victims support programs. These outreach programs provide supportive contact with the bereaved from the initial stages, provide information necessary to handle immediate demands, and provide a framework of contact and follow-up for the future.

First Not to Harm

As in other acute/emergency settings, support provided must be such that it is likely to be of assistance and does not, in itself, further "harm" those affected. For general response in mass casualty situations, as well as individual personal circumstance, the concept of psychological first aid has been useful (NIMH, 2002; Pynoos & Nader, 1988; Raphael, 1977). This involves promoting safety, survival, shelter, and comfort to those affected, helping to bring or keep families together, and protecting them from further harm. It also involves triage of those who may be so acutely affected they cannot function safely. For instance, in the aftermath of a mass violence incident, individuals and groups may be placed at further risk through high levels of arousal, cognitive impairments including dissociation or organic impacts, and behavioral disturbance. This constitutes the A (arousal), B (behavior), and C (cognition), the ABC of psychological first aid and triage.

It is important to not only set in place knowledgeable, compassionate, and effective broader systems of response, as described above, but also to protect those traumatized and bereaved from well-meant but inappropriate and potentially harmful psychological interventions. Stress debriefing processes, including critical incident stress debriefing (CISD) and other forms of psychological debriefing are inappropriate, potentially harmful, and not indicated for acutely bereaved persons (Litz, Gray, Bryant, & Adler, 2002; Raphael & Wilson, 2000). Bereavement counseling which forces bereaved people to talk about their experience and feelings is not appropriate as an acute intervention in the early days and weeks, unless those bereaved seek to talk, or do so in spontaneous ways in response to general support and information to individuals, or possibly in groups. The media image of grief counselors descending on those so bereaved in the earliest stages of their shock and horror represent an inappropriate response. General support is appropriate, but should not push for disclosure, catharsis, or reviewing the loss/trauma experience. These tasks will come at various times for bereaved persons. As noted, sensitivity to "readiness" forms a critical part of both the acute response and the transition to more formal and specific interventions, when these are indicated for prevention or therapy.

Bereavement Support or Liaison Worker

The appointment of a skilled, supportive family liaison officer may be an important provision in the early acute stage, when the need for structured support is indicated. The person in this role helps to negotiate a pathway to deal with what has happened. This role is ideally filled by someone with the following expertise: mental health, trauma, and grief related skills; knowledge of formal processes that may be involved, resources that can be accessed, and how to access these; a capacity to engage with those bereaved, and to offer support in a nonintrusive, practical, and psychologically helpful way. The central issue is *being with* the person through their experience. Self-help organizations, social workers in emergency departments or services; chaplains with pastoral care skills; other mental health or health professionals, are all likely to be of assistance. However, these roles also require recognition of how to integrate psychosocial and practical support; how to relate when the context is not the usual client/professional setting; and how to maintain sensitivity to the needs of the other. Of central importance is the capacity to monitor and manage one's own concerns and feelings of helplessness, without demanding responses or actions that may be inappropriate.

Transition: Assessment, Engagement, Care

In the days and weeks following violent death, when survival is assured for those who have been bereaved, where any ongoing threat of violence is at least to some degree contained, or the bereaved are separated from it, there comes the time to assess the need for care. This will involve some process of assessment of individuals that will take into account the domains indicated above; that is, the specifics of the death and any psychological trauma impacts, and the nature of the grieving process. The vulnerabilities and resilience of those bereaved are key aspects of the assessment, as are past and present events affecting the individuals, their current level of social support, and their readiness. The assessment may help to determine whether either a preventive or therapeutic intervention is required, an intervention is not indicated, or a waiting brief, with monitoring, is the most appropriate course. Several studies have indicated that a significant proportion of those bereaved through the violent deaths of loved ones will be at risk of developing psychopathology (e.g., Lundin, 1984, Murphy, 1996). If the violence has been such as to lead to mass casualties, it is important to plan for a more widespread response that may require group interventions, education, and support. With a single death, individuals and families may be the appropriate focus (Black, Harris-Hendriks, & Kaplan,1992; Rynearson & Sinnema, 1999). Spontaneous or other support groups may be necessary alongside quite specific mental health interventions, particularly where such groups involve individuals with similar experiences. Their capacity to demonstrate role pathways and provide mutual informal support and practical assistance can be invaluable. Planning processes, adequately reflecting numbers affected in large-scale incidents, will require systematic identification of resources (human and other) and processes regarding contact, engagement, and the prioritizing of interventions.

"Therapeutic Assessment" of Individuals

This conceptual framework evolved following experience with those bereaved in a major rail disaster (Raphael, 1979–1980). The intent is to assess the bereaved individuals in ways that are able to gauge their adaptation, to do no harm, and to provide information to inform further decisions about their needs. It is based on a number of research studies, which have found common themes of vulnerability, and to a degree, of resilience (Parkes & Weiss, 1983; Raphael 1977; Stroebe et al, 2001; Vachon, Lyall, Rogers, Freedman-Letofsky, & Freeman, 1980). The assessment is framed around a number of questions/themes which can be evaluated.

1. Can you tell me about the death, about what happened, about the day? This provides information about the *circumstances of the death,*

understanding its detail. This will show how "traumatic" it was in and of itself for those bereaved, how shocking its nature. Not only does this indicate to the bereaved that the clinician is prepared to discuss these circumstances, but also recognizes their significance for the bereaved. It also allows the assessment of affective responses, of avoidance, of rumination, and of the death's reality and impact per se. Frequently this will reveal that the *circumstances* of *violent death* represent stressors at a level commensurate with criterion A of PTSD. This is separate from the grief.

2. Can you tell me about "x," about your loved one? This involves a *story of the relationship*, which may later be expanded and explored. Initially, however, it will indicate the nature of the attachment and to some degree the levels of dependence and closeness, and perhaps ambivalence. It is a snapshot in time, frequently an idealized one in the beginning, but important to query in terms of the *real* relationships involved. Highly ambivalent and highly dependent attachments indicate risk of chronic or complicated grief or other factors that may hinder resolution (van Doorn et al., 1998). It may also indicate the affects, the yearning and longing, the anger, the reality, or otherwise of the loss. The deaths of children have been found in many studies to be associated with the highest levels of grief and potential vulnerability (e.g. Middleton, Raphael, Burnett, & Martinek, 1998).

3. How have you been *feeling*, what have you been *doing?* This will help to identify the degree to which those bereaved are still struggling with survival, where they are at, in terms of the intensity and form of their feelings, and how much they have been able to sustain or return to core functioning. Sleep, appetite, and mood may indicate the person's recovery or ongoing distress. Very high levels of grieving or other psychological distress have been shown to be predictive of poorer outcomes. High distress may relate to heightened arousal or anxiety from traumatization, or to heightened arousal or anxiety from intense separation distress and grief. Identifying the specific contributions of each will be important to inform the basis of intervention.

4. What has been *happening in your life since?* This domain allows for identification of ongoing stressors and their impact. These may range from triggers that remind the bereaved of the traumatic circumstances, to triggers of the absence of their loved one. They may include the perceived and actual support provided in helpful ways, or what was distressing and not helpful in the interventions/responses of others and in the broader context. It will also allow assessment of ongoing or new stressor impacts, including those that have resulted from the violent death, and those that are coincidental. The identification of practical needs is important, since dealing with these may provide a vehicle for further engagement while psychological needs can be dealt with concurrently with these. This process is informed by finding out from those bereaved what is useful to them, and particularly their own

effective strategies, what they have found effective for dealing with major stressors in the past, and how these tools may be mobilized to help the present situation.

5. Formal *questionnaires* can be used for *screening* but need to be understood not only for their reliability and validity, but also for what they will mean to those bereaved in this way and at this early stage. Such measures may provide a baseline, but are probably best utilized in interpersonal contexts of support, explanation, engagement, and making sure they do not harm. A thorough review of available measures highlighted the following (see also Neimeyer & Hogan, 2001):

   Texas Revised Inventory of Grief (TRIG) (Faschingbauer, Zisook, & DeVaul, 1987). A measure of grief based on literature regarding normal and pathological grief and traumatic reactions.

   The Grief Experience Inventory (Sanders, 1980). A measure of somatic and emotional aspects of bereavement.

   Core Bereavement Items (CBI) (Burnett et al., 1997). This is a brief measure of the intensity and course of bereavement experiences.

   Inventory of Complicated Grief (ICG) (Prigerson et al. 1995). This is a brief assessment of emotional, cognitive, or behavioral symptoms of complicated grief.

   Grief Screening Scale (UCLA PTSD Index for DSM-IV) (Rodriguez, Steinberg, & Pynoos, 1999). This is a measure of traumatic bereavement in children and adolescents. It has three independent factors, with measures of positive reminiscing, intrusion of PTSD on the grieving process, and existential loss.

6. *Assessing children and adolescents* is more difficult and should be conducted in a *family context* if possible. Again, if there is a surviving parent then observations of children's response to the death of a family member will be helpful, and can encompass domains as identified above. It should be noted, however, that parents, who are themselves traumatized and grieving, may not be able to recognize the needs of their children (McFarlane, 1987; Raphael, Field, & Kvelde, 1980), or the children's reactions may be delayed until circumstances of security in family/school life are reestablished. In some instances parents may present their children to care as a defense against recognizing and dealing with their own needs. Family assessment may need to take into account the diverse levels and patterns of response to trauma and grief in different family members and the potential impact of complex family dynamics or coping styles (Kissane, Bloch, Dowe, et al., 1996a; Kissane, Bloch, Onghena 1996b).

Engagement

There are many barriers to engagement with people in the community who may not see themselves as in need of help, or as not ready, as coping well, or that others are more needy/deserving of care. These may be realities or defenses against the multiple levels of distress that they fear will overwhelm them if they open the "Pandora's box" of their trauma and grief. This may relate to earlier as well as current deprivations, trauma, and loss. It may relate to an inability to trust those who offer help, perhaps because of past experience with helpers/counselors. It may be that those offering care do not have the sensitivity, empathy, and skills necessary for the task. It is interesting to note that in an early study of outreach after a nightclub fire, Lindy et al. (1983) found that the more skilled, experienced psychotherapists were more likely to be successful in engaging those bereaved traumatically in the aftermath of the disaster. Elements of engagement that may be helpful include:

1. *What is offered*. Practical short-term assistance, assessment, feedback, advice, and information may all be seen as more acceptable than counseling. Nevertheless each of these may be a tool for engagement with more sensitive emotional needs alongside the "acceptable" request. This is all the more so for those who feel that having counseling, care, or therapy may be seen as indicating that they cannot cope. What is offered may be fine tuned in terms of individual needs or the stage of response. Contrary to many popular belief systems, one study showed that emotion-focused counseling was perceived as more helpful to men, and instrumental-focused counseling to women (Schut, Stroebe, van den Bout, & Keijser, 1997). In effect, participants appeared to benefit from increased exposure to a less gender-familiar strategy. It is possible too that one style may be more relevant early and another later. In any case, if the intervention offered recognizes and builds on strengths, it is likely to be less threatening in terms of the individual's confidence in his or her own competence.

   What is offered may be in terms of further assessment, in a mode to deal with trauma, or to assist with grieving. These components may require negotiation and agreement, particularly as the focus of the trauma is the event, while the focus of grieving is the relationship and its loss.

   What is offered is more likely to be acceptable if it is in a context whereby those who are to receive it have a role in defining the things for which they would like assistance. This may ultimately include shared realistic goals, a recognition that coming to terms with something like a violent death will undoubtedly take a long time, and that despite this the intervention may not necessarily be prolonged. Rather, it is a component to assist the journey. Rigid adherence to manual-based approaches is unlikely to be well received in these early stages.

2. *Who is offering engagement?* Skills, wisdom, sensitivity, compassion, and experience are all important. Recognition of, and a respectful response to, the individual's particular need, requires the capacity to take into account the diversity of human pathways through such horror. Language, culture, social distance, and difficulties with differing professional/

personal responsibilities may all make engagement a problem for both parties. Many therapists will avoid too early an intervention: some on theoretical grounds of lack of evidence; others from the discomfort of dealing with someone not unlike the self, with needs, but without a "diagnosis" to reassure that intervention is called for. Experience can help in dealing with these issues, so that engagement is possible with staged goals, expectation of resilience, and a sense of the value of this type of skilled, nonintrusive, yet informed supportive process.

3. *How outreach or offers of intervention are presented.* Public information, help lines, outreach from self-help groups, presentation of interventions as positive and adaptive, packaging of self-help, Web-based, or other intervention strategies may all provide vehicles for and levels of engagement; a "testing the water" as it were, for those in need. Engagement through groups may also be more readily "sold" to some bereaved individuals.

4. *Touching.* Comforting in the emergency and acute phase may involve touching. This can occur physically but more often symbolically as a "holding" of the emotional environment and as a message of basic care. At all times this must occur with understanding and respect for cultural views and appropriateness. Good follow-up may involve touching base by those who have helped in the acute phase, to see how things are going. This type of contact by those who gave early help can provide continuity over time, and support the readiness of people to deal with their trauma and grief.

5. *Costs of recovery.* The availability of human resources, the costs of intervention, and variable funding may make it difficult to be facilitative or may create further barriers to care. Legal processes may also create practical or psychological hurdles to be overcome before those affected can seek care. This is well conceptualized in Rynearson's careful work in this field (2005). This is particularly relevant in circumstances of mass casualty, where much may be promised initially, but proves difficult to sustain over the mid- to longer term.

Care

There are a number of different models of intervention that may be provided either as prevention or treatment. The strong focus on psychological trauma and PTSD has meant that this has often had prominence, with the need to grieve being poorly recognized. Care models include:

Cognitive Behavior Therapy

Exposure for those at high risk in terms of PTSD/traumatic stress syndromes is in line with Bryant, Moulds, and Nixon's (2003) work. These controlled trials showed that those with high levels of initial symptoms, which met criteria for acute stress disorder, could be prevented from developing PTSD and a more prolonged disorder in many instances (e.g., Bryant et al., 2003).

Grief Counseling

Grief counseling is recommended for those with high-risk bereavements, as reported by Lindeman (1944), Raphael (1977), and Vachon et al. (1980). Lindeman's work focused on converting abnormal grief into normal grief, Raphael's model focused on facilitating normal grieving over six to eight sessions, while Vachon's study utilized self-help outreach. Numerous other studies and models exist. A thorough review of such interventions has been conducted by Schut, Stroebe, Van Den Bout, and Terheggen (2001).

Traumatic Bereavement

Interventions for those experiencing both trauma and grief have evolved more recently. They include studies such as those of Shear, involving work with adults (e.g., Shear et al., 2005) and Cohen (2004) in relation to children. Cohen's work highlights a number of modules delivered to parents and children. These covered both trauma- and grief-focused treatment components. The five modules include: traumatic experience; reminders of trauma and loss; bereavement and the interplay of trauma and grief; posttrauma adversity; and developmental progression.

Shear's model, based upon the dual-processing model of Stroebe and Schut (1999), addresses features of both depression and trauma that may be present in adults experiencing complicated grief. Her controlled trial involved a comparison of treatments for complicated grief (Shear et al., 2005). Interpersonal therapy (ITP), originally developed to treat grief-related depression, was modified to incorporate cognitive and behavioral elements to specifically address trauma symptoms. This new approach, complicated grief therapy (CGT), was then compared with standard ITP (N = 95). Randomization of the samples was stratified by treatment site and, within site, by violent (accident, suicide, or homicide) versus nonviolent death of a loved one. One-third of the sample had experienced violent loss. Both treatment approaches were found to improve complicated grief but CGT produced better response rates (51% vs. 28%) and with a more rapid rate of response overall. There was a trend toward CGT producing better outcomes with those who had experienced violent loss, but this did not reach significance due to sample sizes. Future studies with larger samples could determine whether the cognitive–behavioral exposure elements of CGT may particularly benefit those experiencing violent loss.

Raphael and Wooding (2004) have described a clinical model of early intervention for traumatic loss, which deals with the trauma component through the review of the circumstances of the death as above, and a grieving component which reviews the relationship and grieving affects, other stressors, and impacts. This process is very similar to the modular approach described by Cohen (2004).

Complicated and Chronic Grief

These may be diagnosed at a later stage and may require specific interventions to address relationship issues impeding the grieving process or specific trauma effects. Complicated grief of this kind is associated with a more protracted course (greater than six months), more adverse outcomes, and greater treatment complexity. The term itself has been adopted to reflect broad grief phenomena, including nontraumatic grief (Gray et al., 2004). Clinicians working with those bereaved through violence and other traumatic circumstances, increasingly recognize that traumatic stress effects (e.g., death exposure and life threat) must often be dealt with first before it is possible to grieve. Regehr and Sussman (2004) suggest that an integrated, evidence-based approach is likely to entail (1) cognitive restructuring and management of arousal, avoidance, and reexperiencing symptoms associated with trauma stressors; and (2) phased (or parallel) relational therapies which resolve relationship issues and enable a new sense of the relationship and the self.

Social, Role, and Identity Issues

Social, role, and identity issues may be encompassed in any of these interventions or require additional processes, often in group settings. Interventions may be provided for individuals or groups. In either case, however, they will need to be relevant to the extent and nature of the losses incurred through these violent deaths, as well as the resources available in the bereaved person's environment to address the need. These issues of context are well exemplified by Leila Gupta's work with Rwandan children, where she trained primary care community members to be trauma support workers (Gupta, 1999).

The evidence supporting the interventions noted above is variable. They are often open studies and not representative of more violent contexts. Further research is needed to inform these processes, particularly translational research which can move from the randomized controlled trial to the early-phase preventive interventions delivered in real-world social, cultural, and resource contexts, that many who experience death of a loved one require. Many of the themes of therapy in these contexts are to do with narrative (the telling of the story of the death, its trauma, and of the loss). Narrative therapies and psychodynamic and behavioral psychotherapies all support the use of the narrative as a vehicle for assimilation, adaptation, and positive change. However, work with children such as that of Terr (1991) makes it clear that endless replaying may not reflect healing, but rather a fixation to the trauma and the loved one. Rynearson's model of restorative storytelling is one such valid framework to be taken forward. Indigenous peoples have also pursued narrative therapy models to deal with trauma and grief because of their cultural appropriateness (Ober, Peeters, Archer, & Kelly, 2000). Telling of the deceased is also a way of paying tribute to them as the people they were, their legacy, and their incarnation into memory. Many give testimony in books and oral stories, and write of their experiences as catharsis, memory, memorialization, and tribute. Such testimonies are frequently important healing strategies.

Nevertheless there appears to be a common set of observations among those working in these fields. As indicated by Raphael and Martinek (1997),

Lindy, Green, Grace, and Tichner (1983), Cohen (2004), and Raphael and Wooding (2004) there is frequently a need to deal with trauma first and grief subsequently, although there may be significant interactions between these.

Another important issue is where people will present when they have not been identified or provided with outreach content. People may present to private sector providers of mental health care, such as psychiatrists, clinical psychologists, primary care professionals, especially general practitioners or family physicians, to their spiritual advisors, to the legal system, and to the welfare system. Children may present in schools or other childcare settings. Young people may present to youth, drug and alcohol, juvenile justice, or other systems. Thus there is another circle of people who may need to know of trauma, grief, nonclinical, and clinical presentations. They will need to know what to do, when the person may need help, and how and where to refer them. Somatic presentations, suicidal thoughts, depression, and physical illnesses may all be related outcomes, as may other conditions. When treatment for a specific disorder is required, care will also involve the capacity to assess and manage aspects of trauma, grief, and the psychological parameters of violent death.

Many other themes will potentially need to be taken into account if interventions are to support personal growth, recovery, and engagement with life for those affected.

- Anger. These include the anger, even rage, that is associated with such deaths — anger toward those who are deceased and in protest against the abandonment that death entails. There is also rage toward the perpetrators of violence, toward a world in which the sense of personal invulnerability is lost, where safety cannot be guaranteed; and toward those who did not prevent this from happening, or allowed a violent world to exist. Such anger is not only an issue in therapy but also a driving social force after such deaths. Those bereaved may seek justice, revenge, or vengeance. This seeking of action may occur as a constructive social process to enhance safety and lessen violence. Often, however, it can also fuel retribution and the "escalations" of violence typified by the enduring conflicts in Northern Ireland and the West Bank. Ongoing anger reflects a holding-on to the trauma and in a way to the death and the deceased. It may significantly impact on the potential to reengage the positives and hopes for life in the future. Thus it is not only an issue for therapy but also in the longer term adjustment processes.
- *Memory*. Memories of trauma, memories of loved ones, involve complex neural pathways, psychological processes, and social frames of reference. These are being explored in research examining the templates of traumatic memory constellations, how these develop, continue, and are attenuated, and how memories of loved ones are internalized in both positive and negative ways. Psychological interventions inevitably involve helping those affected deal with their memories in ways that

will mitigate the suffering that is associated with them. Social processes
of memorialization may or may not assist.

- *Malevolence.* The violent intent to harm, specifically or generally,
represents a profound stressor. It induces terror and fear in innumerable
human contexts, but remains poorly understood. Coming to terms with
the violent actions of others is a complex psychological task, as well as
a social process. It frequently leads to "splitting" — the ready defining
of the "evil" other and the "innocent" self — although this process
may do little to support adaptation to life's realities. Further research is
needed to address this theme at individual and social levels.

- *Transmission.* Transgenerational impacts and transmission of trauma
and grief may be profound, as exemplified by work with Holocaust
survivors, indigenous populations, and others who have experienced
amongst the deepest of psychological wounds. Interventions for
individuals and communities must also take account of this broader
lens of history. Social programs and restraints, and therapeutic efforts
to heal or forestall the effects of current violence, may be judged ultimately
by their influence a generation hence.

- *Violence.* Violence is an ongoing issue in society. Not only does violent
death occur with frequency, as a trigger to the trauma and grief, but
individuals and society face it daily in some settings, and are preoccupied, even fascinated with it in others. Fascination shows through
media ratings, and crowd behaviors, as an entertainment staple for
some young people, and as individual fantasies and actions. The theme
of personal violence and its meaning will be relevant for individuals, as
will family violence be for families, and group violence for the broader
society. This needs to be recognized as a potential issue in the context
of the mental health therapy that may be provided.

LONGER-TERM ISSUES

Those who have experienced the loss of a loved one in circumstances of
violence will both take their time to progress to an acceptance of the death
and to make meaning of their experience; to take on new identities and roles
such as widow or orphan; to become a different person without the person
who died, and who, through the bonds of attachment, contributed to the
identity of those who were bereaved. The longer-term challenge has often
been conceptualized as needing to deal with the tasks of grieving (Worden,
1991) or the work of grief (Freud, 1917/1957), or perhaps more realistically,
as a journey. After violent death, individuals, families, and communities may
have to deal with a number of common issues into the longer term.

How Do Those Affected Deal with the Changes of Their Lives?

How may health, social, or other strategies be of help? The various approaches
and intervention strategies discussed above offer one set of frameworks. For
mental health and other clinicians they represent an important contribution to

recovery and to the capacity to experience life after such experiences. However, they are only one component.

Memorialization

A simple and common enactment can be seen in roadside crosses and flowers marking the individual circumstances of motor vehicle accidents. Memorials are a powerful personal and societal focus. The candles after the Bali, Madrid, and London bombings, and other circumstances of mass death symbolize loss in the acute period, and anniversaries or ongoing remembrance. Rituals of memorialization may continue, acknowledging both the bereaved and the deceased. Memorialization is complex because it may trigger reexperiencing of the trauma while also reflecting the attachment to the person who was lost, and the sadness and grief for that person or those persons.

Formal structures of memorialization give testimony to those who died and are a focus for those bereaved. For example, the Vietnam Memorial in Washington, DC has come to symbolize, *to be*, the place to review and remember, to deal with trauma, where it can be recognized, where those who have suffered are acknowledged; as a place to pay tribute to all those who died, whose names are inscribed, and to grieve. Ground Zero in New York has come to be imbued with similar meaning and ritual. Support for both personal and societal memorialization facilitates grieving and healing but also requires a sensitive recognition of how it may also trigger painful reminders of the trauma.

Circles of Those Affected

Violent deaths impact not only on those directly and personally bereaved, but also on their communities. They impact too, upon those who most often provide the first response. Police, ambulance, fire services, health, and other emergency responders see it in its acuity and horror. Their own lives may be at risk. They may be secondarily traumatized, and grieve for the loss of children, fellow adult human beings, and their community. Even those specially trained to deal with such events may continue to feel the impact in numerous ways. Just as resilience and strengths need to be recognized alongside care provided, so also strengths of such workers need to be built on and supported to deal with these deaths. Trauma, rotation of tours of duty, buddy systems, support, and supervision can all assist, particularly with emphasis on active strategies which help those involved to recognize both strengths and needs and to seek help when appropriate. Those providing interventions are also in this circle of impact; supervision, case review, and active learning are important supports. Operational reviews may promote active learning and mastery in such circumstances.

Justice, Meaning, and Resolution

One of the most difficult components of individual and community adaptation is that perpetrators may not be found, that uncertainty frequently persists, and that restitution cannot be made. Even if there is a perpetrator, who is found and punished, it may not fulfill the psychological demands of justice for the world to be as it "should" be (or even as it was). Institutions such as the Truth and Reconciliation Commission in South Africa have attempted to address this in one context. Trial and punishment of a murderer may attempt to do so in another. None of these can readily deal with the search for meaning, which asks: why my loved one; why violence; why me? These questions arise in therapy contexts for the individual and in the broader community of those affected by mass violence. Individuals may be supported by recognition and provision for their spiritual needs (D'Souza, 2003) or by faith and religious belief in their attempts to find meaning. But for the majority, other avenues are sought. Preoccupation with vengeance looks to the past and to what cannot be altered. It may lead to ongoing cycles of violence with more violent deaths. Clinical and social processes need to be influenced to steer a more hopeful course for those affected, and acceptance that answers may not be found, justice and resolution may be uncertain, but life will continue.

The Nature of a Safer World

Ultimately the challenge for the individual and the society is the recognition that life cannot always be protected from violence, malevolence, or change. Safety is sought but cannot be guaranteed. One of the difficulties of living with the threat of terrorism, for instance, is the balance of safety/security strategies with the freedom and risk taking that facilitates human growth and development. There are no easy answers except perhaps for the safety that good relationships bring, for the truism of it being better to have loved and lost, than never to have loved at all. But from a strategic, public health perspective the human economic costs of violence need to be urgently addressed. The World Health Organization's 2003 World Report on Violence and Health highlights the need for concentrated action to achieve this (Mercy, Butchart, Dahlberg, Zwi, & Krug, 2003). Such actions, building on research, positive human values, and human rights, offer the most hopeful future and the greatest opportunity for impact on the tragedy of violent death.

REFERENCES

Black D., Harris-Hendriks J., & Kaplan T. (1992). Father kills mother: Post-traumatic stress disorder in the children. *Psychotherapy & Psychosomatics, 57,* 152–157.

Black, D., & Kaplan, T. (1988). Father kills mother. Issues and problems encountered by a child psychiatric team. *The British Journal of Psychiatry, 153,* 624–630.

Bonnano, G. (2004). Loss, trauma, and human resilience. *American Psychologist, 59,* 20–28.

Bowlby, J. (1980) *Attachment and Loss: Vol. 3. Loss: Sadness and Depression.* London: Penguin.

Bryant, R. A., Moulds, M. L., & Nixon, D. V. (2003). Cognitive behaviour therapy of acute stress disorder. A four-year follow-up. *Behaviour Research and Therapy, 41,* 489–494.

Burnett, P., Middleton, W., Raphael, B., & Martinek, N. (1997) Measuring core bereavement phenomena. *Psychological Medicine, 27,* 49–57.

Byrne, G. J. & Raphael, B (1994). A longitudinal study of bereavement phenomena in recently widowed elderly men. *Psychological Medicine, 24,* 411–421.

Campbell, F. R., Cataldie, L., McIntosh, J., & Millet K. *(2004). An active postvention program. Crisis: Journal of Crisis Intervention & Suicide, 25,* 30–32.

Cohen, J. A. (2004). Early mental health interventions for trauma and traumatic loss in children and adolescents. In B. Litz (Ed.), *Early intervention for trauma and traumatic loss.* New York: Guilford Press.

Danieli, Y. (1993). The diagnostic and therapeutic use of the multi-generational family tree in working with survivors and children of survivors of the Nazi Holocaust. In J. P. Wilson & B. Raphael (Eds.), *International handbook of traumatic stress syndromes.* New York: Plenum, p. 889–898.

D'Souza, R. (2003). *Incorporating a spiritual history into a psychiatric assessment. Australasian Psychiatry, 11,* 12–15.

Engel, G. L. (1961). Is grief a disease? *Psychosomatic Medicine, 23,* 18–22.

Faschingbauer, T. R., Zisook, S., & DeVaul, R. (1987). Texas revised inventory of grief, In S. Zisook (Ed.), *Biopsychosocial aspects of bereavement.* Washington, D.C.: American Psychiatric Press.

Freud, S. (1957). Mourning and melancholia. In J.Strachey (Ed. & Trans.), *The standard edition of the complete psychological works of Sigmund Freud* (Vol. 14, pp. 237–258) London: Hogarth Press. (Original work published 1917)

Gray, M., Prigerson, H., & Litz, B. (2004). Conceptual and definitional issues in complicated grief. In B. Litz (Ed.), *Early intervention for trauma and traumatic loss.* New York: Guilford Press, p. 65–85.

Gupta, L. (1999). Bereavement recovery following the Rwandan genocide: A community based assessment for child survivors. *Bereavement Care, 18* (3), 40–42.

Harris-Hendriks, J., Black, D., & Kaplan, T. (2000). *When father kills mother: Guiding children through trauma and grief* (2nd ed.). London: Routledge.

Hodgkinson, P. E. , Joseph, Yule, & Williams (1993). Viewing human remains following disaster: Helpful or harmful? *Medical Science & Law, 33* (3), Horowitz, M. J. (1976). *Stress response syndromes. New York: Jason Aronson,* p. 197–202.

Horowitz, M. J., Siegel, B., Holen, A., Bonanno, G. A., Milbrath, C., & Stinson, C. H. (1997). *Diagnostic criteria for complicated grief disorder. American Journal of Psychiatry, 154,(7),* 904–910

Jacobs, S. (1993). *Pathologic grief: Maladaptation to loss.* Washington D.C.: American Psychiatric Press.

Jacobs, S. C., Kasl, S. V., Ostfeld, A. M., et al. (1986). The measurement of grief. *The Hospice Journal, 2,* 21–36.

Kissane, D., Bloch, S., Dowe, D., Snyder, R., Onghena, P., McKenzie, D., & Wallace, C. (1996). The Melbourne family grief study, I: Perceptions of family functioning in bereavement. *American Journal of Psychiatry, 153,* 650–658.

Kissane, D., Bloch, S., Onghena, P., McKenzie, D., Snyder, R., & Dowe, D. (1996). The Melbourne family grief study, II: Psychosocial morbidity and grief in bereaved families. *American Journal of Psychiatry, 153,* 659–666.

Lindy, J. D., Green, B. L., Grace, M., & Tichner, J. (1983). Psychotherapy with survivors of the Beverley Hills Supper Club fire. *American Journal of Psychotherapy, 37,* 593–610.

Litz, B., Gray, M., Bryant, R., & Adler, A. (2002). Early interventions for trauma: Current status and future directions. *Clinical Psychology: Science and Practice, 9,* 112–134.

Lundin, T. (1984). Morbidity following sudden and unexpected bereavement. *British Journal of Psychiatry, 144,* 84–88.

Maddison, D. & Walker, W. (1967). Factors affecting the outcome of conjugal bereavement. *British Journal of Psychiatry, 113,* 1057–1067.

McFarlane, A. C. (1987). Post traumatic phenomena in a longitudinal study of children following a natural disaster. *Journal of the American Academy of Child and Adolescent Psychiatry, 26,* 764–-769.

Mercy, J. A., Butchart, A., Dahlberg, L. L., Zwi, A. B., & Krug, E. G.(2003). Violence and mental health: Perspectives from the World Health Organization's World Report on Violence and Health. *International Journal of Mental Health, 32* (1), 20–36.

Middleton, W., Burnett, P., Raphael, B., & Martinek, N. (1996). *The bereavement response: A cluster analysis.* British Journal of Psychiatry, 169, 167–171.

Middleton, W., Moylan, A., Raphael, B., Burnett, P., & Martinek, N. (1993). *An international perspective on bereavement related concepts. Australian & New Zealand Journal of Psychiatry, 27, 457–463.*

Middleton, W., Raphael, B., Burnett P., & Martinek, N. (1998) A longitudinal study comparing bereavement phenomena in recently bereaved spouses, adult children and parents. *Australian & New Zealand Journal of Psychiatry, 32, 235–241.*

Mowll, J. (2005). *Viewing the body: Families after disaster.* Presentation to the Second National Consensus Conference: Mental Health Response to Terrorism and Disasters, Sydney, New South Wales.

Murphy, S.A. (1996). Parent bereavement stress and preventive intervention following the violent deaths of adolescent or young adult children. *Death Studies, 20, 441–452.*

National Institute of Mental Health (2002). Mental health and mass violence: Evidence-based early psychological interventions for victims/survivors of mass violence. A workshop to reach consensus on best practices. NIH Publication No. 02-5138. Washington DC: US Government Printing Office
http://www.nimh.nih.gov/publicat/massviolence.pdf

Neimeyer. R.A. and Hogan, N.S. (2001). Quantitative or Qualitative? Measurement issues in the study of grief. In *M. S. Stroebe, R. O. Hansson, W. Stroebe, & H. Schut* (Eds.), *Handbook of bereavement research: Consequences, coping, and care.* Washington, D.C.: American Psychological Association.

Ober, C., Peeters, L., Archer, R., & Kelly, K. (2000). Debriefing in different cultural frameworks: Responding to acute trauma in Australian Aboriginal contexts. In B. Raphael & J. Wilson (Eds.), *Psychological debriefing: Theory, practice and evidence* (pp. 241–253). London: Cambridge University Press.

Parkes, C. M. & Markus, A. (Eds.). (1998). *Coping with loss.* Montreal, Canada: Canadian Medical Association.

Parkes, C. M. & Weiss, R. (1983). *Recovery from bereavement.* New York: Basic Books.

Prigerson, H. G., & Jacobs, S. C. (2001). *Traumatic grief as a distinct disorder: A rationale, consensus criteria, and a preliminary empirical test. In M. S. Stroebe, R. O. Hansson, W.Stroebe, & H. Schut (Eds.)* Handbook of bereavement research: Consequences, coping, and care. *Washington, D.C.: American Psychological Association, p. 613–645.*

Prigerson, H. G., Maciejewski, P. K., Reynolds, C. F. Bierhals, A. J., Newsom, J. T., and Fasiczka, A. (1995). Inventory of complicated grief: A scale to measure maladaptive symptoms of loss. *Psychiatry Research, 59, 65–79.*

Prigerson, H. G. Shear, M. K., Jacobs, S. C., Reynolds, C. F. (1999). Consensus criteria for traumatic grief: A preliminary empirical test. *British Journal of Psychiatry, 174, 67–73.*

Prigerson, H. G., Maciejewski, P. K., Reynolds, C. F., Shear, M. K., Jabcobs, S. C., and Reynolds, C. F. (1995). Inventory of complicated grief: A scale to measure maladaptive symptoms of loss. Psychiatry Research, 59, 65–79.

Pynoos, R. S. (1993). Traumatic stress and developmental psychopathology in children and adolescents. In J. M. Oldham, M. B. Riba, & A. Tasman (Eds.), *The American Psychiatric Press Review of Psychiatry.* Washington, D.C.: American Psychiatric Press.

Pynoos, R. & Nader, K. (1988). Psychological first aid and treatment approach to children exposed to community violence: research implications. *Journal of Traumatic Stress, 1, 445–473.*

Pynoos, R., Nader, K., Frederick, C., Gonda, L., & Studer, M. (1987). Grief reactions in school age children following a sniper attack at school. *Israeli Journal of Psychology & Relationship Sciences, 24, 53–63.*

Raphael, B. (1977). Preventive intervention with the recently bereaved. *Archives of General Psychiatry, 34, 1450–1454.*

Raphael, B. (1979–1980). A primary prevention action program: Psychiatric involvement following a major rail disaster. *Omega, 10,* 211–226.

Raphael, B., Dunsmore, J., & Wooding, S. (2004) Terror and trauma in Bali: Australia's mental health response. *Journal of Aggression, Maltreatment and Trauma,* 9, 245–256.

Raphael, B., Field, J., & Kvelde, H. (1980). Childhood bereavement: A prospective study as a possible prelude to future preventive intervention. In E. J. Anthony & C. Chiland (Eds.), *Preventive psychiatry in an age of transition.* Wiley, New York, 9, 121–143.

Raphael, B. & Martinek, N. (1997). Assessing traumatic bereavement and posttraumatic stress disorder. In J. Wilson & T. Keane (Eds.), *Assessing psychological trauma and PTSD.* New York: Guilford Press, p. 373–395.

Raphael, B., Martinek, N., & Wooding, S. (2004). Assessing loss, psychological trauma and traumatic bereavement. In J. Wilson (Ed.), *Assessing psychological trauma and PTSD* (2nd ed.). (New York: Guilford Press), p. 492–512.

Raphael, B. & Wooding, S. (2004). Early mental health interventions for traumatic loss in adults. In B. Litz (Ed.), *Early intervention for trauma and traumatic loss.* New York: Guilford Press, p. 147–178.

Raphael, B. & Minkov, C. (1999). Abnormal grief. *Psychiatry, 12,* 99–102.

Raphael, B. & Wilson, J. (Eds.). (2000). *Psychological debriefing: Theory, practice, and evidence. Cambridge, UK:* Cambridge University Press,

Regehr, C. & Sussman, T. (2004). *Intersections between grief and trauma: Toward an empirically based model for treating traumatic grief. Brief Treatment and Crisis Intervention,* 4, 289–309.

Rodriguez, A. M., Steinberg, A., & Pynoos, R. S. (1999). *UCLA PTSD Index for DSM IV (Revision 1) Child Version, Adolescent Version.*

Rynearson, E. K., *Psychotherapy of pathologic grief: Revisions and limitations. (1987). Psychiatric Clinics of North America, 10, 487–499.*

Rynearson, E. K. (2005). *The narrative labyrinth of violent dying. Death Studies, 29, 351–360.*

Rynearson, E. K. & McCreery, J. M. (1993). *Bereavement after homicide: A synergism of trauma and loss. American Journal of Psychiatry, 150, 258–261.*

Rynearson, E. K. & Sinnema, C. S. (1999). *Supportive group therapy for bereavement after homicide.* In *B. H. Young & B. D. Dudley (Eds.), Group treatments for post-traumatic stress disorder. The series in trauma and loss., Philadelphia, PA: Brunner/Mazel,* p. 137–147.

Sanders, C. M. (1980). A comparison of adult bereavement in the death of a spouse, child, and parent. *Omega, 10,* 303–322.

Schut, H. A., Stroebe, M. S., van den Bout, J., & de Keijser, J. (1997). *Intervention for the bereaved: Gender differences in the efficacy of two counselling programmes. British Journal of Clinical Psychology. 36, 63–72*

Schut, H., Stroebe, M. S., Van den bout, J., & Terheggen, M. (2001). The efficacy of bereavement interventions: Determining who benefits. In M. S Stroebe,. R. O. Hansson, W. Stroebe, & H. Schut (Eds.), *Handbook of bereavement research: Consequences, coping, and care.* Washington, D.C.: American Psychological Association.

Shear, K., Frank, E., Houck, P. R., & Reynolds, C. F. (2005). Treatment of complicated grief: a randomized controlled trial. *Journal of the American Medical Association, 293,* 2601–2608.

Silverman G. K., Johnson, J. G., & Prigerson, H. G. (2001). Preliminary explorations of the effects of prior trauma and loss on risk for psychiatric disorders in recently widowed people. *Israel Journal of Psychiatry and Related Sciences, 38,* 202–215.

Singh, B. & Raphael, B. (1981). Post disaster morbidity of the bereaved: A possible role for preventive psychiatry. *Journal Nervous & Mental Disease, 169,* 203–212.

Stroebe, M. S., Hansson, R. O., Stroebe, W., & Schut, H. (Eds.) (2001). *Handbook of bereavement research: Consequences, coping, and care.* Washington, D.C.: American Psychological Association.

Stroebe M. & Schut H. (1999). The dual process model of coping with bereavement: Rationale and description. *Death Studies, 23,* 197–224.

Tedeschi, R. G. & Calhoun, L. G. (1995). *Trauma and transformation: Growing in the aftermath of suffering. Thousand Oaks, CA: Sage.*

Tedeschi, R. G. & Calhoun, L. G. (2004). Post-traumatic growth: Conceptual foundations and empirical evidence. *Psychological Inquiry, 15,* 1–18

Terr, L. (1991). Childhood traumas: An outline and overview. *American Journal of Psychiatry, 148,* 10–20.

Vachon, M. L. S., Lyall, W. A. L., Rogers, J., Freedman-Letofsky, K., & Freeman, S. J. J. (1980). A controlled study of self-help interventions for widows. *American Journal of Psychiatry, 137,* 1380–1384.

Vaillant, G. E., (1988). Attachment, loss and rediscovery. *Hillside Journal of Clinical Psychiatry, 10,* 148–164.

Valent, P. (1998). *From survival to fulfillment; A framework for the life-trauma dialectic.* Philadelphia: Brunner/Mazel.

van Doorn, C., Kasl S. V., Beery L. C., Jacobs, S. C., & Prigerson, H. G.(1998). The influence of marital quality and attachment styles on traumatic grief and depressive symptoms. *Journal of Nervous and Mental Disease 186,* 566–573

Worden, J.W. (1991). *Grief counseling and grief therapy.* New York: Springer.

2

Grief, Trauma, and Resilience

GEORGE A. BONANNO

RESILIENCE

Psychological resilience, the capacity for self-stabilization, is essential in adaptively responding to the violent death of a loved one. Later chapters propose preverbal ingredients of resilience and clinical strategies for reinforcement throughout assessment and intervention. As a preamble to this clinical consideration of resilience, the author, a highly creative researcher, defines resilience operationally — as adaptive outcome — "a stable pattern of low distress over time," which can be serially measured, before and after the trauma of death. He presents data from outcome studies substantiating his assertion that resilience is distinct from recovery and is present in about half of loved ones before and after a death has taken place. Though there are few empirical studies of resilience after violent loss, he presents data, including epidemiologic data from World Trade Center survivors, suggesting that the percentage of those who remain resilient following violent death is diminished compared with natural death.

Most of us go about our daily lives with little thought that something bad is about to happen. Unfortunately, bad things do happen. Epidemiological studies indicate that the majority of adults are exposed to at least one potentially traumatic event (PTE) (e.g., a life-threatening accident) in their lifetimes. One of the events almost all of us are forced to confront at some point in our lives, and sometimes at several different points in our lives, is the death of someone extremely close or important to us. More often than not, the death of a loved one is extremely stressful. The death of a spouse or life partner, for example, is consistently ranked at the top of lists of stressful life events (Holmes & Rahe, 1967). Recent research has indicated that when we lose someone of importance to us through a violent death, such as a violent accident, suicide, or homicide, bereavement can be even more painful and protracted, and often involves a particularly thorny combination of symptoms of posttraumatic stress disorder (PTSD) and unremitting depression (Kaltman & Bonanno, 2003; Zisook, Chentsova-Dutton, & Shuchter, 1998).

It is crucial to note, however, that not everyone reacts to loss or traumatic loss in the same way. The available research indicates that, much as with extreme life events in general, people vary greatly in the duration and severity of their grief reactions. Most people feel anxious, confused, and highly distressed within the first few days of a major loss. Some bereaved people, usually 10% to 20%, suffer chronic symptoms of distress and depression for years after the loss. Others experience acute symptoms for several months or longer and then gradually recover and move toward their baseline level of functioning over the course of one or two years of bereavement. However, many and sometimes the majority of bereaved people will tend to experience only brief, short-lived distress reactions and manage to continue functioning at much the same level during bereavement as they had prior to the loss (Bonanno, 2004; Bonanno & Kaltman, 1999).

THREE POINTS ABOUT RESILIENCE

It has been widely assumed in the bereavement literature that relatively mild or minimal reactions to loss are rare and usually indicative of either the lack of a meaningful relationship with the person who had died (Raphael, 1983) or a sort of pathological inability to grieve. For example, one of the most eminent bereavement theorists of the 20th century, John Bowlby (1980), described the "prolonged absence of conscious grieving" (p. 138) as a type of disordered mourning. Similarly, in a major summary of the state-of-the-art bereavement research at the time, Osterweis, Solomon, and Green (1984) concluded "that the absence of grieving phenomena following bereavement represents some form of personality pathology" (p. 18). Middleton, Raphael, and their colleagues (Middleton, Moylan, Raphael, Burnett, & Martinek, 1993) surveyed an international sample of self-identified bereavement experts and found that the majority (65%) endorsed beliefs that "absent grief" exists, that it usually stems from denial or inhibition, and that it is generally maladaptive in the long run. These same bereavement experts (76%) also endorsed the compatible assumption that absent grief eventually surfaces in the form of delayed grief reactions.

To a large extent because of these assumptions, until recently relatively little attention has been paid to the idea that many people might be genuinely resilient to loss. For decades developmental researchers have documented the prevalence of resilience among children growing up in caustic socioeconomic circumstances (Garmezy, 1991; Luthar, Doernberger,

& Zigler, 1993; Masten, 2001; Rutter, 1987). And there have been isolated studies of resilience among adults exposed to potentially traumatic events, most notably the work of Rachman (1978). However, the idea that people might be resilient to the caustic pain of loss has rarely been considered.

This scenario began to change only in the late 1990s, as researchers from a wide range of disciplines in the social sciences and related mental health disciplines embraced bereavement as an important topic of study. In summarizing this literature, I have argued that, although the study of resilience is nascent, the available evidence nonetheless indicates at least three clear and defensible conclusions: resilience to loss represents a distinct and empirically separable outcome trajectory from that normally associated with recovery during bereavement; resilience to loss is more prevalent than generally accepted in either the lay or professional literature; and there are multiple and sometimes unexpected factors that inform the resilience to loss (Bonanno, 2004, in press; Bonanno, Papa, & O'Neill, 2001).

Resilience is Distinct from Recovery

One of the misconceptions about resilience that has plagued research and theory in studies of both children and adults is the idea that resilience is more or less found exclusively within the person. Certainly, as many of the studies I will review in this chapter will attest, there are personality characteristics that do seem to identify and describe "resilient" people. However, as developmental researchers have long observed, resilience is a complex phenomenon resulting from a mix of factors including personality, interpersonal variables, such as supportive relationships, and the temporal characteristics of the stressor (e.g., Garmezy, 1991; Luthar, Cicchetti, & Becker, 2000; Rutter, 1999; Werner, 1995). Thus, people may possess characteristics that suggest resilience but we can only define resilience to loss, or to other potentially traumatic events, in terms of outcome. The psychological study of resilience, therefore, requires that we first operationally define resilience as an outcome following a specified stressor event and then examine the factors that either promote or detract from that outcome.

To this end, in the early to mid-1990s, my colleagues and I inaugurated an ongoing investigation of the resilient outcome pattern following the death of a loved one and the means by which it might be achieved. Our initial studies examined how people coped with the premature death of a spouse at midlife (Bonanno, Keltner, Holen, & Horowitz, 1995; Bonanno, Znoj, Siddique, & Horowitz, 1999). Although based on a small sample, these studies demonstrated that a stable pattern of low distress over time, or resilience, could be clearly distinguished from the more conventionally understood reactions of maladjustment and recovery (see Figure 2.1). In subsequent studies we were again able to empirically distinguish resilience from recovery in older bereaved widows and widowers (Bonanno et al., 2002), in another middle-aged sample of widows and widowers, in a sample of middle-aged bereaved parents, and in a younger sample of gay men who had lost a committed partner to AIDS (Bonanno, Moskowitz, Papa, & Folkman, 2005).

A crucial finding in these studies is that the resilient outcome category remained robust across multiple measures and methods of defining bereavement outcome. As I noted above, among the primary criticisms typically levied against the idea of resilience to loss has been that people who do not show much in the way of protracted grief reactions are either superficially adjusted or pathological, and consequently likely to eventually manifest delayed grief reactions. My colleagues and I have attempted to address these criticisms in several ways. First, across several studies we directly examined the idea that people who show little grief initially will eventually exhibit delayed grief reactions. To date, no empirical study from our own or other research teams has yet to identify delayed grief symptoms in more than just a few participants, and almost always representing only 2% to 3% of the total sample (for reviews see Bonanno & Field, 2001; Bonanno et al., 2002).

In perhaps the most explicit examination of the delayed grief idea, Nigel Field and I (Bonanno & Field, 2001) examined the possibility of delayed grief among a sample of conjugally bereaved individuals who were assessed using multiple measures at multiple time points across the first five years of bereavement. Specifically, we operationally defined and compared the common conceptualization of delayed grief as a robust emergence of symptoms in a form "as fresh and intense as if the loss had just occurred" (Humphrey & Zimpfer, 1996, p. 152), with an alternative perspective that random elevations in symptoms might occur among some individuals who had not previously evidenced symptom elevations as a result of random measurement error. Even the most reliable measurement instruments include some error variance (Nunnally, 1978). Thus, we operationally defined the traditional idea of delayed grief as occurring when a bereaved participant had not shown elevated grief in the early months of bereavement but then did show elevations at one of the later assessments. Because the traditional perspective suggests that delayed grief would emerge in a robust manner, this view predicted that delayed elevations would be evident across multiple outcome measures from the same time point. By contrast, the random measurement error explanation of delayed grief predicted that only a few of the participants who did not show elevated grief in the first months of bereavement would evidence delayed elevations at a later time point, but only on isolated measures. In other words, for these few participants, the delayed elevations would tend to occur on only one of the multiple measures, and thus could be explained simply by measurement error. The results unambiguously supported the random measurement error explanation.

A second way that my colleagues and I attempted to address potential criticisms of the concept of resilience to loss was by examining bereaved participants' adjustment across a range of different outcome measures. The core assessment of adjustment in each of the studies cited above was based on symptom scores from well-validated structured clinical interviews. Specifically, we assessed the symptoms of major depressive disorder (MDD), generalized anxiety disorder

(GAD), and posttraumatic stress disorder (PTSD), as defined by the DSM-IV (APA, 1994), as well as a cluster of symptoms that have been empirically associated with more complicated grief reactions (Horowitz, Siegel, Holen, & Bonanno, 1997). The structured interviews provided an important clinical assessment of grief-related psychopathology. Owing to the seminal role given to these interviews in our research, we included an extensive training period for the interviewers and achieved extremely high levels of inter-rater reliability, for example (Bonanno et al., 2005). In addition, in one set of studies we provided important evidence for the validity of the total symptom score from the interviews by demonstrating its concordance with independent ratings of grief severity provided by experienced therapists who had self-identified as experts in the treatment of bereavement (Bonanno et al., 1995).

It is important to note, however, that resilience is more than the simple absence of psychopathology (Bonanno, 2004, in press). Across these studies, we have shown that bereaved people who exhibit the resilient outcome trajectory as defined by the absence of symptoms were also more likely than other bereaved people to experience and express positive emotion while talking about the loss (Bonanno & Keltner, 1997; Bonanno et al., 1995; Keltner & Bonanno, 1997) and to report gaining comfort from positive memories of a deceased spouse (Bonanno, Wortman, & Nesse, 2004). In addition, resilient individuals were rated as better adjusted than more symptomatic bereaved individuals when evaluated anonymously by their close friends (Bonanno, 2005). Resilient participants' close friends also rated them as better adjusted prior to the loss than symptomatic bereaved participants and when compared to a matched sample of married (i.e., nonbereaved) participants (Bonanno, 2005).

Resilience to Loss is Common

Wortman and Silver (1989, 2001) were among the first to note the somewhat startling fact that there was no empirical basis for the assumption that the absence of distress during bereavement is necessarily pathological. At the time they made this argument, however, there were relatively few longitudinal bereavement studies available. More recent prospective studies have begun to reveal considerable individual differences in grief reactions (see Figure 2.1; for a review see Bonanno & Kaltman, 2001). Generally, a minority of bereaved people, usually between 10% and 15%, will suffer chronic grief symptoms beyond the first year after a major loss. Although this may appear to be a relatively small proportion of the total population of bereaved individuals, given the inevitability of death and loss, even this small proportion underscores the important personal and public health costs of bereavement. I have suggested elsewhere (Bonanno, 2001; Bonanno et al., 2001) that bereavement researchers and theorists have tended to overgeneralize the experience of chronically grieving individuals to the normal population. Thus, as I noted earlier, it has been commonly assumed that the modal reaction to loss is one of acute grief symptoms followed by a gradual return to baseline (i.e., the recovery pattern) and that resilience to loss rarely occurs.

Although until the early 21st century, few studies directly examined this question, when Stacey Kaltman and I (Bonanno & Kaltman, 2001) reviewed the available evidence, it seemed that was not at all the case; rather, across a range of studies the proportion of bereaved individuals who exhibited relatively low levels of depression or distress following loss was always close to or even exceeded 50% of the sample. For example, in a recent study that examined various levels of depression among conjugally bereaved adults, approximately half of the bereaved participants failed to show even mild depression (these individuals endorsed less than two items from the DSM-IV symptom list) following the loss (Zisook, Paulus, Shuchter, & Judd, 1997).

We have also found this to be the case in our own studies where we had explicitly defined a resilient outcome trajectory. Perhaps the most compelling evidence for the prevalence of resilience comes from a large prospective data set from the Changing Lives of Older Couples (CLOC) study. In our first study using these data (Bonanno et al., 2002), we mapped variations in depressive symptoms across time, beginning three years prior to the death of a spouse and continuing to 18 months after the spouse's death. We used several different statistical approaches. No matter how we examined these data, close to half the sample showed a stable low distress profile beginning prior to the spouse's death, as well as relatively few grief symptoms (e.g., yearning, despair) during bereavement. As in previous studies, the low

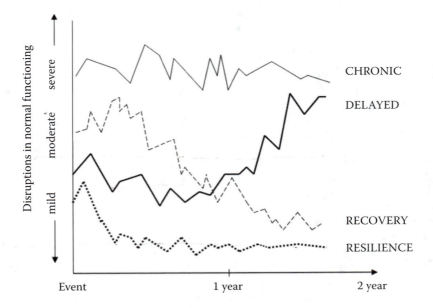

FIGURE 2.1. Prototypical patterns of disruption in normal functioning following loss or potential trauma.

distress pattern was again more prevalent than the recovery pattern (see Figure 2.1) and there was no evidence for delayed grief reactions.

In another set of studies, we defined resilience using normative comparison. In simple terms, normative comparison in these studies involved comparing the level of psychological symptoms in a bereaved sample with the level of psychological symptoms in a comparable sample of married individuals; that is, married people of approximately the same age, gender, and economic status as the bereaved people. It is commonly assumed that literally all psychological symptoms observed after the death of a loved one must be part of the grief reaction; that is, they must have arisen in response to the loss. However, it is possible that at least some of the observed symptoms may have arisen in response to the more general stress that sometimes accompanies major changes like loss, such as new financial troubles or a seemingly overwhelming degree of logistical arrangements. It is also possible, however, that low levels of psychopathological symptoms may arise as part of the normal stress and strain of everyday life and have nothing to do with the loss. Most normal healthy adults from time to time will experience similar symptoms. For example, people worry about finances, their children's performance in school, or their own performance at work. Thus, the normal stress of everyday life can and often does result in brief periods of sleeplessness or edginess or temporarily strain the capacity of our immune systems so that we experience mild physical symptoms. The question is really one of degree, and this is precisely the question addressed by the normative comparison of bereaved people and nonbereaved people.

In one study, we measured individual symptoms from structured clinical interviews in a middle-aged bereaved sample at four and 18 months postloss and in a sample of ostensibly normal, healthy, middle-aged married adults (Bonanno, 2005). This study showed that the married sample had on average about one and a half current psychological symptoms, and that the normal range of variation in these symptoms for the married sample, calculated as the sample mean plus one standard deviation, was four symptoms. In other words, the average healthy married person might exhibit up to four psychological symptoms. When we compared that level of symptoms with the bereaved sample, with both samples matched for age, gender, and economic status, over half (52%) the bereaved sample remained within that same symptom range at both four months of bereavement and 18 months of bereavement. In other words, over half of the bereaved sample exhibited no greater psychological distress or maladjustment than a comparable group of healthy married people. *Look*

We also used the normative comparison approach in a second study involving HIV+ gay men who were in committed long-term relationships and had been providing care to a partner who suffered from and eventually died of AIDS. These men were compared with a matched sample of HIV+ gay men who were also in committed long-term relationships but were neither bereaved nor providing care for a dying partner. This comparison was particularly illuminating because the data for this study had originally been collected in San Francisco Bay area in the late 1980s and early 1990s. Gay men in general tend to show elevated levels of depression. Because of the density of the gay population in the San Francisco area, there was also a community-wide epidemic of grief at that time over the widespread loss of life to AIDS. If this were not enough, the men we considered in this particular study were themselves HIV+, and at the time of the study the antiretroviral medications, which have dramatically prolonged life for people with AIDS, were not yet readily available. Thus, being HIV+ at that time generally meant that one could anticipate a dramatically reduced mortality.

Given the combined nature of these stressors, it was not surprising that the HIV+ nonbereaved, noncaregiver sample were highly depressed. Most men in the comparison group scored near or above the threshold for major depressive disorder. Also as expected, many of the HIV+ bereaved caregivers were also highly depressed. However, similar to the normative comparison with conjugally bereaved people, described above, approximately half of the HIV+ bereaved caregiver sample was no more depressed than the HIV+ nonbereaved noncaregiver comparison sample. Not only did this finding reveal a similar level of resilience as in previous bereavement studies, but it also raised the compelling implication that even elevated levels of depression following the death of a loved one may not necessarily be a direct reaction to the loss. In other words, the elevated depression we observed among many of the HIV+ bereaved caregivers may have been just as likely due to the ongoing stress of being seropositive for a deadly disease that at that time was running rampant through the community.

The Multiplicity of Factors Leading to Resilience

One of the more surprising conclusions to emerge from this research is that there is no single type or way to be resilient. Developmental researchers concerned with children exposed to adverse conditions have long asserted that there are multiple pathways to resilience. In attempting to make sense of these divergent pathways, I have recently attempted to catalogue adult resilience promoting factors into two broad categories: flexible adaptation and pragmatic coping (Bonanno, in press). There is no doubt more to the story. However, these two categories provide a starting point from which to further explore the heterogeneity of resilience.

Flexible Adaptation

At a basic level, it seems apparent that many of the same factors that promote healthy development in children exposed to unfavorable circumstances would also foster resilience in adults confronted with loss. In other words, the characteristics and factors that generally promote health would also likely be recruited in the service of coping with the extremes of adversity. These factors would include, for example, situational or contextual variables, such as supportive relationships, as well as individual difference variables related to personality disposition. Of particular note in relation to the latter are personality variables that suggest a capacity for elasticity or *flexible* adaptation to impinging challenges. Examples of such variables include ego resilience (Block & Block, 1980) and hardiness (Kobasa, Maddi & Kahn, 1982).

Pragmatic Coping

At another level, however, our research has suggested that people who evidence resilience to loss often cope effectively by means that may not be adaptive under normal circumstances. For instance, although considerable research attests to the health benefits of expressing stress-related negative emotions, studies of emotional expression during bereavement have not shown this same result (Stroebe, Stroebe, Schut, Zech, & van den Bout, 2002). What's more, resilient individuals tend to express relatively less negative emotion while discussing the loss compared to other bereaved people (e.g., Bonanno & Keltner, 1997). In explaining these findings, Dacher Keltner and I suggested that the capacity to minimize the expression of grief-related emotions may help to minimize the impact of the loss, while at the same time "increasing continued contact with and support from important people in the social environment" (p. 134).

Findings of this sort underscore a crucial point of departure in comparisons of resilience among children and adults. Whereas childhood resilience is typically understood in response to enduring corrosive environments, resilient coping among adults is more often a matter of coping with an isolated and usually (but not always) brief stressor event. The key point is that whereas corrosive environments require longer-term adaptive solutions, isolated stressor events often oblige individuals to adopt a more *pragmatic* form of coping; a *whatever it takes* approach that may involve behaviors and strategies that are less effective or even maladaptive in other contexts. I have elsewhere referred to these behaviors using the somewhat vague but perhaps more evocative phrase, *coping ugly.*

The heterogeneity of resilience is illustrated by a subset of the bereaved participants from the CLOC study, discussed earlier. This group had high levels of depression, neuroticism, and marital conflict before the spouse's death. However, after the spouse's death they improved markedly and in fact were indistinguishable from participants evidencing a more stable low distress pattern (Bonanno et al., 2004). We observed a similar pattern in a recent study of bereavement and attachment style (Fraley & Bonanno, 2004). Adults identified as having a secure attachment style are generally trusting in their relationships, and not surprisingly these individuals showed a resilient trajectory during bereavement. However, a resilient trajectory was also observed among bereaved subjects with a dismissive–avoidant style (i.e., a tendency to minimize the importance of the relationship). In fact, dismissive–avoidant subjects coped as well as securely attached subjects and both groups were no more symptomatic than a comparable sample of married individuals. This is not to deny that dismissive–avoidant attachment comes with a potentially serious price tag: compromised intimacy. However, as these findings clearly indicate, it also appears to be quite pragmatic during bereavement and carries the benefit of effective coping with loss.

Another pragmatic pathway to resilience is illustrated in research on the trait dimension of self-enhancement. Taylor and colleagues (Taylor & Brown, 1988) have argued persuasively that self-enhancing biases (e.g., overestimating one's positive qualities) are a natural and beneficial aspect of human cognition. However, some people tend to rely on such biases more than others, and this tendency has costs as well as benefits. For instance, trait self-enhancers cope effectively in a laboratory stress-challenge paradigm (Taylor, Lerner, Sherman, Sage, & McDowell, 2003), but also score high on measures of narcissism and tend to evoke negative reactions in other people (Paulhus, 1998).

When the world turns ugly, however, self-enhancers appear to have a genuine coping advantage. In one set of studies, our research team examined self-enhancement among a bereaved sample dealing with the premature death of a spouse, some of whom had died from violent means (Bonanno, 2004). In this study, trait self-enhancement was positively associated with ratings of adjustment made by mental health experts. However, untrained observers also developed more negative impressions of self-enhancers. Nevertheless, these negative social impressions did not appear to interfere with self-enhancers' ability to cope effectively. Secondary analyses showed that self-enhancement was particularly adaptive for bereaved individuals coping with the more pernicious losses due to violent death. For participants who had lost a spouse to natural causes, self-enhancement showed a modest inverse predictive association with PTSD symptoms across time. However, for participants who had lost a spouse to violent death, self-enhancement was considerably more strongly and inversely predictive of PTSD symptoms across time. Indeed, the PTSD levels for violent-loss bereaved participants high on self-enhancement were almost indistinguishable from natural-loss bereaved participants, whereas violent-loss bereaved participants who were low in self-enhancement had considerably elevated PTSD compared to the other groups. We have observed similar patterns of findings in studies of self-enhancers coping with more purely traumatic events (Bonanno et al., 2005).

RESILIENCE AFTER THE SEPTEMBER 11 TERRORIST ATTACK

The question of resilience following loss due to violent death or following other potentially traumatic events presents a crucial imperative for further research (e.g., Litz, 2005). Unfortunately, there has been relatively little data available from which to examine this question. Only a few studies have identified traumatic loss reactions, and these studies have not yet considered resilient outcomes.

The only study currently available to address this issue comes from epidemiological data on the September 11 terrorist attacks on the World Trade Center (WTC) in New York City. In an ambitious study, Galea and colleagues managed to obtain a large probability sample of people living in or near New York City at the time of the September 11 attack (Galea, Ahern, Resnick, et al., 2002; Galea, Resnick, Ahern et al., 2002; Galea et al., 2003). The final sample (N = 2752) adequately represented the broader New York population, as evidenced by its close resemblance to the mostly available census data for the area. Although the probable PTSD prevalence for the New York metropolitan area during the first six months after the attack was estimated at 6.0% (Galea et al., 2003), PTSD estimates were considerably higher among people most directly exposed during the attack.

As part of a collaborative project, these investigators and I attempted to examine resilience across differing levels of exposure (Bonanno, Galea, Bucciarelli, & Vlahov, in press). Of particular interest to our discussion in this chapter, it was also possible to examine resilience among people who had lost loved ones in the attack. In determining the cut-off for resilience in this study, we attempted to use the same normative comparison approach as my colleagues and I had employed in some of the studies discussed above. Because this was an epidemiological data collection on a large sample, however, only self-report and phone interview data were available and the primary outcome measure was PTSD symptoms. The PTSD diagnosis is comprised of 17 symptoms and includes several nonspecific symptoms (e.g., difficulty sleeping) that may be present even in the absence of trauma exposure. In an earlier study, we had assessed PTSD symptoms in the absence of trauma exposure in one of our married comparison groups, and found that the normal range in this group was two or fewer PTSD symptoms (Bonanno, 2005). However, we decided to err on the conservative side and follow studies of subthreshold depression, which have typically set a more conservative criterion for the absence of depression as one or zero symptoms (Judd et al., 1997). This same criterion has also been used to determine resilience during bereavement (Zisook et al., 1997). Therefore, because we did not have the multiple outcome measures customary in our previous studies, we adopted the relatively conservative criterion for resilience as one or zero PTSD symptoms. We also defined a mild/moderate trauma response as two or more PTSD symptoms in the absence of the PTSD diagnosis. We then assessed the proportions of the sample exhibiting resilience, a mild/moderate trauma response, or PTSD across different exposure categories.

The results clearly indicated widespread resilience across virtually all levels of exposure during the six months after the September 11 attack. Even among the groups with the most pernicious levels of exposure and highest probable levels of PTSD, the proportion that were resilient never dropped below one third. This was also true of people who had lost friends or relatives in the attack. This group had a probable PTSD proportion of 11.8%, which is somewhat higher than the national average for PTSD following potentially traumatic events (e.g., Kessler, Sonnega, Bromet, Hughes, et al., 1995). However, slightly over a third (37%) of this group exhibited mild to moderate trauma symptoms while over half (51.2%) evidenced the resilient outcome of one or zero trauma symptoms.

Few would argue with the characterization of the loss of a friend or relative in the September 11 attack on the World Trade Center as a loss due to violent death. Nonetheless, it should be stressed that there was great variability in this category in terms of the specifics and the level of closeness in participants' relationships with the lost persons. Of potentially greater interest to our concerns here was an additional finding from this same study indicating a considerably higher PTSD prevalence among people who lost a friend or relative in the attack *and* witnessed the attack in person. Compared to the 11.8% probability of PTSD prevalence for loss in general, people who lost someone and witnessed the attack in person had almost three times as much PTSD; probability of PTSD for this group was estimated at 31.3%. Approximately the same proportion of people in this group with mild to moderate trauma symptoms (35.4%) did not differ meaningfully from the group that lost a friend or relative but did not directly witness the attack. However, resilience among the loss group who witnessed the attack in person fell to 33.4%.

Together these findings suggest two important conclusions. First, the level of resilience to loss is clearly reduced when bereavement occurs in the context of the most violent and potentially traumatic losses. Second, although as this study showed, such exceptionally pernicious losses result in exceptionally high levels of psychopathology and do reduce the proportion of the sample showing resilience, it should be underscored that resilience was not eliminated. Far from it; the fact that resilience was still exhibited by a third of the sample is quite remarkable given that almost the same proportion of the sample had evidenced PTSD.

There were obvious limitations to this study; most notably, although the measure of PTSD used in the study had adequate reliability and validity, the necessity of using phone interviews made it impossible to conduct more thorough clinical judgments about functioning or about the relative absence of PTSD symptoms. Similarly, the epidemiological nature of the study meant that there could only be a limited score of measures, and for that reason our operational definition of resilience was also necessarily restricted. We did, however, explore using either a more stringent or more liberal definition of resilience, and this did not meaningfully change the basic pattern of results. At minimum, however, these findings suggest the durability of human resilience to loss under even the most pernicious conditions, and beg for further research in this area.

CONCLUSION

Clearly there is much more to learn about the topic of resilience during bereavement. Because we have for so long ignored resilient functioning, it is still a relatively poorly understood phenomenon. An obvious imperative is to learn how resilience or the factors that inform it may vary across different types of losses. Another important avenue worthy of exploration would be the ways that resilient individuals experience the earliest weeks and months of bereavement, a period for which we have clinical insights but relatively little empirical data. Retrospective reports from the CLOC study indicated that most participants, including those exhibiting resilience, experienced at least some yearning and emotional pangs in the early months after the loss (Bonanno et al., 2004). The repeated measurements from the AIDS caregiver study (Bonanno et al., 2005) revealed that resilient individuals were highly distressed in the first two weeks of bereavement. How resilient individuals manage to maintain stable functioning despite having experienced such disequilibrium remains an open and relatively poorly understood question.

Perhaps one of the most important implications of the study of resilience is that it may lead to new intervention strategies for those who fare less well during bereavement. Unfortunately, this issue is not as simple as it may seem. If resilient behaviors are traitlike, then such behaviors may not be easily inculcated in others. And, given the costs associated with some resilient traits, such as self-enhancement, the advantage of imitating resilient individuals may be questionable. A possible avenue toward reconciling this issue is suggested, however, by the evidence linking resilience to flexible coping. Recent experimental evidence from our laboratory indicates, for example, that adjustment among New York college students depended not so much on the use of any particular regulatory mechanism but rather, on the flexibility to use whatever regulatory mechanism might most clearly satisfy the demands of the stressor situation (Bonanno, Papa, Lalande, Nanping, & Noll, 2005). In contrast to the rigidity implied by pragmatic coping, it seems entirely plausible that flexible coping strategies could be taught to others. These issues suggest an obvious imperative for further research and clinical exploration.

Finally, there is the enormous question of ethnic and cultural variations in resilience during bereavement. Western, independence-oriented countries tend to focus more heavily than collectivist countries on the personal experience of grief (Bonanno et al., 2001). However, little is yet known about the extent that loss and trauma reactions might vary across cultures. A comparative study showed that bereaved people in China recovered more quickly from loss than did bereaved Americans (Bonanno, Papa, et al., 2005). However, as is culturally appropriate, the Chinese also reported more somatic complaints than Americans. These data raise the intriguing question of whether resilience has different meanings in different cultural contexts or, perhaps even more intriguing, whether different cultures may learn from each other about effective and not so effective ways of coping with extreme adversity.

REFERENCES

Block J., H. & Block, J. (1980). The role of ego-control and ego-resiliency in the organization of behavior. In W. A. Collins (Ed.), *The Minnesota Symposia on Child Psychology* (vol. 13, pp. 39–101.). Hillsdale, NJ: Erlbaum.

Bonanno, G. A. (2001). The crucial importance of empirical evidence in the development of bereavement theory: Reply to Archer (2001). *Psychological Bulletin, 127*(4), 561–564.

Bonanno, G. A. (2004). Loss, trauma, and human resilience: Have we underestimated the human capacity to thrive after extremely aversive events? *American Psychologist, 59*(1), 20–28.

Bonanno, G. A. (2005). Clarifying and extending the construct of adult resilience. *American Psychologist, 60*(3), 265–267.

Bonanno, G. A. (2005). Resilience in the face of potential trauma. *Current Directions in Psychological Science, 14,* 135-138

Bonanno, G. A. & Field, N. P. (2001). Examining the delayed grief hypothesis across 5 years of bereavement. *American Behavioral Scientist, 44*(5), 798–816.

Bonanno, G. A. Galea, S., Bucciarelli, A., & Vlahov, D. (2006). Psychological resilience after disaster: New York City following the September 11th terrorist attack. *Psychological Science, 17,* 181–186

Bonanno, G. A. & Kaltman, S. (1999). Toward an integrative perspective on bereavement. *Psychological Bulletin, 125*(6), 760–776.

Bonanno, G. A. & Kaltman, S. (2001). The varieties of grief experience. *Clinical Psychology Review, 21*(5), 705–734.

Bonanno, G. A., & Keltner, D. (1997). Facial expressions of emotion and the course of conjugal bereavement. *Journal of Abnormal Psychology, 106*(1), 126–137.

Bonanno, G. A., Keltner, D., Holen, A., & Horowitz, M. J. (1995). When avoiding unpleasant emotions might not be such a bad thing: Verbal autonomic response dissociation and midlife conjugal bereavement. *Journal of Personality & Social Psychology, 69*(5), 975–989.

Bonanno, G. A., Moskowitz, J. T., Papa, A., & Folkman, S. (2005). Resilience to loss in bereaved spouses, bereaved parents, and bereaved gay men. *Journal of Personality and Social Psychology, 88*(5), 827–843.

Bonanno, G. A., Papa, A., Lalande, K., Nanping, Z., & Noll, J. G. (2005). Grief processing and deliberate grief avoidance: A prospective comparison of bereaved spouses and parents in the United States and the People's Republic of China. *Journal of Consulting and Clinical Psychology, 73,* 86–98.

Bonanno, G. A., Papa, A., & O'Neill, K. (2001). Loss and human resilience. *Applied & Preventive Psychology, 10*(3), 193–206.

Bonanno, G. A., Wortman, C. B., Lehman, D. R., Tweed, R. G., Haring, M., Sonnega, J., et al. (2002). Resilience to loss and chronic grief: A prospective study from preloss to 18-months postloss. *Journal of Personality & Social Psychology, 83*(5), 1150–1164.

Bonanno, G. A., Wortman, C. B., & Nesse, R. M. (2004). Prospective patterns of resilience and maladjustment during widowhood. *Psychology & Aging, 19*(2), 260–271.

Bonanno, G. A., Znoj, H., Siddique, H. I., & Horowitz, M. J. (1999). Verbal-autonomic dissociation and adaptation to midlife conjugal loss: A follow-up at 25 months. *Cognitive Therapy & Research, 23*(6), 605–624.

Bowlby, J. (1980). *Attachment and loss.* New York: Basic Books.

Fraley, R. & Bonanno, G. A. (2004). Attachment and loss: A test of three competing models on the association between attachment-related avoidance and adaptation to bereavement. *Personality & Social Psychology Bulletin, 30*(7), 878–890.

Galea, S., Ahern, J., Resnick, H., Kilpatrick, D., Bucuvalas, M., Gold, J., et al. (2002). Psychological sequelae of the September 11 terrorist attacks in New York City.[see comment]. *New England Journal of Medicine, 346*(13), 982–987.

Galea, S., Resnick, H., Ahern, J., Gold, J., Bucuvalas, M., Kilpatrick, D., et al. (2002). Posttraumatic stress disorder in Manhattan, New York City, after the September 11th terrorist attacks. *Journal of Urban Health, 79*(3), 340–353.

Galea, S., Vlahov, D., Resnick, H., Ahern, J., Susser, E., Gold, J., et al. (2003). Trends of probable post-traumatic stress disorder in New York City after the September 11 terrorist attacks. *American Journal of Epidemiology, 158*(6), 514–524.

Garmezy, N. (1991). Resilience and vulnerability to adverse developmental outcomes associated with poverty. *American Behavioral Scientist, 34*(4), 416–430.

Holmes, T. & Rahe, R. (1967). The social adjustment scale. *Journal of Psychosomatic Research, 11*, 213–218.

Horowitz, M. J., Siegel, B., Holen, A., & Bonanno, G. A. (1997). Diagnostic criteria for complicated grief disorder. *American Journal of Psychiatry, 154*(7), 904–910.

Humphrey, G. M. & Zimpfer, D. G. (1996). *Counseling for grief and bereavement.* Thousand Oaks, CA: Sage publications.

Judd, L. L., Akiskal, H. S., & Paulus, M. P. (1997). The role and clinical significance of subsyndromal depressive symptoms (ssd) in unipolar major depressive disorder. *Journal of Affective Disorders, 45*(1-2), 5–17.

Kaltman, S. & Bonanno, G. A. (2003). Trauma and bereavement: Examining the impact of sudden and violent deaths. *Journal of Anxiety Disorders, 17*(2), 131–147.

Keltner, D. & Bonanno, G. A. (1997). A study of laughter and dissociation: Distinct correlates of laughter and smiling during bereavement. *Journal of Personality & Social Psychology, 73*(4), 687–702.

Kessler, R. C., Sonnega, A., Bromet, E., Hughes, M., et al. (1995). Posttraumatic stress disorder in the national comorbidity survey. *Archives of General Psychiatry, 52*(12), 1048–1060.

Kobasa, S. C., Maddi, S. R., & Kahn, S. (1982). Hardiness and health: A prospective study. *Journal of Personality and Social Psychology, 42*, 168–177.

Litz, B. T. (2005). Has resilience to severe trauma been underestimated? *American Psychologist, 60*, 262.

Luthar, S. S., Cicchetti, D., & Becker, B. (2000). The construct of resilience: A critical evaluation and guidelines for future work. *Child Development, 71*(3), 543–562.

Luthar, S. S., Doernberger, C. H., & Zigler, E. (1993). Resilience is not a unidimensional construct: Insights from a prospective study of inner-city adolescents. *Development & Psychopathology, 5*(4), 703–717.

Masten, A. S. (2001). Ordinary magic: Resilience processes in development. *American Psychologist, 56*(3), 227–238.

Middleton, W., Moylan, A., Raphael, B., Burnett, P., et al. (1993). An international perspective on bereavement related concepts. *Australian & New Zealand Journal of Psychiatry, 27*(3), 457–463.

Nunnally, J. C. (1978). *Psychometric Theory* (2ⁿᵈ Ed.). New York: McGraw-Hill.

Osterweis, M., Solomon, F., & Green, F. (Eds.). (1984). *Bereavement: Reactions, consequences, and care.* Washington, D.C.: National Academy Press.

Paulhus, D. L. (1998). Interpersonal and intrapsychic adaptiveness of trait self-enhancement: A mixed blessing? *Journal of Personality & Social Psychology, 74*(5), 1197–1208.

Rachman, S. J. (1978). *Fear and courage.* New York: Freeman.

Raphael, B. (1983). *The anatomy of bereavement.* New York: Basic Books.

Rutter, M. (1987). Psychosocial resilience and protective mechanisms. *American Journal of Orthopsychiatry, 57*(3), 316–331.

Rutter, M. (1999). Resilience concepts and findings: Implications for family therapy. *Journal of Family Therapy, 21*(2), 119–144.

Stroebe, M., Stroebe, W., Schut, H., Zech, E., & van den Bout, J. (2002). Does disclosure of emotions facilitate recovery from bereavement? Evidence from two prospective studies. *Journal of Consulting & Clinical Psychology, 70*(1), 169–178.

Taylor, S. E. & Brown, J. D. (1988). Illusion and well-being: A social psychological perspective on mental health. *Psychological Bulletin, 103*(2), 193–210.

Taylor, S. E., Lerner, J. S., Sherman, D. K., Sage, R. M., & McDowell, N. K. (2003). Portrait of the self-enhancer: Well adjusted and well liked or maladjusted and friendless? *Journal of Personality & Social Psychology, 84*(1), 165–176.

Werner, E. E. (1995). Resilience in development. *Current Directions in Psychological Science,* 4(3), 81–85.

Wortman, C. B. & Silver, R. C. (1989). The myths of coping with loss. *Journal of Consulting & Clinical Psychology, 57*(3), 349–357.

Wortman, C. B. & Silver, R. C. (2001). The myths of coping with loss revisited. [references]. In M. S. Stroebe, R. O. Hansson, W. Stroebe, & H. Schut (Eds.), *Handbook of bereavement research: Consequences, coping, and care* (pp. 405–429). Washington, D.C.: American Psychological Association.

Zisook, S., Chentsova-Dutton, Y., & Shuchter, S. R. (1998). PTSD following bereavement. *Annals of Clinical Psychiatry, 10*(4), 157–163.

Zisook, S., Paulus, M., Shuchter, S. R., & Judd, L. L. (1997). The many faces of depression following spousal bereavement. *Journal of Affective Disorders, 45*(1–2), 85–94.

3

Family Resilience After Violent Death

ALISON SALLOUM AND EDWARD K. RYNEARSON

FAMILY SYSTEM

Surveys of bereaved adults and children share a common finding — that family support is sought before any other. Perhaps the presence of family is a primary resource of resilience because of the ingredients of kinship resilience, familiar stabilizing patterns of verbal and nonverbal interactions that restore the sense of safety, cohesion, and hope for survival that have developed over years within the family matrix. However, the kind and degree of kinship resilience is unique to each family before and after a violent death. Regardless of the family capacity for resilience, it is important to reinforce *it,* particularly so for the sake of dependent children. The authors outline practice guidelines to include family members in restoration after the violent death through a supportive family assessment and specific sessions during intervention. Since 20% of homicides are perpetrated by one family member upon another (i.e., intrafamily homicide), a final section of the chapter focuses on strategies for reinforcing resilience in remaining family members.

Word of the violent death of a family member usually comes as a traumatic announcement — a mandated notification by police or medical examiner or a military officer. The brutal news of the dying cascades from family member to family member, all of whom gather for reassurance in the stabilization of proximity, cohesion, and kinship.

The family assembles in those early days to join in timeless rituals of
kinship retelling ("What happened?"), caregiving ("Are you OK?"), and
rites of respectful farewell for the deceased — preparing their remains and
participating in their memorial and funeral.

Resilience is implicit within a family that has a history and narrative of
caring kinship. As remaining family members assemble and retell the dying,
a kinship narrative may be summoned and enacted between family members
that kindle:

- hopeful belief systems
- nurturant behaviors
- communications of mutual respect
- problem-solving strategies (Walsh, 2003)

These patterns of stabilizing beliefs and interactions are resilient kinship
activities through which the family strives to maintain its unity and integrity
despite the meaningless and horrific dying. By interacting in a family-based
network of coherence and hope, kinship reassures each member that they
are not alone during this time of disintegration, but are bonded in the challenge of surviving the violent dying together.

And this family matrix may include summoning the voice of the deceased
to invoke their resilient presence:

- (name of the deceased) wouldn't want us to dwell on this;
- they would want us to remember them when they were alive;
- they would want us to go on with living;
- they would want us to celebrate what a great life they had.

Because violent dying is usually the product of a human act, it is followed
by an imperative, extrafamily investigation to find whoever was at fault, and
once found to try and punish that person, to reestablish a sense of honor,
safety, and justice to the family and community.

The family may welcome the imperative demand for investigation, retaliation, and retribution from the surrounding community because it promises to
satisfy the family member's own need for an active response to nullify his or
her self-blame and virtual impotence over the dying event. However, the formal
investigation, and, if a perpetrator is found, trial and verdict, often promises
more than it is able to deliver, and moreover guarantees that the history of the
family and the victim is no longer private or respectfully treated.

DISRESPECT, RETALIATION, AND RETRIBUTION

To cause a violent death may be the most supremely disrespectful act of
all, an active repudiation of the life of the victim and the life of the
family. While retribution (to restore the honor of the family) and retaliation
(to restore the honor of the victim's life) are fundamental psychological and

social responses to violent dying, the family is legally barred from carrying them out. Stabilizing themselves within the unity of the family from intense trauma and separation distress, family members are additionally preoccupied in understanding how this dying happened and who is willingly or negligently responsible.

Violent dying demands a formal, criminal–judicial inquiry to establish culpability and punishment, but there is no role for the family in this search for truth and justice. The media, police, medical examiner, local court, or military tribunal carries out an investigation of the dying, while the family helplessly watches. When one or several of its members become enraged by the combination of disrespect to the family and a feeling of impotence, the unity of the family can be threatened by "acting out" murderous rage at the perpetrator (if identified) or by the disillusionment at the betrayal, by the surrounding agencies of police and court, of the family's trust in those entities to restore their honor and compensate them for their loss.

Specific types of violent death are associated with differing levels of disrespect for the victim leading to divergent responses of retaliation and retribution:

Accidental dying from an impersonal act of nature, in the absence of human intention, negligence, or disrespect, is not associated with intense family or community retaliation or retribution.

Accidental dying from a human act of commission (drunk driving) or omission (unregulated industrial pollution) is associated with negligence, but without personal premeditation or malice, and may be followed by a family demand for retaliation and retribution, but the criminal–judicial inquiry and response will be slow and not robust.

Suicidal dying while lethal and intentional, cannot punish or exact retribution from the perpetrator who was a member of the family. Once the police establish the dying as suicidal, the inquiry providing a "how and why" to the dying becomes the lonely ordeal of the family — sometimes so painful to begin or accept that the family insists the dying was homicidal.

Homicidal dying is personally motivated and disrespectful, associated with intense community and family responses of retaliation and retribution, and followed by a vigorous institutional inquiry that includes retribution for the family and death or prolonged imprisonment for the perpetrator.

Terrorist killing of innocent civilians, though politically motivated and impersonal, may be viewed as homicidal by community and family members who demand retribution and retaliation against not only the terrorist(s) but federal and metropolitan authorities and institutions failing to prevent the attack.

Military dying of personnel in combat may be violent and mutilating but the soldier combatant willingly placed herself or himself in "harm's way," and the family may view her or his dying as heroic and self-sacrificing in protecting fellow combatants and country. The death of fire and police personnel carries a similar meaning of self-sacrifice that is recognized by elaborate ceremonies of memorial and burial.

Dying of innocent civilians in combat is a common occurrence, accounting for over 90% of warfare deaths, which cannot be buffered by ideals of heroism, nationalism, or ceremony. While impersonal and nonintentional, the killing of noncombatants disregards and disrespects the life of the victim and the victim's family and is followed by strong demands for retaliation and retribution, resulting in violent insurgencies and reprisals.

LITERATURE REVIEW: FAMILY RESILIENCE AND VIOLENT DYING

Unfortunately, the literature is sparse on the effects on the family of violent dying, and there are no reports on the specific effects of investigation, retaliation, or retribution on long-term family adjustment. Studies specific to the measurement and maintenance of resilience within the family after violent dying have not been reported. While the resilience of family kinship is real and supports the traumatized family, its definition and measurement are challenging and complex.

The term *resilience* has been inconsistently defined by scholars, and debates continue about the stability of resilience, the longitudinal effects, the multidimensional characteristics, and about whether the construct is one involving personal traits or dynamic processes (Luthar, Cicchetti, & Becker, 2000). Nevertheless, a broad definition of resilience is that it is "a dynamic process encompassing positive adaptation within the context of significant adversity" (Luthar et al., 2000, p. 543). Resilience after violent dying does not preclude some family members from typically experiencing acute traumatic stress reactions in the immediate aftermath, experiencing profound longings for the deceased, or experiencing challenging long-term adjustment to the numerous changes. Indeed, when a loved one has died violently, distress within the family is to be expected, but the dynamic processes of kinship resilience over time (i.e. shared hopeful belief systems, nurturant behaviors, communications of mutual respect, and engaging in problem-solving strategies) can provide immediate stabilization and long-term support to promote resilient families so that they are enabled to engage in living and commemorating the life of the deceased, despite the horror associated with violent death. As Walsh (2003) states, "resilience involves key processes over time that foster the ability to 'struggle well,' surmount obstacles, and to go on and live and love fully" (p. 1).

The available family therapy literature discussing the aftermath of violent dying searches for pathology instead of resilience — dysfunctional responses in dysfunctional families highly troubled before the violent death. This anecdotal finding, the association of high familial distress after violent dying, with antecedent history of intrafamilial abuse, neglect, psychiatric disorder, and treatment, is consistent with studies of individual vulnerability to violent dying.

Unfortunately, there is no specific family treatment protocol (replicable agenda or procedure) that has been tested for complicated bereavement after violent death or diagnostic criteria for establishing indications for family intervention. Instead, there are clinical reports of nonspecific interventions or theoretical approaches, such as transitional family therapy (Horwitz, 1997); empowerment and strengths perspective; risk and resilience research; narrative therapy (Wall & Levy, 1996; Levy & Wall, 2000); contextual therapy with narrative therapy (Temple, 1997); psychoanalytic methods (Parson, 1995); and the use of psychosocial development, social learning theory, and cognitive–behavioral strategies (Burman & Allen-Meares, 1994). These case studies of family therapy after violent death use specific theoretical approaches to discuss associated improvements, but there remains a lack of rigorously designed, empirically based investigation.

The lack of research evidence verifying the significance of family therapy after violent dying, does not detract from the pragmatic importance of including family members in a supportive intervention. The gathering of family members to promote kinship resilience is basic in supporting a traumatized family. This support takes place by reinforcing attitudes of mutual respect and encouraging open, accurate, and nurturing communications between remaining family members.

THE FAMILY ALLIANCE

The programmatic involvement of family members in psychological support after violent dying began decades ago when peer-led support groups formed. The leaders intuitively recognized the salience of family resilience and encouraged family participation.

This vital engagement of family in peer-led support illustrates that maintaining the potential for engagement with the entire family after violent death fosters an alliance with the kinship network, and engagement with that "networking" may play an important role in restoring individual members of the family as well as restoring the integrity of the family unit.

Practice Guidelines for Maintaining Family Resilience

Individual family members often ask for help for their individual distress, not for family therapy, after a relative has died violently. Despite family discord, they see themselves as the problem rather than the family. Family conflict may have been a source of high distress for the family member long before the violent death. In unusually abusive and chaotic families the violent death may have been precipitated or even committed by another family member. However, regardless of its dysfunction, the highly distressed family member needs the family, or its remnant, to maintain some show of unity in countering the underlying chaos and helplessness implicit in the disintegration caused by violent dying.

In the early months following a violent death the family reserves its energies for the day-to-day survival of caring for one another and returning to routines of work, play, and reengagement with life. There is neither time nor energy for the family to deal with further disruption accompanying the expression of divisive feelings or the acting out of discordant relationships.

Resilience Assessment

A highly distressed family member (most commonly the mother), actively seeks intervention for herself or a child in the family, and once that person is stabilized and agrees to an evaluation, the clinician may request a family visit.

When the young, dependent child is the primary client, the parent who initiated the consultation may contribute important information about the child's family prior to clinical contact and the parent can share with the clinician any concerns about the child. Clinicians can offer reassurances about typical developmental responses and encourage parents to provide additional comfort to the child during this time. In addition to providing education and encouraging nurturing interactions, other concerns of parents or issues to be raised by clinicians such as parenting, communication, and behavioral changes may need to be discussed before meeting with the child or as a family. In addition, since violent dying can unsettle or in some cases shatter a child's sense of safety, discussion about ways to strengthen the child's sense of safety may need to be prioritized, and there are numerous ways that sense of safety can be bolstered (see below for strategies for parents to help children feel safe).

Creating a Sense of Safety for Children

- Establish family routines and rituals (especially comforting ones at bedtime)
- Talk with the child about what it means to feel safe
- Provide honest information in a developmentally appropriate manner
- Limit exposure to distressing content
- Remain open to ongoing questioning
- Provide reassurances that the parents will take care of the child
- Be emotionally available to respond to the child's emotional needs
- Participate in activities that calm and relax the child
- Balance between being too lenient and too strict — provide appropriate limits
- Identify or create a place where the child can feel safe (use in vivo and imaginary exposure to the safe place)

Some parents may be withholding information about the death from the child as a way to "protect" the child from the horror and grief. If this is occurring, clinicians and parents should discuss how parents can provide honest, open communication about the death that is developmentally appropriate.

Clinicians may also inquire if the parenting and disciplining have changed since the death. It may be that parents have either become more lenient (feeling sorry for the child) or more strict (feeling scared that something bad may happen to the child) since the death, and discussion about how parents may find a more balanced approach may be indicated. In the wake of the chaos caused by the violent death, parents may not have reestablished old routines and structures within the family. Clinicians should inquire about this as bedtime rituals and a sense of structure to family life can assist with stabilization of the child. During this discussion inquiring how the child and family engage in activities (such as sports, taking walks, or going to the park, a restaurant, a movie, or family gatherings, etc.) to take "breaks" from the stress is important, because recreation is an excellent approach for all family members to manage stress. Recreation can also provide an avenue for children to feel a sense of mastery and control in their lives, which may be lessened due to the violent death.

Upon the first visit with the child, the parent, in the presence of and in collaboration with the clinician, needs to explain the clinician's role to the child. Additionally, it is important for parents to give the child permission to talk with other family members and clinicians about what has happened. With all family members present, the family is told that the purpose of the evaluation is to assist the clinician in clarifying the strengths of the family rather than uncovering problems.

There is no rigid format to follow during a resilience assessment. To place the visiting family members at ease the clinician is the first to speak and tries to set a relaxed tone. An opening to the session may include a message of thanks for their willingness to gather as a family to help the clinician and one another after the violent death, emphasizing that this meeting will help family members to see each others' needs more clearly.

The clinician reassures the family members that they are not on a hot seat. They can choose to speak or remain silent. Also, the clinician lets members know that if a family member begins to speak and becomes too overwhelmed, it is all right to stop or to take a break until the distress diminishes. When the member is able and ready he or she can resume sharing with the family and clinician.

During the initial meeting, family members are asked to introduce themselves, to clarify what they feel would ease the distress within the family or of the family member who has been identified for treatment, and how the family might provide that support. If they want to talk about the dying, they are encouraged to retell not only the dying events in their own words (and sometimes their narratives of the dying are unique and divergent), but *t* include their beliefs about death (spiritual or religious).

In the ebb and flow of the conversation, the clinician sometimes finds herself or himself in the privileged position of initiating a long delayed communicative process of resilience that didnot begin at the time of notification or in those early days when the family gathered. For whatever reason, the family could not openly engage in a retelling or enact a kinship narrative of resilience.

Though signs and symptoms of psychopathology may be observed during the assessment, they are not probed or pursued. Indeed, during this early phase of stabilization when dysfunctional thoughts, feelings, or behaviors are disruptive of family cohesion, the clinician may interrupt a family member to explain that the purpose of the evaluation is informational, not confrontational.

As the session draws to a close, the clinician asks each member for his or her feedback and actively responds to their questions and evaluations. The session ends with the clinician emphasizing the observed resiliencies of the family, and recommends their continuance and reinforcement (see list below for some signs of family resilience after violent death). This is also the time to suggest corrective insights about family attitudes and behaviors that are interfering with the process of mourning and trauma resolution. It is helpful too to tell the family that every family member, including children, benefits from an open communication of what is known about the dying and what might support each member in adjusting to the death. Emphasizing that there is no "right" way to grieve is an important clarification — that each person follows his or her own direction and time frame in adjusting to death that cannot be compressed or erased.

When children and adolescents are part of the family, it is important for the clinician to underscore that due to developmental differences as well as individual uniqueness, the way in which a child or adolescent expresses grief may differ vastly from that of adult family members, and this is to be respected. For example, a six-year-old may engage in family discussion about the deceased, but he or she may only participate briefly before wanting to return to playing. While developmentally, young children may not be able to tolerate long periods of discomfort and pain and may grieve in "spurts," parents may misinterpret this behavior as not caring or disrespectful. Adolescents may engage with the family in reminiscing about the deceased, but they may not turn to the family for all of their emotional support. Some youth may seek emotional understanding outside the family, such as from their peers (including girlfriends or boyfriends). In addition, with adolescents some of the inner struggles of the loss and meaning of the death may be confined to personal writings and journals. Parents are cautioned against believing that adolescents, who are often placed in the position of being young adults, may not need the comfort and nurture of parents.

Signs of Family Resilience After Violent Death

Communications of Mutual Respect
- Able to reminisce as a family and create a family narrative about the life of the deceased.
- Able to tolerate individual family members reminiscing.
- Able to share a family narrative about the violent death and loss, as well as construct a family narrative about the deceased while honoring individual narratives about the meaning of the deceased in the lives of individual family members.

- Family uses humor in a respectful manner, one which brings smiles and laughter to all.
- Family members understand and respect that each person's relationship to the deceased is unique and respects how each family member expresses his or her grief.

Hopeful Belief Systems
- Talks about and utilizes spirituality or belief systems that offer hope, peace, or understanding.
- Hopeful narratives and belief systems about death and life.
- Continues to have visions of future.
- Does not allow stigma or guilt to become the predominate belief.

Nurturing Behaviors
- Recognizes the importance of kinship and uses family support.
- Has support system outside the family.
- Able to "take breaks" and find moments where the mind is not consumed with thoughts of death or loss.
- Able to have conversations with deceased and stay connected to presence and finds strength in this.
- Able to share pain and feelings of loss together.
- Adjusts and becomes flexible to roles of deceased being filled by the other family members.
- Provide comfort to one another.
- Adults able to recognize emotional state of children and acknowledge their grief.
- Adults able to take care of one another in familiar, supportive ways.
- Safety and protection of all family members is priority.
- Utilizes family culture and rituals to provide stabilization and connection.
- Engages in healthy activities for the family: balanced meals, time for exercise, and recreation.

Problem-Solving Strategies
- Acknowledges changes and losses as a result of the death.
- Thinks of creative approaches to solve new problems and includes others in brainstorming solutions.
- Able to utilize family and outside resources to address problems.
- Aware of rights and becomes informed about how to interact effectively with different systems.
- Able to discern the pros and cons of making major life changes after the death.

It is quite common for families, even families who have a history of open emotional expression, to try to protect other family members from experiencing additional distress due to worrying about each other. This relational worry can become pervasive among various subgroups within the family: child-parent; parent-parent; sibling-sibling; extended family-family. If open communication and acceptance of expression of feelings does not seem to be occurring or tolerated within the family, it is helpful for clinicians to wonder aloud with the family if this may be occurring. For example, the clinician may state, "You know sometimes even the most loving and close families find it difficult to talk and share with each other after a violent death. This type of silence often occurs in an attempt by family members to try to protect each other and to prevent each other from worrying about the other person. I wonder if this has been occurring within your family?" If any family member confirms this common occurrence, the clinician continues to explain that silence within the family, which may be on some level helping family members cope, may in fact prevent healthy communication which may be needed to foster the family's strengths and resiliencies. Finally, the clinician suggests that the family might return for another informational session when the clinician, the patient, or other family members feel another gathering would be helpful to them.

In protocol-based interventions, family members (and this may include close friends as well) are included in a family session. This session is scheduled toward the end of the time-limited intervention to consolidate the therapeutic gains now shared with the patient's family and supportive friends. Clarifying these changes in open session allows supportive family members and friends to play an active part in celebrating and maintaining the therapeutic changes.

Resilience Reinforcement

There are several clinical complications specific to violent dying that affect family dynamics and resilience, and indicate meetings between the treating clinician and the family as a whole or selected members:

1. A meeting with a clinician is indicated when a family member, particularly a dependent child, is feeling unsafe or unsupported, and is unable to articulate his or her distress or identify anyone within the family who they can "go to" for stabilization.

Debra was shot by her husband, and as a result of the gunshot lived for five years as a paraplegic before dying. Prior to Debra's death, her mother, Ms. Ruth, took care of Debra and her two children: Geraldine who was aged 12 and Reginald who was aged six. After Debra died, it became too difficult for Ms. Ruth to continue to care for the children. Therefore, Geraldine went to live with her paternal grandparents as she had requested, and Reginald rotated between staying with Ms. Ruth sometimes and staying with his maternal aunt. However, due to financial difficulties, Ms. Ruth moved out of her home and began living sometimes with her daughter who was caring for Reginald, and at other times with another child who lived in a neighboring city, thus leaving Reginald to live full time with his aunt. Ms. Ruth had heard from her daughter that Reginald was not doing well in school and she had contacted a clinician who had visited with her family two years earlier when Debra was alive. The clinician attempted to meet with

Reginald and his aunt, but due to his aunt's schedule (attending college and working in the evenings) several visits were canceled. The clinician gained permission from Ms. Ruth (who was currently living with her other child in another city) to meet with Reginald at school.

Reginald remembered the clinician and was excited and ready to meet. During the session, the clinician asked Reginald to "draw a picture of something he wanted to tell a story about." After he drew the picture of himself watching his mother's burial and a picture of a home, the clinician wrote his story about his picture. His story was "I love my mom, I love my grandma, will you be my new mom?" As a result of meeting with Reginald and seeing his picture and hearing his story, the clinician wondered if the difficulty Reginald was experiencing was not only due to the grief for his mother, but more because he felt there was no one he could "go to" and no one was identified as his primary caregiver. Prior to meeting further with Reginald, the clinician shared these thoughts with Ms. Ruth and her daughter. Both acknowledged that their shared efforts to take care of Reginald may have resulted in times when neither one of them were focused on his needs. This realization helped the aunt to take a more active parenting and maternal role with Reginald.

---

2. A meeting with a clinician is called for when one or several members (usually young males) of the family are at high risk to engage in active retaliation against the presumed perpetrator, presenting potential trauma and legal chaos for the family, and a medical-legal risk for the clinician, who is responsible for notifying the authorities of serious risk of retaliation.

Ms. Johnson called a community-based grief and trauma program seeking a counselor to talk with her about whether her grandchildren (ages five and three) should attend their mother's funeral. Ms. Johnson explained that her daughter, Susan, had been found stabbed to death in the neighborhood park and that the daughter's husband (the children's father) was the suspected perpetrator, but charges had not been brought. The clinician met with Ms. Johnson at her home and talked with her about ways to prepare the children for the funeral and ways to help them. During the meeting Ms. Johnson's other adult children, a daughter and two sons, were at the home and listened to the conversation. The clinician sensed the silence among the adults and asked to talk with all of them about common reactions of children and of adults. During the meeting the clinician explained that thoughts about retaliation, especially when the legal system is delayed, are bound to surge for some of the family members and that these thoughts are often associated with intense feelings. The clinician explained that while these thoughts may be normal, such actions may result in another family member's death or incarceration. The clinician paused to observe the family's reactions and to allow them to talk about this. After some silence, the daughter, perhaps recognizing the body language of her two brothers, sensed that her brothers had already talked about killing their brother-in-law. She looked at both of them and said, "don't do it." She and her mother were able to let them know that they did not want them to retaliate for fear of one of them dying and also that their religion did not condone this action. They pleaded further by explaining that retaliation would not bring Susan back nor would it bring honor to their sister or to their family. The brothers gave them their word that they would not kill their brother-in-law.

This family meeting with open discussion about retaliation seemed to bring a sense of relief to the family and an awareness of the power, strength, and bond within the family. After the funeral the clinician continued to meet weekly with the young children and the grandmother to allow the children an opportunity to express their feelings about the loss of their mother and father (the children had not seen their father since their mother died) and to strengthen the relationship between the grandmother and the children.

After some months of little contact from the police department, the adult family members with the help of the clinician set up a meeting with the homicide detective on the case. The family was told that the case had been transferred to the cold case unit and that due to a lack of evidence they could not arrest the children's father, who the family confidently thought had killed Susan. Despite the profound anger and frustration with the criminal justice system that failed to provide any legal resolution, the family's support for one another provided the necessary stability for family members to continue to commemorate the life of Susan and for the family to continue engaging in life.

---

3. When a family member (usually the mother) assumes an overprotective role with surviving family members through compulsive, overdetermined, "checking" behaviors to ensure proximity and safety, a meeting with a clinician can be helpful.

The therapist who referred Maggie was concerned that she would not attend the interview without her daughter and mother in the same room with her. Since her son's homicide six weeks before, she would not allow them out of her sight. A psychiatrist assured the therapist that he wanted to meet with all of them during the first visit. The three of them stood as one when he introduced himself. Maggie was in the midst of a panic attack and looked stricken while her mother and daughter looked to the psychiatrist with a combination of desperation and relief.

All of them spent the next hour in family consultation trying to establish where and how they might reassure Maggie that she and her daughter were protected. They dreaded returning to their house, which had been transformed into a death scene after they had watched Maggie's son murdered on the front porch. Maggie's older sister had urged them to move in with her until they could begin looking for another place. They called her from the psychiatrist's office, and it was decided that they would go there that afternoon. Maggie agreed to start on a low dose of an antianxiety medication to control her panic attacks and insomnia and to meet after the weekend.

It was agreed that it was mandatory that Maggie's daughter return to school and arrangements were to have one of her schoolmates escort her to and from her aunt's house so Maggie knew she was not alone.

At the next meeting Maggie and her mother attended without the daughter. Maggie was markedly improved as a result of the combination of the move and the physical effect of the medication. Without the panic, she had slept for the first time since her son's murder and was beginning to feel less disintegrated. She no longer felt a pervasive dread of imminent death and could appreciate that she and her daughter could survive what had happened.

---

4. When a family member (usually the mother) assumes an overdetermined role of isolated caregiver for surviving family members (particularly surviving children) without recognition of her or his own need for resilience, a meeting with a clinician is advisable.

Charles, a 17-year-old, came to see a psychiatrist at his mother's insistence. His older brother, Herb, had committed suicide four months before and Charles had carried on his normal routine as if nothing had happened. He was willing to come to see the psychiatrist in order to reassure his mother, but didn't think that he needed help.

After visiting with Charles and his parents, the psychiatrist suspected that he was serving as a psychiatric authority to reassure his parents that he was safe. Charles and the psychiatrist agreed that he was, and the psychiatrist also presumed that Charles was threatened by being identified as potentially suicidal. He had been so closely identified with Herb that he needed some distance from the way he had died. They reviewed what they might expect in their adjustment as a family and they agreed to consult with the psychiatrist again in several months — or sooner if there was any difficulty.

Six months later Charles's mother again requested a consultation. Charles remained stable and was focused more on the future than the past after deciding to attend a small college on the East Coast, and was looking forward to the transition.

But Charles was concerned about his mother. Now that he had decided to attend school across the country, he recognized that his departure for college was going to be very distressing for her.

The psychiatrist asked to see Charles's mother Barbara, by herself, and within minutes she began to cry for the first time since Herb's death and admitted that she needed some support for herself outside of the family. The psychiatrist suggested that she return to see one of his associates. He didn't want to place himself between them, as a shared therapist and listener, unless the three of them were meeting together to retell the same story. The psychiatrist suspected that her retelling was very different from Charles's version, and that she needed her own private opportunity to come to terms with her own distress. However, the psychiatrist emphasized that he remained available for a family session if that would be of support for her. Since the family interactions were solid and supportive at this point, there was no urgency.

Dynamics after Intrafamily Murder

Of the solved murders in the United States (about 62% solved in 2002), 21.5% of the murder victims were killed at the hands of a family member. The majority of these victims were adult females who were killed by their husbands, but all types of familial victim–offender relationships occur, such as parent killing child, wife killing husband, extended family member killing family member, and sibling killing sibling or parent (Durose et al., 2005). The prevalence of a family member killing another family member may be significantly higher if the term *family member* is defined by the family and not by biology or law, since boyfriends, girlfriends, and friends are often considered "family" and engage in familial relationships and patterns.

It is difficult to imagine that kinship resilience can be present within a family where one family member murdered another. Indeed, the more central theme is the past pathology and chaos that led to the death and the current psychopathology of surviving family members. However, the circumstances, perception, and health of certain family members prior to the murder can lead to moments, or for some families, stable patterns of resilience. Some factors, in addition to the signs of resilience discussed earlier in this chapter, that may bolster resilience after intrafamilial murder include familial relations with limited conflict and hostility; recognition, acceptance, and appropriate expression of a range of feelings; and the ability to identify and change past harmful relational patterns.

Hostility within the family or extended family is a common theme after intrafamilial murder, especially when one spouse or partner kills another. Members of each family of origin often band together to defend the perpetrator or the victim and define how and why the murder occurred. Occasionally, one family member may reach across to someone in the other family and offer condolences or understanding, especially if there was a history of known domestic violence. However, when hostility and family conflict becomes the central pattern, surviving children may be caught in the middle and forced by family members to "take sides" with the alleged perpetrator or the deceased. In the midst of this conflict, families often elaborate on definitive narratives about each spouse or partner, become closed to hearing other views, and disallow dissenting opinions from the children. Families that are aware of these patterns and can take steps to disentangle themselves and the children from opposing hostile sides can help strengthen the kinship resilience and the surviving children's resilience.

In the midst of trial proceedings of a woman who allegedly killed her husband and custody hearings among two grandmothers over the eight-year-old surviving boy, the paternal and maternal grandmothers agreed to avoid any negative conversations about the boy's parents. The grandmothers also agreed that they would not discuss with the surviving child their own opposing beliefs about how and why the murder occurred. Instead both grandmothers told him how much they both loved him, agreed on a visitation schedule, and told him that they were there to talk with him or listen to him if he wanted to talk about his parents. They mutually consented to providing the child with a child therapist to allow him an opportunity to express himself.

Surviving family members may make it clear to other family members how they are feeling, such as expressing anger and profound sadness, yet some members may also be experiencing feelings that they are ashamed or scared to share, such as ambivalence about the death, guilt, or relief that the person is dead. If family members can recognize that given the circumstances surrounding the death, a range of feelings may actually be common responses, they will be more likely to establish open communication rather than an atmosphere of closed communication without expression of feelings.

A 15-year-old boy shot and killed his father who was physically attacking his mother. He had called the police, but they did not respond, and when the violence escalated and his father went aggressively toward him, he shot him. With the help of a clinician the boy and his mother were able to talk about the guilt they both felt: each took sole blame for the death. They also both talked about feeling ambivalent about the death: on the one hand the violence had ended and they felt a sense of relief, but on the other hand they missed him, and they could talk about the man they both loved, especially when he was not drinking and being violent. With the open expression of feelings the boy and mother were able to provide support to one another.

Intrafamilial murder often takes place in a historical context of domestic violence where familial dynamics of conflict, control, and abuse are common themes. Even after the family member who was the batterer is killed at the hands of another member, prior dynamics that the deceased played a central role in may linger within the family, reoccur in another familial relationship, or may reoccur with the next generation. Perhaps the most common example of the violent pattern continuing is when the aggressive battering partner is killed and the surviving partner engages in another relationship with a person who is also abusive. Another example that is more subtle is when the batterer is killed and the surviving partner and one of the surviving children engage in similar relational negative patterns that emulate the relationship

of the batterer and surviving partner. This reoccurrence of old negative relational interactions may occur due to various reasons, such as the child identifying with the deceased and being angry with the surviving partner, and
therefore taking on the prior role of the deceased. Alternatively, the child
triggers memories in the surviving partner and in turn that partner engages
with the child as if the child were the batterer (the deceased).

A woman who was in a violent relationship for years shot her husband to death
in self-defense. Their son, age five, whose behavior was aggressive prior to the
death, became even more aggressive and defiant (a common response of a child
who has witnessed domestic violence). When the mother would respond to her
child's disobedient behavior she would become enraged and feel as if it were
her husband being demanding and abusive toward her when it was actually her
five-year-old son being defiant. While trying to discipline the child, the mother
would overreact and lash out toward him. On one occasion she found herself
starting to choke her child. With the help of a clinician she recognized that she
was becoming triggered by her son (who had the same name and looked like the
deceased) to memories of violent interactions with her husband. After identifying this pattern the mother was able to use cognitive–behavioral strategies to
change this pattern and to learn to provide appropriate parenting to her son.

Frantuzzo and Mohr (1999) report that children exposed to domestic
violence are at risk for experiencing problems including, but not limited
to, conduct problems, aggressive behavior, difficulty concentrating, poor
academic and intellectual functioning, depression, low self-esteem, and
anxiety. In addition children who witness domestic violence are also at risk
for developing posttraumatic stress symptomatology (Kilpatrick & Williams,
1997; McCloskey & Walker, 2000) as are children who witness the murder of
one family member by another (Eth & Pynoss, 1994; Malmquist, 1986).

When one parent kills another the magnitude of secondary losses is
enormous. Many of these children may end up living with relatives or in
foster care (Kaplan, Black, Hyman & Knox, 2001; Lewandowski, McFarlane,
Campbell, Gary, & Barenski, 2004), which means they will move from their
homes and neighborhoods and leave friends and familiar settings. Some
of these children have in fact lost both parents, with one being dead and
the other in jail or perhaps both dead, such as in a murder-suicide. These
children need to be in environments that provide consistent patterns of
stabilizing interactions that foster kinship resilience.

SUMMARY

Patterns of stabilizing beliefs and interactions (hopeful belief systems,
nurturant behaviors, communications of mutual respect, problem-solving
strategies) are the ingredients of resilient kinship activities through which

the family strives to maintain its unity and integrity after violent dying. Maintaining and reinforcing resilient kinship is restorative for highly distressed family members. Caregivers and clinicians can enlist the family as allies in support during assessment and intervention and more particularly with support and intervention for dependent children.

Despite its lack of empirical verification, family resilience is an important resource of psychosocial stabilization for the telling and restorative retelling of the violent dying and the nonverbal behaviors and attitudes that ensure a sense of proximity and safety.

REFERENCES

Burman, S. & Allen-Meares, P. (1994). Neglected victims of murder: Children's witness to parental homicide. *Social Work, 39,* 28–34.

Durose, M. R., Harlow, C.W., Langan, P. A., Motivans, M., Rantala, R. R., & Smith, E. L. (2005*). Family violence statistics: Including statistics on strangers and acquaintances.* Washington, D.C.: U.S. Department of Justice, Office of Justice Programs, Bureau of Justice Statistics, [NCJ207846]

Eth, S. & Pynoos, R. (1994). Children who witness the homicide of a parent. *Psychiatry, 57,* 287–306.

Frantuzzo, J. W. & Mohr, W. K. (1999). *Prevalence and effects of child exposure to domestic violence. The future of children, 9.* Los Altos, CA: The David and Lucile Packard Foundation.

Horwitz, S. H. (1997). Treating families with traumatic loss: Transitional family therapy. In C. R. Figley, B. E. Bride, & N. Mazza (Eds.), *Death and trauma: The traumatology of grieving* (pp. 159–191). Washington, D.C.: Taylor and Francis.

Kaplan, T., Black, D., Hyman, P., & Knox, J. (2001). Outcome of children seen after one parent killed the other. *Clinical Child Psychology and Psychiatry, 6,* 9–22.

Kilpatrick, K.L. & Williams, L. (1997). Post-traumatic stress disorder in child witnesses to domestic violence. American Journal of Orthopsychiatry, 67, 639-644.

Levy, A. J. & Wall, J. C. (2000). Children who have witnessed community homicide: Incorporating risk and resilience in clinical work. *Families in Society, 81,* 402–411.

Lewandowski, L. A., McFarlane, J., Campbell, J. C., Gary, F., & Barenski, C. (2004). He killed my mommy! Murder or attempted murder of a child's mother. *Journal of Family Violence, 19,* 211–220.

Luthar, S. S., Cicchetti, D., & Becker, B. (2000). The construct of resilience: A critical evaluation and guidelines for future work. *Child Development, 71,* 543–563.

Kaplan, T., Black D., Hyman, P. & Knox, J. (2001). Outcome of children seen after one parent killed another. *Clinical Child Psychology and Psychiatry, 6,* 9–22.

Malmquist, C. P. (1986). Children who witness parental murder: Posttraumatic aspects. *Journal of the American Academy of Child Psychiatry, 25,* 320–325.

McCloskey, L. A. & Walker, M. (2000). Posttraumatic stress in children exposed to family violence and single event trauma. Journal of the American Academy of Child and Adolescent Psychiatry, 39, 108-111.

Parson, E. R. (1995). Post-traumatic stress and coping in an inner-city child: Traumatogenic witnessing of interparental violence and murder. *Psychoanalytic Study of the Child, 50,* 272–307.

Temple, S. (1997). Treating urban families of homicide victims: A contextual oriented approach. *Family Process,36,* 133–144.

Wall, J. C. & Levy, A. J. (1996). Communities under fire: Empowering families and children in the aftermath of homicide. *Clinical Social Work Journal,* 24, 403–414.

Walsh, F. (2003). Family resilience: A framework for clinical practice — theory and practice. *Family Process, 42,* 1–18.

4

Spiritual Essentials

JANICE HARRIS LORD

SPIRITUAL FRAMEWORK

Spirituality, belief in a realm of reality beyond that generally experienced by the five senses, can be a significant resource of stability following violent death. Surveys document that bereaved family members turn to personal prayer, church attendence, and pastoral counseling long before consulting a mental health clinician. Regardless of their perspectives on spirituality, caregivers should not disregard the reestablishment of meaning offered by the belief that the spirit of the deceased is at eternal and peaceful rest — detached from the horror and helplessness of his or her dying. The author of this chapter (both a therapist and a pastoral counselor) highlights the clinical relevance of spirituality after violent death by providing a brief description of various spiritual beliefs about death followed by specific funeral and memorial practices. Two clinical cases illustrate the author's application of clinical/spiritual support and intervention. Techniques and exercises for spiritual/clinical stabilization are outlined for moderating distress, diminishing the trauma of the dying narrative, and reconnecting with meaning and living through a group intervention.

For many people, spiritual faith feels like the one constant they can cling to when their loved one has been ripped from them. For most, however, their beliefs make a slow transition from a state of naiveté before the tragedy, to critical questioning of previously held understandings that didnot "work," to a postcritical stability that incorporates or assimilates the tragedy into some, but not all, of their long-held spiritual assumptions. Like other transitions in grief, spiritual transformation takes time. As the caregivers companion family members through the spiritual aspects of trauma grief, they can eventually help them reach a new understanding of resilience from within, reconstruct the meaning of their loved one's death, and reconnect with life as wiser, yet scarred, pilgrims. Let's begin with a couple of true stories of persons whose spiritual reactions to a violent death vary.

Bob and Jane had two daughters, Cindy and Meredith. Bob is a conservative Christian and was deeply distressed when Jane converted to Islam. In fact, this stress was a crucial factor in their decision to divorce. Jane remarried and maintained custody of the girls. One evening as Jane, her new husband, and the girls were traveling, they discovered that they were lost and pulled off the side of the road to make a phone call. While stopped, they were rear-ended by a speeding and intoxicated driver, killing Meredith and injuring Cindy. Jane insisted on a Muslim funeral and burial, which included ritually washing Meredith three times and wrapping her in a white cloth for burial. She was not embalmed or otherwise "prepared." Following prayers, she was buried directly into the ground facing Mecca without the benefit of casket or vault, as is Muslim custom. Bob's fury over his daughter's burial erupted in numerous violent outbursts, and he continues to lament that his daughter was "buried like a dog." He remains inconsolable, refusing to learn about the values underlying Muslim burial customs and seeking to prevent other family members from obtaining such knowledge. He refuses to participate in a trauma grief group and appears to believe that the only way to honor his daughter's life is to remain angry.

Don and Julie reacted to their son's death differently. Each had been married before, and Julie brought her only son, Kris, into the marriage when he was a small boy. Don was like a father to Kris. They were somewhat active in a Christian congregation, and Julie's personal spirituality was particularly deep and abiding. She prayed every day that the angels would protect her child from harm. Kris was popular in school, enjoying a fairly charmed life, and decided to join the Air Force after attending two years of college. He was deployed to Iraq, and managed to make it back home safely, an accomplishment the family credited to God. Kris, too, was hit by an intoxicated driver shortly after his return. He was on life support for 42 hours before his parents followed the directive set forth in Kris' will to not be kept alive through the use of machines. The family's immediate focus was on the unfairness of what happened, but Julie, especially, entered into deeply distressing spiritual turmoil. Had God not heard her prayers for Kris' protection? If God had heard them, why were they no longer honored? Julie had to reconfigure her theology or abandon it altogether. Even though furious with God, she remained slightly open to spiritual guidance. She and Don read books, they attended a trauma grief group, and they talked with other spiritual people, but did not reconnect with a faith community. Julie wrote letters to Kris in her journal, and eventually allowed him to "write back" in a group session. Don, too, participated in this exercise and used a similar exercise to allow Kris to write a

Mother's Day message to Julie. Both remain open to spiritual messages from Kris and from God. While still deeply saddened by Kris's death, sometimes verging on the threshold of depression, their spiritual connection has become deeply satisfying. Following is a note Julie sent to their friends as she and Don approached a motions hearing to suppress evidence in the trial of the man who killed their son:

In the past I shared what happened in court with you after we returned home. This time, I am writing to ask for your prayers before we go and while we are there. I ask that you pray for Light in this situation. I ask that you surround and fill the courthouse with God's Light, Love, and Life. I ask that you help us to have faith — to KNOW that there is ONE power and that power is God. I know the power of "when two or more are gathered..." and I thank you all in advance for your prayerful support.

When they returned from the trial, Julie wrote:

There was a marked difference in the courtroom yesterday. Knowing that everyone was praying for light made us aware of God's Light and helped us remain calm. We continue to be so grateful for your ongoing prayer support.

Spirituality and religious practice are significant parts of the lives of many Americans. The September 5, 2005 issue of *Newsweek* reported on a random survey of 1,004 adults, which found that 79% described themselves as "spiritual," and 64% said they were "religious." Among religious or spiritual activities, 64% said that they pray. Their primary purposes in praying were "to seek God's guidance" (27%) and "to thank God" (23%). A full 67% said they believe that when they die, their souls will go to heaven or hell.

A national survey of 20,000 parents whose child had died found that while most of them relied primarily on their own families for comfort, 60% of them turned to their clergy (NFO Research, 1999). Likewise, a study of 8,200 victims of crime in Texas revealed that most turned to family and friends, but ranked clergy higher than victim advocates and as high as doctors and prosecutors as useful helpers (Crime Victims Institute, 1998). A survey of 1,423 victims of drunk driving crashes (75% with a loved one killed; 25% injured or with a loved one seriously injured) found that 67% frequently sought spiritual comfort (Mercer, Falkenberg, & Lorden, 1999).

Of those who seek counseling in the aftermath of tragedy, many are not only comfortable with therapists who incorporate spirituality into their practice, but actively seek out therapists who do so. In a national random survey of 1,000 people, 83% said their spiritual faith and religious beliefs were closely related to their mental and emotional health. Among African Americans, 97% said they were closely related. More preferred a pastor or person with religious training than a secular professional mental health counselor. Of those who said they would seek the services of a mental health counselor, 69% said it would be important to them that the counselor represented spiritual beliefs and values (Woodruff, 2001).

Some caregivers, particularly if they receive public funding for their programs, may have been instructed to avoid discussion about spirituality because of "separation of church and state" concerns. George W. Bush's administration has pushed the envelope on this issue, seeking clarification about what is and is not allowed. The First Amendment itself does not mention the phrase "separation of church and state." The Amendment simply reads, "Congress shall make no law respecting an establishment of religion or prohibiting the free exercise thereof." It does not guarantee freedom *from* religious expression but it guarantees freedom *of* religious expression. The forefathers came from England where the Church of England dominated the country. They wanted to be sure that no one religion would ever again dominate the law of the land and that every citizen would have the full right to express his or her religion.

While individuals retain the right of religious expression regardless of the setting, the Bush administration has sought to clarify the separation issue:

- Government-funded programs cannot discriminate against program participants on the basis of religion, a particular religious belief or practice, or choice to participate or not to participate in religious activity.
- Inherently religious activities (such as prayer, worship, worship instruction, or promotion of any single faith) must be provided separately in time or location from government-funded services. (28 C.F.R. Parts 38.1 and 38.2)

Those receiving government funding may identify spiritual assistance resources and outreach to faith-based groups to assure informed referrals (Vargas, 2005).

Most mental health practitioner codes of ethics now include spirituality or religion. For example, religion is mentioned five times in the 1999 revision of the Code of Ethics of the National Association of Social Workers, usually in the context of competency, diversity, and nondiscrimination; that is, "Social workers should obtain education about and seek to understand the nature of social diversity and oppression with respect to race, ethnicity, national origin, color, sex, sexual orientation, age, marital status, political belief, *religion*, and mental or physical disability" (NASW, 1999).

SPIRITUALITY IN THE IMMEDIATE AFTERMATH

While the focus of this book is beyond the crisis, it is important to recognize what trauma does to people immediately and how the faith community can help long before surviving family members reach out to mental health professionals. Faith leaders are crucial in the immediate aftermath because they provide unique services other caregivers are unable to give. Faith leaders are granted immediate access to families at the scene of the death, to ER staff at the hospital, to the medical examiner, and to the funeral home director. These sources can provide valuable information to clergy and, thereby, to the family. When faced with events that make no sense, families are desperate for valid and reliable information that their faith leader may be able to obtain even when they cannot.

Faith leaders bring calmness and stability to a traumatic situation because they are representatives of the Divine. As long as they do not make naive theological pronouncements about why the tragedy happened, they can bring a helpful dimension to the event. Without speaking many words, they present a sense of authority that points beyond the present. Commonly referred to as "the ministry of presence," the fact that they have come results in many distraught families clinging to them with words like, "I'm so glad you're here now."

Clergy are generally the only professionals who work with both the family and the funeral director to plan the funeral or memorial service. They become trusted caretakers of the body through performing death and burial rituals. They provide both words and deeds believed to ease the passage of souls into the next realm. For those who believe that baptism is a requirement for salvation, clergy can perform this ritual before or after the death. Anointing with oil and specific blessings or rites of passage assure family members that everything that could be done for their loved one was done. All of these practices retell the trauma story in a spiritual framework. In so many ways, how we tell it is how it is. As survivors begin to tell the trauma story in a spiritual framework, they usually experience more peace and hope.

Faith leaders can remain valuable team players with mental health professionals throughout long-term services. Family members of those who died violently are usually willing to sign a release so that their mental health professional and faith leader can work together, coeducating each other as they support both spiritual and emotional resilience. The faith community should continue to provide support to the family indefinitely, long after the therapeutic counseling relationship ends. Faith communities provide not only spiritual support, but social, physical, and financial support as well. Faith leaders can monitor and encourage avoidance of self-destructive measures such as substance abuse, and other high-risk behaviors and addictions. Many faith-based experiences such as prayer, worship services, and home visits create opportunities for hope, a key ingredient of resilience (Flach, 1990; Wolin & Wolin, 1993).

Every mental health provider should develop a well-researched referral list of faith leaders from the major religious groups in the community who are also educated, or willing to be educated, about trauma grief. Since unique circumstances of the death, the death notification, and the funeral and burial experiences are likely to surface in a counseling relationship, these cross-discipline relationships can be crucial in assuring more spiritually sensitive mental health counseling and more mentally and emotionally sensitive spiritual guidance. Faith leaders must learn enough about trauma that they will not underestimate or overspiritualize trauma grief symptoms. Faith-related scriptures and rituals can help, but they do not always. Rabbi George Stern points out that faith leaders must be aware of aspects of their teachings that lend themselves to interpretations that can be harmful for surviving family members (Stern, 2004). They must be willing to educate themselves about other faiths and other beliefs within their own faiths where questions of interpretation arise. Faith leaders must be competent and prepared to make referrals to the mental health community when it is warranted.

The following information about death and dying rituals among minority faiths in the United States is introductory only, but may provide basic guidelines for spiritual sensitivity among mental health professionals and faith leaders. Particularly following mass community disasters, spiritual caregivers may be called upon to assist those of faiths other than their own. The wisdom of Mahatma Gandhi may serve well in this regard. Gandhi believed that there is a divine truth that transforms all cultures and religions, and that this truth is beyond the ability of anyone to know completely, given our limitations as human beings. This belief represents the attitude family members may find very helpful as they bring up their spiritual concerns.

BASIC MULTIFAITH DEATH AND DYING RITUALS

The faiths addressed here are arranged in chronological order based on perceived origin.

Native American Spirituality

Most of the more than 200,000 Native Americans who live in the United States are deeply spiritual, with no intention to separate out the spiritual from the natural. They believe that the spirit of the deceased is just as alive after the death of the body as it was before, and that the spirit remains very accessible. People came from the spirit world and return to it, so the next realm of experience is not new for them. Rituals vary among the more than 500 tribes in the United States, but better known ones, such as smoking the peace pipe and performing the Sun Dance, engage the practitioner with the spirit world where communication with deceased ancestors is common. Anatomical donations and autopsy are very difficult concepts for most traditional Native Americans, and they will want rituals conducted by medicine men, medicine women, or elders before the cutting. The number four holds significance for most Native Americans (four winds, four directions, four colors: red, black, yellow, white), and many do not bury their dead until four days after the death. Navajos and some other tribes do not speak the name of the deceased during these four days because they believe it may call the spirit back into the body. Most Native Americans are buried in the earth rather than cremated, in order that the body may return to the dust of the earth to once again contribute to the cycle of natural life. Criminal justice involvement, a common requirement following a violent death, is difficult for many Native Americans, who are traditionally more interested in restoring harmony than seeking retribution. They may be just as concerned about rehabilitating the offender as they are in helping the surviving family members. They usually prefer that cases be addressed in Tribal Courts, where circle sentencing, family conferencing, and more restorative practices are common. However, if the death was a homicide, it will more than likely be tried in the federal justice system, which may be very difficult for Native Americans to connect with in emotional terms.

For more information about Native American spirituality, consider reading Vine Deloria's book, *God is Red: A Native View of Religion* (2003) and Ed McGaa's book, *Mother Earth Spirituality: Native American Paths to Healing Ourselves and the World* (1990).

Hinduism

Like Native Americans, Hindus claim that theirs is the oldest religion with roots going back about 8,000 years to the advanced Indus Valley civilization. About a million Hindus now live in the United States, an increase of 237% since 1990. Inner, introspective, personal spirituality is more significant to Hindus than external religious practice.

Traditional Hindus believe that the soul leaves the body within a short time after death, after which the body is impure. They are eager for the body to be cremated as soon as possible because, until the body is consumed by flame, the soul may choose to reenter it rather than proceed on to its next realm of existence. The body is bathed with pure water, hair and nails are clipped, basil leaves are placed in the mouth, and for women in some Hindu communities, a piece of gold or precious stone is placed in a body orifice. Traditionally, the body is wrapped in white unbleached cotton cloth, but more modern Hindus may dress the body in a sari or business suit. The body is usually viewed by the family as soon as it is prepared, and cremation is accomplished within 24 hours of the death. Ashes are scattered into water, and those able to do so will send their loved one's ashes to be scattered over the Ganges River in India.

Anatomical donations are prohibited because the karma (effect of all human thoughts, words, and deeds) of the deceased is believed to be stored in the organs; thus a new recipient would receive the good or bad karma of the deceased. Further, the continued presence of the organ may make it more difficult for the soul of the deceased to let go of its attachment to the body. Likewise, autopsy is very difficult for Hindus because of disturbance of the organs and because immediate cremation is desired. Hindu families remain in the home and mourn from eight days to a month, the time they believe it takes their loved one's spirit to depart. Spirits with much positive karma are believed to enter a new body relatively soon, working their way toward enlightenment. Troubled spirits, for example those who died violently, too young, or after betrothal but before marriage, may wander for years until appeased by rituals and eventually allowed to enter another body.

For more information about Hinduism, go to www.hindu.org/htl and view issues of *Hinduism Today*, or go to http://www.himalayanacademy.com/ basics and view the document, "Ten Questions People Ask About Hinduism … and Ten Terrific Answers."

Buddhism

Buddhism developed out of Hinduism in India in the 6th century B.C. More than 4 million Buddhists live in the United States, an increase of 170% since 1990. Most Buddhists do not acknowledge a Supreme Being outside the self but, like Hindus, seek eventual enlightenment. The word *Buddha* means "enlightened one" or one who has become released from cycles of reincarnation and is fully "awake." Buddhists believe that a calm, focused state of mind at the moment of death is important in determining the quality of rebirth, and they want the body to remain in a quiet, peaceful environment, undisturbed for several hours after the death except for prayers and rituals conducted by a Buddhist priest or monk. These prayers and rituals are believed to be more important for the passage of the soul to the next life than the family's access to the body, a commonly encouraged Western practice. Obviously, violent deaths are particularly troublesome for them. They, like Hindus, are deeply troubled by anatomical donation or autopsy.

In most Buddhist families, the body is cleansed and dressed and remains in the home until a funeral takes place three to five days later, after which it is cremated. Mahayanan Buddhists, however, cremate immediately. Buddhists observe prayers and rituals throughout a 49-day period following the death called *Bardo*, the time they believe it takes for the spirit of the deceased to be reborn into a new body. However, when a person has died under unsettling circumstances, such as a violent death, this period may be longer than 49 days because violent death "closes the spiritual eyes." Space pervades, and the spirit remains close to the body, requiring special prayers over time for the spirit to finally detach from the body.

For more information about Buddhism as it relates to death, consider reading Rimpoche Nawang Gehlek's book, *Good Life, Good Death* and go to http://www.tricycle.com and view issues of the magazine, "Tricycle: The Buddhist Review."

Judaism

Judaism developed about 4,000 years ago and has decreased 11% since 1990 to about 5 million members in the United States. The only common religion in the United States to decrease rather than increase, the decline is generally attributed to intermarriage.

Judaism was the first religion to believe in one God and to discount the idea of numerous reincarnations. Jewish death rituals emphasize reality, simplicity, and respect for the body, stemming from their conviction that human beings are created in the image of God. Jews generally oppose cremation, preferring natural decomposition of the body in the ground. They do not usually embalm, and autopsy is forbidden unless required for legal reasons. When autopsy is mandatory, Jewish law requires all body parts to be placed back in the body.

The body is generally taken to a funeral home where a team of two or three Jewish persons of the same gender, often from the deceased's synagogue, cleanse it in a ritual called *tahara.* All adornments, such as dentures and nail polish, are removed to assure that the body leaves the world in as pure a state as it entered it. Traditionally, the body is dressed in a white, seamless linen or muslin shroud including a shirt, pants, belt, and a hoodlike covering for the head, the front of which is like a veil. Many Reform Jews are dressed in ordinary clothing, but the men may also wear prayer shawls and yarmulkes. Plain, wooden coffins are desired.

The body is not left alone until burial 24 to 48 hours later. Following 9/11, Jewish college students in New York City were deeply troubled by the collection of unidentified body parts and, to assure that no Jewish body parts were unattended, they stood vigil beside the refrigerated semitrucks until they were moved to another location for attempted identification.

Traditional Judaism does not support public viewing, and visitation of the family, other than direct relatives, is not encouraged until after burial. Postburial begins a three- to seven-day period of mourning called _shiva_ which assures that the dead person is honorably respected. A mourning ritual of a minyan of 10 or more people is observed, leading into a more private period of mourning that extends beyond shiva (_shloshim)._ Following a Jewish death, charitable donations are more appropriate than flowers. Visitors to the gravesite during the first year often place small stones on the grave to show that they have visited. The headstone is usually set at the one-year anniversary. Temples and synagogues have memorial boards at the front of the worship area with lights by the name of each deceased member which are illumined during their death anniversary month. Jewish people focus more on leading a good life in this world than on the afterlife. Some believe the spirit lives on after death, and some do not. For those who do, one's position in the afterlife is believed to be a function of the good the person did while living.

For more information on Judaism and death, consider reading *The Book of Jewish Sacred Practices* by Irwin Kula and Vanessa Ochs or go to http://www.jewishlights.com to review a number of books on Judaism.

Islam

Those who practice Islam are called Muslims. The Holy Book of Muslims is the Qur'an, which contains the message the Angel Gabriel delivered to the Prophet Muhammad 632 years after Christ. Islam is the second-largest faith practiced in the United States, following Christianity. The number of Muslims in the United States has more than doubled since 1990, with about 7 million practitioners.

Muslims believe in one God whom they call Allah. It is the same God worshipped by Jews and Christians, but the name "Allah" is Arabic. The ultimate concern of every Muslim is to be offered a place in Paradise following death. Muslims do not embalm, and cremation is forbidden. They believe that after death, the soul briefly leaves the body for questioning by the Angel of Death and then returns to the body where it remains until Judgment Day. The ritual cleansing of the body is similar to the Jewish *tahara*, but the body is washed three times rather than once, the final time with camphor-infused water. The body is wrapped in unstitched white cotton cloth and wrapped with cloth ties around the waist, head, and feet. The extra binding prevents the cloth from unwrapping when the body is placed in the ground for burial without casket or vault. It also defines the head so that the body can be placed on its right side with the face toward the east (Mecca). The funeral in the mosque consists only of prayers from the Qur'an. After the burial, family and friends stay with the family for a three-day official mourning period, sometimes more if needed. Children who die under the age of seven are believed by Muslims to enter Paradise unquestioned, as do those who die unexpectedly as a result of violence. In these cases, only a short prayer is required. For those facing Judgment Day, all behaviors of the individual during earthly life will be revealed on that day and the individual will be sent to one of seven levels of Paradise or seven levels of Hell. Suicide is forbidden in Islam and is considered a mortal sin earning eternal damnation.

To learn more about death and Islam, consider reading *The Remembrance of Death and the Afterlife* by Abu Hamid Al-Ghazali and T. J. Winter or go to http://www.IslamiCity.com.

Christianity

Christianity is not addressed in this chapter because it is by far the most commonly practiced religion in the United States. Numbering more than 150 million, followers of Christ are affiliated with more than 2,000 denominational and nondenominational branches of Christianity. It would be impossible to address the wide variance of Christian beliefs and practices. It is crucial that Christian caregivers not assume that a person who identifies as "Christian" believes and practices the same as he or she does. Exploration is always necessary because the variation between more fundamental Christians and more modernized or liberal Christians may be broader than differences between Christians and practitioners of other faiths.

SPIRITUALLY SENSITIVE MENTAL HEALTH PRACTICE

If a mental health caregiver wishes to become more spiritually sensitive, the place to begin is to identify one's own spiritual values and beliefs. Even people who self-identify as atheists or agnostics have a belief system about religion. Unless this is clarified, it is easy to be critical of those expressing other belief systems, even though the resistance may be somewhat unconscious.

All human beings are most comfortable with others who believe the same things they do, and it is extremely easy to impose one's own spiritual values on surviving family members without being aware of it. Once cognizant of those values and able to articulate them, the caregiver can more easily recognize that someone else's spiritual values may differ but need not be judged.

The next step is to determine when to refer to another caregiver if a family member's spiritual values differ significantly from the caregiver's. If spirituality does not become a focus of the counseling relationship, this may not become an issue. On the other hand, since spirituality is often a key component of resilience (sometimes detrimental to it) as clients deal with violent death, too great a discomfort level can impede the therapeutic relationship, and even the content of caregiving.

It is important to develop inclusive spiritual language that does not seem foreign or offensive to a person of another faith. For example, the word *clergy* is not used in Native American spirituality, Hinduism, or Buddhism. These groups are more comfortable with *faith leader* or *spiritual teacher*. The term *Bible* is used only in Christianity. Jews use the terms *Torah* and the *Talmud*. What Christians commonly call the *Old Testament* is more respectfully referred to as *The Hebrew Bible* when speaking with Jews. Muslims' Holy Book is the *Quran*. Buddhists and Hindus use the term *Sacred Texts*. Christians worship in a *church*, but followers of other faiths worship in a *faith community, house of worship, temple, synagogue, mosque,* or *meditation center.*

SPIRITUAL PRACTICES FOR MODERATING STRESS
DURING TRAUMA GRIEF

The first task of the caregiver is to maintain a sense of humility in seeking to understand the family member's spiritual perspective. If that perspective is helpful for the family member, it is totally irrelevant whether or not the caregiver agrees with it. It is to be honored and respected. Theological debate may have its place, but not when a person is in crisis. Respecting a family member's spiritual journey is much more than tolerance. It extends to genuine appreciation of differences, and requires caregivers to seek clarity and understanding. On the other hand, if the family member's spiritual beliefs seem dissonant with what he or she is now experiencing emotionally, these beliefs may be explored just like any other troubling issue. Inquiring gently about such matters is generally appreciated.

If the family member brings up spiritual matters, a positive reaction might be, "I'd like to hear more about that" or "Would you like to help me understand more about that?" If the family member responds positively, the caregiver should let the family member know that this will be a collaborative effort and that he or she is interested in learning about how the family member's spirituality has been affected by the violent death.

Spiritually sensitive caregivers operating with government funding may wonder how to let family members know that they are comfortable dealing with spirituality issues and yet remain within government guidelines. Dr. Harold G. Koenig, Associate Professor of Psychiatry and of Medicine at Duke University Medical Center (Koenig, 2002), educates physicians about how to take a spiritual history, and his guidance may serve other fields well. He points out that (1) the questions should be brief and take only a few moments to ask; (2) the questions should be easy to remember so they may be asked at the most appropriate time (usually within the context of a social history); and (3) the information is all about the patient's (family member's) beliefs and has nothing whatsoever to do with the physician's (caregiver's) beliefs.

Conducting a brief spiritual assessment may be all that is required for some family members. When asked a few simple questions, some will make it clear that they do not wish to include spiritual concerns in their work with their caregiver. Those who do, however, will feel validated because the inquiry has been gentle and respectful.

Some unassuming questions that may encourage family members to begin talking about their spiritual concerns include:

"What is the most important thing in your life right now?"
"What has been meaningful and helpful to you as you have tried to cope with your loved one's death?"
"How are you feeling within yourself?"
"What has strengthened you as you as you deal with this violent death?"
"Have certain people been especially supportive and helpful?"

If responses to these questions are not spiritually oriented, that's fine. Spirituality will not need to be brought up again unless the family member does so. If the responses are spiritually oriented, continue to explore the family member's answers like any other information to help assess their strengths, resources, and stressors.

If the caregiver is comfortable addressing spirituality more directly, the following three questions, developed by Dr. Dale Matthews, Associate Professor of Medicine at Georgetown University (Matthews & Clark, 1999), are direct but do not violate government guidelines.

"Is religion or spirituality important to you?"
"Do your religious or spiritual beliefs influence the way you look at what has happened to you and your family?"
"Would you like to include religion or spirituality in the work we do together?"

Obviously, if the answer to the first question is "no," it need not be further explored. The second question offers the opportunity for the family member to express how religion or spirituality may have shaped the way he or she experiences and tells his or her trauma story. It can also inform the caregiver about religious restrictions on medical treatment or pharmacology, and about how the family member understands justice and forgiveness, which may influence his or her level of involvement with the justice system, if it is required.

If disappointment in faith leaders or the faith community comes up, listen carefully and supportively. As the family member explores these issues, he or she may come to realize that, even though the things said or done may not have helped, they were probably well-intentioned.

In his book *Spiritual Diversity in Social Work Practice: The Heart of Helping* (Canda &Furman, 1999), Dr. Edward Canda distinguishes between four categories of spiritually sensitive caregiving which have been adapted for this chapter. He would place the issue of a family member's disappointment in his or her faith community in category two and, with permission, collaborate with his or her faith leader to work on the problem.

TABLE 4.1
Ethical considerations for using spiritually based activities

Conditions for determining spiritual reactions	Options for spiritual reactions
Family member expresses no interest in spirituality	Caregiver's relationship with the family member may demonstrate spiritual values (respect as one created by God, for example) though not specifically addressed. Caregiver may engage in private spiritual activity, such as praying for the family member at home, but does not further explore spirituality unless the family member brings it up.
Family member expresses interest in exploring spirituality	The above, plus: Caregiver may explore spirituality issues to the degree competent. Caregiver refers family member to outside spiritual resources.With permission, caregiver may collaborate with outside spiritual resource.
Family member and caregiver have developed a spiritually sensitive relationship	The above, plus: Caregiver may accept invitation of the family member to attend a religious ritual outside working hours such as a memorial event (paying attention to spiritual and cultural customs about actually participating).
The above, plus the caregiver also has relevant spiritual qualifications such as having completed Clinical Pastoral Education or is an otherwise licensed or certified clergy person or pastoral counselor	The above, plus: Caregiver may initiate spiritual activities with caution.

In summary, spiritual tools that moderate stress during early stages of trauma grief include: (1) development of a sense of humility in learning about the family member's spirituality thus strengthening rather than diminishing the caregiving relationship; (2) gentle inquiry during assessment about the role of spirituality in the family member's reaction to the violent death; and (3) guidance of the family member, either alone or with his or her faith leader, to address disappointments the family member may have experienced within the faith community.

SPIRITUAL PRACTICES FOR RESTORATIVE RETELLING

Once the caregiving relationship is comfortable, and strengths contributing to resilience have been identified, family members may feel safe enough to begin sharing their trauma stories and exploring ways to reframe them into something more positive. If connections or reconnections with an affirming faith community have been made, it is good to ask the family member from time to time how his or her faith community is helping (or hurting). Caregivers must be careful not to push family members toward restorative imagery until the trauma imagery has been ventilated and explored. Otherwise, they may feel that their pain is being discounted. To simply restate a very stressful life event in new, more positive words trivializes a very painful, complex process into nothing more than a cognitive coping strategy. They must hear that, even though the caregiver is not jumping into the trauma story, it is important and will be shared in many ways when the time is right. Over time, the telling will change into a new orientation, a genuine new understanding — not just a different way of stating it (Neimeyer, 2001).

While the following tools may be used in individual sessions or in trauma grief group, the examples are described for a group setting.

To continue gradual and indirect movement toward restorative retelling, the caregiver might ask the family members to bring pictures, videotapes, audiotapes, baptismal certificates, and other mementos to help the caregiver and other group members get to know the person who was killed. Restating the positive attributes of the deceased as the stories are told can help family members recognize the energy associated with those attributes as something that goes on. A more defined biography of the person who died becomes constructed as the stories are shared with others (Walter, 1996).

The Air Force had put together a large collage of pictures of Kris that Don and Julie displayed on an easel in their living room. As they told their trauma grief group the stories surrounding each picture on the collage, they seemed more happy than sad at the remembrances. The stories brought back to mind a living son and all his vivaciousness. Group members affirmed Kris' life with comments like, "He must have been a really kind and giving person." In future sessions, group members often recalled Kris's positive attributes with comments like, "Knowing that Kris was a kind and giving person, I'm wondering what you think he would have done in this situation." The question brought Kris' values and energy back into the here and now in a constructive way.

At the end of the trauma grief group session where members brought their loved one's pictures and mementos, the caregiver made this comment, "Not making any assumptions about whether this is true or not true, some people believe that our souls or spirits come into our bodies to accomplish something, and when that mission is accomplished, it is ok for them to leave." She then asked, "If you were to believe that, what do you think your loved one's purpose might have been?" Don and Julie smiled, knowing their answer immediately. It was to be of service to others and to show us all the "lighter" side of life.

Quote

It is surprisingly common for family members to react the same way. They can answer the question with little pondering. The question goes beyond intellectual theological discussion to the heart of the matter. It makes no difference whether or not they believe it theologically. They have developed a way to speak of the meaning of their loved one's life and death, and have phrased it in a simple way that can be repeated time and time again. For some, it may be the first time they have spoken of the death in a way other than the criminal justice account, the medical account, or the media account. It also leads to an opportunity to reflect on how the meaning of their loved one's life and death has now been appropriated into their own values, characteristics, and behaviors (Vickio, 1999).

In a group session following the one with the pictures and mementos, the caregiver pointed out that some people believe it is still possible to communicate with the spirits of their loved ones. Group members who were skeptical were asked to pretend that this is possible for the exercise. Each group member was given several sheets of paper and a pencil, and asked to write a letter to their loved one. They were encouraged to keep writing, even though they might be tempted to stop because the exercise could seem like a stretch for their cognitive beliefs. The caregiver gave them the following prompt to help them begin: "Dear (deceased's name), Since you left I...."

Prompt

When they had finished, group members were told to remain silent and, in the same frame of mind, turn the paper over and allow their loved one to write back. The prompt was, "Dear (Mom/Dad, etc.), I've been watching you and...."

This exercise is both emotional and spiritual, and most people react to it very warmly. If they want to generally share their letters or read them aloud verbatim, the messages are reinforced. Some will choose to keep them private. These exercises lead very naturally into an inquiry such as, "What *are* your beliefs about an afterlife?" For those with a strong belief in the continuation of the soul or spirit, it can be enlightening to state that many surviving family members feel that they receive a visitation of some sort from the person who died. Asking if they have had this experience frees those who have had one to be able to talk about it without fear of being questioned or labeled. A risk of doing this in a group is that those who have not had

TABLE 4.2
Spirituality graph

Level of Spirituality										
10										
9										
8										
7										
6										
5										
4										
3										
2										
1										
Age	5	10	15	20	25	30	35	40	45	50+

such an experience will wonder why they have not. This can be handled by asking, "If you were to have such a visitation, what's your best guess as to what Johnny would want to communicate to you?"

This chart (see Table 4.2) provides family members the opportunity to look back over their life spans and recall periods of high and low spirituality. Some will note particular life events that they felt contributed to their highs and lows. This exercise can put their current crisis into perspective with previous crises in their lives and bring back to mind how they eventually experienced some relief and recovery from former lows.

A similar exercise with the same goal is more like an art therapy experience and will require various sizes and colors of paper and art supplies. Rather than using the graph, family members will freely draw Spiritual Life Maps of mountains and valleys, intense and more profuse experiences, throughout their spiritual journeys. They will work on their maps in silence and then explain them to the group when all are finished. Like the graph, maps offer the opportunity to explore spiritual changes that took place when their loved one was killed and the direction of spiritual growth or decline since then.

These exercises set the stage, in terms of process, for one or more Death Scene Imagery artwork sessions. As described in previous chapters, facing the actual death scene may have been avoided by some, while others may have felt driven to look at death scene investigation photos and autopsy photos and reports in an effort to fit the puzzle of missing information together. A family member should never be pushed to do this artwork if he or she is not ready to do so, but it has been the author's experience that nearly all will participate to the degree they are able to face their reality.

Some are ready to make a literal drawing, but may find it difficult to color or paint blood red.

Julie drew Kris lying in the street with blood around his head because his most serious injury was to his head, and she knew that head wounds bleed heavily. Even though she had not seen photos of the death scene, it was an image that she often pictured in her mind.

Others may totally spiritualize their artwork by drawing angels, streams of light, or other spiritual imagery believed to have manifested at the moment of death. Regardless of the content, sharing the artwork with the group tends to be an emotional experience but a cathartic one. When tears emerge, a gentle reminder to the group that, "We cry only because we need to cry" normalizes the experience and provides support.

Although not recommended too early, the Gratitude Journal has been shown to decrease depression (Pennebaker, 1997). If suggested too early, clients may feel that the pain of their traumatic experience is not being acknowledged. It is hard to feel grateful when it feels like the world has come to an end. When the time seems right, the family member is asked to set aside a certain time each day to write down five things he or she is grateful for. This turns the focus from the destruction of the death to some reconstruction of beliefs and affirmation of good. It can also serve as a retelling and a reframing of the trauma in a more positive light — for example, "I am grateful for the gift of memory because I will remember certain things about my loved one for the rest of my life and, eventually, I will be able to smile again when I remember them." For people of faith, these expressions of gratitude can seem like prayer. Some find it helpful to list the five gratitudes and follow them with five laments or petitions. Even without the prayer format, the expressions often have spiritual content.

SPIRITUAL PRACTICES FOR RECONNECTION

Eventually, reestablishing connections with the faith community and its events feels right and good for most families. Those disappointed in the lack of support offered by their faith leader or faith community may avoid returning to church/synagogue/mosque/temple. After a period of absence, they may feel uncomfortable going back even though they feel drawn to do so. Rather than suggesting a full return to all activities, the caregiver might suggest that the family return only to particular services or rituals that hold special meaning for them. They are more likely to find these spiritually uplifting, and just showing up will break the ice for a greater comfort level at other events or activities.

If the relationship between the family member and his or her faith leader has become distant, encourage the family member to schedule an appointment with the faith leader to explain his or her disappointment and offer suggestions about how the faith community might have been more helpful. Most faith leaders will be very open to this as long as the information is given from a perspective of explaining hurt and disappointment rather than blaming or accusing.

If the family member continues to withdraw and isolate from the faith community but wants to try to reconnect spiritually, encourage him or her to invite a person to lunch who has been spiritually supportive in the past. During this time, honest spiritual struggles can be expressed and support given.

Bibliotherapy is another excellent tool for helping family members develop new or more accommodating faith perspectives. While many books on death line the shelves of bookstores, few include trauma death material and even fewer bring the spiritual component into traumatic dying. Following are a few suggestions: *Lament for a Son* by Nicholas Wolterstorff (1987) is an honest expression of a Lutheran theologian's faith struggle as he deals with the sudden death of his 25-year-old son, Eric. Three other good books on the death of children that include Christian spiritual components are John Munday and Frances Wohlenhau-Munday's book, *Surviving the Death of a Child* (Fran's daughter was murdered) (1995); *The Worst Loss* by Barbara D. Rosof (1994); and *When Good-Bye is Forever: Learning to Live Again After the Loss of a Child* by John Bramblett (1991), whose Two-year-old son was accidentally killed. Janice Harris Lord's book *No Time for Goodbyes: Coping with Sorrow, Anger, and Injustice After a Tragic Death* (2006) focuses specifically on sudden, violent death and includes spiritual aspects.

Both Don and Julie both read *Lament for a Son* and reported at their trauma grief group that it had validated many of their feelings because in expressing his emotional reactions, the author articulated Don's and Julie's as well.

Another significant reconnection activity is organizing an annual memorial observance to honor trauma death victims. These memorials help family members validate their experiences to the broader community and express the personal meaning or growth they have noticed in themselves since the deaths. The telling of their stories often includes spiritual aspects, usually described as a means of transcending their tragic experiences. Mothers Against Drunk Driving and other groups that deal with trauma deaths have offered Candlelight Vigils at Christmas/Hannukah time for years as a means of remembering loved ones at an emotionally laden time of year and expressing hope for a less violent future.

CLOSING THOUGHTS

In time, bereaved family members find that beginning to reach out to other more recent survivors can bring significant healing. Holocaust survivor Eli Wiesel has said that the best way to overcome despair is to reach out to someone else in despair. Many crime victim assistance programs as well as faith communities link newer surviving family members with those who have become more seasoned as a means of establishing hope.

Some family members find it particularly helpful to personally address convicted violent offenders. Mothers Against Drunk Driving developed a Victim Impact Panel program where those whose loved ones were killed by an intoxicated driver speak on panels to offenders ordered by the courts to attend the panel presentation as a component of their sentences. These efforts to reach beyond one's own experience to help others or to prevent future violence are particularly meaningful to many family members.

Viktor Frankl lost his family in the Holocaust, one of the most violently traumatic events in world history. He noticed that among other concentration and death camp residents, basic spiritual and emotional perspectives became exaggerated. Those with spiritual and emotional supports and resiliences in place became even more altruistic, sharing their turnip with someone else even though it may have meant decreasing their own life span. Others stole a turnip, knowing that it would decrease the life span of someone else. Frankl (1997) points out that while he had no control over what happened to him and his family, he had a very great deal of control over how he would react to it. His spiritual resilience helped him survive even as he reached out to others in despair.

REFERENCES

Bramblett, J. (1991). *When good-bye is forever: Learning to live again after the loss of a child*. New York: Ballantine Books.

Canda, E. R. & Furman, L. D. (1999). *Spiritual diversity in social work practice*. New York: Free Press.

Crime Victims Institute (1998). *The impact of crime on victims: Final report*. Austin, TX: Office of the Attorney General.

Deloria, Jr., V. (2003). *God is red: A native view of religion*. Golden, CO: Fulcrum.

Flach, F. (1990). The resilience hypothesis and posttraumatic stress disorder. In M. E. Wolf & A.D. Mosnaim (Eds.) *Posttraumatic stress disorder: Etiology, phenomenology, and treatment*. Washington, D.C.: American Psychiatric Press.

Frankl, V.W. (1997). *Man's search for meaning*. New York: Pocket Books. (Original work published 19xx)

Gehlek, R. N. (2001). *Good life, good death*. New York: Penguin.

Koenig, H. G. (2002). *Spirituality in patient care*. Philadelphia: Templeton Foundation Press.

Kula, I. & Ochs, V. (2001). *The book of Jewish sacred practices*. Woodstock, VT: Jewish Lights.

Lord, J. H. (2006). *No time for goodbyes: Coping with sorrow, anger, and injustice after a tragic death*. Burnsville, NC: Compassion Books.

Matthews, D.A. & Clark, C. (1999). *The faith factor*. New York: Penguin.

McGaa, E. (1990). *Mother Earth spirituality: Native American paths to healing ourselves and the world*. New York: HarperCollins.

Mercer, D., Falkenberg, S., & Lorden, R. (1999, Winter). Spirituality and drunk driving victimization. *MADDVOCATE, 13*, 22.

Munday J. & Wohlenhaus-Munday, F. (1995). *Surviving the death of a child*. Louisville, KY: Westminster John Knox

NASW (National Association of Social Workers) (1999). *NASW code of ethics*. Washington, D.C.: National Association of Social Workers.

Neimeyer, R. A. (2001). Searching for the meaning of meaning: Grief therapy and the Process of reconstruction. *Death Studies, 25*.

NFO Research (1999, November/December). When a child dies: A survey of bereaved parents. *The Forum, 25* (6), 1–10.

Pennebaker. J. (1997). *Opening Up*. New York: Guilford. *Newsweek*. (2005, August 29/September 5). Where we stand on faith. *Newsweek*, 48–49.

Rosof, B. D. (1994). *The worst loss: How families heal from the death of a child*. New York: Henry Holt.

Vargas, O. (2005, March 10). *Task force for faith based and community initiatives, Office of the Deputy Attorney General*. Workshop Handout at Fourth National Symposium on Victims of Federal Crime sponsored by U. S. Department of Justice, Atlanta, Georgia.

Vickio, C. (1999). Together in spirit: Keeping our relationships alive when loved ones die. *Death Studies, 23*, 161–176.

Walter, T. (1996). A new model of grief: Bereavement and biography. *Mortality, 1*, 7–25.

Wolin, S. J. & Wolin, S. (1993). *The resilient self: How survivors of troubled families rise above adversity*. New York: Villard Books.

Wolterstorff, N. (1987). *Lament for a son*. Grand Rapids, MI: Eerdmans.

Woodruff, C. R. (2001, Spring). New national survey affirms desire for pastoral counseling. *Currents, 39*, (2), 2.

5

Fragmented Stories: The Narrative Integration of Violent Loss

JOSEPH M. CURRIER AND ROBERT A. NEIMEYER

Narrative Framework

Storytelling is so embedded in our kind that the authors suggest we be labeled *homo narrans* and not simply *homo sapiens*. Humans establish coherence and meaning through the ordering of events into a narrative template; however, the narrative of a violent death of a loved one is so incoherent and meaningless that its retelling invalidates both the life narrative of the teller and the deceased. The authors offer a brief, scholarly review of constructivist theory as a basis for explicit narrative procedures outlined and applied in a case presentation that not only reduces symptoms and reestablishes function, but enlivens the teller through and beyond the violent death narrative. Their description and theoretical analysis of the self-destructive fixation of the dying narrative, and its reconstruction, is resonated and reworked in every subsequent chapter that includes a narrative case presentation.

For violently bereaved individuals, the inveterate human quest for significance can resemble more of a curse than a romantic ideal. These survivors not only feel the burden of grief, but many also reside in the shadows of one philosopher's claim that human beings are "condemned to meaning" (Merleau-Ponty, 1962). Healing from bereavement resulting from homicide, suicide, or a mutilating accident confronts people with the challenge of reconstructing meaning in the face of unspeakably meaningless events. With the aid of an illustrative clinical vignette, this chapter will provide a constructivist–narrative conceptualization of the impact of traumatic loss and briefly suggest a handful of psychotherapeutic concepts for helping survivors integrate the experience and mend the narrative fabric of their lives.

MEANING AND PSYCHOTHERAPY: THE NARRATIVE TURN

The human propensity to construct stories out of life's lessons and events has been gaining increasing attention since the mid-1980s (Bruner, 1986 Howard, 1991; Mair, 1988 Neimeyer, 1999 Polkinghorne, 1988 Sarbin, 1986a). Some scholars have even called for a shift away from the predominant objectivistic paradigm in psychology by designating narrative as the "root metaphor" for the discipline (Sarbin, 1986b). The epistemological framework of constructivism provides the scaffolding for this narrative approach (Neimeyer & Mahoney, 1995; Neimeyer & Raskin, 2000 Rosen & Kuelwein, 1996). Central to this maturing relationship between constructivism and narrative is the premise that human beings are natural storytellers who possess the creativity and relationality to narrate their lives in both intra- and interpersonal spheres (Gonclaves, 1994a, 1994b Russell, 1991). Thus, according to this perspective, human beings implement a storytelling structure as they proactively seek a sense of coherence and continuity in the inchoate flow of lived experience (Neimeyer, 1995).

So pervasive is the human penchant toward narration that some scholars have suggested that our species might appropriately be labeled not simply *homo sapiens*, emphasizing our effort to seek knowledge, but more specifically *homo narrans*, stressing our tendency to organize such knowledge in storied form (Hermans, 2002). And so basic is this predilection that it is reflected at the level of a widely distributed network of identifiable neural structures that subserve autobiographical memory and the narrative construction of accounts (Neimeyer, Herrero, & Botella, 2006; Rubin & Greenberg, 2003). Indeed, a capacity for storytelling seems to develop in tandem with children's consciousness of self and their gradually elaborating understanding of others, capacities that are already surprisingly sophisticated by the time they reach school age (Nelson, 2003). In this sense narration serves as a critical bridge not only in weaving life experiences into a coherent, self-organizing whole, but also in spanning self- and other-consciousness through the construction of social shared accounts, drawing on a repertory of culturally shaped themes, symbols, and preferred narrative conventions (Neimeyer & Levitt, 2001).

Stories, therefore, represent a primary human "way of knowing" (Bruner, 1986) or "assimilating structure" (Mancuso, 1986), with the absolute *telos* being the construction of meaning (Gonclaves, 1995). At its most fundamental level, narrative is the form by which everyday experiences are modulated and processed to construct a meaningful story of one's life, thereby making personal identity ultimately a narrative achievement. That is to say, a cohesive sense of self becomes organized in the stories we tell to and about ourselves, the stories that relevant others tell about us, and the stories we enact in their presence (Neimeyer, 2006). For a narrative to be successful in endowing experience with meaning, however, it must project a valued endpoint building on life events that are congruent with this implicit goal (Gergen & Gergen, 1986). An integrated narrative further encompasses the dimensions of setting, characterization, plot, and theme, thereby providing an orientation to the respective *where* and *when, who, what*, and *why* of the life story (Neimeyer, 2000). A breakdown in any of these components can disturb one's psychological equilibrium and engender painful difficulties with meaning-making (Neimeyer, 2000, 2001).

The "narrative turn" has also influenced the theory and practice of psychotherapy. Contemporary theorists and clinicians from a diversity of orientations have advocated for conceptualizing the therapeutic process in narrative terms (Gonclaves, 1994a, 1994b; Russell, 1991; Smith & Nylund, 1997; Terrell & Lyddon, 1996; White & Epston, 1990). Nonetheless, psychotherapists have long employed the concept of story to comprehend their efforts with clients. For example, Schafer (1980), a psychodynamic theorist, has likened the process of making interpretations to "narrating" or "retelling" the client's story in the safety of the therapeutic relationship. Additionally, Spence (1982) has argued that the aim of any form of psychotherapy is not the uncovering of "historical truth" but the creation of "narrative truth," being the construction of a personal account that makes sense and allows the client to live a meaningful life. Other key tenets of the narrative approach include "reauthoring" of the life story, identifying themes, deconstructing meanings, and viewing the therapist as simultaneously the audience, coconstructor, and editor of the client's story (McLeod, 1996; White & Epston, 1990). As we now narrow our focus, we propose that a central goal of psychotherapy with survivors of violent loss is to help them integrate these fragmenting experiences more adequately and to promote the ongoing revision and expansion of their life narratives over time.

THE CASE OF TAMICKA: WHEN WORDS ARE NOT ENOUGH

During what surely felt like a routine walk home from school, Nine-year-old Tamicka and her two older siblings' customary chatter quieted as they noticed smoke billowing on the not-so-far-off horizon. Their pace quickened to a steady run as they reached their block, caught up in the excitement and rising anxiety from the crowd converging on their street. Rounding the corner in horror, the three children saw that the burning house was their own, though it was growing scarcely recognizable as a burned-out shell. Tamicka began screaming and attempted to run to the still-flaming ruins to ensure the safety of her remaining family members, only to be barred from entering by one of the firemen present at the scene. Tamicka and her siblings were then forced to watch in silent helplessness as the fire completely eradicated the house, and in so doing, drastically altered their lives forever.

The fire resulted from their mother's poor decision to leave the two youngest brothers unattended earlier that morning when she went to the store to buy liquor. Tragically, Tamicka's two brothers were not able to escape and they perished in the flames. Moreover, as the months slowly passed, Tamicka and her two older siblings needed to accommodate another painful revision in the storyline of their lives: their mother was becoming more and more "sick" from relying on alcohol and would not regain custody and care for them again. During this time, Tamicka's outward demeanor changed to reflect the smoldering ashes of her prior identity, and she increasingly withdrew in sullen silence. Unlike the grief of her older siblings, Tamicka's distress did not abate with time, nor did her school performance return to its previous level. Ultimately she was referred for therapy at a mental health clinic serving inner city families.

Following a couple of largely unsuccessful months of attempting to help Tamicka in therapy, I (JMC) was both perplexed and pleased when she assertively picked up a box of Legos™ at the start of one of our sessions. To this point, Tamicka had remained vigilantly guarded with her thoughts and feelings, expressing nothing about the deaths of her siblings or the abandonment by her mother, which were now nearly two years in the past. Instead, without any visible display of emotion or eye contact, she would enter the room compliantly and sit nervously in the same chair each week. She had given tentative indications of enjoying cards and drawing, though she often grew too unfocused to finish these activities. Based on her uncustomary display of excitement this day in holding up the box overfilled with Legos, I validated for her that many children find them to be more helpful than simply talking and encouraged her to try building something.

Considering the earlier scene of incineration and death, I experienced hope and concern when Tamicka expressed in a shaky voice, "Maybe … I'll build a house." With ever increasing focus and deliberation, she used the next three sessions to complete her project. It was then that Tamicka first located two Lego figurines, which she affectionately named "Sally" and "Bill," and eagerly distributed one of the characters to each of us. For starters, Tamicka claimed exclusive ownership of the house as Sally, but reassured me that she still hoped that Bill would come to visit with her each week. Over subsequent sessions, the characters' friendship deepened, mostly through collaborating on further renovations and additions to the house. However, a promising dialogue also emerged between the characters around such previously disavowed subjects as Sally's painful losses, problems in school, scary dreams, lack of friends, and an unremitting feeling of hopelessness and fears about the future.

Despite Tamicka's increasing sense of authorship in the narrative with Sally and Bill, she still chose periodically to demolish and reconstruct the house. Notably, these instances always followed a break in our weekly routine, such as after a holiday or time of illness. Through this recurrent pattern,

Tamicka communicated without words that this house not only represented the ongoing consolidation of her fragmented story, but it also served as a tangible symbol of our relationship. For this reason, I was honored when Sally trusted Bill to move into the house. The characters then made renovations that safely modified the house into something resembling a duplex. However, following several sessions with this living arrangement, Sally grew dissatisfied with its awkwardness and voiced a desire to again reconstruct the house so that she and Bill did not have to live on opposite sides of the wall that still separated them.

Soon after construction was completed, Tamicka spontaneously brought her own voice into the play narrative. Specifically, she expressed with strong conviction the wish for us to now build a time machine in which the characters could return to the past to save her parents from drinking and using drugs at the hands of the "evil dealers." Over the ensuing months, the characters traveled back and forth in time to wage gruesome and victorious battles against the forces of evil that plagued her parents. Through the repetition of these time voyages, Tamicka also added further layers to the story in using the characters to not only save her own parents, but also to rescue the parents of other children from villains and possible disasters. In so doing, Tamicka gradually integrated a newer and more satisfying self-narrative as courageous, strong, and the triumphant protector of other children's stories, rather than her previous identification as a passive and helpless bystander to her younger brothers' deaths and mother's abandonment.

Tamicka's increased cohesiveness and resilience generalized to other important areas of functioning as well. For example, she came to radiate a sense of pleasure and strength that led to more participation in the foster family and the formation of meaningful friendships with neighborhood girls. She also voiced no longer having "scary dreams," and her academic performance improved to the point that she was able to stay at grade level, something that earlier seemed to be an impossibility. Tamicka additionally began to assume a leadership role among her peers and younger family members. During our termination process, she reflected aloud with excitement and slight puzzlement that she was not only having much more fun in her life, but also was surprised that many of her new friends were coming to her with their own problems to draw upon her newfound wisdom and compassion for others.

EXPERIENCING VIOLENT LOSS — NARRATIVELY SPEAKING

As the above vignette demonstrates, few experiences present a more complex synergism of anguish and grief than losing a loved one to violent death. Factors that give rise to this sense of distress include intense emotions (e.g., shock and horror), extreme stress, the grotesqueness of the dying experience, the untimeliness of the death, and the surrounding social context. Also, violent losses occur without warning, thus destroying survivors' anticipations of future selves and plaguing them with posttraumatic imagery (Rynearson,

2001), regardless of whether they were present at the death scene. From a constructivist–narrative perspective, these events become traumatic for survivors insofar as they defy attempts at narrative processing. The occurrence of violent loss particularly carries the risk of fragmenting at least two of the central features entailed in constructing a meaningful sense of self: (1) the plot, and (2) the thematic structure of one's existence. Put differently, experiencing violent loss disrupts the narrative processes relevant to organizing historical events, as well as destroying the fundamental assumptions that endowed the life story with significance. Therefore, we use the terms *emplotment* and *thematic deconstruction* to describe the devastation that violent loss can have on the life narratives of the bereaved.

Emplotment   — What

In narrative terms, the specific process of integrating historical events into a completed and comprehensible account is captured in the term *emplotment* (Neimeyer & Levitt, 2001). Briefly defined, emplotment is the overarching activity of a narrative that enables "sense making" and the capacity to organize sometimes random life events (Davis, Nolen-Hoeksema, & Larson, 1998; Neimeyer & Anderson, 2002). The experience of trauma arises when circumstances elude the capacity for emplotment (Stewart & Neimeyer, 2001; Widgren, 1994). Used in this way, "plot" then refers to the intelligible whole that governs the succession of events in our lives, thus underscoring its function in integrating disparate events with the overall story (Ricoeur, 1980). Violent death resists integration into life's implicit plot structure, as reflected in the yearning and meaninglessness that is commonly expressed by survivors (Davis, Wortman, Lehman, & Cohen Silver, 2000). For example, Tamicka had no way to make sense of the loss or envision her own fate as the enormity of devastation associated with the fire was literally incomprehensible in terms of her life narrative to that point. Moreover, Tamicka's earlier positive developmental trajectory was interrupted by this failure of emplotment, and she grew more and more confused as time moved forward.

As these observations suggest, experiencing violent loss highlights the reciprocal and sometimes fragile relationship between narrative and time (Ricoeur, 1980; Spence, 1982). If the traumatically bereaved person is to be successful in integrating the loss event into his or her personal history, then the loss experience must become more than an isolated, singular happening; it must be woven into the larger narrative fabric of the survivor's life. Consequently, emplotment involves ordering events, giving them a beginning and an end, and connecting them to other life experiences, thereby engendering a sense of self-continuity in time. Sadly, violent loss can destroy this "unifying thread of temporality" (Stolorow, 2003). In other words, these types of events have a unique place in memory in that they resist narrative integration within the neocortex (Siegal, 1995), while still pervading the survivor's consciousness with troubling and fragmented aspects of the initial experience (Sewell & Williams, 2001).

Thematic Deconstruction — Why

Beyond these obstacles to emplotment, experiencing violent loss can also devastate the fundamental themes or beliefs that give significance to one's existence. Whereas the work of emplotment relates to sorting out *what* actually happened, the themes of a narrative refer to its *why* or the explanatory underpinnings that thread the historical events through with deeper meaning. However, it is the essence of traumatic experience that it radically shakes a survivor's "absolutisms" (Stolorow, 1999), "assumptive world" (Janoff-Bulman, 1992; Kauffman, 2002; Parkes, 1971), or "organizing life themes" (Stewart & Neimeyer, 2001). Experiencing violent bereavement similarly can lead to thematic deconstruction of the survivor's meaning system, decimating such taken-for-granted themes as security, predictability, and trust, perhaps permanently perturbing a survivor's previous sense of "being-in-the-world" (Stolorow, 1999).

Unfortunately, this process of thematic deconstruction also exposes the survivor to an unsettling alternative thread of themes for organizing his or her personal identity. Some of these new constructs are that the universe is random and unpredictable and that no safety can be guaranteed in life. Additionally, as in Tamicka's case, when the tragedy is the result of the intention or neglect of other people, one's sense of trust in others can be radically undermined, even as one is forced to confront one's ultimate powerlessness. This dismantling of previous assumptions of continuity and safety further disrupts the coherence of one's life narrative over time, as the survivor now has learned that self-continuity can dissolve at any moment (Neimeyer, 2000; Stolorow, 1999). Based on his work with survivors of the Hiroshima disaster, Lifton (1964) aptly portrays this deconstruction process:

> One might say that [the Hiroshima] survivors have imbibed and incorporated the entire destruction of their city, and in fact the full atomic bomb experience. But they have found no adequate ideological interpretation — no spiritual explanation — that might release them from this identification, and have instead felt permanently bound by it. (p. 201)

Coupled with the struggle to emplot a singular act of violence that the world had then not thought possible, Lifton highlighted the reverberations from the invalidation of the Hiroshima survivors' taken-for-granted beliefs about themselves and their larger psychosocial worlds.

Our own research with recently bereaved individuals has corroborated these observations (Currier, Holland, Coleman, & Neimeyer, 2006). When compared to over 1,200 natural death survivors, we discovered that the nearly 500 survivors of homicidal, suicidal, and accidental deaths we studied indicated poorer adjustment on all but one of nine completed measures. The most robust finding pertained to obvious difficulties with "sense-making" (Davis et al., 1998; Neimeyer & Anderson, 2002), the ability to formulate an explanation or comprehensible narrative of the loss experience, among the violently bereaved subset. As with Lifton's study of the people of Hiroshima, these survivors were still reporting to have made "very little sense" of their loss an average of 12 months postloss. Notably, a failure in sense-making persisted as the strongest distinguishing feature between the naturally and violently bereaved groups, even when compared to such other important factors as complicated grief symptomatology (Prigerson & Jacobs, 2001), which was also elevated.

FORMS OF NARRATIVE DISRUPTION

Narratively speaking, violent loss outpaces emplotment and invalidates thematic assumptions, breaching both the *what* and the *why* of the survivor's life narrative. From a narrative standpoint, these breakdowns transpire most strikingly at the level of the *self-narrative*: "an all-encompassing cognitive-affective-behavioral structure that organizes the 'micro-narratives' of everyday life experiences into a 'macro-narrative' that consolidates our self-understanding, establishes our characteristic range of emotions and goals, and guides our performance on the stage of the social world" (Neimeyer, 2006, p. 70). Violent loss compels survivors to revise their self-narratives as a means of both integrating the enormity of the loss experience and adapting to the changed circumstances of their lives. In this section, we outline three possible avenues along which the self-narrative becomes profoundly disrupted, and by implication how the arduous passage toward reconstruction might proceed.

Narrative Disorganization

It is widely accepted that memories encoded under conditions of traumatic distress are underorganized and qualitatively different from typical memories (Siegal, 1995; van der Kolk & van der Hart, 1991). From a physiological perspective, immersion in such horrific experiences as Tamicka's witnessing the burning of her home floods the brain with neurotransmitters, thus engraving vivid sensory memories of the event that can be fused with troubling emotions of terror, despair, or helplessness (Siegal, 1995; van der Kolk & van der Hart, 1991). Contrary to the more linear "cortical" recollections of events, traumatic memories are held at the level of the amygdala in the form of fragmented and disturbing images, sensations, and emotions that reside "beneath" the level at which conscious narrative processing takes place. Instead, when later events occur that bear some resemblance to the cues associated with the loss experience (e.g., the smell of smoke, the sight of flames, the sound of sirens), rapid appraisal processes associated with this part of the limbic system trigger hyperarousal and increased vulnerability to intrusive memories alternating with avoidance behaviors (Horowitz, 1997). In keeping with this conceptualization, investigators have demonstrated long-term reexperiencing symptoms among groups of violent loss survivors

(Green et al., 2001; Kaltman & Bonanno, 2000; Murphy, Braun, et al., 1999; Murphy, Johnson, Chung, & Beaton, 2003).

Construing this physiological disorganization in narrative terms, these memories are viewed as being "prenarrative" (Neimeyer, 2002) in that the recollections fall outside the domain of autobiographical and other conscious memory processes (Siegal, 1995). As a result, violent bereavement can leave the survivor with a recurrent and disorganized stream of images — witnessed or imagined — that are radically at odds with the implicit plot structure of his or her prior life story (Stewart & Neimeyer, 2001). Unlike events that are more easily emplotted, however, traumatic loss resists integration into life's "master narrative" (Neimeyer, 2002). As a result, the experience remains as an isolated and unprocessed collection of fragmented memories that also can negatively shape the anticipation and elaboration of future events (Sewell & Williams, 2001, 2002). Conversely, when memory reaches an ideal narrative form, these self-regulatory problems do not occur because the affect is connected to and contained in a specific episode or sequence (Widgren, 1994), thus enabling the maintenance of coherence and continuity in the self-narrative (Neimeyer & Levitt, 2001).

Narrative Dominance

This second category of disruption focuses on the pathogenic role of socially, politically, or culturally enforced accounts of an individual's or group's identity (White & Epston, 1990). In brief, these dominant narratives "colonize" an individual's sense of self, limiting identity possibilities strictly to those that are externally governed or "problem-saturated" (White & Epston, 1990). This form of narrative disruption characteristically marginalizes more fragile, preferred accounts of self, while simultaneously stealing "authorship" for the individual's life story. In contrast to disorganized narratives, which result in "fragmented construing" (Sewell, 1996) and an incoherent sense of self and world, dominant narratives can be viewed as being far *too cohesive* in that they organize an individual's self-narrative under a single, all-consuming label or description. "Disenfranchisement" (Doka, 2002) of survivors can further add to the "assignment" of dominant narratives at a cultural level. For example, Tamicka's struggle to accommodate the previously foreign and often stigmatized designation of "foster child," following the dissolution of her biological family, can be seen in these terms, as she no longer could perceive herself as her mother's "little princess" or "just like all the other kids." Fortunately for Tamicka, the additional prospect of being branded a "problem child" or "emotionally disordered" was ultimately avoided by her successful experience in therapy.

In the aftermath of violent loss, narrative dominance can occur at intrapersonal as well as interpersonal levels, when a survivor's sense of identity becomes dominated by the nucleus of a "traumatic self" (Stewart & Neimeyer, 2001). Instead of allowing for the integration of newer, more positive emotional experiences, the "traumatic self" elaborates subsequent life experiences that are congruent with its darker themes, functioning as a kind of mental magnet for "attracting" and "holding onto" later experiences that confirm the unfairness of life, the dangerousness of the world, and the brokenness of the self. Furthermore, the dominance of a posttraumatic identity can be generalized to other personal and social experiences, sometimes causing the repetition or reenactment of the traumatic theme with friends and loved ones. Such enactments might include unconsciously identifying oneself as a "victim" in intimate relationships or guiltily sabotaging attempts at personal growth or contentment after the loss experience. Although Tamicka initially was at risk for internalizing a dominant narrative of powerlessness in the wake of the loss of her home and her brothers, she ultimately was able to recover her "voice" and sense of competence in both play therapy and in her broader social world.

Narrative Dissociation

The third form of narrative disruption entails the dissociation of the traumatic memory, which blocks aspects of it from both conscious awareness and narration in the social context. This detachment involves "silent stories" (Neimeyer, 2006) that resist acknowledgment in the public sphere, and often even the private world of their primary protagonist. Used in this way, "dissociation" implies both a breach of sociality and a rupture in the interpersonal sphere of meaning-making, as well as a dissociative blocking or compartmentalizing of awareness in a classical psychodynamic sense. In most instances of narrative dissociation, each implies the other, as the attempt to prevent a traumatic or painfully incongruent private event or story from finding expression in critical relationships requires and reinforces a hypervigilant form of self-monitoring and segregation of threatening private memories, and vice versa. In these instances, the "silent story" also ensures that any spontaneous offer of support will eventuate in "empathic failure," as the most relevant aspects of the plot structure of the traumatic narrative will remain hidden, unintegrated, and without social validation (Neimeyer & Jordan, 2002). However, as Tamicka's story will shortly underscore, if the potentially supportive persons can remain patient as the survivor of violent bereavement gradually risks disclosure of the dissociated narrative, the result can be a piecemeal movement toward genuine openness, congruence, and emotional responsiveness both at the level of the self-narrative and between the self and others.

Despite the heartfelt concern of foster parents, extended family, school staff, and case managers, Tamicka largely cleaved to subjective safety at all costs through the silencing of her traumatic story. She initially compromised the capacity for narrative integration by briefly feigning a hollowly upbeat attitude of "everything is great!" When this façade soon collapsed, Tamicka began to "space out" and grew more vigilant in isolating herself, through such "solutions" as constantly sleeping and always staying by herself. Not surprisingly, these behaviors eventually came to engender more than concern in the interpersonal sphere; her caregivers and other parental figures became angered by Tamicka's worsening condition and concurrent refusal to receive their best attempts at helping. Thus, the storm resounded all the louder and her increasing distress betrayed Tamicka's staunch efforts at denial and disavowal. However, through an alternative passage to reconstruction in therapy, Tamicka used the play narrative and therapeutic relationship to "rebuild" a sense of coherence and continuity, and in the process she integrated several positive possibilities for her personal and social identity.

HOW THEN SHALL WE HELP? CLINICAL IMPLICATIONS

The foregoing constructivist–narrative conceptualization carries several important implications for treatment of survivors of violent loss. First, it assigns a central role to the survivor's selfhood and how fundamental narrative processes can be disrupted or shattered by the violence of the loss experience. This underscores the importance of not limiting attention to familiar psychiatric symptoms such as depression or anxiety, instead giving equal attention to the underlying narrative significance of the survivor's distress. For example, in an effort to account for Tamicka's difficulties, a child psychiatrist assigned the diagnoses of major depressive disorder and attention-deficit/hyperactivity disorder. Although these categories did function to "legitimize" Tamicka's suffering so that helpful medication could be secured, they did not speak to the changed reality of her life following her tragic losses. As an increasing evidence base builds for a diagnosis of complicated grief in cases like Tamicka's (Prigerson & Maciejewski, 2006), there is hope that psychiatric diagnosis following violent death might become somewhat more relevant to the themes of disrupted trust, loss of purpose and direction, decimation of meaning, and the struggle to move forward in life that are criteria for this disorder (Neimeyer, 2006b). Still, a purely psychiatric approach is unlikely to provide the subtle and individualized conceptualization of distress necessary to guide treatment in a particular case. Narrative methods such as the *loss characterization*, in which survivors write an unstructured essay from a third-person standpoint about who they are "in light of their loss," can be useful in suggesting particular narrative gaps and themes that can then become the focus of therapy (Neimeyer, Keesee & Fortner, 2000).

A second clinical implication is that treatment of violent loss survivors does not simply involve identifying the ways in which their personal narratives of the traumatic events are incomplete. Although fleshing out and mastering the story of the loss might well be a critical part of treatment, genuine integration of the loss further implies the survivor's ability to place the "micronarrative" of the loss experience in the broader "macronarrative" of his or her life (Neimeyer, 2006a). In other words, psychotherapy should ultimately help bridge the survivor's pre- and postloss selves. One approach to assessing the need for such work is the *time line interview*, which contextualizes the loss experience in the flow of the survivor's overall self-narrative, and charts the degree of meaningful elaboration of past, present, and future events (Neimeyer et al., 2000).

A third clinical heuristic arising from this framework is to promote subjective mastery of the event through explicit narrative procedures. For example, therapeutic opportunities for *retelling* stories of violent death can play an important role in the integration of loss, whether in professional therapy or in specially constructed community support programs (Rynearson, 2001). Likewise, the use of *journaling* to express and explore the trauma narrative as a means to achieve healing insights and perspectives has proven helpful in reducing physical and psychological symptoms of maladjustment, even when these narratives are never shared with others (Neimeyer & Anderson, 2002; Pennebaker, 1997; see Neimeyer, 1999, for several variations on journaling methods specific to bereavement). The utility of this approach is also compatible with the report by Shear and her colleagues (Shear, Frank, Houck, & Reynolds, 2005) of a randomized controlled trial for complicated grief therapy, the focus of which involved an evocative relating, recording, and review of the narrative of the loss, in the context of reorganization of future life goals. However, it is worth emphasizing that not all "retelling" needs to take place in words alone, as such nonverbal or supplemental methods as *movement, music,* the *visual arts* (Bertman, 1999), *sand-trays* (Dale & Lyddon, 2000), and other forms of play therapy can help children in particular express and enact narratives of violent loss in ways that words cannot. Tamicka's elaborate use of block play in the context of professional psychotherapy illustrates this point.

All the same, we maintain that narrative repair does not necessarily require formal psychotherapeutic interventions. Indeed, one of the hallmarks of constructivist approaches in general is their nonpathologizing and strength-oriented approach to helping clients (Neimeyer & Bridges, 2003). The growing literature on resilience among the bereaved argues against the overzealous assumption that all survivors of violent loss will require professional psychotherapy to achieve the work of narrative integration (Bonnano, Wortman, & Nesse, 2004). In fact, if controlled studies of grief therapy are to be believed, offering clinical services to bereaved persons who are coping adaptively could be ineffective (Jordan & Neimeyer, 2003).

Data from our own large-scale study of violent bereavement bear on the general question of the type of support needed in such cases. We found that nearly 90% of 1,032 bereaved students reported having someone in their family or social environment to whom they could talk about the loss, whereas only 10% sought the help of a psychotherapist (Currier et al., 2006). Furthermore, the violently and naturally bereaved did not differ with respect to perceptions of being supported. In keeping with a "resilient systems approach" (Neimeyer, 2005), our conceptualization stresses the benefits of utilizing the collective healing forces in survivors' cultural institutions (e.g., church and faith communities, neighborhoods, schools). However, the existing research on the effectiveness of grief therapy does suggest that professional interventions can be specifically helpful for bereaved individuals at risk for complication, which would include those suffering traumatic loss (Jordan & Neimeyer, 2003). Thus, a community-based model that would provide narrative support to those who seek it, while also screening vulnerable individuals over a period of several months for possible professional referral, is likely the most sensible course of action (Neimeyer, 2002).

SUMMARY

Whatever the context of narrative work, a meaning reconstruction approach grounded in constructivist principles is particularly well suited to addressing these needs over the duration of the restoration process (Neimeyer, 2001). The aims of such an approach encompass not only *ameliorative* goals (e.g., symptom reduction) and *restorative* goals (e.g., resumption of preloss functioning), but also *elaborative* goals (e.g., developing beyond the time at which the event took place; Harter & Neimeyer, 1995). Because we believe that the healing of the survivors entails adapting to their changed postloss reality, some of these elaborative goals in therapy include the construction of new selves, reorganization of social ties, and rebuilding of one's "assumptive worldviews" (Janoff-Bulman, 1992; Parkes, 1971). As Tamicka's case illustrates, such changes can help survivors of violent loss move from posttraumatic stress to posttraumatic growth (Calhoun & Tedeschi, 2006), "rewriting" accounts of loss in a way that not only the stories, but also their authors, become more whole.

REFERENCES

Bertman, S. L. (Ed.). (1999). *Grief and the healing arts*. Amityville, NY: Baywood.

Bonanno, G. A., Wortman, C. B., & Nesse, R. M. (2004). Prospective patterns of resilience and maladjustment during widowhood. *Psychology and Aging, 19*, 260–271.

Bruner, J. (1986). *Actual minds, possible worlds*. Cambridge, MA: Harvard University Press.

Calhoun, L. & Tedeschi, R. (Eds.) (2006), *Handbook of posttraumatic growth: Research and practice*. Mahwah, NJ: Lawrence Erlbaum.

Currier, J. M., Holland, J. M., Coleman, R. A., & Neimeyer, R. A. (2006). Bereavement following violent death: An assault on life and meaning. In R. Stevenson & G. Cox (Eds.) *Perspectives on Violence and Violent Death*. Amityville, NY: Baywood.

Dale, M. A. & Lyddon, W. J. (2000). Sandplay: A constructivist strategy for assessment and change. *Journal of Constructivist Psychology, 13*, 135–153.

Davis, C. G., Nolen-Hoeksema, S., & Larson, J. (1998). Making sense of loss and benefiting from experience: Two construals of meaning. *Journal of Personality and Social Psychology, 75*, 561–574.

Davis, C., Wortman, C. B., Lehman, D. R., & Cohen Silver, R. (2000). Searching for meaning in loss: Are clinical assumptions correct? *Death Studies, 24*, 497–540.

Doka, K. (Ed.).(2002). *Disenfranchised grief*. Champaign, IL: Research Press.

Gergen, K. J. & Gergen, M. M. (1986). Narrative form and the construction of psychological science. In T. R. Sarbin (Ed.), *Narrative psychology: The storied nature of human conduct* (pp. 22–44). New York: Praeger.

Green, B. L., Krupnick, J. L., Stockton, P., Goodman, L., Corcoran, C., & Petty, R. (2001). Psychological outcomes associated with traumatic loss in a sample of young women. *American Behavioral Scientist, 44,* 817–837.

Gonclaves, O. F. (1994a). From epistemological truth to existential meaning in cognitive narrative psychotherapy. *Journal of Cognitive Psychotherapy, 7,* 107–118.

Gonclaves, O. F. (1994b). Cognitive narrative psychotherapy: The hermeneutic construction of alternative meanings. *Journal of Cognitive Psychotherapy, 8,* 105–125.

Gonclaves, O. F. (1995). Hermeneutics, constructivism, and cognitive–behavioral therapies: From the object to the project. In R. A. Neimeyer & M.J. Mahoney (Eds.), *Constructivism in psychotherapy* (pp. 155–168). Washington, D.C.: American Psychological Association.

Harter, S. L. & Neimeyer, R. A. (1995). Long-term effects of child sexual abuse: Toward a constructivist theory of trauma and its treatment. *Advances in personal construct psychology* (Vol. 2, pp. 225–265). Greenwich, CT: JAI.

Hermans, H. (2002). The person as motivated storyteller. In R. A. Neimeyer & G. J. Neimeyer (Eds.), *Advances in personal construct psychology* (pp. 3–38). New York: Praeger.

Horowitz, M. J. (1997). *Stress response syndromes* (3rd ed.). Northvale, NJ: Aronson.

Howard, G. (1991). Culture tales: A narrative approach to thinking, cross-cultural psychology, and psychotherapy. *American Psychologist, 46,* 187–197.

Janoff-Bulman, R. (1992). *Shattered assumptions: Toward a new psychology of trauma.* New York: Free Press.

Jordan, J. R. & Neimeyer, R. A. (2003). Does grief counseling work? *Death Studies, 27,* 765–786.

Kaltman, S. & Bonanno, G. A. (2003). Trauma and bereavement: Examining the impact of sudden and violent deaths. *Anxiety Disorders, 17,* 131–147.

Kauffman, J. (2002). *Loss of the assumptive world: A theory of traumatic loss.* London: Brunner-Routledge.

Lifton, R. J. (1964). On death and death symbolism: The Hiroshima disaster. *Psychiatry, 27,* 191–210.

Mair, M. (1988). Psychology as story telling. *International Journal of Personal Construct Psychology, 1,* 125–137.

Mancuso, J. C. (1986). The acquisition and use of narrative grammar structure. In T. R. Sarbin (Ed.), *Narrative psychology: The storied nature of human conduct* (pp. 91–110). New York: Praeger.

McLeod, J. (1996). The emerging narrative approach to counseling and psychotherapy. *British Journal of Guidance and Counselling, 24,* 173–185.

Merleau-Ponty, M. (1962). *Phenomenology and perception* (Colin Smith, Trans.). New York: Routledge.

Murphy, S. A., Braun, T., Tillery, L., Cain, K. C., Johnson, C. L., & Beaton, R. D. (1999). PTSD among bereaved parents following the violent deaths of their 12- to 28-year-old children: A longitudinal prospective analysis. *Journal of Traumatic Stress, 12,* 273–291.

Murphy, S. A., Johnson, C. L., Chung, I. J., & Beaton, R. D. (2003). The prevalence of PTSD following the violent death of a child and predictors of change 5 years later. *Journal of Traumatic Stress, 16,* 17–25.

Neimeyer, R. A., (1995). Client-generated narratives in psychotherapy. In R. A. Neimeyer & M. J. Mahoney (Eds.), *Constructivism in psychotherapy.* Washington, D.C.: American Psychological Association.

Neimeyer, R. A. (1999). Narrative strategies in grief therapy. *Journal of Constructivist Psychology, 12,* 65–85.

Neimeyer, R. A. (2000). Narrative disruptions in the construction of self. In R. A. Neimeyer & J. Raskin (Eds.), *Constructions of disorder* (pp. 207–242). Washington, D.C.: American Psychological Association.

Neimeyer, R. A. (Ed.). (2001). *Meaning reconstruction and the experience of loss.* Washington, D.C.: American Psychological Association.

Neimeyer, R. A. (2002). Traumatic loss and the reconstruction of meaning. *Journal of Palliative Medicine, 5,* 935–942.

Neimeyer, R. A. (2006a). Re-storying loss: Fostering growth in the posttraumatic narrative. In L. Calhoun & R. Tedeschi (Eds.), *Handbook of posttraumatic growth: Research and practice* (pp. 67–80). Mahwah, NJ: Lawrence Erlbaum.

Neimeyer, R. A. (2005). Widowhood, grief and the quest for meaning: A narrative perspective on resilience. In D. Carr, R. M. Nesse, & C. B. Wortman (Eds.), *Late life widowhood in the United States* (pp. 227-252). New York: Springer.

Neimeyer, R. A. (2006b). Complicated grief and the quest for meaning: A constructivist contribution. *Omega, 52,* 37-52.

Neimeyer, R. A. & Anderson, A. (2002). Meaning reconstruction theory. In N. Thompson (Ed.), *Loss and Grief* (pp. 45–64). London: Palgrave.

Neimeyer, R. A. & Bridges, S. (2003). Postmodern approaches to psychotherapy. In A. Gurman & S. Messer (Eds.), *Essential psychotherapies* (2nd ed., pp. 272–316). New York: Guilford.

Neimeyer, R. A., Herrero, O., & Botella, L. (in press). Chaos to coherence: Psychotherapeutic integration of traumatic loss. *Journal of Constructivist Psychotherapy, 19,* 127–145.

Neimeyer, R. A. & Jordan, J. R. (2002). Disenfranchisement as empathic failure: Grief therapy and the co-construction of meaning. In K. Doka (Ed.), *Disenfranchised Grief* (pp. 95–117). Champaign, IL: Research Press.

Neimeyer, R. A., Keesee, N. J., & Fortner, B. V. (2000). Loss and meaning reconstruction: Propositions and procedures. In R. Malkinson, S. Rubin, & E. Witztum (Eds.), *Traumatic and nontraumatic loss and bereavement* (pp. 197–230). Madison, CT: Psychosocial Press.

Neimeyer, R. A. & Levitt, H. (2001). Coping and coherence: A narrative perspective on resilience. In S. Snyder (Ed.), *Coping with stress* (pp. 47–67). New York: Oxford University Press.

Neimeyer, R. A. & Mahoney, M. J. (1995). *Constructivism in psychotherapy.* Washington, D.C.: American Psychological Association.

Neimeyer, R. A. & Raskin, J. (Eds.). (2000). *Constructions of disorder.* Washington, D.C.: American Psychological Association.

Nelson, K. (2003). Narrative and the emergence of a consciousness of self. In G. D. Fireman, T. E. McVay, & O. J. Flanagan (Eds.), *Narrative and consciousness: Literature, psychology and the brain* (pp. 17–36). New York: Oxford University Press.

Parkes, C. M. (1971). Psycho-social transitions: A field for study. *Social Science and Medicine, 5,* 101–115.

Pennebaker, J. W. (1997). Writing about emotional experiences as a therapeutic process. *Psychological Science, 8,* 162–169.

Polkinghorne, D. E. (1988). *Narrative knowing and the human sciences.* Albany, NY: State University of New York.

Prigerson, H. G. & Jacobs, S. C. (2001). Traumatic grief as a distinct disorder: A rationale, consensus criteria, and a preliminary empirical test. In M. S. Stroebe, W. Stroebe, & R. O. Hansson (Eds.), *Handbook of bereavement research* (pp. 613–645). Washington, D.C.: American Psychological Association.

Prigerson, H. G. & Maciejewski, P. K. (2006). A call for sound empirical testing and evaluation of criteria for complicated grief proposed for DSM-V. *Omega,* 9–19.

Ricoeur, P. (1980). Narrative time. *Critical Inquiry, 7,* 169–190.

Rosen, H. & Kuelwein, K. (Eds.). (1996). *Constructing realities.* San Francisco: Jossey Bass.

Rubin, D. C. & Greenberg, D. L. (2003). The role of narrative in recollection: A view from cognitive psychology and neuropsychology. In G. D. Fireman, T. E. McVay, & O. J. Flanagan (Eds.), *Narrative and consciousness* (pp. 53–85). New York: Oxford University Press.

Russell, R. L. (1991). Narrative in views of humanity, science, and action: Lessons for cognitive science. *Journal of Cognitive Psychotherapy, 5,* 241–256

Rynearson, E. K. (2001). *Retelling violent death.* Philadelphia, PA: Brunner-Routledge.

Sarbin, T. R. (1986a). *Narrative psychology: The storied nature of human conduct.* New York: Praeger.

Sarbin, T. R. (1986b). The narrative as a root metaphor for psychology. In T. R. Sarbin (Ed.), *Narrative psychology: The storied nature of human conduct* (pp. 3–21). New York: Praeger.

Schafer, R. (1980). Narration in the psychoanalytic dialogue. *Critical Inquiry, 7,* 29–53.

Sewell, K. W. (1996). Constructional risk factors for a post-traumatic stress response after a mass murder. *Journal of Constructivist Psychology, 9,* 97–108.

Sewell, K. W. & Williams, A. M. (2001). Construing stress: A constructivist therapeutic approach to posttraumatic stress reactions. In R.A. Neimeyer (Ed.), *Meaning reconstruction and the experience of loss* (pp. 293–310). Washington, D.C.: American Psychological Association.

Sewell, K. W. & Williams, A. M. (2002). Broken narratives: Trauma, metaconstructive gaps, and the audience of psychotherapy. Journal of Constructivist Psychology, 15, 205–218.

Shear, K., Frank, E. Houck, P. R., & Reynolds, C. F. (2005). Treatment of complicated grief: A randomized controlled trial. *Journal of the American Medical Association, 293,* 2601–2608.

Siegal, D. J. (1995). Memory, trauma, and psychotherapy: A cognitive science view. *Journal of Psychotherapy and Research, 4,* 93–122.

Smith, C. & Nylund, D. (Eds.). (1997). *Narrative therapies with children and adolescents.* New York: Guilford.

Spence, D. P. (1982). *Narrative truth and historical truth: Meaning and interpretation in psychoanalysis.* New York: Norton.

Stewart, A. E. & Neimeyer, R. A. (2001). Emplotting the traumatic self: Narrative revision and the construction of coherence. *The Humanist Psychologist, 29,* 8–39.

Stolorow, R. D. (1999). The phenomenology of trauma and the absolutisms of everyday life: A personal journey. *Psychoanalytic Psychology, 16,* 464–468.

Stolorow, R. D. (2003). Trauma and temporality. *Psychoanalytic Psychology, 20,* 158–161.

Terrell, C. J. & Lyddon, W. J. (1996). Narrative and psychotherapy. *Journal of Constructivist Psychology, 9,* 27–44.

van der Kolk, B. A. & van der Hart, O. (1991). The intrusive past: The flexibility of memory and the engraving of trauma. *American Imago, 48,* 425–454.

White, M. & Epston, D. (1990). *Narrative means to therapeutic ends.* New York: Norton.

Widgren, J. (1994). Narrative completion in the treatment of trauma. *Psychotherapy, 31,* 415–423.

6

Meaning Making for Survivors of Violent Death

MARILYN PETERSON ARMOUR

MEANING MAKING

Symbolic meaning can accompany practices of spiritual and narrative retelling to counterbalance the incoherent cognition of the violent dying; however, this chapter suggests that beyond revision of thought, meaning is also "made" through deliberate action — by performing intentional, meaningful acts. The performative dimensions of meaning making are categorized by the author as (1) declarations of truth; (2) fighting for what is right; and (3) living in ways that give purpose to the loved one's death. The author presents insights from an empirical study of family members after homicide clarifying the model of performative meaning making with case illustrations and clinical recommendations for its reinforcement. The "pursuit of what matters" is the driving force of this performative response and contributes to the coherence and continuity of self. More manifest in the later phase of bereavement after violent dying, meaning making with its deliberate commitment to the future is active and interpersonal.

Few events are more seismically traumatizing than the loss of a loved one to murder. Besides the horror that someone willfully and violently took life away from another, homicide survivors quickly learn that the dominant social narrative makes the state the surrogate victim and harm done by offenders to victims is handled as if it is harm done by offenders to the state. Homicide survivors become invisible as the agenda of the criminal justice system, the media's interpretation of the facts, and the community's response construct the public meaning given to the tragedy. Too often, they are cruelly left alone to face the abject grief, rage, and sense of violation that accompanies the abhorrent act of murder. As their meaning systems implode, they enter a netherworld where they fight to find footing.

Neimeyer (2001) contends that meaning reconstruction in response to loss is the central feature of grieving. Studies of traumatically bereaved mourners suggest, however, that meaning making based on traditional definitions of the process may not occur because violent death is irrational and meaningless (Davis, Wortman, Lehman, & Silver, 2000; Rynearson, 2001). Specifically, meaning making has been narrowly construed as "making sense" based on a cognitive system of appraisal about the nature of the event or as an existential search for meaning and purpose in life. Populations who are blocked from finding meaning in these ways may use other methods both to counter the incoherence inherent in violent acts and rebuild meaning where little seems to exist.

The chapter draws upon the results of a previously published qualitative study of 14 families of homicide victims (Armour, 2002) to elaborate on the concept of meaning making grounded in action as reflected in the accounts of these family members. Discussions of the "meaning of meaning" have drawn attention to the performative dimension of meaning making beyond the predominant cognitive conceptualization that dominates most research (Neimeyer, 2000). This chapter adds a specific demonstration of the relevance of performed meanings in the case of a distinctive population of the bereaved. Moreover, since the deeds that mark the journey for homicide survivors are often done in reaction to being in the public eye, meaning making is both an intrapersonal and interpersonal endeavor.

LITERATURE REVIEW

The search for meaning after stressful events is a common and essential task (Park & Folkman, 1997). Successful adaptation, however, depends upon achieving congruence between the appraised meaning of a current situation and long-standing global beliefs about order and purpose, including estimates of benevolence, a sense of fairness and predictable order, and evaluations of one's self as worthy. Severe stressors such as unexpected, unnatural, and violent death can challenge the global meaning system at its most fundamental level since beliefs about how and why things happen no longer seem tenable (Janoff-Bulman, 1992; Park & Folkman, 1997). Theorists generally agree that people make efforts to bridge the gap by finding reasons for what happened or discovering benefit and purpose in the occurrence (Davis, Nolen-Hoeksema, & Larson, 1998; Murphy, Johnson, & Lohan, 2003; Park & Folkman, 1997). Making attributions about causality falls within the framework of meaning-as-comprehensibility and refers to sense making. Deriving perceived benefit falls within the framework of meaning-as-significance and refers to a new appreciation for life.

Neimeyer and Anderson (2002) contend that people who have experienced traumatic loss use these two dimensions, among others, to assimilate the loss by constructing a coherent self-narrative that preserves a sense of continuity about who they have been and are now. The ability to find meaning has far ranging consequences. Realizing benefit in the loss influences adjustment and adaptation (Murphy et al., 2003). Without resolution, for example, traumatic grief, anxiety, and depression predict negative health outcomes including cancer, heart trouble, high blood pressure, and negative eating habits (Prigerson et al., 1997).

Indeed, studies show that many persons have difficulty making sense of violent death or other traumatic events or pulling back far enough to find a silver lining in catastrophic acts. According to Lehman, Wortman, and Williams (1987), 64% of parents who lost a child in a motor vehicle accident were not able to make sense of the loss four to seven years after it occurred. In a sudden infant death syndrome (SIDS) study described by Davis, Wortman, Lehman, and Silver (2000), 66% of parents who had lost a child to SIDS were unable to find meaning at 18 months postloss. Murphy et al. (2006) determined that 43% of parents whose child suffered a violent death from accident, suicide, or homicide were not able to find meaning after five years. The largest percentages of parents unable to find meaning were parents of children dying from suicide (61%) or homicide (66%). Moreover, parents of homicide victims showed the greatest distress.

Although speculative, the difficulty in finding meaning may be attributed to problems with reflection, incoherent realities, and the lack of a supportive and accepting audience for meaning reconstruction. Rynearson (2001) theorizes that the "disintegratory effects of traumatic imagery and avoidance impair the more reflective demands of acknowledging and adjusting to the loss" (p. 260). Consequently, methods of meaning making that require reflection may not be accessible to mourners who have extensive trauma distress. Neimeyer, Prigerson, and Davis (2002) suggest that the ability to reconstruct a personal world of meaning rests on fitting traumatic loss into an underlying assumptive base on which the self-narrative depends. The extinguishing of that base leaves mourners void of a meaning base from which to create a coherent story. Moreover, Rynearson (2001) contends that achieving coherence is blocked by the paradox of trying to integrate a story about living from a violent dying that continues to pulse. Therefore, meaning making by assimilating the loss into an existing self-narrative may not be possible. Neimeyer et al. (2002) assert that meaning making is not a private affair but is pursued at the juncture of self and society. The significance of the loss can be affirmed or contested, congruent or discrepant, upheld or disconfirmed through interactions with other reference groups. The ability to make meaning by constructing a coherent account of bereavement may, therefore, be dependent on a supportive and validating social milieu. People suffering from disenfranchised losses such as homicide receive little or no ritual support from the community (Doka, 2002; Neimeyer & Jordan, 2002). Consequently, the ability to make meaning can be thwarted by their stigmatized social status and the meaning given to the death by others.

Persons who cannot find meaning are more likely to suffer from complicated bereavement. Murphy (1999) found that 30% of parents of children who died violent deaths have no trauma diminishment. They suffer persistent thoughts of reenactment, remorse, retaliation, and overprotection of other family members. Moreover, those parents who could not find meaning were less well off relative to mental distress, marital satisfaction, and physical health status than those who found something positive in the experience. Neimeyer et al.(2002) claim that complicated bereavement can be viewed as "the inability to reconstruct a meaningful personal reality" (p. 235). Symptoms are viewed in terms of a struggle to integrate the meaning of the loss. They are not effectively reduced by interpersonal psychotherapy or tricyclic antidepressants. Additionally, the study of bereaved parents whose child has suffered a violent death found that personal and family prayer and church attendance did not improve outcomes over time (Murphy, Johnson, Lohan, & Tapper, 2002). Although participation in a support group seemed to make some difference, mutual support also did not aid in the reduction of mental distress and PTSD.

The examination of meaning making may need to include other dimensions that have been eclipsed by the focus on cognitive appraisals or existential quests for significance in the loss. Neimeyer and Anderson (2002) suggest exploring the ways in which people make meaning in the stories they construct for themselves and others. J. W. Pennebaker (1997; J. Z. E. Pennebaker & Rime, 2001) has shown that narrative journaling about traumatic experiences seems to improve mood and reduce health complaints. Rynearson (2001) has developed a model for retelling violent death that helps the mourner to disengage from the futile search for coherence in the imaginary story of violent dying and build resilience by reconnecting with living memories and experience beyond the event of the dying.

Neimeyer and Anderson (2002) have also added identity reconstruction as a dimension of meaning making that occurs as a consequence of the transition between the past and the present. Identity reconstruction may have more application to traumatized populations that deal with violent death since meaning making is associated with fundamental change that requires "relearning the self" and "relearning the world" (Atiig, 1996, 2001). Indeed, meaning making grounded in action may be an important mechanism for promoting positive reconstruction of the self. As this chapter describes, it is used by some families of homicide victims to confront posthomicide challenges while discovering and testing out latent resources in a changed world.

Meaning reconstruction is a form of adaptive coping. It has traditionally been equated with cognitions and intrapsychic processes (Neimeyer, 2000). Moreover, it is considered to be a result of shifts in perception. Studies have shown that finding meaning occurs less often for persons dealing with violent death (Davis, Wortman et al., 2000; Murphy, Johnson, & Lohan, 2003). Consequently, it is important to examine other dimensions of meaning making that may be less direct but still central to the construction of coherent accounts. This chapter describes how families of homicide victims made meaning through behaviors that had symbolic significance. Instead of *finding* meaning, the metameaning of the behaviors was inferred.

BACKGROUND

The finding of the performative dimension of meaning making comes from an earlier family-focused study of the posthomicide experience (Armour, 2002). Fourteen families who had experienced the homicide of a family member were recruited from three sites. The total number of participants was 38, of whom 92% were Caucasian, 5% were African American, and 3% were Korean American. Mean length of time since the homicide was 7.5 years (range = 18 months–23 years, SD = 5.59). Data were collected through one two- to four-hour, open-ended interview with each family. Interviews were audiotaped and transcribed for analysis.

A qualitative approach is appropriate for research that seeks to systematically examine unexplored areas such as the lived experience of homicide survivors. The study used a hermeneutic phenomenological paradigm to guide the research approach. This specific qualitative method was selected because it had the ability to expand what was known about the subjective experience of homicide survivors beyond the traditional focus on homicide trauma; identify patterns and core meanings that survivors attach to their loss; illuminate the interactional processes by which meaning was made; and attend, as described by Neimeyer (2000), to the tacit and preverbal as well as explicit and articulate meanings hinted at by vocal tones, gestures, and emphases.

In the data analysis, themes were assigned and clustered based on a line-by-line and holistic reading of interview transcripts and accompanying materials as well as cross-case comparisons. Out of the clustered themes, essential themes were determined using the process of imaginative variation (Giorgi, 1985, 1997). Imaginative variation is a process whereby the researcher takes a concrete example of a thing, and imaginatively subtracts one feature, then another, discovering in the process which features are essential and which are not. Essential themes were determined by both the researcher and one of two consultants to the study after they collaboratively reviewed each cluster of themes to first find the essence of the phenomenon and then evaluate whether or not the essence was core to the lived experience of the participants. A qualitative computer research program (*Atlas-ti*, Version 4.16) was employed to recode the transcripts according to the essential themes and retrieve the quotes to substantiate and describe the findings. The findings were validated by the researcher who repeatedly read and tested the initial descriptions of the essential themes against (1) alternative interpretations; (2) accounts from family members of homicide victims who were not research participants; (3) facilitators for homicide support groups who wrote anonymous responses after reading the findings; and (4) research participants who anonymously rated the applicability of each essential theme to their experience using a five-point rating system. In this study, meaning making was depicted by the following essential theme: "the intense pursuit of what matters is the meaning in my life." There were 48% of the participants who indicated that this theme completely represented their experience and 35% who felt it substantially represented their experience (Armour, 2002).

Two consultants monitored the entire research process. The first consultant was a psychologist who reviewed the audiotapes for subjective bias in the researcher's questions and responses, substantiated the determination of essential themes, and reviewed the findings against the associated quotes from the transcripts. The second consultant was a specialist in hermeneutic phenomenology and reviewed methodological procedures, essential themes, and descriptions of the themes.

CHARACTERISTICS OF MEANING MAKING GROUNDED IN ACTION

"The intense pursuit of what matters" is a form of coping comprised of intentional acts that have symbolic meaning. Its implied purpose is to restore or find meaning in a changed life through problem solving or striving to attain visionary goals. Although acts are geared toward desirable results, meaningfulness related to the posthomicide experience rests primarily on the process of the pursuit rather than the specific outcome. Over time, engagement in numerous meaning making ventures reconstructs a self-identity as homicide survivors both "relearn the self" and "relearn the world" (Attig, 1996). Narratives about their actions in response to the posthomicide experience facilitate this reauthoring of the self.

For homicide survivors, meaning making grounded in action has attributes that are shaped by the trauma: (1) The meta meaning of behavior is to reestablish a moral order by deliberately reacting to what matters as a consequence of the murder. (2) The meaning making initiative is generated by intrusive stimuli such as insensitive responses from friends or violations of privacy by the media, which compel reactions that are either self-protective or encompassing of a survivor mission. (3) Meaning making is comprised of many small acts that can occur within hours of the death notification and continue throughout the posthomicide experience. (4) The attainment of meaning is a by-product of a focused striving to attend to that which is deemed significant. These characteristics suggest that the performative dimension of meaning making is a form of coping in response to the appraised meaning of posthomicide events. As such, the meaning making endeavor is both interpersonally and intrapersonally interactional.

METHODS OF MEANING MAKING GROUNDED IN ACTION

This chapter is an explication of one essential theme from the previously published study that serves as an example of meaning making grounded in action. It is labeled by the phrase, "The intense pursuit of what matters is the meaning in my life." Manifestations of the theme include (1) declarations of truth; (2) fighting for what's right; and (3) living in ways that give a sense of purpose to the loved one's death. Each of these manifestations is conveyed in two ways: (1) Declarations of truth are conveyed by (a) declarations that expose hypocrisy, and (b) declarations of self-determination. (2) Fighting for what's right is conveyed by (a) fighting for what's mine, and (b) fighting to correct what's wrong. (3) Living in ways that give purpose to the loved one's death is conveyed by (a) using my experience to benefit others, and (b) living life deliberately in an effort to give positive value to the homicide. These categories are not discrete. For example, a particular act might include both declarations that expose hypocrisy and a fight to correct what was wrong. Moreover, individual homicide survivors might use some methods more often than others.

DECLARATIONS OF TRUTH

The bereaved (i.e., who have lost a loved one to violent death) construct narratives that are punctuated with commentary, opinions, and beliefs about the real truth of what happened in posthomicide events. The certitude with which they express their convictions is guided by an internal sense of integrity that gives strength and direction to their journey. In their pronouncements, they symbolically claim their right to see things as they are, reveal hidden motives behind other people's behavior, and decide things for themselves separate and apart from the opinions of others.

Declarations that Expose Hypocrisy

Homicide survivors make statements that show the incompetence, ignorance, and hypocrisy of others. Their incisive comments penetrate pretense and assert truth as they see it. Declarations are based on seeing life through a moral lens that separates what is genuine from what is false. The pronouncements scrutinize the motives of others so that homicide survivors can be protected from further harm. Their recounting of personal injustices dealt them or others justifies their anger and lets them claim their worth as undeserving victims of crime.

In the following example, family members expound on the incompetence of the police chaplain who advised them to forgive the murderer. They claim their own authority by mocking his patronizing and controlling behavior, exposing his incompetence, and disqualifying his legitimacy as a valid cleric in their lives. Their anger implicitly establishes their worth as vulnerable survivors who deserved better treatment.

Family member 1: Well this chaplain was a jerk. It's like he's got his little personal mission or something. He volunteers. He is not paid. He spoke very quietly. He delivered the news and just told us briefly, very briefly what had happened. And then he said (voice measured and soft imitating the chaplain), "You know I need to tell you now that as you go through this whole process that you got to think about forgiveness. Maybe not right now but somewhere down the line ya gotta think about forgiveness."

Family member 2: We all wanted to (yelling) *plaster* the man. Nobody is ready to hear that once they had just heard the news. It just seemed arrogant. We are Catholic. We have our faith. We didn't need anyone (sounding insulted) *preaching* to us. It was presumptuous, like he knew more than we did and he was (slapping hand with fist) going to get it to us right now. I've got my one chance to hook into this family and I'm going to do.

Family Member 3: Well and anybody who has dealt with homicide for any period of time knows that forgiveness (singsong voice) doesn't come for a while. The thought doesn't even hit your head until you are ready for it.

Family Member 1: When?

Family Member 3: If you're ready for it. At that point I don't think any of us were....

Family Member 4: No one who hasn't been through this has the right to say that [about forgiveness] to anyone. Even someone who has been through it would know they don't have the right to say that to someone. You don't tell someone else, "You have to forgive." You just, you don't do that.

A father, whose 13-year-old daughter was killed by a serial rapist, exposed the government's negligence in releasing a dangerous criminal from prison and not monitoring his whereabouts. As he shows that the government was culpable in his daughter's death, he implicitly claims that her death was preventable and the government is inept in its ability to protect its citizens. Moreover, the unrelenting quality of his anger is justified because there is no way to undo his loss.

The long and the short is after the rapist was caught, we found out that he had been in Hollingswood State Prison for two and a half years and had been let out nine months earlier on good behavior. He had been there for the rape of three other young girls. We find out that when he was released he was supposed to go to a halfway house. He never went to that house and the police never looked for him. So he broke his parole and was a felon but they didn't look for him. They didn't even post that he was missing. That really irritated us and still does today. Because the government screwed up I lost my daughter. And that will never settle with me.

Declarations of Self-Determination

Homicide survivors take positions that are grounded in moral precepts and the meanings they assign to particular situations. The beliefs that undergird the survivors' declarations provide them with a source of energy and motivation. A sense of having reduced choices drives them to act on their own behalf, because they find that who they are and what they believe do not fit cultural prescriptions or the expectations of others. They realize that their destiny is to stand alone and apart from the crowd. Their commitment to following their own path creates a sense of wholeness.

In the following example, a sister draws her own conclusions about why she cannot continue to hate the boy who senselessly murdered her brother. In her decision to hate or not hate, she realizes that the true victims in her revenge fantasy would be the many innocent people, like her, whose lives she would hurt if she hurt the murderer. She speaks from this moral imperative in ordering others to move in a different direction.

When Bobby (*pseudonym*) died the person that killed him should have hated him. There should have been more of a reason. There wasn't, which made it all the more pathetic. There was (said emphatically) *no … reason.* Bobby is gone now. This person is happy because the person they didn't like is gone. But who did you actually hurt? Bobby? No. You hurt all of the people that are [left]. All of us, that's who you hurt. So by my hurting Cal — because that's what I wanted to do so bad, to kill him — I'm not hurting Cal. I'm hurting all of his. I started realizing I can't (loud voice) *hate* this person anymore, I can't (loud voice) *want* to kill this person anymore because what am I going to get from it? (loud voice) *Nothing.* No satisfaction. I'm still not going to get Bobby back. And look how many people's lives I'm going to (loud voice) *hurt* if I hurt him. That's what I say to people now. "You can't do that." The old saying "two wrongs don't make a right" is so true. You're not going to get anything back.

An African-American mother controlled what information she learned from the media, and who and what she would believe about her son's murder, by steadfastly electing to blank out her television screen. Instead of succumbing to pressure, she chose her own path by going to reliable sources for information about her son's death.

I never seen, I never seen it on TV. I never saw any of the news reports. An' all they were sayin was there was a body left at Seton Hospital. I guess I never seen, I never seen, I didn't see any of it on TV. Someone would call me and say, "Latoya, look right now. It's comin' on channel such and such an' I'd sit there and it would not come on my TV. It never came on my TV. I never saw it at all. Yah know, they would call and say, "Well did yah know he was shot multiple times?" An' I said, "No." So I hung up and I called my sister [for the information].

Verbal assertions reshape the narrative and the meaning given to the death by others. Declarations show the dissonance between what is and what's professed. They also illuminate the necessity for autonomy in decision making due to the solitary and uncommon circumstances that comprise each person's experience.

Fighting For What's Right

Homicide survivors feel ill-treated by the actions of others. In response, they forcefully assert themselves by holding others accountable and claiming what is rightfully theirs. Their interventions become symbolic statements about the importance of their experience and their right to be seen. Their actions help reestablish a moral and principled world.

Fighting for What's Mine

Homicide survivors are forced into interactions with the public that rob them of important rights and deprive them of their justifiable privilege to define and control their realities. What they fight for underscores what matters to them. The convictions they act on are fueled by moral indignation and passion for what is theirs to hold onto, correct, or take back. Fighting is a form of self-preservation to minimize more losses. Asserting their needs makes who they are visible to others.

In the following example, a father breaks through the dispassionate courtroom climate to claim and celebrate his victory over the murderer. His applause redefines the occasion as joyous rather than somber, reestablishes that he, rather than the state, is the aggrieved party, and congratulates the judge, jury, and prosecution on a job well done. His applause also provokes a reaction from the murderer that validates the father's gain and presence as a force with which to be reckoned.

So now the whole courtroom is still absolutely quiet. Nobody has even moved. And I want to jump and scream so bad, I'm ready to wet my pants. And nothing is happening. Now the judges are not leaving, but kind of packing up to leave. The jury is taken out. The defense attorney is starting to pack his belongings. The guards are coming in to take Brandel and cuff him back up and finally I started clapping. Then everybody broke loose and Frank Brandel turned around and whipped me the bird. And I thought, "I did it. I finally got to the guy. I finally got to the asshole (laughs). I finally got to this guy." They hauled him off and then we just exploded.

Two sisters formed a pact not to let any psychotherapist take away or alter their reality with drugs. They fought for the right to have intense reactions by insisting that the therapist not pathologize their appropriate responses to their father's murder. As they reassured the therapist that they would monitor their suicidal proclivities, they took back the power to determine their dangerousness.

Sister 1: They all tried to put me on drugs.

Sister 2: This lady mentioned it and encouraged it. But when I refused she said that was okay. 'Cause I kept telling her that there is nothing wrong with me. I am supposed to be fucked up. "My dad, you know, was butchered. I am supposed to be messed up. When I am going to kill myself I'll let you know." I promised her that.

Sister 1: That's one thing we all agreed on. We did not want to do that. We didn't want to be on Prozac™.

Sister 2: "No, you can't take that away from me."

Fighting to Correct What's Wrong

Homicide survivors respond viscerally to situations they recognize as wrong and work to wake others up to the realities they see clearly. In their dedication to stop or prevent more harm, they demand what is due them, admonish others for their poor performance, and enlighten people who are ignorant. Their ability to recognize wider issues prompts them to hold others accountable for the part they play in creating pain. By teaching lessons or monitoring behavior, they seek to control what happens to them and reestablish order. Righting the wrong makes them feel strong and worthwhile.

In the following example, a family took offense at the funeral director's insensitivity to their loss. They chose to correct his behavior with a question that simultaneously registered their insult, mocked his priorities, and served as commentary on the absurdity of the situation. Moreover, their question held him accountable for making cost more important than human life, human feelings, and human interaction.

Family Member 1: He was the epitome of an asshole. He was a jerk from the get-go, we walked in the place and he was a jerk (hitting hand with fist) right now.

Family Member 2: He never even said, "I am sorry for your loss." Typical words given to anybody who has lost [a loved one]. No, didn't even recognize [our loss] and he knew the situation. Never ever recognized anything. Just said (horridly) "Well, come on."

Family Member 3: We're going through book after book and form after form and of course they are trying to sell you the world here at the funeral home. We are bargain hunters. (laughs) And of course if you can't use a coupon or if you can't get it on clearance or on sale, you just don't do it right.

Family Member 2: He was bugging me. The guy was bugging me. He had this long list and he said, "This will cost this much." (angry/fed up voice) And he kept his head down. He (said loudly) *never* looked at us. This will cost this much. This will cost this much ... He never looked at us. And finally I said, (serious question) "Do you take coupons?" (laughter) It just came out.

A mother implored attendees at her son's funeral to stop killing each other by lecturing them and singing a solo about their halfhearted efforts to end violence. She used herself to poignantly remind them that she could no longer help her son but they still had a chance. She implicitly directed the attendees to use her son as an object lesson and to lessen the needless loss of his life by turning things around.

I just wanted to be able to say something to the young people. And I saw that as an opportunity of being able to do that. 'Cause I begin to talk and I let them know that there was nuthin' that I could do for my child. Nothing more I could do for them. But I could let them know that they've got a chance and that they need to stop all the killing and just come together and love one another. I begin to sing a song called "Stop Going Through the Motions." I don't even know if it meant anything to these young people because they are all young and doin' their own thing. I just knew that I had to sing it. I don't know if the words mean anything to the young people. But the older people that was there. I'm sure that they understood. I, I hope it said somethin' to the younger people.

"Fighting for What's Right" consists of actions that take personal ownership or attempt to manage outcomes. Most often, they occur in response to feeling powerless or a lack of control.

LIVING IN WAYS THAT GIVE PURPOSE TO THE LOVED ONE'S DEATH

Homicide survivors feel a fierce commitment to their loved one. Besides being incensed by the needless loss of life, they value what his or her life now stands for. Their pain and outrage propel them in directions that provide purpose and create meaning out of a senseless act. Choices about how to live become testimonies to the fact that their loved one's life mattered as do the lives of others, including themselves.

"Others can benefit from my experience": Homicide survivors grow wise quickly and feel called to give because they know the territory others must cross. Their generative acts, though life-giving, validate their loss and what they have been through. By converting the bad that happened to them to good in contributing to the world, they transcend their own trauma. Helping others provides a way for them to meaningfully fit in the world and makes them feel worthwhile.

In the following example, a mother shared all she has left of her son with young delinquents in an effort to shock them into valuing their own lives. She carefully read the labels the police put on the envelopes that contained her son's personal effects and showed the condition of the clothing he was wearing when he was shot. The bonding that happened between her and these adolescents validated the significance of her son's death, affirmed her and her mission, and produced transcendent feelings of happiness.

This is all I had left of my son. A pair of tennis shoes and a pair of underwear that had no blood on them. He loved this little chain he had on. And you see how it's broken up, with a shot? Here's his earring. It was found on the ground. It was all I had. Look at this — "Homicide" — you know, ugh, ugly. "Personal Belongings — your number" "Days on Deceased"; "$13.37." That money's still in here. I won't be touching it. This sock still has the dirt where he fell. See, I use these in my little talks to the kids. That's my shock bag. These groups of young kids are sitting there like this (gestures), you know, thugs. And I just love every one of them. I hug them. And I tell them exactly about my son. I said, "My son went the same path as you. I'd like to see you [back] here in a year." They hugged me. I'm totally, totally committed to them. Driving home tonight from that group, I just get warm, like affirmation, and I always say to myself, "Have you ever had such a good feeling? Genuine feeling?" And I say that every time after [the group]. I'm just, I'm high on life driving home through the ghetto.

A mother attended a homicide support group to buttress survivors with the truths that had helped her maneuver through the aftermath of her son's death. Recognizing their vulnerability to their own self-condemnation and the judgments of others, she used her own experience to draw a map that anticipated the challenges and furnished a set of guiding principles that freed them to value their own process. She underscored what matters by being repetitious.

I went to Parents of Murdered Children for a period of time and I basically went to help others. That was my basic rule for going. I was there to help some of the people through it and to let them realize that you always try to blame yourself — what if, what if I, what if I — and just to let them realize that they couldn't have helped it. They couldn't have helped it. Number one is they are going to have problems on the first year of the holidays and number two is don't let anybody tell you how long you can grieve. People will say, "Well, you ought to be over it by now." I told that to a friend of mine. I said, "Don't let anybody tell you how long you should grieve. That's an individual thing. It's your thing. So when they come up to you and say, "Well aren't you over it," just look at them and laugh. Also, I said, "You are going to be driving down the street and thinking of something and you are going to start crying while you are driving," and I said, "Don't worry about it. Don't worry about it. That's what's going to happen. Just, just do it."

Living Life Deliberately Gives Me a Sense of Purpose

Homicide survivors intentionally make life-altering decisions out of a resolve to live in a different way. Convictions about what matters now move them into virgin territory where they determine to be proactive or make something important happen. Following through requires a deep commitment to themselves and what they believe. The actions the survivors take give them a sense of personal completion that helps generate wholeness and satisfaction.

In the following example, a mother decided to mother her dead son by attending and becoming a visible presence at every hearing held for the eight boys who killed him. She watched over her son and his welfare by sitting in for the victim and making the court system, as well as the boys, accountable to her. This deliberate act of dedication helped complete her as a mother and publicly established her loss and deep love for her son.

Mother: I don't know how many hours I spent in the courtroom but it was a ton because I went to every hearing they had for anything. I felt it was important that Nate was represented there. If they had to look at me and explain to me what they were going to do then probably we would get the best outcome we could get. I think maybe it helped them work a little harder. The judge looked at me every day and he knew who I was and he would check through the attorneys whether or not I was aware and OK with certain things. It did matter and my thought was that I always have wanted to be there for my kids and so this was my last time for Nate. He would expect it and it's something that I would do. I was still an important part in Nate's death. I was in his life and then in his death just to hold the system accountable, make sure that he wasn't just a number or an empty face, that he had impacted our lives and that he was important and that the best thing should come from the system.

A father pushed through a barrier by challenging himself to find the courage to make his loss and the murder of thousands of others visible. Although "coming out" was difficult, he realized that he had to answer to himself and accept unabashedly what had happened to him and who he was now. His decision to no longer hide helped resolve his shame and cemented his decision not to be controlled by people's discomfort.

I remembered coming back on the plane from [the national meeting of Parents of Murdered Children] and I was really enthused about doing things. And then the next year I went to Chicago to the second one and I was coming back the same way on the plane. I had bought this big red bumper sticker to put on my car the first year and as I was coming back from Chicago I said, "Well, you haven't done anything in a year." Anyway the next morning after I finished [breakfast], I put that on the car and it's been on every car I've ever had ever since. It was a hard thing to do at first but it's like so many things. [People] come up a lot when I park and somebody will look at it and … say, "That's a strange…." They don't know what to do. It just says Parents of Murdered Children. And it's bright red. You can't miss it. And I just decided, it's sort of like with the gay issue when I didn't tell that we had a gay son. So I just thought, "That's going to be your problem, not mine." Like I say, that's who we are now.

Living in ways that give purpose to the loved one's death consists of acts that aim to transcend the negativity or senselessness of the loved one's violent death. These undertakings either benefit others or give significance to the survivor's life.

DISCUSSION

The essential theme labeled as "the intense pursuit of what matters" has three manifestations that use different behaviors to cope with the negative conditions created by homicide. Declarations of truth consist of pronouncements that define territories of insincerity and personal autonomy. Fighting for what's right is comprised of acts that respond to specific injustices. Living in ways that give purpose to the loved one's death encompasses acts that transcend the murder in a life-affirming way. These behaviors occur in response to negatively appraised meanings. Studies of traumatic death suggest that certain negative conditions such as death imagery or shattered worldviews may impede finding meaning as sense making or benefit finding (Davis et al., 2000; Janoff-Bulman, 1992; Rynearson, 2001; Rynearson & McCreery, 1993). However, the negative meanings given to events by the homicide survivors in this previously published study helped elicit meaning-making behaviors connected to naming truth, problem solving, and the revamping of life goals. It is possible that these behaviors establish or reinforce a sense of mastery and control in the midst of conditions that may not be within a person's control. A sense of accomplishment may generate positive affect to help bolster homicide survivors through the otherwise arduous journey. Moreover, the accumulation of actions over time may give family members a base from which to construct coherent narratives in which their experience is central.

Meaning making associated with the "the intense pursuit of what matters" occurred on both an intrapersonal and interpersonal level. The intrapersonal level consisted of the survivor's appraisal of self and other, including the significance to the survivor of his or her behavior. The interpersonal level consisted of actions done in response to external events and meaning made in interaction with others, including family, friends, representatives of social institutions, and others in the community. These two levels show that the performative dimension of meaning making may use both personal construct theory (Kelly, 1955) at the intrapersonal level and the theory of social constructionism (Gergen, 1998; McNamara & Gergen, 1999; Shotter, 1996) at the interpersonal level to explain how meaning making occurs. Personal construct theory is built on the premise that the individual seeks to understand his or her environment by attributing unique meanings to the data of his or her experience (Neimeyer, Epting, & Krieger, 1984). Social constructionism maintains that psychological reality is socially constructed and that meanings are realized through joint action or the continuously unfolding relations occurring between ourselves and others (Berger & Luckmann, 1966; Shotter, 1996).

PSYCHOLOGICAL IMPLICATIONS OF MEANING
MAKING GROUNDED IN ACTION

Meaning making serves to reestablish the coherence and continuity of the self by reducing the dissonance created by the conflict between pre- and postrealities. Rynearson (2001) contends that looking for life-generating meaning in the violent death itself cannot reduce the dissonance. Data from the study of homicide survivors suggest that they decreased the dissonance by intensely pursuing "what matters now" in relationship to the homicide. Specifically, their ability to act in accordance with their beliefs creates an internal resonance that is self-affirming. Consequently, when homicide survivors confront someone who has made an insensitive comment, they act in ways that are congruent with their upset and the meaning assigned to that person's behavior. The sense of agency required by such a pursuit, and the feeling of completion that comes from addressing what matters, produces a sense of coherence that gives order, meaningfulness, and comprehensibility to the interaction. The internal experience of the individual is that "I make sense." This unity may counter the dissonance that can otherwise fragment the self.

The intense pursuit of what matters also creates a sense of continuity since the accumulation of individual acts about what matters provides an ongoing history from the time of the trauma to the present. Moreover, the formation of causal linkages between meaningful acts generates movement and directionality from event to event. Frequently, the response to each event grows out of the response to the event that preceded it. The internal experience of the individual is that "I go on." Continuity of self, marked by significant acts, affirms the existence of a person in historic time. Consequently, when a homicide survivor repeatedly visits the victim's grave, he or she establishes a pattern of remembrance that validates his or her ongoing love and commitment never to forget. Because the persistence required by this ritual is marked by time, the homicide survivor may experience a sense of personal endurance that is self-stabilizing and counters the despair associated with emptiness.

The pursuit of what matters contributes to the coherence and continuity of self. The intensity that fuels that pursuit is powerful because it provides an experience of self as enlarged due to the presence of strong emotions, clarity of purpose, and strength of commitment.

Additionally, pursuits related to what matters help establish a social identity because many of them involve interactions with others who also have a stake in the murder and how it is portrayed. Sometimes these pursuits are expressed through internalized conversations with key players or constructive activities that can benefit other people. More often these pursuits occur in reaction to unexpected events that compel homicide survivors to take action in order to minimize harm or prevent additional losses to themselves or others. Encounters, for example, with representatives of social institutions, the community, family, or friends, can be, in effect, meaning-making arguments or conversations over who has the power to decide outcomes or define and determine how the murder, the homicide victim, and the family will be perceived. A daughter's struggle, for example, with the coroner for information about the extent of her father's wounds is thus a fight for the power to control access to information that rightfully belongs to her. These struggles for personal justice can be ironically empowering in that they force homicide survivors to think and act in ways that are determinative of their new social identity. By intensely pursuing what matters, homicide survivors, therefore, lay the foundation for another kind of membership in the community.

The intense pursuit of what matters by homicide survivors attempts to make order and establish control through acts of inferred meaning. Besides creating a sense of personal coherence and continuity, these acts, in concert with other people, further the development of a social identity and construct new ways to belong. Therefore, identity reconstruction as formulated by Neimeyer and Anderson (2002) is inherent to this process as homicide survivors are compelled to live differently in a changed world.

ADVANCING MEANING MAKING IN CLINICAL PRACTICE

Homicide survivors may not recognize that meaning making is occurring because meaning itself may be a by-product of and imbedded in numerous or small actions. Moreover, meaning making is usually not deliberate. Rather, it is generated in reaction to intrusive stimuli. Consequently, the clinician's role is to recognize those behaviors that may be manifestations of the intense pursuit of what matters and help clients identify with the symbolic meaning inferred by the behaviors. This process amplifies the importance of seemingly minor acts and highlights the intentionality and deeper meaning behind them. It promotes identity reconstruction because it helps clients identify with what they themselves have created.

The clinician's ability to advance meaning making rests on waiting for significant events to emerge during client sessions, distinguishing those cues that indicate the client's pursuit of what matters, and responding in ways that elevate and encourage the pursuit. During a therapy session, a sister whose brother had been killed by his wife began to express anger toward her church after she discovered that it set aside a week in recognition of prisoners' rights but gave no such attention to victims' needs. She made a casual remark about having written down her complaint anonymously on the church bulletin and stuffed it in the church donation box for someone to find. The clinician recognized the importance of the client's anger and the declaration she was making to expose what, for her, constituted unfair or hypocritical behavior. The clinician also understood that the issue of victim invisibility is central to the stigma and alienation generally felt by homicide survivors. The clinician therefore assumed the role of compassionate witness to the client's story in order to honor the magnitude of the injustice and the symbolic meaning of her protest. Then the clinician countered the client's attempts to minimize the significance of her behavior by suggesting that, in fact, her "minor" act was important because she was trying to educate the church about the experience of victims and their right to be seen. As such, the client was fighting to correct what was wrong. The clinician inferred from this behavior that the client, though apprehensive, might consider making herself a more visible advocate. The clinician therefore proposed a hypothetical meeting with the pastor about the church's need to counter social stigma and injustice by also recognizing victims of crime. Although the clinician understood that the client might not want to meet with the pastor now or ever, the planning for such a meeting underscored the importance of the client's initial pursuit and used the direction from the client about what matters to help the client contemplate additional choices that would extend the sense of mission. Several months later, the client announced that she had a productive meeting with the pastor who knew nothing about the experience of homicide survivors. The pastor subsequently agreed to designate another week during the year to crime victims and their needs.

A clinician's ability to recognize the behavioral indicators of meaning making helps clients honor their own emotional process and the importance of living more deliberately. The accumulation of acts over time gives them the base from which to construct coherent narratives that make their experience central. The clinician's role, therefore, is to be a watchful observer, a witness to outwardly inconsequential events, an interpreter of the symbolic significance of client's actions, and an advocate for constructive and instrumental behavior.

CONCLUSION

The performative dimension of meaning making may be a particularly relevant arena to explore in dealing with traumatized populations who otherwise struggle to cognitively reconcile images of violent dying with memories of tenderness or acts of destruction with global beliefs about a benevolent world. Family members of persons who have died from suicide, been killed in motor vehicle crashes, or been the casualties of medical negligence may pursue what matters by using some of the meaning-making processes noted in this chapter. Victims traumatized by physical, sexual, and emotional abuse may also use mechanisms such as declarations of truth or fighting for what's right to redress the violation and reconstruct their lives. Furthermore, people whose worldviews are threatened by the meaninglessness of a particular event may exercise some of the behaviors that comprise "the intense pursuit of what matters" as a response to those situations that have no redemptive value.

Meaning making grounded in action has been portrayed as activism in relation to behaviors performed by persons who have been traumatized (Office of Victims of Crime Bulletin, 1998). Although this categorization recognizes the significance of empowering behavior, it assigns a function to behavior that may not adequately represent the meaning that the behavior signifies. For example, the concept of activism may exclude behavior that is not aimed at changing social conditions. Moreover, because activism assumes some level of premeditated planning, it may not reflect impulsive behavior generated by unexpected and volatile situations or behavior generated by an impromptu rather than integrated self (Langer, 1991). Finally, the concept of activism embodies the formation of noble goals and may not be inclusive enough of practices that create provisional meaning in small ways (Debats, 1998).

Future research is needed to examine how populations who deal with different kinds of trauma use or add to the processes described in this chapter. Additional studies on homicide survivors are needed both to replicate findings and examine the performative dimension of meaning making by culturally diverse groups. An important area for clinical practice is whether the processes that comprise "the intense pursuit of what matters" build resilience in response to trauma. Literature on posttraumatic stress indicates that people can thrive as a result of coping with stress (Calhourn & Tedeschi, 2001; Tedeschi, Park, & Calhoun, 1998). Disruptions in worldviews force fundamental changes in belief systems and the reordering of priorities. Coping effectively with traumatic events may result in closer relationships, new coping skills, and enhanced personal resources. Finally, research on trauma and meaning making grounded in action should examine the relationship between meaning making, social context, and the nature of the trauma. Many of the processes used in the intense pursuit of what matters reflect the public nature of dying by homicide. Populations traumatized by conditions other than homicide may also face distinctive challenges and create unique meaning-making responses grounded in action.

REFERENCES

Armour, M. P. (2002). The journey of homicide families: A qualitative study of their post homicide experience. American Journal of Orthopsychiatry, 72, 372–382.

Attig, T. (1996). How we grieve: Relearning the world. New York: Oxford University Press.

Attig, T. (2001). Relearning the world: Making and finding meanings. In R. A. Neimeyer (Ed.), Meaning reconstruction and the experience of loss (pp. 35–53). Washington D.C.: American Psychological Association.

Berger, P. L., & Luckmann, T. (1966). Social construction of reality: A treatise in the sociology of knowledge. Garden City, NY: Doubleday.

Calhourn, L. G. & Tedeschi., R. G. (2001). Posttraumatic growth: The positive lessons of loss. In R. A. Neimeyer (Ed.), Meaning reconstruction and the experience of loss (pp. 157–172). Washington D.C.: American Psychological Association.

Davis, C. G., Nolen-Hoeksema, S., & Larson, J. (1998). Making sense of loss and benefiting from the experience: Two construals of meaning. Journal of Personality and Social Psychology, 59, 561–574.

Davis, C. G., Wortman, C. B., Lehman, D. R., & Silver, R. C. (2000). Searching for meaning in loss: Are clinical assumptions correct? Death Studies, 24, 497–540.

Debats, D. L. (1998). Measurement of personal meaning: The psychometric properties of the Life Regard Index. In P. T. P. Wong & P. S. Fry (Eds.), The human quest for meaning: A handbook of psychological research and clinical applications . Mahwah, NJ: Lawrence Erlbaum.

Doka, K. (2002). Disenfranchised grief: New directions, challenges, and strategies for practice (2nd ed.). San Francisco: Jossey Bass.

Folkman, S. (1997). Positive psychological states and coping with severe stress. Social Science Medicine, 45, 1207–1221.

Gergen, K. J. (1998). Social theory in context: relational humanism. Available: http://www. swarthmore.edu/SpcSci/kgergen 1/text6.ht.

Giorgi, A. (1985). The phenomenological psychology of learning and the verbal learning tradition. In A. Giorgi (Ed.), Phenomenology and psychological research (pp. 23–85). Pittsburgh, PA: Duquesne University.

Giorgi, A. (1997). The theory, practice, and evaluation of the phenomenological method as a qualitative research procedure. Journal of Phenomenological Psychology, 28, 235–260).

Janoff-Bulman, R. (1992). Shattered assumptions: Towards a new psychology of trauma. New York: Free Press.

Kelly, G. A. (1955). Personal construct theory. New York: W.W. Norton.

Langer, L. L. (1991). Holocaust testimonies: The ruins of memory. New Haven, CT: Yale University Press.

Lehman, D. R., Wortman, C. B., & Williams, A. F. (1987). Long term effects of losing a spouse or child in a motor vehicle crash. Journal of Personality and Social Psychology, 52, 218–231.

McNamara, S. & Gergen, K. J. (1999). Relational responsibility: Resources for sustainable dialogue. In S. McNamara & K. J. Gergen (Eds.), Relational responsibility: Resources for sustainable dialogue. Thousand Oaks, CA: Sage.

Murphy, S. A. (1999). PTSD among bereaved parents following the violent deaths of their 12-to-28-year old children: A longitudinal prospective analysis. Journal of Traumatic Stress, 12, 273–291.

Murphy, S. A., Johnson, I. C., Lohan, J., & Tapper, V. J. (2002). Bereaved parents' use of individual, family, and community resources 4 to 60 months after a child's violent death. Family and Community Health, 25, 71–82.

Murphy, S. A., Johnson, L.C., & Lohan, J. (*in press*). Finding meaning in a child's violent death: A five-year prospective analysis of parents' personal narratives and empirical data. Death Studies.

Neimeyer, R. A. (2000). Searching for the meaning of meaning: Grief therapy and the process of reconstruction. Death Studies, 24, 541–550.

Neimeyer, R. A. (2001). Reauthoring life narratives: Grief therapy as meaning reconstruction. Israel Journal of Psychiatry & Related Sciences, 38, 171–183.

Neimeyer, R. A. & Anderson, A. (2002). Meaning reconstruction theory. In N. Thompson (Ed.), Loss and grief (pp. 45–64). New York: Palgrave.

Neimeyer, R.A., Epting, F. R. & Krieger, S. R. (1984). Personal Consonal Constructs in thanatology: An introduction and research bibliography. In F. R. Epting & R. A. Neimeyer (Eds.) *Personal Meanings of Death*: Applications *of personal construct theory to clinical practice* (pp. 87-94).

Neimeyer, R. A. & Jordan, J. R. (2002). Disenfranchisement as empathic failure. In K.Doka (Ed.), Disenfranchised grief: New directions, challenges, and strategies for practice. San Francisco: Jossey Bass.

Neimeyer, R. A., Prigerson, H. G., & Davies, B. (2002). Mourning and meaning. Mareican Behavioral Scientist, 46, 235–251.

Office of Victims of Crime Bulletin (1998). New directions from the field: Victims' rights and services for the 21st century — Victim's rights. (Vol. 2). Washington, D.C.: U.S. Department of Justice, Office of Justice Programs, Office for Victims of Crime.

Park, C. L. & Folkman, S. (1997). Meaning in the context of stress and coping. Review of General Psychology, 1, 115–144.

Pennebaker, J. W. (1997). Opening up: The healing power of expressing emotions. New York: Guilford.

Pennebaker, J. Z. E. & Rime, B. (2001). Disclosing and sharing emotion: Psychological, social, and health consequences. In M. S. Stroebe & R. O. Hansson (Eds.), Handbook of bereavement research: Consequences, coping, and care (pp. 517–543). Washington, D.C.: American Psychological Association.

Prigerson, H. G., Bierhals, A. J., Stanislav, V. K., Raynolds, C. F., Shear, M. K., Day, N., Beery, L. C., Newsom, J. T., & Jacobs, S. (1997). Traumatic grief as a risk factor for mental and physical morbidity. American Journal of Psychiatry, 154, 616–623.

Rynearson, E. (2001). Retelling violent death. Philadelphia: Brunner-Rutledge.

Rynearson, E. K. & McCreery, J. M. (1993). Bereavement after homicide: A synergism of trauma and loss. American Journal of Psychiatry, 150, 258–261.

Shotter, J. (1996). Social construction as social poetics: Oliver Sacks and the Case of Dr, P. Available: http://www.massey.ac.nz/~ALock/virtual/sacksdrp.ht.

Tedeschi, R. G., Park, C.L., & Calhoun, L. G. (1998). Posttraumatic growth: Positive change in the aftermath of crisis. Mahwah, NJ: Erlbaum.

7

Considering Medication Use in the Wake of Traumatic Experience: Neurobiology, Affect Dysregulation, and the Psychiatrist as a Witness Who May Also Prescribe

RICHARD A. CHEFETZ

NEUROBIOLOGY AND PSYCHOPHARMACOLOGY

The author of this chapter, "a psychiatrist who does a lot of long term work with people who have been severely wounded by life," continues the tone of thoughtful reflections on meaning on the topic of neurobiology and medication. He begins with a mythic reference to Chiron, the wounded healer, as a model for the empathic caregiver and "empathically" presents a wondrously wise simplification of the neurobiology of affect, autonomic nervous system function, an understanding of the experiential dimensions of affect, the meaning of medication, the value of learning from placebo success, and some of the "tricks of the trade" in prescribing psychotropic agents. Later in the book, when authors refer to the neurobiology of trauma and grief and pharmacotherapy, the reader will have a much fuller understanding of its fundamentals because of this chapter.

Once upon a time, in a faraway land, there lived a centaur named Chiron, half-man and half-horse. He was not well liked by his brother centaurs. While they preferred the arts of war, drinking, and bawdy socializing, he studied the world, marveling at its complexity and diversity. He became a student of the flow of life in the plants and animals of the world, so much so that he discovered their healing properties, a magic that grew indifferently in the fields and soil around his home. He became a knowledgeable healer. After a while, the gods of Olympus took note of his skills, his qualities as one who was especially learned about medicinal plants, and asked him to tutor their children in the ways of the world. He gave of himself generously, and the gods bestowed immortality upon him, in payment for his services.

One evening, during a drunken meal, his jealous brothers fought. In the melee, a magic arrow plucked from the quiver of an unsuspecting Achilles was shot into Chiron's knee. While he was immortal and the ensuing infection could not kill him, it nevertheless caused unremitting pain and foul suppuration. He wished to die from his wounds and end his suffering. The gods would not take back his immortality, and so he continued to suffer.

There are a number of different versions of how Chiron dealt with his pain. Regardless, the ancients clearly intended that there be a story about a healer, who would also be a person who knew pain — intimately and relentlessly. Such a model also fits the modern clinician, a wounded healer (Guggenbuhl-Craig, 1971). This is the starting point for appreciating the dilemma we face as we try to understand the hearts and minds of those who have been wounded; we have to face our own wounds, and know our own pain if we are going to be of service in healing the wounds of others. It is also true, that in making conscious our own wounds as healers, we may come to know the gifts of the wounded, who often offer healing to the healer. At times, it is only in the willingness of a healer to accept such a gift from one who is wounded that healing can occur. It is this particular tension within us all that is our companion as we consider an approach to the use of medication as an adjunct to healing the wounds of a person's mind, body, and soul when he or she has been a witness to violent death. How do we understand our patients in the midst of their pain? How do we ensure that psychopharmacologic prescribing follows the dictum: "First, do no harm"? And what is it, after all, that we will be treating? Let's start our quest by defining the landscape in which we will journey.

I will be describing not simply how to choose a medication, but how to think about understanding what is happening in a person who is seeking help after being a witness to an emotionally overwhelming event. I believe that to do the best we can do for our patients we need to combine the art of prescribing with the arts of psychotherapeutic understanding. In what follows, I will be describing the way I work with people who hire me to help them figure out if medication would be useful to them. I wish I had worked this way years ago. I suppose I'll just keep practicing, as my old friend Jack

Hardy used to chide me. If I practice long enough, then maybe I'll finally get it right!

WHAT IS A TRAUMA?

The definitions of trauma in the *Diagnostic and Statistical Manual of Mental Disorders* (DSM-IV-TR; American Psychiatric Association, 2000) rely upon a kind of consensus view of what constitutes a violent experience before labeling it a trauma. There is the need to make an assessment of whether or not the event in question involved actual or threatened death or serious injury, or a threat to the physical integrity of self or others, and that the response involved intense fear, helplessness, or horror. The main focus is on the size/power of the event, and secondarily on an emotional response.

There are additional psychological factors to consider too. What distinguishes an acute stress disorder from a posttraumatic stress disorder, by definition, is the initial presence of symptoms of dissociation in the peritraumatic period (Cardena & Spiegel, 1993) (Classen, Koopman, Hales, & Spiegel, 1998): emotional numbing, narrowed conscious awareness (e.g., being in a daze), derealization (the world is not real or has an unreal quality), and depersonalization ("I am not in my body, I am feeling unreal, or somehow feel not connected to my body"). All of these particular symptoms modify our ability to know feeling, emotion. Affect is the great contextualizer of experience (Chefetz, 2000a). If it is absent, then experience loses its "punch." The form in which affective experience is altered distinguishes one kind of dissociative response from another. In thinking about trauma and grief, we might do well to begin by considering alterations in the psychological metabolism of affect, the stuff out of which feelings come, and a matching definition of trauma. It is in the "feeling" of a trauma that the impact is experienced.

I believe that it is most parsimonious to have a definition of trauma that relies upon how we understand the affective dimensions of being human, rather than a consensus agreement on whether or not an event is awful enough to consider it traumatic and whether or not there has been a generic response. What is most problematic about trauma is the specific effect it has on human relatedness. None of us is so capable that we are able to live for long in isolation. Severe trauma impairs the ability to communicate with others on both narrative and emotional levels (Ledoux, 1996; Metcalfe & Jacobs, 1996; Rauch et al., 1996). Furthermore, severe trauma wounds self-regard, identity, and the ability to link affect, somatic sensation, and action scripts, and integrate this traumatic narrative into the longer narrative of a person's life. When the trauma is interpersonal, rather than as a result of a weather disaster, for example, additional experiences of shame, humiliation, terror, and basic loss of trust in other humans may be salient (Bromberg, 1998; Krystal, 1988; Liotti, 1999 Lyons-Ruth, 2003; Lyons-Ruth, Bronfman, & Parsons, 1999; Main & Morgan, 1996; Ulman & Brothers, 1988; van der Kolk, 1994; van Ijzendoorn, 1995). In this chapter,

I will use the following definition of trauma: *Trauma is the experience of an event or ongoing circumstances that an individual can neither assimilate nor accommodate into his or her existing world/self/other view, resulting in the impairment of basic capacities to know feelings and thoughts, maintain a coherent sense of self/identity, and manage relationships with others while living productively in community.* From this perspective, if we are to understand trauma more intimately, then we need to start with the basics of how we experience ourselves and the world.

UNDERSTANDING THE BASICS OF EMOTION: NEUROANATOMY FOR THE UNINITIATED

We can understand a lot about traumatic experience if we know something about our brains, and the wider nervous system. If we work with accurate metaphor rather than trying to absorb technical details of our brain's structure, then the neuroanatomically naïve clinician can gain a knowledgeable foothold that will inform his or her clinical work.

"Feeling" is to interpersonal relationships as sensation is to "touching the world." Feeling provides inward sensing while our five senses provide outward sensing. We sense into relatedness by having consciousness for inward sensing, feeling, in response to being present with another person. We can quickly feel something about someone to the extent that we have a pretty clear notion as to whether it might be okay to ask a particular stranger for directions in a busy railway station. There are other people we might easily avoid, even without realizing we are doing that. But we use our feelings, call it intuition, to guide our choices in life. When we try to think our way through a busy situation we may be left overwhelmed with the detail that feeling cuts right through to a conclusion.

What are feelings? Consider the language of emotion: "light-hearted," "weighed-down depressed," "nauseous with fear," "flushed with shame," "dancing with joy!" Emotional language often contains reference to our bodies. I prefer to use the word *affect* to refer to the somatic experiences associated with what will later be named as a specific "emotion," and eventually be experienced as a specific "feeling." The emotion is the named construct of a psychophysiologic flow that results in consciousness of a feeling. These feelings arise out of affects that are representative of the somatic stirrings associated with an ongoing physiologic experience in life. Affects team up like the mixing of the winds and blow us in one direction or another as we talk about feeling "moved" to take action.

Amygdala: sorts affects by intensity, not "good" or "bad" qualities

The amygdala is an almond-sized organ that sits in the center of the brain, below the anatomic location of the massive thinking, sensing, and moving centers of the cerebral cortex, the part of the brain that looks like a convoluted maze from the outside. The amygdala is part of a more primitive collection of brain organs that process affect. In particular, the amygdala seems to register fear. In fact, overly intense affect seems to be roughly equivalent to fear. We have all either heard or experienced someone saying that, "Things are just too intense and happening too fast, for me to be comfortable. I just can't take it all in." From our metaphorical perspective, that's the amygdala doing its work by sending signals that tell us to slow down before we blow our fuses. Too much excitement/surprise can cause fear. Too much intense affect can frighten us (Demos, 1995). Moreover, when the amygdala is overwhelmed, it seems that not only might we experience fear, but we also may find ourselves unable to speak (Rauch et al., 1996). The functional expressive aphasia occurs not only when we are frightened, but we can become speechless with joy! Remember, amygdala regulation of rising affect is about *intensity* of feeling, not good or bad feeling. In my clinical experience, this notion of sorting affect by intensity has been very useful in understanding why traumatized people don't tolerate too much of anything. They seek to avoid intensity, good or bad, happy or sad. Social and interpersonal withdrawal is the result. Understanding the neurobiology of affect can inform our clinical experience, and also help educate our patients in a way that relieves shame. The person who is speechless in their abuse, or witnessing of trauma, may have a neurobiologic circuit breaker open, rather than a failure of will or complicity in an outrage against their humanity.

Hippocampus: sorts "everyday" affects, provides time and spatial sense, as well as short term memory

The hippocampus sits adjacent to, and curls first behind and then in front of the almond-sized amygdala. In the simplified heuristic we are developing, this two-organ association is in the emotional center of the brain. The hippocampus plays a central role in sorting experience. If we are having a pretty good day, then the amygdala can take a break and let the hippocampus just sort things in regular memory by connecting to the language and mathematically oriented centers of the left brain, the left cerebral cortex. There is both a left and a right hippocampus and amygdala, but you don't need to know what they do, for our purposes. What I really hope you'll remember is that while hippocampal circuits connect with left brain language centers, amygdala circuits tend to go both to emergency circuits in the brain, and also to right brain circuits like visual, auditory, tactile, gustatory, and olfactory centers. Hippocampal connections are what lawyers and engineers rely upon. Amygdala connections are what artists and dancers coax into consciousness. There is one other amygdala connection of major significance in this discussion: centers that coordinate fine movement, in the cerebellum (a small area of cortex at the back of the brain that doesn't look convoluted like cerebral cortex, but instead looks like a modestly small ball of knitting wool). The take-home point is this: *traumatic experience tends to be encoded and then recalled in right brain and cerebellar regions.* Left brain language centers are not necessarily accessed when the amygdala is activated from being

Yes

overwhelmed with fear. *Trauma narratives are written in our bodily sensing experience, not our considered thoughts.*

You probably already get the drift of where this is leading. Hippocampally mediated experience is language dependent, and the more intense kinds of experience tend to be laden with sensory data. In fact, I've already noted evidence that when things get too intense, we lose our language skills, but we maintain our sensory impressions. We can't always speak during trauma experience, but we don't stop sensing. Since hippocampal processing of experience is bypassed when amygdala circuit breakers pop, we then have traumatic experience filtered through a sensorial symphony that may sound more like a kindergarten class that's been let loose to have unbridled play with the instruments of a chamber orchestra. Not only that, but cerebellar memory creates an odd kind of memory for position sense during traumatic experience. Dance and movement can kindle memory of trauma. It can also help us to heal, as our movement therapists know. The repetition in communal dancing is more than the good feeling of being together; it is, in my view, reestablishing healthy memory for movement that supersedes the proprioceptive memories of traumatic events and helps us remember what "normal" was about. We get back to our "roots," and we also change the hierarchy of recent cerebellar memories. We remember how to be ourselves when we engage in our communities.

What does stress/trauma do to the processing of emotion and experience?

Amygdala and hippocampal sorting of experience leads to memory in the right and left brain cerebral cortical "libraries" that are respectively sensorial and linguistic. (The emotional library is in the orbito-frontal cortex, behind our eyes, if you must know!) Stress changes function. Our ability to link cognition with emotion is impaired with trauma. When this unlinking occurs, we can call it a *dissociation of function.* Dissociation of cognitions and affects leads to an *inability to contextualize and formulate a coherent narrative for experience.* With this loss of narrative, there is limited ability to truly "know" what has happened. The lack of a coherent narrative for experience limits our human ability to review our lives and to grieve our losses. *Impaired grieving is at the core of what makes an experience traumatic rather than a source of resilience. Impaired grieving might therefore be thought of as at least a partial function of dissociation of the elements of experience.*

Look

When affective experiencing is impaired, and we can't really understand what has happened to us, not only is our ability to grieve impaired, but our ability to modulate new experience suffers. Our human tendency to be alert to danger becomes a caricature of itself, and we may lose our ability to sort threatening versus nonthreatening experience. Everything may be interpreted as containing threat. The hyperarousal and startle of posttraumatic disorders may be the result of this kind of process, both psychologically, and with its physiological correlates. After enough traumatic experience, the tendency is to expect trauma, and to physiologically move toward the extremes: hyper- or hypoarousal. Each of these has its own problems. However, in some ways, the hyperaroused person has an advantage. We have reasonable pharmacologic intervention to calm a nervous system in distress, but it is much more difficult to intervene psychopharmacologically when someone is hypoaroused: emotionally numb, depersonalized, and derealized.

In this section on neurobiology I have hoped to accomplish two things. First, I have illustrated the fundamental role of affect in both routine and traumatic experience, as well as its neurobiologic basis, and second, I have shown how a clinical appreciation of neurobiologic processes can change what we say to our patients and potentially relieve them of some of their pain. Yes, we can contrive neurobiologic explanations for the existence of transference, but the real value of this knowledge, in my opinion, is that it can *change the way we work with our patients.*

ADJUSTING THE SENSITIVITY AND SELECTIVITY OF THE NERVOUS SYSTEM: AUTONOMICS

The earth's atmosphere is filled with all manner of electromagnetic radiation, some of which we know as radio waves. If we try to tune in to our favorite station, we need to be right on the channel, or we end up listening to static, mostly random radio waves from things like sunspots, electrical transmission wires, and so on. If we have a good tuner, the sound is clear because we can select a signal and stay right on the station. And if the tuner is really sensitive, we can pick up distant signals and have a greater variety of stations to entertain us. Ideally we'd have a tuner that is both really sensitive, and really selective. It's the same for our nervous systems. Our ears and eyes, for example, have limits to their sensitivity and selectivity. Just try and follow a conversation in a noisy train station and you will get my point. Likewise, our brains have to decide what to listen to and what to ignore. A traumatized person will tend to either be shut down (hypoarousal), or on full alert (hyperarousal). The hyperaroused person has the problem of being so tuned in to every signal they perceive that they are quickly overwhelmed in any place that is not isolated. Moreover, the hyperarousal may extend to bodily sensing. In this case, everyday signals from a body begin to be interpreted as if they were catastrophic signals.

For example, a woman with hypochondriasis regularly sought the help of her doctors, complaining of serious and threatening pains in many different places in her body. Her doctors could never figure out what was wrong, but her pleadings for help often meant extra medical tests, expense, and some danger from experimentation with new treatments. After long discussion about her symptoms, it became clear that even as a child, she was bereft of anybody understanding her bodily experiences. Nobody ever helped her to calm down when she was hurt, and worse, her mother was herself terrified of her becoming ill. With each new sensation of everyday function that she noticed, she would panic.

[handwritten: We need both sensitivity & selectivity in CNS function]

Her nervous system was lit up like a fireworks display. She was engaged in full catastrophe living, but really, from her hyperaroused alertness, only feeling *the sensations of normal function*. She had the highest sensitivity to signals from her body, but no selectivity; she couldn't make out the difference between useful information and noise. If she was absorbed in a task, she felt better because she didn't notice she was feeling things in her body. It took about a year of working with this model for her hypochondriasis to remit.

Likewise, a chronically frightened woman developed a series of changes in her right arm including alterations of circulation, with mottling of her skin, pain in several fingers, exquisite painful sensitivity to light touch, and muscle stiffness. She met criteria for a complex regional pain syndrome. All of these changes were mediated by her autonomic nervous system. Not only was she frightened, but she was totally furious about mistreatment in both her childhood family and her adult workplace. It took a very long time for her to be willing to notice that when she became angry her pain increased dramatically, and that using hypnosis helped her pain to remit, temporarily.

The sympathetic nervous system is the division of the autonomic system that regulates this sensitivity/selectivity. It tends to speed things up and maintain alertness. There is a counterbalancing system, the parasympathetic, and it tends to slow things down. The prototype drug for the sympathetic system is adrenalin, and for the parasympathetic system it is atropine. Increased sympathetic tone is a common finding in posttraumatic disorders and is directly related to hyperarousal. However, when the nervous system can't shut out "static," it overreacts and exhausts a person's physical and emotional resources. Since the autonomics have direct connections to the emotional centers of the brain, our feelings have a very profound effect on our bodies through activation of the sympathetic nervous system. This is a major source of what stress does to bodies through a relentlessly hyperactive sympathetic response.

HYPOAROUSAL AND DEPERSONALIZATION

What about hypoarousal? People who are withdrawn into a physiologic shell don't appreciate being asked to leave their "safe place." For example, let's think about depersonalization. The studies done on its physiology are relatively unrevealing, though there are some brain regions that have increased activity during depersonalization (out of body experience). However, little is actually known about the physiology of depersonalization. It does seem that it represents a state of hypoarousal secondary to painful psychological experience and initial hyperarousal (Simeon, 2004). There is no particular established treatment for depersonalization, and the value of psychotherapy in its treatment has not been established (Khazaal,

Zimmermann, & Zullino, 2005). However, in my clinical experience the problem of the relative hypoarousal of depersonalization responds, slowly, to the establishment of a safe interpersonal relationship. Depersonalization, feeling not in one's body, feeling unreal in relation to one's self, is often associated with derealization, feeling unreal in relation to one's surroundings. While most people talk about "out of body experience" as the primary symptom of depersonalization, my observation is that this overstates the gravity of the experience. There are many less dramatic examples, including not feeling outside one's body, but strangely not being able to feel inside either, feeling just behind one's body but not really outside.

The problem of depersonalization becomes somewhat understandable through the lens of the neurobiology of affect proposed earlier. Affective instability, terror, leads to "giving up" somatic experience as a way to down-modulate feeling. The cost is a sense of not feeling real, not having a sense of being in one's body, being detached. For those persons whose bodies have been the scene of unspeakable abuse, shame, humiliation, or injury, the cost of not having a body may not seem so high. It is when there is enough healing in a person's life that the lack of attachment to one's physical self becomes painful. There is a longing to connect with being in the world.

It is the indescribable numbing pain of depersonalization that is often a motivating factor that brings people with depersonalization to treatment. Treatments which reduce anxiety and psychic pain seem to be helpful. Pharmacologic intervention is often of limited benefit, if any, in my experience. An offer of relatedness, in a psychotherapeutic environment, may seem a scant hope. However, it is a powerful medium of healing. The central problem beyond affect dysregulation in the secondary hypoarousal of depersonalization is a history of toxic relatedness to people. The "solution" to this is a healthy relationship that is offered, and can be taken up bit by bit, often over many years. The toxic relatedness may not be easy to discern, but a careful history may be quite revealing (Lyons-Ruth, 2003).

AFFECT DYSREGULATION AS A WAY OF LIFE

What is perhaps most sad about repetitive trauma and chronic complex bereavement is that our minds unconsciously learn how to achieve some protection from pain, and the protection is often painful in and of itself. In this scenario, the addictive behaviors associated with impaired grief, which are so much a part of psychiatric practice, become more intelligible. For example, bulimia often follows the pattern of eating until a stomach is impossibly, painfully bloated. At that point, all affective attention becomes focused on the pain. The bulimic then has a clear reason upon which they can focus their understanding that they are in "pain." Their psychic pain becomes "visible" in their physical pain, while this "sleight of mind" remains unconscious. Additionally, the physical pain acts as an all consuming and compelling distraction from any thought or feeling. With purging, the bulimic will often report achieving a kind of trancelike or dissociative "swoon," and a period of sleep, afterward. With that sleep, wakefulness follows that may be a little disoriented, and is very much like someone having pressed the reset button on their computer after a "screen freeze." The bulimic knows the behavior is self-destructive, but it is also one of the few ways she or he can get effective relief from her or his psychological pain.

There are countless variations on this theme of managing a deep unconscious pain by creating and modulating one that is palpable on the surface. Pharmacologic efforts to interrupt the paradoxical self-soothing qualities of self-destructive actions must be aimed at the source of the deep pain in order to have any real efficacy. The same is true regarding the sources of grief. Selective serotonin reuptake inhibitors (SSRIs), cause a loss of affective awareness. Less arousal relieves the urge to repetitively engage in self-harming behaviors that are generated by hyperarousal. In my experience, affect dysregulation is at the center of addictive behaviors, just as it is at the core of the relentlessness of intractable grief. The grief may take on an affect regulatory function, and become a "necessary" means with which to maintain psychological equilibrium. This intractable grief is no different from intractable shame that acts as a protection from the intense pain of overwhelming loss, helplessness, and terror.

WHAT IS ANXIETY?

I find it a useful heuristic to think of anxiety as related to specific emotions as color is related to blue, green, red, and so on. Anxiety is undifferentiated affect that is both a striving for conscious expression and blocked from reflective awareness and coherence. Feelings don't happen without training. We learn to feel via the special socialization processes in infancy that are described as right brain learning (Schore, 2003). We teach our children how to be emotionally competent. That said, states of anxiety often represent particular feelings that for one reason or another can't make their way into consciousness. For example, there is shame-anxiety, anger-anxiety, sadness-anxiety, fear-anxiety. This is all modulated to some extent by the sympathetic nervous system.

Autonomic nervous system "tone" is reflected in our "gut" feelings. The gastrointestinal (GI) tract has more neurons than any other place outside the brain. It is literally wrapped from mouth to anus in a "neural stocking mesh." After all, the GI tract is a place where the outside world "enters" our body. There would be few things of more "concern" to an organism. Gut feelings are eliminated, for example, by the pain of bulimic bingeing, and if the gut feelings are related to chronic anxiety over an unresolved loss, then the bingeing can be thought of as an affective banishing act mindlessly perpetrated to eliminate feeling. Gut feelings may be thought of as responsible for bowel activity that leads to diarrhea when frightened, or vomiting when seeing something disgusting. Anxiety may be slight or profound. Either way it is associated with specific affects that are often partly modulated by autonomic factors.

People can learn the somatic activation patterns that are associated with each of the affects and the associated felt "feelings" during a careful psychotherapeutic investigation. It is a short step from body consciousness to using the names of feelings, if a clinician focuses on that. It is amazing how many people are not at all conscious of their bodies as a source of useful information about how they are feeling. They are not numb, they are just not focused. If this kind of exploratory psychotherapeutic option is not available to help people learn to know their feelings, name them, and work with them, then medication becomes a necessary route. Ancillary treatments such as hypnosis, acupuncture, or meditation may substitute quite well for psychopharmacologic intervention, in some cases. Pharmacologic solutions that inhibit feeling are not helpful. However, that said, overwhelming anxiety can be a bigger problem than the potential for emotional numbing in psychopharmacological treatment. The point is that you need to be aware of both the psychological cost and benefit if you engage in prescribing.

IDEAL DRUGS AND THE REALITY OF PSYCHOTROPIC AGENTS

An ideal psychotropic medication would target a symptom, remove it, have no effect on any other mode of physiology, no side effects, not require more than one dose to do its job, and return an individual to a natural state of being within a day. Real life is much more complicated. The reality is that prescribing an agent to reduce anxiety, for example, usually means balancing relief of anxiety with inducing sleep, decreasing physical agility, decreasing mental alertness, or creating a sense of physical lassitude that can precipitate a depression. Pregnant women may be at increased risk of having children with birth defects from the use of benzodiazepines, and newborns with circulating benzodiazepines may have altered temperature regulation, decreased medical consciousness, and other dangerous side effects.

Recent literature reviews suggest that there may be less risk to the unborn child from most antidepressants than was previously thought (Lattimore et al., 2005), but there is also clarity that these drugs will pass through breast milk to infants (Iqbal, Sobhan, & Ryals, 2002). Nobody really knows if the amounts cause a significant effect or not for the infant. What would you do if you were depressed or anxious, grieving, and nursing an infant, your only child? The wisdom of the situation would seem to be to avoid medications when possible, and use the lowest possible doses, avoiding dosing regimens that cause major peak blood levels by spreading out doses, avoid dosing just before breasts are filling with milk, and having a well-informed partner in decision making.

In adults, agents to relieve depression routinely mean weighing the potentials for agitation versus somnolence, weight gain or loss, dry mouth, and, with SSRIs, a penalty for suddenly running out of a drug that creates an unpleasant, but not fatal, withdrawal syndrome characterized by increased anxiety and somatic sensations that patients have described as "small, fleeting, electric like 'shocks'". Lower doses of many of the SSRIs are useful for anxiety (e.g., sertraline at 25 mg daily, or fluoxitene at 10 mg each morning). These effects may start within a day, in contrast to the several weeks it might take for antidepressant activity. Venalfaxine is an excellent antianxiety agent at 12.5 mg three times daily, though it is best known as a powerful antidepressant. However, its withdrawal syndrome is very unpleasant.

SUICIDE AND MEDICATION

There is significant controversy about whether or not some antidepressants increase the risk for suicide. Traditionally, any antidepressant may cause the unfortunate experience of giving a severely depressed and lethargic person a sudden burst of physical energy prior to lifting their mood. This means that someone without the energy to kill themselves may feel strong enough to do the deed, long before his or her mood improves. Patients need to be warned about this potential. Visiting frequently with suicidal patients, making contact by telephone, involving family members, and hospitalization may all be important options. If a particular medication is going to make things worse, careful and regular contact with depressed patients, after starting medication, will often catch an untoward event. Each clinician needs to find his or her own style, tailored to what the patients need.

PSYCHOPHARMACOLOGIC TRANSFERENCE

The problem with psychotropic prescribing is that it works. I say that because I know it works, and is extraordinarily useful, sometimes lifesaving. You can read the statistics with little effort, I won't repeat them here. What is most striking is the extent to which placebos often work as well, or simply a little less often than medication (Bootzin & Bailey, 2005; Kradin, 2004), but still achieve significant response rates in many studies. In many respects then, they are the ideal drug: no side effects, no toxicity, and they relieve the target symptom. My sense is, however, that placebos work best when expertly prescribed. What does that mean for prescribing nonplacebo, real medication? Whatever dose of medication is prescribed, its efficacy will reflect the qualities of relatedness between the prescribing physician and the patient. I suppose that's not mainstream psychopharmacologic thinking, but it is my observation. Moreover, proper follow-up in the first few days after prescribing, initiated by the psychiatrist, creates a level of collaboration and expectation that facilitates the efficacy of medication. What I really want to know is this: What is it in those placebos that make them so effective? So far as I can tell, it is the feeling of being with the prescribing clinician: a dash of hope, a pinch of confidence, a flourish of respect and validation for a person's pain, and a generous and spiritually grounded regard for the dignity of the patient.

PSYCHOPHARMACOLOGIC COUNTERTRANSFERENCE

During the years when I was a rural family physician in the foothills of the Blue Ridge Mountains of Virginia, I would sometimes meet people while traveling. It always warmed my spirit to hear them say how wonderful they thought I was for being a country doctor! When I became a psychiatrist, the response of most people, upon hearing of my professional work, was a curtain-dropping: "Oh." End of conversation. To say that never affected me would be an outright lie. I have learned to agree that I'm a "shrink," but quickly add that I'm the kind of shrink that shrinks problems, not people!

In the midst of emotional crisis, psychiatrists are called in to work their magic and fix things. I sure wish I had half the magic people think I have. Actually, I have to be careful to not believe the good press I do get. I don't have much magic at all. I pretty much just have me, and an occasional medication that might do some good. I don't really feel very magical when making an assessment of someone's suicidality. Instead, I feel pretty intensely, and have to work hard to make hard decisions and believe in the potential for healing in the souls of the deeply wounded.

In my 45 hours, or so, of direct patient care each week, when levels of grieving reach a certain point, it gets very hard to really listen, focus, respond, validate, and emote. At the end of some days, a gentle hug from my lovely wife, a psychoanalyst, often is accompanied by a sense of my armor falling like scales to the floor. I'm usually unconscious of the extent to which I withdraw to protect myself from feeling more overwhelmed than I already am during my work day, but my sharpest patients pick it up in a flash and ask if I've had a hard day. How aware of being overwhelmed are you? What do you do to take off your armor? What do you do to cultivate having a life of your own? At what point of feeling overwhelmed do you stop listening "between the lines." In working with a grieving and suicidal person, it is sometimes the pause in response to a question of mine that opens a whole vista of suicidal planning. I need to listen for the pause that kills. I need to hear it loud and clear, and I need to ask about it without reservation or hesitation. I need to be able to listen, and to know when I've stopped.

Regardless of what is going on in my life, or in my mind at the moment in which I am with my patient I need to *be* with them. Is that magic? Maybe. It might be magic for someone who hasn't had anybody look at them and engage his or her eyes for a year or a life. Sometimes it seems that there's nothing other than honestly being present and being a genuine and truthful witness to the grief that pours into the room, swimming, floating, staying with my patient until the wave recedes. That doesn't always fit into an appointment schedule, so I make the schedule fit the patient. Sometimes I make an effort to ensure that particular patient is the last to be seen before a lunch break, or the end of the day if I know what's coming.

Psychopharmacologic prescribing is less about the best drug you can pick to treat depression or anxiety, and more about making a connection with patients so that you can be clear that they need a medication or not, and if so, what drug "their lives" would pick if they were doing the choosing. I don't think I am belaboring this by saying it yet another way. I see too many patients who have never "met" their psychiatrist before to just be casual about this issue. I hold the standard of care in being a psychiatrist as inclusive of the psychiatrist as witness, not just as technician who assesses and prescribes.

SOME SPECIFIC PSYCHOPHARMACOLOGIC INTERVENTIONS IN THE TREATMENT OF ACUTE AND CHRONIC GRIEF

What Is the Target Symptom?

I want to know enough about the specific details of a symptom to know how to assess a change that might occur from use of a medication. If anxiety occurs every day at about 5 p.m., then I want to know the patient's associations to 5 p.m., as well as to understand why he or she needs coverage for that anxiety around that time. *I want to know where they feel anxiety in their body.* I want them to be conscious of it too, so that their anxiety loses its mysteriousness and becomes something that their unconscious mind is trying to convey in the language of the body. It's the same process of desensitization to panic attacks by teaching people about the adrenalin response, the chemistry of adrenalin, and the reality that once there is a release of a jolt of adrenalin, it will be 20 minutes before the adrenalin jitters go away, even if the thing that incited it is long gone. Anxiety about being angry, unconsciously wanting to yell or scream, and having chest pain from splinting intercostal muscles is much easier to understand than just "being anxious."

If patients tell me they are depressed, but they have no way of telling me what that means, then I may not end up treating them with an antidepressant. If they don't particularly have a disturbance of mood, concentration, appetite and sleep habits, then I would wonder out loud why they think/believe they are depressed. I wouldn't dismiss the idea that there was something wrong in their lives, but I would want to see if they could name what it was. I would want to make a careful assessment for alexithymia, and understand if their lack of words for their moods and feelings is related to a traumatic event, childhood, family constellation, or early patterns of parental discourse. Perhaps their lack of words for mood is related to such high levels of chronic anxiety, or emotional numbness that they are among the "living dead." An antianxiety regimen might make more sense in that case than an antidepressant. Of course, you might consider using imipramine, even if it is out of fashion, and treat both.

A recently referred patient with intractable depression for over 20 years was indeed socially withdrawn, unable to work, unable to talk with people, and had failed to gain any improvement with all the psychopharmacological agents a competent Manhattan psychopharmacologist had prescribed, as well as a course of ECT. The patient and her family were fully enamored of the medical model of treatment that saw depression as a brain disorder that had little to do with living life in a family with "every advantage." After an hour with her, I discovered that she was one of the most shame-laden people

I had ever met. As a child, her socially prominent and privately drunken mother had begun cursing her and telling her she was worthless from about age two onward. Depression is especially resistant to treatment when it is what the patient complains of, but not the actual source of a person's distress. It's not that she wasn't depressed, but she was so ashamed that any effort to help her understand herself was not going to succeed without addressing that feeling. I don't believe we will ever have a psychopharmacologic solution for shame. It's just not in the nature of being human. No antidepressant worked, in this case, nor was it tolerated. An antianxiety agent has at least had some limited success.

I recommend going further in discerning the quality of sleep than to simply note if there is a depressive pattern of early wakening, or an anxious–depressed pattern of difficulty falling asleep. Why? Sleep disturbance is the sine qua non of posttraumatic disorders. It is also implicated in the genesis of fibromyalgia, and related syndromes (Mease, 2005). The quality of sleep is very important. While REM sleep is associated with flaccid musculature and dreaming, non-REM dreaming is associated with traumatic stress and nocturnal movement (Ross, Ball, & Dinges, 1994). Beds look like battlefields after a night of restless non-REM dreaming. A careful history can be revealing. With a history suggesting non-REM dreaming, treatment for anxiety makes a lot of sense.

What about the quality of anxiety? Not all anxiety is created equally. Most importantly, anxiety is often felt in different physical locations by different persons. For example, anxiety associated with suppressed rage, in my experience, is often associated with chest pain. Shame anxiety is often associated with nausea and stomach upset. Fear is often associated with a sense of swelling in the throat or a need to urinate. Sadness anxiety is often associated with fullness in the upper chest and throat. Regardless of my specific observations, the physical manifestation of the anxiety is quite idiosyncratic to the psychology of the individual. Affects that arise in the body, but are never expressed, simply build up (Krystal, 1988). Somatic expressions of anxiety often lead medical clinicians on long chases for diseases that are not there. If psychopharmacologic approaches are all that are available to impact these symptoms, then patients may feel quite encouraged when a careful history and target symptom elicitation will allow them to notice small changes in their symptom complex that herald additional healing. It also provides a way to discern small changes in anxiety rather than having to rely upon all-or-nothing results of anxiety treatment where anxiety is either present or absent after an intervention.

PERSONAL OBSERVATIONS ON DRUG SIDE EFFECTS

The material that follows is based upon my personal observation; it is not referenced. In the hands of another psychiatrist, observations may differ. Readers should use their own judgment in considering these options for treatment.

Sertraline tends to make people a little drowsy, can be associated with mild nausea, initially, and does better when prescribed at bedtime. Fluoxitene tends to wake people up, give them psychomotor energy, and is better prescribed, in my experience, in the morning. Citalopram tends to be neutral in regard to activation. Sertraline and paroxitene can cause weight gain, especially paroxitene, and so someone who is having trouble eating and has lost weight is a good candidate for those drugs. Don't give drugs to women that make them gain weight. It decreases compliance. Doxepin stimulates appetite and can relieve some depression even at 10 mg doses, especially when combined with an SSRI. Generally, interactions between cytochrome p450 related enzymes preclude simultaneous use of SSRIs and tricyclic antidepressants (TCAs) because the latter can have a four- to tenfold increase in expected blood level with associated toxicity. However, that's also potentially good news if you prescribe a standard dose of fluoxitene with 10 mg of desipramine, or Sertraline with 10 to 25 mg of imipramine. If the SSRI fails, then augmentation with a low dose of a TCA may be just the thing that tweaks someone's brain into a healthier place. Nefazodone in combination with Sertraline may also be highly effective. Remember that nefazodone may have a desipramine-like effect, and so orthostatic hypotension is a potential side effect, even in low doses. Essentially, each of these TCA/SSRI pairs acts as a dual serotonin/norepinephrine agent. Venlafaxine's success may be related to this. However, I believe that the art is to find the lowest dose of medication that will work. Low doses of both SSRIs and TCAs in combination keep side effect profiles low, and may be highly efficacious. *Always get a blood level of a TCA in combination with an SSRI if going above 25 mg or so.* The tenfold increase in TCA blood level is a real possibility in combination with SSRIs.

Prescribing benzodiazepines to reduce anxiety holds the promise of relief of anxiety as well as the likelihood of dependence after sustained dosing that would establish a steady state. This is usually attained after five to six half-lives of drug degradation. For example, Ativan may have its effect reduced by half in two to four hours, and would do little for someone with anxiety all day long. Ativan treatment would encourage a person with a history of sustained anxiety to be thinking about getting another dose, worrying when the short-lived drug effect will tail off, and, generally, increase anxiety as a paradoxical side effect. Clonazepam has a half-life of 16 to 18 hours and like temazepam, may therefore require only twice daily dosing, or less. This is much more suited to dealing with daytime or nighttime, anxiety. Giving someone just a little bit less medication than they need, or assuring that the drug effect will wear off while he or she is still anxious is an excellent way to undermine effective treatment and create drug seeking behavior. Giving "just a little more" than someone needs to get a proper drug effect goes a distance to assuring that the patient will feel the drug is working, the psychiatrist knows what he or she is doing, and that he or she can expect to maintain relief from his or her symptoms, thereby reducing anxiety from secondary benefits of a thoughtful treatment. Giving inadequate medication

for pain or anxiety is, in my experience, certain to encourage drug-seek- *Logic*
ing behavior. What's the point of giving less if it creates more trouble for the
patient? Why restrict medication if it risks loss of efficacy? I am not in favor of
"drugging" people, nor am I in favor of playing "bait and switch" by promising one thing and delivering another. Ideally, our patients should have the
drug effect they need, with a little bit of margin so that they experience some
resilience in their drug regimen.

There are some situations where a person's anxiety is so over the top that
benzodiazepines and antidepressants fail to give relief. In those situations,
low doses of atypical antipsychotics, risperidone, olanzapine, or ziprasodone,
may be helpful. Doses of 0.25 or 0.50 mg of risperidone, or 2.5 mg of olanzapine are often useful in subduing terror. Doses below recommended doses
for the treatment of psychosis are the rule of thumb. Ziprasodone has an
odd increase of sleepiness at lower doses, 40 mg or below. This remits by
80 mg daily, and may be profound. It is an excellent antidepressant. It may
cause QT wave elongation, an electrocardiographic diagnosis, and should be
monitored properly. Risk of tardive dyskinesia is lower in these drugs than
with classic antipsychotic agents. Metabolic effects of these drugs related to
fat metabolism, glucose metabolism, and prolactin secretion may be significant. It is important for clinicians to become familiar with these effects and
to discuss them with their patients.

Antihistamines are an inexpensive and effective group of agents that may
decrease anxiety, and often induce sleep. While they do cause dry mouth,
drugs like diphenhydramine have a very high LD_{50} (50% of people die at
the lethal dose) and so are safe to give with relative impunity. Even when
fancier agents are available, it's been very pleasing to use this class of drug
with confidence when nothing else is around, or nearly everything else has
failed: 100 mg of diphenhydramine gets most everybody some sleep. That's
always a relief.

Each psychiatrist becomes familiar with various and sundry tricks of
the trade. The suggestions given here feel like a necessary part of talking
about the use of medication in the treatment of grief, even though the
emphasis of this chapter has been more on understanding psychopharmacologic prescribing than the specifics of doing it. Regardless, perhaps some
of my personal experience in prescribing will be helpful to some readers.

SOME THOUGHTS ON GRIEF, COMMUNITY, AND THE PSYCHIATRIST AS WITNESS

Psychiatrists need to grieve too. There, I've said it. Each day there is a
burden that each clinician picks up, and it must also be put back down. Some
days it feels like my sadness does not stay on the ground where I put it; I find
it in my pockets, in my hands, on my mind, stuck like chewing gum to the
bottom of my soul. It's not that all days are like this, but many are. A patient
sent me a poem about her losses:

THE MEADOW

by Kate Knapp Johnson
   Half the day lost, staring
at this window. I wanted to know
just one true thing
about the soul, but I left thinking
for thought, and now —
two inches of snow have fallen
over the meadow. Where did I go,
how long was I out looking
for you? who would never leave me,
my withness, my here.

Losing sight of one's soul, one's witness, one's "here," is a pain that has no measure. We work in community, and sometimes it is only in the community of psychiatrists, psychologists, social workers, and psychotherapists of all stripes that we can find someone who knows the pain of being a professional and a witness.

There are no professional witnesses. It is part of the paradox of being a clinician who is capable of being a witness. I do not use my training to witness; I use my humanity. Still, there are times when having listened and spoken from my heart, I give my head a chance to speak and make connections out loud that magnetize lost souls, bringing them first into orbit around their owners, and eventually to reunion.

It is in the company of a small trusted group of colleagues that grieving is often facilitated. Five of us have been meeting for nearly 10 years, once a month, for 90 minutes. All seasoned traumatologists, we don't need to explain the context of our work to each other. We are so familiar with the countertransference patterns of our lives that it is very hard to hide for too long with my trusted friends. If you don't have a community of colleagues locally, form a group. Or, if you really are working in isolation, then try an online group. There are a number of clinical societies for trauma clinicians. Some of them have online listservs. A well-moderated online discussion can be a thick lifeline in the tumult of a trauma practice.

In this chapter, I emphasize a gamut of thinking about the neurobiology of affect, autonomic nervous system function, understanding the experiential dimensions of affect, the meaning of medication, the value of learning from placebo success, and some of the tricks of the trade in prescribing psychotropic agents. It's an eclectic approach by a psychiatrist who does a lot of long-term work with people who have been severely wounded by life, as well as psychopharmacologic consultation for the patients of a small group of independent nonpsychiatrists whom I know. I will not prescribe for patients of clinicians I don't know well. I need to be able to trust the treating therapist or see a patient frequently when he or she is distressed. I care about my work, and if you've read this far, I wager you do too!

REFERENCES

American Psychiatric Association (2000). *Diagnostic and statistical manual of mental Disorders* (4th ed., text rev.). Washington, D.C.: Author.

Bootzin, R. & Bailey, E. (2005). Understanding placebo, nocebo, and iatrogenic treatment effects. *Journal of Clinical Psychology, 61*(7), 871–880.

Bromberg, P. M. (1998). *Standing in the spaces*. Hillsdale, NJ: Analytic Press.

Cardena, E. & Spiegel, D. (1993). Dissociative reactions to the San Francisco Bay Area earthquake of 1989. *Amercian Journal of Psychiatry, 150*, 474–478.

Chefetz, R. A. (2000a). Affect dysregulation as a way of life. *Journal of the American Academy of Psychoanalysis, 28*(2), 289–303.

Chefetz, R. A. (2000b). Disorder in the therapist's view of the self: Working with the person with dissociative identity disorder. *Psychoanalytic Inquiry, 20*(2), 305–329.

Classen, C., Koopman, C., Hales, R., & Spiegel, D. (1998). Acute stress disorder as a predictor of posttraumatic stress symptoms. *American Journal of Psychiatry, 155*, 620–624.

Demos, V. (Ed.) (1995). *Exploring affect. The selected writings of Sylvan S. Tomkins*. New York: Cambridge University Press.

Guggenbuhl-Craig, A. (1971). *Power in the helping professions*. Dallas, TX: Spring.

Iqbal, M., Sobhan, T., & Ryals, T. (2002). Effects of commonly used benzodiazepines on the fetus, the neonate, and the nursing infant. *Psychatric Services, 53*(1), 39–49.

Khazaal, Y., Zimmerman, G., & Zullino, D. (2005). Depersonalization — Current data. *Canadian Journal of Psychiatry, 50*(2), 101–107.

Kradin, R. (2004). The placebo response: Its putative role as a functional salutogenic mechanism of the central nervous system. *Perspectives in Biological Medicine, 47*(3), 328–338.

Krystal, H. (1988). *Integration and self healing: Affect, alexithymia, and trauma*. Hillsdale, NJ: Analytic Press.

Lattimore, K., Donn, S., Kaciroti, N., Kemper, A., Neal, C., & Vazquez, D. (2005). Selective serotonin reuptake inhibitor (SSRI) use during pregnancy and effects on the fetus and newborn: A meta-analysis. *Journal of Perinatology, 9:*, 595–604.

Ledoux, J. (1996). *The emotional brain*. New York: Simon & Schuster.

Liotti, G. (1999). Disorganization of attachment as a model for understanding dissociative psychopathology. In J. Solomon & C. George (Eds.), *Attachment disorganization* (pp. 291–317). New York: Guilford.

Lyons-Ruth, K. (2003). Dissociation and the parent-infant dialogue: A longitudinal perspective from attachment research. *Journal of the American Psychoanalytic Association, 51*(3), 883–911.

Lyons-Ruth, K., Bronfman, E., & Parsons, E. (1999). Maternal frightened, frightening, or atypical behavior and disorganized attachment patterns. In J. I. Vondra & D. Barnett (Eds.), *Atypical attachment in infancy and early childhood among children at risk* (Serial No. 258, *64*(3), 67–96). Chicago: University of Chicago Press.

Main, M. & Morgan, H. (1996). Disorganization and disorientation in infant strange situation behavior: phenotypic resemblance to dissociative states. In L. K. Michelson, & William J. Ray (Eds.), *Handbook of dissociation: Theoretical, empirical, and clinical perspectives* (pp. 107–138). New York: Plenum Press.

Mease, P. (2005). Fibromyalgia syndrome: Review of clinical presentation, pathogenesis, outcome measures, and treatment. *Journal of Rheumatology* (Suppl.), *75*, 6–21.

Metcalfe, J. & Jacobs, W. J. (1996). A "hot-system/cool-system" view of memory under stress. *PTSD Research Quarterly. 7*, 1–3.

Rauch, S. L., van der Kolk, B. A., Fisler, R. E., Alpert, N. M., Orr, S. P., Savage, C. R., Fischman, A. J., Jenike, M. A., & Pitman, R. K. (1996). A symptom provocation study of posttraumatic stress disorder using positron emission tomography and script driven imagery. *Archives of General Psychiatry, 53,* 380–387.

Ross, R., Ball, W., & Dinges, D. (1994). Motor dysfunction during sleep in posttraumatic stress disorder. *Sleep, 17*(8), 723–732.

Schore, A. N. (2003). *Affect regulation and repair of the self.* New York: W.W. Norton.

Simeon, D. (2004). Depersonalization disorder: A contemporary overview. *CNS Drugs, 18*(6), 343–354.

Ulman, R. B. & Brothers, D. (1988). *The shattered self: A psychoanalytic study of trauma.* Hillsdale, NJ: Analytic Press.

van der Kolk, B. A. et al. (1994). Trauma and the development of borderline personality disorder. *Psychiatric Clinics of North America, 17*(4), 715–731.

van Ijzendoorn, M. H. (1995). Adult attachment representations, parental responsiveness, and infant attachment: A meta-analysis on the predictive validity of the adult attachment interview. *Psychological Bulletin, 117* (3), 387–403.

Part II

Restorative and Clinical Interventions

8

Exorcising Ghosts: The Counting Method and Traumatic Death Imagery

FRANK M. OCHBERG

FUNDAMENTALS OF INTERVENTION

The visual image of the reenactment of a violent dying may become an agonizing icon of terror and helplessness for bereaved loved ones. When the image persists for months, intruding upon daily thoughts and interrupting sleep with its terrifying recurrence, it may become a primary source of trauma distress and a first priority for intervention. The clinical management of traumatic imagery has produced a multitude of treatments — usually followed by some degree of positive response. The introduction to this book emphasized that the "mechanism" of an effective intervention is most probably nonspecific; that is, various treatments of trauma and grief are successful not so much from their unique model or technique(s), but because they are based upon common principles of stress moderation, reconstructive and imaginal exposure, and meaningful reengagement. The author of this chapter developed a remarkably parsimonious intervention model (neurobiological encoding of trauma memory) and procedure (the Counting Method) with documented effectiveness; however, its effectiveness is presumably not only associated with the procedure of counting, but is based also upon a trusting relationship and the three common principles of stress moderation, reconstructive and imaginal exposure, and meaningful reengagement.

O, answer me…. why the sepulcher
Wherein we saw thee quietly inurn'd
Hath op'd his ponderous and marble jaws
To cast thee up again.

— (*Shakespeare, Hamlet,* Act I, Scene iv)

Unnatural death has, too often, an unnatural life. The image of the lost one returns with haunting and disturbing intensity — hence belief in ghosts and other fantasies, reified into enduring myth. The reality of posttraumatic imagery is no myth, however. To lose a loved one to murder, suicide, or frightful accident, to the butchery of war and genocide, is to risk obsessive rumination on the death itself — its causes, its pain, its immediate consequences — rather than to remember, albeit mournfully, the one who once lived. How are we posttraumatic therapists to help our clients and patients dislodge this demon — the reappearing image of a loved one's death?

This chapter draws upon an illustrative case and explains a particular method to modify and ameliorate traumatic death imagery. Elsewhere, I have discussed a general philosophy of posttraumatic therapy (Ochberg, 1988, 1993a) and the application of a measured reexperiencing technique within this framework (Ochberg, 1993b). Many others have elaborated concepts and theories to explain why traumatic memories are so indelible and debilitating (van der Kolk & Fisler, 1995). Two concepts strike me as particularly helpful when considering the legacy of unnatural death. First is Edward Rynearson's discussion of reenactment, which he variously calls reenactment fantasy, imaginary reenactment, or the reenactment story. This applies to loved ones who learned of, but did not witness, the murder. Based upon hundreds of direct observations and a theory that is both descriptive and dynamic, Rynearson (2001) explains the survivor's preoccupation with the murder scene.

In my experience, it is most often the male of our species who nurses this image, allowing it to motivate a search for evil with a focus on the perpetrator. Our criminal justice system builds on this male preoccupation, relegating surviving kin to the role of witness for the state. Little attention goes to rights and remedies for victims; so much to apprehending, prosecuting, and punishing offenders (Herman, 2000).

Visit a chapter meeting of Parents of Murdered Children (Tedeschi & Calhoun, 2003). It is 90% female. Fathers and brothers, husbands and boyfriends come for a session or two, but the mothers and sisters return months and years later, sharing stories, nurturing newcomers, focusing on the emotionally wounded rather than on the murderer, and the crime itself. This gender generality is not absolute. Many mothers focus on the killer who stole a life. Many fathers help other fathers grieve. My point is not the gender difference, but rather that there is a difference between the work of grief and the work of comprehending and apprehending criminals. Grief interferes with detection and prosecution. Dedication to the work of criminal justice

Grief vs.
prosecution

interferes with grief. We drift toward specialized roles and concentrate on one process or the other.

In sum, Rynearson explains the phenomenon of obsessive reenactment in close kin and significant others who experience unnatural death. This reenactment serves a function — assuring attention to crime; increasing the probability that crime will not pay; extending the "long arm of the law" through space and time. Whether the crime scene is communal or individual, we never forget. We remember the Maine, the Alamo, 9/11; we remember the context of the death of the individual we lost. The image of death is a biological and a cultural icon. It illuminates the path toward justice — often in biblical terms, "an eye for an eye," and it obscures the path through grief toward emotional acceptance, equilibrium, and health.

A second construct, best explained by Chris Brewin (2003), illuminates a different but related dimension. Brewin posits that the human brain contains two separate memory systems, situationally accessible memory (SAM) and verbally accessible memory (VAM). The verbally accessible memory system is the set of pathways that connects our speech center, our forebrains, both hemispheres, and, in moderation, our limbic systems, so that we can voluntarily recover a piece of personal history. We can replay it for our own consumption, explain it to another, and do so without suffering an attack of overwhelming anxiety, rage, or depression. VAM is coherent, it contains autobiographical memory. SAM is, by definition, unattached to language. It is aroused by sensation and situation such as the Musak in an elevator that played during a rape or an assault. Without conscious recognition and without words to describe the connection, a sound or a smell can evoke a deadly image. Sometimes the image is unseen but the feeling of dread and horror is elicited. The body remembers. Much of Freudian psychology is based upon similar theory: unconscious "memory" drives neurotic behavior. Therefore, making the unconscious conscious breaks the chain. But posttraumatic therapy is not usually Freudian because most of our patients have memories that are all too conscious. These memories burst into awareness and shatter one's equanimity, one's sense of security. The memory has accurate intensity. Our job is to help our patients make these conscious memories less conscious — not so frequently and so unexpectedly the focus of awareness.

Does this mean converting SAM to VAM? According to Brewin (personal communication, September 2005) it is not entirely appropriate to think of trauma memories literally moving from SAM to VAM, or as one memory system converting to the other. Rather he proposes that both systems coexist, and that the act of focusing attention deliberately on a traumatic image copies information from the SAM to the VAM system. In the presence of trauma reminders, there is a contest between the two systems. When VAM succeeds in dominating SAM, a person experiences control over traumatic memory. The memory still has strong meaning and disturbing feelings are remembered, but the PTSD symptoms of flashback and dysphoric, intrusive recollection are not present to a disabling degree. When, conversely, SAM dominates, clinically significant episodes of intrusive reexperiencing symptoms are, indeed, present and profound. Some form of therapy to modulate and master this overactive SAM is needed.

A previously traumatic memory, copied from SAM to VAM, is less likely to spring forth unbidden with disturbing intensity.

How does one copy a trauma memory from SAM to VAM? Verbalization — talking it through — is not necessarily the way. But the ability to speak of the trauma without disabling emotion is a goal, and is evidence of significant progress. The concept is attractive because it directs the therapist and the client toward acceptance rather than denial. It confirms a line in The Survivor Psalm (Ochberg, 1993a): "I may never forget but I need not constantly remember."

SUE AND BRANT

I met Sue and Brant in November 2001, two weeks after their 20-year-old son, Alex, was murdered. His death was particularly brutal, with multiple stabbings and near beheading. The killer was an older, unstable, ne'er-do-well who shared a rental home in Lansing, Michigan with Alex and one or two others. Alex left high school in his senior year and was taking a detour through late adolescence with odd jobs and overuse of alcohol. His dad described him as good natured, whimsical, strong, slightly lost, yet closely connected to a loving family. Brant was the last person, other than the murderer, to see Alex alive.

He had stopped by the rental home at 9 p.m. on November 10, to deliver a message, while Sue sat in the car. Alex had been drinking but was not drunk. Within an hour the phone rang at Brant and Sue's house and a policeman told them their son was dead.

The leader of the local Parents of Murdered Children group referred Brant and Sue to me. Both saw me together 14 times and I saw Brant alone once, Sue alone twice. On one occasion the family of four came to my office — mother, father, a daughter in college, and one in high school. Eventually Sue and Brant joined the Michigan Victim Alliance, telling their story to students of journalism, medicine, and criminal justice. Sue helped me introduce third- and fourth-year psychiatry residents to issues discussed in this chapter.

In the beginning both Sue and Brant were consumed by their son's murder. They learned from police investigators about the crime scene and the reconstruction of motive: a long simmering argument erupting into rage. They absorbed the actual method: a sudden attack with a kitchen knife, multiple stabbings and slashes, a throat wound, and probably a postmortem attempt at decapitation.

We did not dwell on these details, but spoke instead about the impact on Alex's sisters, about insomnia and nightmares, of Sue's deep depression, and Brant's concern for her. The couple sat together on a small sofa, husband always comforting wife. They spoke openly about the loss of sexual interest, not as a problem but as a fact. He had images of the murder scene, but not flashbacks. She had horrifying flashbacks to the moment of notification and then to the sequence of images that formed in her mind at the time. These images changed as she learned more and were accompanied by palpitations and shortness of breath.

I wanted to see Brant alone to probe for symptoms, but he revealed nothing beyond grief and combinations of anger and self-blame that seemed proportional to the extreme circumstances. He felt he should have done more to help Alex concentrate on studies, make better choices, and avoid a lifestyle that placed him at risk. But Brant overcame self-blame soon enough. With Sue, he established a scholarship for C students in honor of his C-student son.

Sue had full-blown PTSD. She read about the diagnosis and appreciated my instruction on the nature of the disorder. "It made me feel normal," she later explained to a class of medical students. She readily accepted and clearly benefited from Celexa®, 20 mg a day, Trazodone®, 50 mg at night, and Xanax, 1 mg three times a day. The Celexa® helped alleviate black moods that kept her in bed. The Trazodone allowed her to sleep through the night without nightmares or early morning wakening. The Xanax diminished the frequency and intensity of panic-laced intrusive recollections. She had intrusive recollections six weeks after the murder, so I offered a form of modulated reexperiencing called the Counting Method. This exposure technique has been described in articles and videotapes (Johnson & Lubin, 2005; Ochberg, 1993b, 1996; Ochberg, Johnson, & Lubin, 1996), and evaluated in comparison with EMDR and prolonged exposure (Johnson & Lubin, 2006). Although not as thoroughly investigated and promulgated as those other techniques, I find it simpler and as effective.

USING THE COUNTING METHOD

First, I explained to Sue that we had reached a point of comfort with each other, of trust and familiarity, and we could now schedule a time for her to deliberately "turn on the tape." She would remember, without words, that horrible moment of receiving the news of Alex's death. I told her that I would count out loud to 100 and while I was counting, she would remember. "When I am counting in the 40s and 50s and 60s, you will go through the worst of your recollection and feelings," I said. "When I get to the 90s, you should be sure to be remembering a time when you felt more secure," I added.

I explained that after she finished this silent memory we would talk about what she just remembered. She agreed and we set a date: December 20, 2001.

Sue arrived punctually, and sat in a comfortable chair in subdued light. After five minutes of relatively pleasant catching up, I reviewed the instructions for the counting method and we began. During my counting to 100 she did not cry, but by the count of 60 she had a grimace on her face and her lids drooped. Her body seemed tense.

After the counting I took these notes as she spoke:

Home that night ... pajamas on ... washed face...
The phone rang ...
Alicia from the basement ...
Voice on the other end panicky.
Alex not breathing!
Another call about crime scene tape.
I thought BAD ...
Brant ran upstairs.
Instinctively BAD ...
Policeman on the phone, "I don't like to do things this way. Your son died."
We just ran around the house.
What do we do? Didn't know what to do.
Youngest daughter heard.
Should we call our other daughter? Family?
Leslie knew something was wrong.
Advocates came.
Seemed so long.
Alicia and I were staring and waiting on the front porch. No shoes or socks.
Police car screaming up the street, three more behind.
I wanted him to tell me, "We are still working on him," but he had an
    awful look.
Advocates were very nice.
Called my sister (who lived) on the other end of the block. She came down.
Disbelief.
Called the rest of the family.
All there. A blur.
Police took us to the station.
Statement. 2 a.m.
Came back. Family left 3:30.
Fell asleep 5.
Awake 6 to 6:30.
Next couple of days a blur. Family, people coming and going. Funeral
    arrangements. Surreal. Unbelievable.
Not being able to see Alex was hard.
Saturday to Tuesday was a long time not seeing him.
Then we did. Girls screamed.
I felt a little peace come over me. He looked nice. Peaceful. I could hug
    him. Healthy. Young. That night, peaceful.
Then visitation, funeral.
So many people. Nice tribute to Alex and to us. Blur. So much going on.
    That day at the funeral they closed the casket. I didn't want that. That
    was the hardest moment — other than finding out.
Funeral, sermon, nice service. Church almost full. Walked across the
    street to the cemetery. 65 degrees. Sunny.

There was more. Sue went on, adding thoughts that came to mind as she spoke, not necessarily thoughts that came during the 100 seconds of counting. For example, her sister-in-law brought 25 colored balloons and one white balloon, off by itself. "That was Alex," she smiled. A cousin brought firecrackers (that was Alex, too). Sue recalled seeing one little scratch on the side of Alex's face, but no other signs of violence.

She told me then of the detective describing Alex's wounds to Brant, including a gash six inches long and two inches deep that severed both jugular veins and the esophagus. "All I can picture is this man over him, making sure he did the job, standing there with a bloody knife."

The Counting Method has four distinct phases. We had completed three. ←
First, we had discussed the method, reviewed how and why it could help, and scheduled a session at a time that suited her and that came after she had made some progress in therapy. Second, I had counted to 100 while she allowed herself to remember the worst of the traumatic experience, closing with the comfort of seeing Alex at peace, touching him, and walking from funeral to cemetery in the sun. Third, she recounted what she remembered (and more). During this phase, she did cry.

Now it was my turn to read back to her what she had said and what I had managed to capture in a furious scribble on a yellow pad. This is a phase not just of rote recounting, but of adding words of respect and comfort. I have no record of what I said, but it probably included the fact that she was able to do this difficult task. "You turned the tape on and you ran it through the worst memories," I would have observed. I usually comment on the points in the trauma story that are disturbing and the parts that carry hope, meaning, and connection to others. I would have pointed out, one way or another, that Sue was on her way to grieving the loss of her son, enjoying the memory of his personality, and overcoming the horror of his final few minutes alive.

AFTER THE COUNTING

A visit with Brant alone, Christmas, New Year, and a family visit came next, with conversation about a raft of issues including minor physical ailments and the emotional problems of Sue's parents. Of course we spoke of the holiday season without Alex, but the family did manage to generate some holiday spirit, using the idea that "Alex would want it that way."

On January 11, 2002, I noted, "Good!! She (Sue) has overcome trauma imagery and PTSD but has empty feeling and deep sadness — I'd call it normal grief, profound …."

Technically, Sue had PTSD, with anxiety, numbing, and at least one unwanted memory per month for several months. But she didn't feel that her mind had a mind of its own, as many of my traumatized patients feel. She was extremely sad, not haunted or obsessed. As the trial loomed ahead and she knew she would be in the same room as the killer, she became angry. I liked the anger. It was clear, reasonable, and better than depression or confusion.

Did the counting make a large difference in Sue's progress? It is never easy to tell just what element of therapy makes the most impact, and therapy itself is just one part of the healing process. Sue felt the counting did matter significantly. Before, she doubted that she would ever be free of visions of Alex's violent death. She thought that she would hear what some call "the death knock"— the moment of notification — over and over and over.

I believe that we, Sue and I together, shared the experience of her SAM — her situationally accessible memory — and we shared it in silence as I counted. She could tolerate a self-induced replay of her worst moments because the experience of therapy had become familiar. Sue later said that she loved to come to my office because it felt safe and comforting. Not all trauma patients feel that way. Therapy and therapists can symbolize forced encounters with personal demons. Many PTSD patients avoid therapy for that reason.

The timing of the Counting Method is very important. It requires clinical judgment, not just the consent of the client. In Sue's case, we got there quickly for several reasons. Brant was such a source of security during the initial visits that the therapy room became an oasis for all of us. We made progress with appropriate use of education about PTSD, and about the criminal justice system (it didn't hurt that I had been an adjunct professor of criminal justice and knew quite a lot about the county court procedures). We used humor when it was tasteful and reasonable. Just thinking about Alex's sense of humor could make all of us smile. I prescribed medication and that ameliorated some symptoms.

So by the time we engaged in the Method, Sue was on an upward course, improving her mastery of her own condition.

The themes uncovered during the counting and the following discussion were interesting and, in some ways, typical. Three peaks of negative experience stand out: First, she had the terror of learning her son was murdered. This caused shock and dissociation. She used words such as *blur, incredible,* and *surreal.* Second, she learned of his death struggle and his antemortem and postmortem wounds. This caused horror. Third, she saw the casket close and left his sight and touch forever. This caused grief and emptiness.

With some patients, repeat counting sessions are helpful, focusing on such individual peaks of experience until they are mastered and diminished. Sue didn't need that.

Several peaks of positive experience were revealed. Family and friends came in large numbers and Sue felt she and Alex were well regarded, embraced by so many caring people. The white balloon remains an image of Alex's individuality. The firecrackers, brought to his funeral, elicit a smile for Alex and for those who were able to introduce some sparkle into a somber ceremony. Alex at peace, restored to an image of health and youth, was seen during counting, and is now more vivid than Sue's imagined "memory" of his mortal wounding.

In Brewin's terminology, Sue did copy her trauma memory from one mental system to another. It didn't happen all at once during a Counting

Method session. It happened over time for many reasons, one of which was a technique of moderated memory.

At the time of this writing, three and a half years later, Sue and Brant have enough time and distance from those terrible weeks at the end of 2001 and the beginning of 2002 that they can help other victims of violence contend with the impact of human cruelty. We have become friends and colleagues through this work. An encounter with a student or a peer who seeks information about violent death, will stir up some bad feelings in Sue or Brant. But they find the gratification of helping others is worth the price of feeling reexposed to trauma. Sue does not have PTSD now.

ADDITIONAL APPLICATIONS OF THE COUNTING METHOD

In several additional instances, I have observed patients use the Counting Method to explore and assimilate traumatic memories of violent death. These involve suicide, accident, war, and murder.

> The mother of a young police officer found her son in his apartment after he had shot himself following a break-up with his fiancée. In the counting session, the mother focused on her view of her son's bare heel, the first thing she saw upon pushing open his door. This image led to all the rest, including her shock and grief.
>
> A trucker, forced over the center line by a drunk driver of an oncoming car, collided with an SUV and six passengers died, including children. He still has PTSD, but flashbacks to the scene are now less frequent and intense.
>
> A veteran of the first Gulf war, during his second Counting Method, recovered a hitherto unremembered sensation of stepping on the body of an Iraqi soldier he had killed. He cried during the counting and during the discussion immediately afterward, expressing horror and anger. "Why did the lieutenant order me into the bunker (wearing night vision goggles) to kill the sleeping soldiers?" he said.
>
> Another member of the Michigan Victim Alliance retold, after counting, the terrible day when intruders held him and his fiancée at gunpoint, executing her and sparing him. His images of death have abated but he still cannot sleep through the night without Trazodone.

As in Sue's case, each of these survivors had intrusive, debilitating reexperiencing symptoms. In several instances, my patient felt he or she was going to die, but the haunting image was (and, for some, remains) the death of another. The "other" was a stranger to the soldier and the long distance hauler, but a loved and cherished one to the mother and the fiancé. All claimed some mastery, some relief after the counting. None wanted more than three sessions. Few (including others not mentioned here) came close to Sue in depth of support from marriage, family, and community. Sue's community included a large, active extended family, her church, and the Michigan Victim Alliance.

AFTERWORD

It troubles me when too much is made of the use of a specific therapeutic technique, after a literally life-shattering experience. Neither counting nor EMDR nor prolonged exposure transforms the witness from one who feels haunted and disabled, sometimes dehumanized, to one who is sadder, wiser, and restored to emotional health. But these guided journeys through traumatic memory do transform the memory from a personal demon that strikes with little warning and overtakes the theater of private thought, to a manageable, bitter truth.

The question as to what form of therapy best modulates traumatic memory has interested and perplexed clinicians and investigators in the trauma sciences for decades. Two of the most thoroughly researched approaches are Edna Foa's method of prolonged exposure (Foa & Kozak, 1986; Foa, Molnar, & Cashman, 1995; Foa, Rothbaum, Riggs, & Murdock, 1991) and Francine Shapiro's EMDR (Shapiro, 1989). As this chapter goes to press, so does an article by David Johnson and Hadar Lubin (2006), documenting their research at Yale, in which they compared prolonged exposure, EMDR, and Method Counting. Johnson and Lubin brought Foa and me to the Yale-New Haven Veteran's Administration Hospital in 1994 where we trained trauma therapists in each technique. Therapists attended official EMDR training sessions sponsored by Shapiro. Later, these therapists were randomly assigned to treat outpatients in a trauma clinic. Each clinician used each method, again by random assignment, one method to one patient at least three times in a brief, six- to nine-session course of treatment. Patients were also placed on a waiting list, untreated. Using objective and subjective outcome measures, all treatments provided improvement significantly better than placement on a waiting list. There were no meaningful differences in outcome due to the treatment technique that was applied. The authors concluded that, by the law of parsimony, the Counting Method is simplest and therefore preferable. But simplicity seldom sells: Complex theories and methods have long lives and fervid adherents. One relatively small study will not and should not change the field.

I recall a lively debate during the revision of the PTSD diagnosis from DSM-III to DSM-III-R in the mid-1980s. Some thought PTSD belonged in the chapter on dissociation, because the cardinal feature was an alteration in consciousness, short of psychosis, changing the subjective nature of the experience of self and environment. Others, a majority, held for inclusion with the anxiety disorders, since extreme arousal was such a profound element of the original experience and the episodic aftershocks. Now we have evidence of a memory distortion at the heart of PTSD: a failure to apply the correct measure of distance to personal recollection, so that terrible events are too close, too present, too frightening in their apparent proximity and power.

The surviving witness of another's violent dying is subject to all of these dimensions of disability and more. They have endured biological reality and often human cruelty.

They are, for a period of time, free of the fantasies we mortals use to insulate ourselves from inevitable loss and death.

We therapists work with the tools our patients grant us to exorcise their ghosts:

Their connections to others who love them.
Their humor, spirit, and character.
Their biological resilience.
Their trust in us to sit with them as they have a sharp look at what they wish they'd never seen.

REFERENCES

Brewin, C. R. (2003). *Posttraumatic stress disorder: Malady or myth*. New Haven, CT: Yale University Press.

Foa, E., Molnar, C., & Cashman, L. (1995). Change in rape narratives during exposure therapy for posttraumatic stress disorder. *Journal of Traumatic Stress, 8*, 675–690.

Foa, E. B., Rothbaum, B. O., Riggs, D. S., & Murdock, T. B. (1991). Treatment of posttraumatic stress disorder in rape victims: A comparison between cognitive–behavioral procedures and counseling. *Journal of Consulting and Clinical Psychology, 59*, 715–723.

Foa, E. & Kozak, M. (1986). Emotional processing of fear: Exposure to corrective information. *Psychological Bulletin, 99*, 20–35.

Herman, S. (2000). *Seeking parallel justice: A new agenda for the victims movement* Washington, D.C.: National Center for Victims of Crime monograph.

Johnson, D. R. & Lubin, H. (2005) The Counting Method as exposure therapy: Revisions and case examples. *Traumatology, 11*(3), 189–198.

Johnson, D. R. & Lubin, H. (2006). The Counting Method: Applying the rule of parsimony to the treatment of posttraumatic stress disorder. *Traumatology, 12* (1), 83–99.

Ochberg, F. (1988). *Post-traumatic therapy and victims of violence*. New York: Brunner/Mazel.

Ochberg, F. (1993a). Posttraumatic therapy. In John P. Wilson & Beverley Raphael (Eds.), *International handbook of traumatic stress syndrome*, 773–783. New York: Plenum Press,

Ochberg, F. (1993b). *The counting method*. Videotape. (Reviewed by John Wilson., *Psychotherapy, 30* (4), 705, 1993; Janet Bell, *Journal of Traumatic Stress, 8* (1), 197–199, 1995. Available from Gift from Within, 800-888-5236)

Ochberg, F. (1996). The counting method. *Journal of Traumatic Stress, 9*, 887–894.

Ochberg, F., Johnson, D., & Lubin, H. (1996). *The counting method: Training manual*. (Available from Post Traumatic Stress Center, New Haven, CT).

Rynearson, E. K. (2001). *Retelling violent death*. Philadelphia: Brunner-Rutledge.

Shapiro, F. (1989). Efficacy of the eye movement desensitization procedure in the treatment of traumatic memories. *Journal of Traumatic Stress, 2*, 199–233.

Tedeschi R. & Calhoun, L. (2003). *Helping bereaved parents: A clinician's guide*. Philadelphia: Brunner-Rutledge. See also http://www.pomc.org

van der Kolk, B. & Fisler, R. (1995). Dissociation and the fragmentary nature of traumatic memories: Overview and exploratory study. *Journal of Traumatic Stress, 8*, 505–526.

9

Treatment of Complicated Grief Following Violent Death

KATHERINE SHEAR, BONNIE GORSCAK, AND NAOMI SIMON

EVIDENCE-BASED INDIVIDUAL THERAPY

This chapter begins with an in-depth review of a biobehavioral model of complicated grief expanding upon the theoretical insights introduced in chapter 1 and clarifying its differentiation from posttraumatic stress disorder (PTSD) and major depressive disorder. The model maintains that a recurrent intrusive image of the dying is typical of complicated grief, independent of the mode of dying. The authors then describe a time-limited, individual intervention with a protocol and agenda of 10 sessions that reinforces "restoration coping," while engaging in imaginal exposure with memories of the deceased, and finally prepares for termination of treatment. A case presentation dynamically illustrates the phenomenology of complicated grief before and during intervention, including an imaginal, two-way "conversation" with the memory of the deceased. The authors also present highlights of an impressive, rigorously designed study demonstrating the effectiveness of their treatment.

INTRODUCTION

People naturally shrink from the idea of a loved one's violent death, as even the thought of such an event is fraught with anguish. Faced with the reality of such a loss, it is remarkable that most people are resilient, finding a pathway back to vital, if more sober, engagement in ongoing life. An unfortunate minority of bereaved people do become caught in the chronic, persistent post-loss stress condition designated as either *complicated* (the term used here) or *traumatic* grief. It may be that the violent death of a loved one is more likely than a natural death to result in chronic postloss stress. However, data suggest that the form and progress of grief is similar, regardless of the manner of death. A very close relationship to the deceased appears to be a greater risk factor than the circumstances of the death (Langner & Maercker, 2005).

In our NIMH-funded treatment study (MH60783; Shear, Frank, Houck, & Reynolds, 2005) we found no difference in baseline scores on the Inventory of Complicated Grief (Prigerson, et al. 1995), among those with complicated grief following violent compared to nonviolent death from natural causes. We treated people whose loved ones died following suicide, homicide, and violent accidents using the same approach as those who suffered from complicated grief (CG) following natural death. The treatment we devised to help these people was confirmed as being efficacious in our randomized controlled trial with similar outcomes for those bereaved by violent or natural death (Shear et al., 2005). Through this work and the research of others, we have come to believe that there is a natural process of coping with significant loss that can go awry, regardless of the circumstances of death. When this happens, the resulting postloss stress disorder (complicated grief) has a remarkable consistency. We understand this condition as a problem of stalled progress of the commonly occurring acute grief reaction. Therefore, the objective of our intervention is to free the natural process of grief so that it will progress to an integration of the loss.

A BIOBEHAVIORAL MODEL OF GRIEF

Grief is the painful but universal complement to love and attachment. Close attachments are ubiquitous and very important in our lives. We gain emotional support from people we love. We share with them our sense of personal history and our dreams and plans for future happiness. People we love anchor our lives, and contribute to the rhythms of everyday life. There is even evidence that these relationships help regulate our physiological functioning. Given the critical importance of close attachments, it follows that there is an inborn biobehavioral response to help us adjust to the loss of an attachment figure. We used our own observations and reports in the literature to develop a model of this adjustment. This model, based on extensive review of the grief literature, interactions with research and clinical colleagues, and observations of ourselves and our patients, provides the theoretical underpinnings of a treatment for the condition of complicated grief. In discussing this model we use terminology in the manner suggested by Stroebe and others (Stroebe, Stroebe, Abakoumkin, & Schut, 1996).

Bereavement is defined as the state of having lost someone close, and grief is the psychological response to bereavement. Just as each love relationship is unique, so too each grief reaction is distinct. However, most people who lose a loved one experience a period of acute grief that has certain common features. This reaction is intensified and much more severe following a violent death (Lindemann, 1944). Upon learning of the violent death of a loved one, there is almost always an immediate sense of shock and disbelief. This is quickly followed by waves of intensely dysphoric emotions and/or numbness. There is a sense of profound sadness, usually intermixed with rage, guilt, fear, and other difficult feelings. Highly emotional pangs of grief recur frequently over the first days, weeks, and months after the death.

In the initial period after a death, feelings of yearning and longing for the person who died, preoccupation with thoughts and memories of the deceased, and feeling drawn to reminders of the person dominate the mind of the bereaved person. At the same time there is a strong tendency to avoid reminders that are too painful. Additionally, there is diminished overall interest in ordinary activities. These highly charged feelings and unfamiliar behavior patterns often feel uncontrollable and unwelcome, especially to a person who is usually emotionally controlled or those who are frightened of uncontrolled emotions.

Fear of one's own reaction, intense self–criticism, or unrealistic expectations of the course of grief can lead to inhibition of the natural progress of a grief reaction. The sense of betrayal that can accompany urges to reengage in a new life can also impede the progress of grief. By contrast, acceptance of the death and one's own wide-ranging emotions is fundamental to the gradual process of integration of the reality of the death into the mind of the bereaved person.

Loss of a loved one is intensely stressful in itself. Yet this difficult event carries in its wake a myriad of associated life stressors. Grief researchers have noted that adjustment to loss entails coping with all of these stressors. An interesting model posits that two processes occur side by side in the everyday life of a bereaved person (Stroebe & Schut, 2005). One of the processes is loss oriented and entails thinking about the deceased, looking at pictures, imagining how they would respond to different situations, and thoughts or even ruminations about the death. A range of loss-related emotions, most prominently sadness, are contained in this process.

A second process is restoration oriented and entails adjustment to a world in which interaction with the deceased loved one no longer occurs. Loss of this interaction leads to countless secondary changes associated with the loss. Prominent among these is emotional loneliness, a state that has been shown to be associated with a range of negative long-term outcomes (Stroebe, Stroebe, & Abakoumkin, 2005; Stroebe, Stroebe, Abakoumkin, & Schut, 1996). Other stresses associated with the restoration focus include the need to take on tasks previously managed by the deceased, requirements to manage changes in role functioning, and dealing with practical matters necessary to reorganize life without the loved one present.

An interesting feature of Stroebe and Schut's loss- and restoration-oriented coping model is the postulation of a dynamic process of oscillation between loss- and restoration-focused attention that they consider central to effective coping. Similar to the oscillation posited by Horowitz et al. (Horowitz, 1974; Sundin & Horowitz, 2003) in managing traumatic stress, such a process entails deploying attention to processing of a painful emotion or solving a given problem, alternating with turning attention away from that emotion or problem. Attention to a given stressor thus alternates between engagement and avoidance. This creates an oscillating process of revisiting a problem and setting it aside. Such oscillation would provide a helpful regulatory mechanism in coping with difficult stressors. Our treatment model accepts this proposition.

Given effective coping, the acute grief reaction gradually subsides, perhaps following a damping, pendulum-like course (Bisconti, Bergeman, & Boker 2004). There is debate in the literature regarding what takes the place of acute grief. Some have proposed "completion," "resolution," or "detachment" as the desired outcome of successful grief (Weissman, Markowitz, & Klerman, 2000), but this idea is no longer generally accepted. Most investigators have concluded that grief is not completed or resolved. Instead, the reaction to loss is a permanent state, though its intensity and quality change. George Eliot provides an eloquent description of integrated grief when she writes in *Adam Bede,*

> For Adam, though you see him quite master of himself, working hard and delighting in his work after his inborn inalienable nature, had not outlived his sorrow — had not felt it slip from him as a temporary burden, and leave him the same man again. Do any of us? God forbid. It would be a poor result of all our anguish and our wrestling if we won nothing but our old selves at the end of it — if we could return to the same blind loves, the same self-confident blame, the same light thoughts of human suffering, the same frivolous gossip over blighted human lives, the same feeble sense of that Unknown towards which we have sent forth irrepressible cries in our loneliness. Let us rather be thankful that our sorrow lives in us as an indestructible force, only changing its form, as forces do, and passing from pain into sympathy — the one poor word which includes all our best insight and our best love. (p. 72)

Thus, in our model, acute grief is gradually transformed to a state of integrated loss, which is comprised of a permanent collection of thoughts and memories of the deceased, with which a bereaved person has a variable degree of ongoing commerce. A range of feelings, images, attitudes, and beliefs related to the deceased are still accessible, though no longer preoccupying. There is renewed interest in ongoing life, and other people again become important. Rehearsing of recollections gradually recedes into the background of ongoing life. Over time, the emotional valence of memories of the deceased tends to shift toward a more positive tone for many individuals (Bonanno, G. A., Wortman, C. B., Nesse, R. M., Prospective patterns of resilience and maladjustment during widowhood. *Psychol Aging.* 2004 Jun;19(2):260–71. et al., 2001).

Integrated grief is associated with little or no avoidance of reminders of the person who died. Nevertheless, at certain anniversaries, in the face of new loss, in the context of a fresh life event, an old loss can again come to the fore with associated painful emotions and preoccupying thoughts and memories. In such situations, though, the upsurge in grief-related thoughts and feelings is transient and subsides within a relatively short period of time. This differs from the situation of the group of bereaved people for whom the integration of the loss is never achieved. Instead, the progress of grief is impeded and a prolonged period of acute grief ensues. The result is the chronic, persistent syndrome of postloss stress disorder currently called *complicated grief.*   " Stuck grief "

CLINICAL FEATURES OF COMPLICATED GRIEF (CG)

A surprisingly consistent postloss stress disorder occurs as one of the complications of bereavement. This condition of complicated grief can be reliably identified using the Inventory of Complicated Grief (Prigerson et al., 1995). We have characterized symptoms experienced by bereaved individuals so identified using a structured clinical interview. Factor analysis of this interview (Shear et al., in preparation) indicates symptoms can be categorized into the four groups: (1) painful feelings of separation distress; (2) difficulty coping with ongoing life; (3) guilty feelings related to the deceased; and (4) avoidance behaviors.

Once established, it appears that symptoms of CG are similar following a violent death and following death resulting from a long, progressive illness. Furthermore, such symptoms can be very chronic and persistent, causing significant distress and impairment for decades. In cases of CG that present long after the death of a loved one, there is sometimes a superficial adjustment to everyday life, but upon discussion of the loss, typical CG symptoms are endorsed. Individuals who presented for treatment years after the loss show evidence of being highly emotional and report long-standing interference in work and relationships, beginning at the time of the death. In comparison to the usual range of grief responses, the persistence and stability of acute postloss distress in complicated grief is remarkable. It may be that this invariant picture is related to loss of the normal flexibility of response. Rather than an oscillating pattern of engagement with loss- and restoration-related problems, it appears that both preoccupation and avoidance are prominent and not synchronized effectively.

Several features stand out in our clinical observations and in the literature as characteristic of patients suffering from CG. There is persistence of a range of easily evoked painful emotions associated with reminders of the death or the person who died. Positive emotions, often also present, are nevertheless quickly drowned by anguish associated with the loss. Against a background of persistent and noticeable sorrow, there are intermittent pangs of very intense painful emotion. Emotional pain is accompanied by inability or refusal to accept the death and rumination over why it happened, what could have prevented it, or how it is unfair and wrong.

Ruminations sometimes center on how wonderful the person was, how much the grief-stricken person needed his or her loved one, and how empty and meaningless the world is without this person. Joyous feelings and comforting thoughts in relation to the deceased are tinged with bitterness or remorse, even after many years of bereavement. There is little interest and pleasure in recreation because the loved one cannot share in the fun. Satisfaction in accomplishments is absent or spoiled because this person is no longer present to participate or contribute. Painful as it is, the person with CG resists the idea that grief could diminish, fearing that painful CG sadness is all that is left of his or her loved one, and believing the tie to the deceased lessens in proportion to the lessening of the person's pain. A father had the image that his dead son was like a ship that has left the harbor. The father told us he needed to hold tightly to a rope tied to the ship (his metaphor for his grief) to prevent the vessel from disappearing forever over the horizon and his son being lost forever.

Sometimes there is an idea that the intensity of pain is proof of the intensity of love, and, by extension, if the pain is less, so is the love. A woman became alarmed as she experienced relief of her intense pain upon the accidental death of her sister, saying she feared her heart might turn cold. Others experience themselves as disloyal if they find pleasure or enjoyment alone or with others. Many who endorse this feeling say they know that their loved one would not want them feel this way. Still, they are unable to convince themselves that living their own lives is not a betrayal.

A case example provides an illustration of this condition.

THE CASE OF KAREN M

Karen presents for treatment of grief 12 years after the murder of her husband. She is a generally pleasant, middle-aged woman with a full range of affect, though she sprinkles the interview with mildly hostile comments. Upon being asked to talk about her husband she becomes very tearful, weeping freely as she relates how wonderful their marriage was, how her husband Jim was her soul mate, and how devastated she was by his death at age 53. She explains that he died from a gunshot wound during a robbery in a convenience store where he had stopped to purchase a cup of coffee around 4 p.m. one day. She says he never drank coffee in the afternoon and she doesn't know why he decided to get coffee that day. Her emotions escalate further as she relates this part of the story. "Why," she sobs hysterically, "why did he have to go there? Why did he need coffee that day of all days!"

After regaining control of her emotions, she says that she doesn't know why she still gets so emotional. She says she is disappointed in herself because she still feels so distraught about this loss. She explains that she has participated in many support groups and has seen three different therapists since her husband's death. She is currently taking an antidepressant medication.

She thinks that all of this has helped her a little, but that no one really can help her because her husband is gone and his death was horrible and senseless. She challenges the therapist to explain how he would feel if this had happened to him. Still, she is tired of suffering like this. Her life has become so constricted that she rarely experiences pleasure. She would like to feel better.

Karen describes how she has kept her husband's home office and his tool room intact for more than a decade. She still refuses to let anyone sit in his favorite armchair in the living room, and long ago moved her own things out of the master bedroom of the house. She currently lives in three of the six rooms of their home. She feels estranged from her two daughters and her son even though she wishes she could be close to them, especially since they have children. She does push herself to see them on a weekly basis, but she can't really enjoy the time she spends with them. The same is true of her old friends. She sees these friends only rarely and only because they continue to call. When she is with them, she feels incomplete, and is flooded with troublesome emotions. She often has a strange sensation that Jim is present, explaining that it is almost like a phantom limb. Being with her friends also evokes intense feelings of sadness, anger, and envy. She is disappointed in herself that she still has these feelings. She has a small group of new friends, all of whom also have a murdered spouse. They understand that they all feel the same way, and while this is comforting, it contributes to her feeling of futility about change. She believes these friends are the only ones who can understand what she is going through.

Karen does not date because she feels this would be a betrayal of her husband, even though she says she knows he would not agree. In fact, early in their marriage they once had a discussion about how each would want the other to fall in love like this again if one of them died. Karen often thinks about this conversation, wondering if it was a premonition. Still, she can't bring herself to see other men. She spends many hours every week ruminating about how beautiful their life was together, imagining being with him again, or feeling angry and bitter about the way he died. She says it's irrational, but she can't help thinking that this was somehow her fault. She knows it is ridiculous, but she often asks herself why she didn't warn him, or call him and ask him to come home early that day. She still has a hard time believing this really happened, and not infrequently she has a strong sensation that he will come home, as he always did, and she will wake up from this nightmare. She knows this is foolish and sometimes berates herself for being so stupid.

While she spends much time in reveries about Jim, she also avoids reminders of his loss. She avoids going to their favorite restaurant and to many other places they enjoyed together. She refuses to go near the hospital where the ambulance brought her husband that day. She thinks they could have saved him if the doctors had acted more quickly. She never goes shopping downtown because the store where she used to buy her clothes is across the street from the convenience store. She has visited the cemetery only twice since Jim died. She feels guilty about this, but she can't bear to think of her husband lying in the ground.

Overall, Karen says that the way her life is going, she thinks she might has well have died with Jim. Sometimes she strongly wishes that she did. She takes medication for hypertension and osteoarthritis, though she developed high blood pressure only after the murder. When her feelings of futility are very strong she skips her medication, though her doctor has told her this could be dangerous. She says her religious upbringing keeps her from trying to take her own life. She used to attend church regularly, but she lost her faith after Jim died. What kind of God would allow such things to happen? Why did this happen to her when she was the one who attended church regularly? Why not those people who are really bad? Given her sense of disappointment and abandonment, she can no longer bring herself to go to services. Her daughters are very worried about her and convinced her to seek treatment again, even though her own feeling is that it is unlikely anyone can help her since no one can bring her husband back.

A recurrent intrusive image of the death, or an image of the loved one around the time of the death, is a feature of CG. A mother whose son died by suicide was plagued by visions of him hanging from a tree. A man whose brother died of cancer saw his brother's eyes, crying yellow tears. A woman whose spouse died of a chronic illness had recurrent images of his emaciated body. Some people have the idea that they were somehow to blame or that they could have acted in some way to prevent this death, or at least to mitigate the suffering of the deceased.

Most people with CG try to avoid reminders of their loved ones. They may leave rooms of possessions untouched, stay away from the cemetery or place of disposition of the remains, or avoid talking about the deceased to family and friends. A woman whose granddaughter died had never visited the grave and could not remember where the child was buried. A man whose wife collected antiques kept several households full of objects for years until he was treated. A woman who received her medical care at the hospital where her daughter died stopped going to the doctor after her daughter's death; she could not bring herself to go into the building. A man whose beloved wife had died could not watch a movie as this was something they had done regularly together. An elderly woman refused to eat oatmeal because this was the breakfast she and her husband had shared for decades. A father could not bear to listen to the music his son enjoyed.

Some people with CG fear losing control of their emotions. One woman changed jobs so she would not have to answer questions about her loss. Often friends and family are similarly reluctant to engage in such conversation. One family put away all the pictures of their nephew whenever his father visited.

Given the avoidance, it is perhaps puzzling that preoccupation with articles attached to the deceased or with special music or scrapbooks also occurs. Some individuals with CG refrain from involvement in any activities that are not directly connected to the lost loved one. Others spend hours at the cemetery every day. Some become very involved with Internet or in-person support groups, spending large amounts of time discussing how difficult this loss has been, or trying to help others. For some patients, the main objective of avoidance behavior is an attempt to refrain from becoming preoccupied.

Karen explains that as soon as she has contact with something that belonged to her dead husband she is caught up in a lengthy reverie, thinking,"Jim, oh, Jim. I remember when you wore this. You looked so handsome. You were so very special. Why did you leave me? How I miss you! Where have you gone? How did this happen? I can't bear my life without you," and so on, ending with intensifying pain.

Many individuals with CG feel drawn to objects associated with the deceased. Thus, both avoidance and preoccupation contribute to the cluster of behavioral symptoms commonly seen in this condition. It is also common for painful feelings of estrangement to interfere with social functioning. The bereaved person feels an unfamiliar self-consciousness with acquaintances and old friends, and relatives are perceived as reminders of shared times, or as secret critics, evaluating how the person is doing with his or her grief. Friends and relatives eventually begin to feel frustrated and helpless and grow impatient. Powerless to comfort the patient, they turn to avoidance or sometimes gentle confrontation over the need to "get over this loss and move on in your life." However, the patient is equally powerless to relinquish her or his symptoms and often feels quite hurt and angry about the growing lack of sympathy. The result is a further increase in the feeling of isolation.

Individuals with CG often feel they are at the end of their rope, and any additional problem will be too much to deal with. On occasion, the person completely shuts down. A woman called begging us to see her husband, who had "become a different person" since the death of his son. He had shepherded the family business into bankruptcy, and he was unable to engage emotionally with his wife or other family members. A bereaved wife had lost her job because of a medical problem and was unable to complete disability papers or medical insurance documents. As a result, she barely had enough money to survive. Sometimes the person appears to the outside world to be functioning, but he or she will be emotionally unavailable and feel like a shell.

Complicated grief shares some features with DSM-IV mood and anxiety disorders (APA, 1994). Yet it is important to distinguish CG from these conditions. Major depressive disorder (MDD) and CG have different risk factors, different clinical correlates, different temporal courses, different responses to tricyclic antidepressants, and different outcomes. Sadness and loss of interest or pleasure in CG are focused on missing the loved one, while these feelings are pervasive with MDD. Suicidality is as likely to be related to joining the loved one as it is to feelings of hopelessness or self-devaluation.

CG also resembles PTSD. However, a postloss stress syndrome differs in important ways. The nature of the event is loss of a positive, sustaining relationship rather than exposure to violence. PTSD separation distress (e.g., yearning or searching for the deceased) is not prominent in PTSD while it is a core symptom cluster in CG. The unbidden, intrusive thoughts about and longings for the deceased appear to have a dual origin in the trauma of the loss, and in a wish — growing out of separation anxiety — to be reunited with him or her. The most prominent and consistent affect in CG is sadness, in contrast to prominent fear in PTSD. Avoidance is more complex and variable in CG. Perhaps most telling, many people with CG do not meet criteria for PTSD. Thus, we judge CG to be a distinct disorder, and we developed a targeted treatment to alleviate the symptoms.

COMPLICATED GRIEF TREATMENT

The CG treatment model is based on the conceptualization of adjustment to loss we have described above. CG is thought to develop because the usual progress from acute grief to integrated loss is impeded. The goal of the treatment is to free ("unblock") the natural grief process. Put another way, the person with CG is not coping effectively with an important loss. We seek to help people improve their coping effectiveness. We draw upon Stroebe and Schut's ideas about dual process coping and structure the treatment sessions so that each encompasses a focus on both loss and restoration coping. Furthermore, we incorporate some attention to religious and spiritual coping. While we attended to spiritual issues throughout our studies, recent work with a local church has refined our ideas about how this can be done. We include a discussion of spiritual evaluation and intervention here. The treatment we devised integrates interpersonal psychotherapy (IPT) for depression and cognitive–behavioral treatment of PTSD. Similar to IPT, our treatment has an introductory, middle, and termination phase.

Introductory Phase

During the first three introductory sessions, the therapist takes a history that includes inquiry about the relationship to the deceased, the story of the death, the course of grief since the loss, and the state of current relationships. The patient is given a handout describing usual grief and the symptoms of complicated grief. A grief monitoring diary is introduced, and the patient completes this weekly throughout the treatment.

The therapist provides an overview of the treatment and its rationale. The concept of loss-oriented and restoration-oriented coping is explained, and the therapist describes procedures from each track that continue side by side. As a part of the restoration-oriented focus, work is begun on establishing personal goals. Loss-oriented procedures of revisiting and imaginal conversation with the deceased are explained. In the remainder of this chapter we highlight the main components of our approach using the case of Karen M as an example. We focus on procedures used in the middle phase of the treatment. We provide a general sense of the rhythm of the treatment.

Middle Phase

The middle phase of treatment begins with session 4. During this session the procedure we call "imaginal revisiting" is introduced. This technique, derived from work by Foa and her colleagues (Foa & Rothbaum, 1998) entails asking the patient to close her eyes and tell the story of the death as though it is happening in the present. The story begins at the time the patient first learns of the death and proceeds until she leaves the body (if present) or until the end of that day. The story is tape recorded and the patient is invited to take the tape home and listen to it on a daily basis. The story is limited to 15 to 20 minutes. During this time the therapist monitors the subjective units of distress (SUDS) level, asking the patient to rate this on a 0 to 100 scale. SUDS levels are reported every two to four minutes during the story, especially when distress level escalates.

Imaginal revisiting is highly evocative and almost always results in SUDS levels of 100 for most of the period of telling the story for the first time. As a result, we use a standard procedure to debrief and then to "put away" the story. Following the end of the story, or after 15 minutes (whichever occurs first), the therapist asks the patient to stop and open her eyes. The therapist asks the patient to talk about how this went and what she observed. The patient is encouraged to reflect on her experience. Following this debriefing, the therapist asks the patient to imagine the story is on a videotape and invites her to imagine herself rewinding the tape and putting it away. The SUDS levels are checked after this. At this point, the discussion turns to plans for self-care and rewards.

The therapist asks the patient to plan to reward herself for the hard work of the treatment. They discuss what kinds of rewards might be best. These are activities that the patient enjoys. The patient is asked to take especially good care of herself during this treatment, by treating herself gently psychologically and by physically taking care. In addition, as often as daily, if possible, the patient is asked to reward herself. This may be by going to a good movie, reading a good book, going for a walk, taking a relaxing bath, or purchasing a wanted item. Self-care is an important component of this treatment. In addition the therapist discusses personal goals.

Personal goals in this treatment are long term. The patient is asked to think about what she would want for herself if the grief could be magically dispelled. She is encouraged to think about things that would make her life pleasurable and satisfying. This may be a long-standing goal that was set aside for awhile. It may be something that could not be pursued when the deceased was alive. It may be something the patient and deceased planned to do together. Once such a goal is identified, the therapist works with the patient to decide how she will know if she is making progress on the goal, who can help her, and what barriers she anticipates. This approach is derived from techniques used in motivational enhancement therapy (Miller & Rollnick, 2002; Zweben & Zuckoff, 2002). At each session, the therapist helps the patient decide on some concrete steps to take toward these goals.

Revisiting is continued for at least three more sessions with the aim of reducing the overall distress in telling the story, identifying the parts that are particularly difficult ("hot spots"), and helping the patient reflect on the narrative of the story. Questions such as how the deceased was feeling, whether he suffered, whether he knew how much the bereaved person loved him, often arise in this context. These questions are then used in the imaginal conversation, described below. The therapist provides direct support and cheer leading during the period of imaginal revisiting. When warranted, direct praise is provided. In fact, we believe it requires enormous courage to participate in these emotionally evocative exercises and patients do not always give themselves credit for this. It is important for the therapist to do so.

After the third revisiting session, the therapist adds the first of a series of five memories forms that consist of a series of questions about the deceased. Memories forms are completed at home and reviewed in the following session. The therapist also invites the patient to bring in pictures of the deceased at this time. The first memories form is "Favorite Memories." This is followed by "Things I Still Think About," "Most Favorite Memories," "Some Difficult Times," and "All Kinds of Memories." The therapist spends time in the beginning of each session reviewing and discussing the past week's memories form as well as the grief monitoring diary. During this period situational revisiting exercises are also planned and implemented.

After SUDS levels are noticeably reduced during revisiting and there is a coherent narrative of the story of the death, the therapist invites the patient to have an imaginal conversation with the deceased. Revisiting the death will always be a difficult and emotionally evocative exercise, so the expectation is not that the SUDS levels will be low. Rather, it is important that there is a reasonable level of comfort in telling the story and that the distress during the telling is noticeably less than in the beginning. The goal is for the patient to feel free to think about the death from time to time. This is important in case these thoughts are needed for revising the mental representation of the deceased to incorporate the death (Shear & Shair, 2005). We work with the patient to feel comfortable with thinking about the death and also with setting aside those thoughts.

The imaginal conversation with the deceased is a powerful component of our treatment. This procedure entails asking the patient to again close her eyes and imagine she is with the deceased at a time close to his death. She is invited to imagine that she can talk with him, even though he has already died, and that he can hear and respond. The patient is reminded that we do not believe this is literally true, but rather that we can imagine such a scenario. The patient is further invited to talk with the deceased to tell him anything she wishes to say to him or ask him about that he might be able to answer. Typically patients express their love at this point. Often they ask how the person is doing, if he is frightened, or if he is at peace. Frequently, too, there are questions about whether the deceased thought the patient did enough, whether the deceased knows how much the person loves him, and such.

The therapist then invites the patient to take the role of the deceased and to respond. The bereaved person, speaking for the deceased, usually reflects the same loving comments that the patient expressed to him. Imagining the voice of the deceased, the bereaved person usually answers the questions in a positive way, affirming the love between them and the strength of the relationship.

Again, imagining the deceased is speaking, the patient usually reassures herself that the deceased person is at peace. The net result of this exercise is that the patient feels deeply reassured and connected to the deceased. This exercise is usually done once or twice, but occasionally is repeated during several more sessions, if the patient feels she has more to say.

The therapist elicits SUDS levels during and after the imaginal conversation, as is done with the revisiting exercise. When the conversation is over, the therapist asks the patient to reflect on how this went. The conversation is debriefed. However, we do not usually conduct the imagery exercise to put the story away. Instead, the therapist transitions, as always, to a discussion of plans for self-care, rewards, daily monitoring, and situational revisiting exercises, and ends with a discussion of progress on goals.

The final three sessions of the treatment are focused on termination. During this period, the rationale for the treatment is reviewed, progress is assessed, and plans for the future are discussed. The permanent nature of grief is underscored and the idea that even when integrated, an important loss can provoke a temporary upsurge of grief at vulnerable times. One way bereaved people get into trouble is when they chastise themselves or worry about having transient periods of increased symptoms. The therapist works with the patient to help her understand that such difficult periods are natural and do not indicate that the person is back where she started. During the last three sessions any questions are answered and any residual problems are addressed. Feelings about the ending of the treatment are discussed.

Often the idea of ending the treatment evokes a feeling of leaving the deceased person in the room with the therapist. In reflecting on the progress she has made, the patient recalls how much more dominant the deceased was in her everyday life at the beginning of the treatment. Sometimes the patient interprets the receding of this dominance as breaking a bond with the deceased. The therapist encourages the patient to see this differently. The loss is now integrated into the ongoing life of the patient instead of "sitting on top of her," weighing her down. The therapist emphasizes the fact that the patient has a strong and deep sense of connection to her loved one, which incorporates the full richness and complexity of their relationship. Rather than the intense focus on the death and the period of loss, memories can now be more fluid and satisfying. The therapist encourages the patient to accept the passing of acute grief as a natural process of adjustment. Discussion of any feelings about leaving the therapist is also invited.

COMPLICATED GRIEF TREATMENT STUDY

The treatment described in this paper was subjected to a randomized controlled trial, funded by NIMH (Shear et al., 2005). This study enrolled 95 individuals who had been bereaved for at least six months. Mean time since the death was about two years. Thirty-one (33%) lost a loved one to a violent death. Approximately 27% lost a spouse, 27% lost a parent, 27% lost a child, and 18% lost a close friend or another relative. All participants scored over 30 on the ICG; mean score was 45. Most (88%) were women and white (77%). Mean age was 48. Forty-five percent met criteria for current major depression and 49% met criteria for current PTSD.

Participants were randomly assigned to receive either complicated grief treatment or interpersonal psychotherapy for a period of approximately 16 weeks. Therapists were all master's- or doctoral- level clinicians with at least two years of experience. They underwent extensive training in the treatment they provided and attended weekly supervision sessions throughout the study period. Assessments were conducted by independent evaluators and self-report.

Results indicated better response for complicated grief treatment than for IPT. Specifically, among the entire randomized group, 51% of those treated with complicated grief treatment compared to 28% of those treated with IPT, were judged responders chi-square = 5.07, df = 1, p < 0.024. Twelve IPT and 15 CGT participants dropped out of treatment. For those who completed the treatment, 66% treated with CGT and 32% of those with IPT were responders. A survival analysis indicated that time to response was shorter for CGT.

Karen M's Treatment

The therapist obtained the information about Karen's relationship with her husband in the introductory sessions of the treatment. He learned that Karen had been married at age 22 and had her first child a year after the wedding. Jim was her high school sweetheart and she had stopped seeing him after they graduated because he wanted to see other women. She was devastated by this but gradually began to date and thought she was beginning to have fun when she ran into him at a party. He asked her to dance and they left the party shortly thereafter, leaving their dates to fend for themselves. She recalls the next phase of their relationship as the most romantic period in her life. They spent as much time together as possible and loved being in each other's company. They began socializing with their old group and everyone loved seeing them together again. After about six months they announced their engagement. Karen remembered their wedding as being the most wonderful day of her life. She described the early period of their marriage and the time after their children were born. Jim was very uncomfortable with small children and he seemed to suddenly have a lot more demands on his time after their oldest daughter was born. She bore some resentment about this, and even wondered for awhile if he was having an affair. However, as the other children were born and grew older, it became clear that Jim was infatuated with his children. His oldest daughter was the apple of his eye and his son, the middle child, was his pride. He was a gentle, loving father to all of his children, and Karen forgot about her irritation with him. The children were 19, 17, and 14 when he died. Karen does not know how she managed after that. Some of the time is only dim in her memory. Her own older sister and their mother stepped in and took charge and without them, she thinks there would have been a real disaster. Now though, it seems that the children have coped better with this death than she has.

Her oldest daughter was married at age 23 and has eight-year-old and six-year-old sons. Her son married six years ago and his first child was born shortly thereafter. He has three other children. The youngest is six months old. Karen's youngest daughter is engaged to be married. Karen is close to all of her children, especially her son, but she feels an uncomfortable sense of distance from them at the same time. In particular, her son reminds her so much of his father that she sometimes has to leave when she is at his house visiting. Her oldest daughter is a little bossy and seems cold to Karen.

The therapist describes the model for understanding usual grief and complicated grief and explains how the treatment is designed to help get complicated grief back on track. He gives Karen the handout. Karen is interested in these ideas. Although she has participated in support groups and grief therapy, much of this is new to her. She has never been told that her symptoms could be diagnosed. Rather, others have told her that she experienced a terrible loss and she will need to deal with it in her own way. She finds it strangely reassuring to think this might not be quite right. The explanation the therapist provides sounds reasonable. The handout makes a lot of sense to her and helps her feel a little more hope.

Karen is interested in the idea that she should think about her own personal goals. She remarks that she is not really sure she ever did that. Then she begins to recall that during the period after high school when she and Jim had stopped seeing each other, she had begun to be interested in computers. She had gone to work as a secretary because her family was short of money, but she was considering applying to community college in the evening to study computer programming. She had always done well in math and she seemed to have some aptitude for computers. She brightened as she recalled this phase of her life, commenting, "Gee. I haven't thought about that for a really long time." With the therapist's encouragement, she considered whether she might still be interested in learning about computers. She wasn't so sure, but she decided to give it more thought. She agreed to look on the Internet for possible jobs and see if there were any that intrigued her, even if she was not qualified to apply right now.

In the fourth session, the therapist introduced the revisiting exercise. Karen expressed fear and trepidation about agreeing to do this very emotional procedure. She asked what would happen if this made her worse. The therapist responded by telling her that this was possible, though not so likely, beyond a possible brief period in the beginning. He reassured her that he would be available to her in any case, that she could call him between sessions if she needed to, and that he would help her as best he could. She agreed to proceed. The first revisiting session was extremely emotional and the therapist stopped it after only 10 minutes. He praised her extensively and helped her debrief the story and then put it away. They discussed self-care and rewards and Karen agreed to visit her daughter and play with her grandchildren at least three days a week. She also said she would spend some time just reading by herself. This is something she enjoys but often tells herself is a waste of time. The session ended with a focus on goals work. SUDS level at the end of the session was 60.

The next three revisiting sessions went well and by the end of the fourth session, SUDS level was 70 for most of the story and jumped to 100 at the moment just after Jim was shot, when one of the survivors had reported he cried out, "Oh my god I am shot. I can't breathe! I can't breathe!" Karen repeatedly sobbed hysterically when she got to that part of the story. In the debriefing she explained that she has this terrible feeling that he was so frightened and alone at that moment and she hates thinking of him that way. The therapist works with her to help her recall that the medics arrived almost immediately after that and quickly put an oxygen mask on him and stayed with him, talking with him. After discussing this a number of times, Karen began to realize that the idea of Jim being frightened and alone was scaring her so much that she lost track of the progress of the story. She now realized that there was likely very little time when this occurred. When she returned after this session, she said she felt better than she had in a while.

After several weeks of considering computer jobs and thinking about her future, Karen decided she would like to learn to be a network administrator. She thought this would be a job where she would interact with people and also have responsibility for computer work. She liked the idea of being in a service job. She said her brother-in-law worked at a company that had an intranet and he was friendly with the people in the IT group. He might be able to help her learn more about the job and the training she would need. By the end of the treatment, Karen had met a woman she liked at her brother's company and they were seeing each other socially. This woman also had become a mentor in helping Karen plan her application to a local trade school where she could learn the skills needed to do a computer networking job. She described this as one of the most interesting things she has done in a long time.

Karen's progress on revisiting, and her work with different kinds of memories of Jim led to a marked improvement in her mood and she began reporting periods of time when she really had fun with her grandchildren. Her daughter had asked her if they had found a new medication because her mother seemed so much brighter and so different. Karen was ready for the imaginal conversation. This exercise was difficult for her. It again evoked strong feelings and a SUDS level of 80 as she began imagining herself talking with Jim. She told him how much she loved him and missed him and said she hoped he was at peace and in heaven. He "answered" in her imagined response by affirming his love for her as well. He said though that he did not really miss her because he felt himself with her all the time. She imagined that he said, "Things are different up here in heaven. The world is peaceful and good and you don't really have the same kind of problems you have when you are alive on earth." Karen then asked him several other questions and again responded as though she were him. At the end of this "conversation" she reported feeling a strange and powerful sense of closeness to Jim. She said she felt relieved.

By the end of her treatment Karen is no longer experiencing reveries and has begun to dispose of Jim's clothes and other possessions. She is using all six rooms of the house and considering whether she will move back into the master bedroom. She is no longer susceptible to painful musings and recollections when reminded of Jim. She approaches his belongings in a practical way, keeping a few things of value and disposing of the rest. She now has a strong sense that Jim was with her much of the time, and she sometimes takes opportunities to "talk with him" in her mind, seeking his advice or comfort. She tells the therapist that she feels like a different person. She says she feels more hopeful and alive than she has felt in a very long time. In fact, she feels different from the way she has previously felt. She is very grateful and repeatedly says she never thought this would be possible.

To protect confidentiality, this case is a composite of patient presentations coalesced into a single case presentation. Karen is an example of the kind of patient and treatment that we have seen in our treatment center. Clearly, this would be considered a highly successful treatment and not all patients respond as well. However, many do, and we believe it is important for therapists to know this kind of approach can be helpful.

REFERENCES

Bisconti, T. L., Bergeman, C. S., & Boker, S. M. (2004). Emotional well-being in recently bereaved widows: A dynamical systems approach. *Journal of Gerontology: Psychological Sciences, 59b*, 158–167.

Bonanno, G. A., Wortman, C. B., Nesse, R. M., Prospective patterns of resilience and maladjustment during widowhood. Psychol Aging. 2004 Jun;19(2):260–71.

Eliot, G. (1849). *Adam Bede*. New York: Harper & Brothers.

Foa, E. B. & Rothbaum, B. O. (1998). Treating the trauma of rape: Cognitive-behavioral therapy for PTSD. In *Treatment Manuals for Practitioners*.

Horowitz, M. (December, 1974). Stress response syndromes. Character style and dynamic psychotherapy. *Archives of General Psychiatry, 31*(6):768–781.

Langner, R. & Maercker, A. (2005). Complicated grief as a stress response disorder: Evaluating diagnostic criteria in a German sample. *Journal of Psychosomatic Research, 58*, 235–242.

Lindemann, E. (1944). Symptomatology and management of acute grief. *American Journal of Psychiatry, 101*, 141–148.

Miller, W. R. & Rollnick, R. (2002). *Motivational interviewing: Preparing people for change* (2nd ed.). New York: Guilford.

Prigerson, H. G., Maciejewski, P. K., Reynolds, C. F., Bierhals, A. J., Newsom, J. T., Fasiczka, A., Frank, E., Doman, J., & Miller, M. (1995). Inventory of complicated grief: A scale to measure maladaptive symptoms of loss. *Psychiatry Research, 59*, 65–79.

Shear, M. K. Frank, E., Houck, P., & Reynolds, C. F. (2005).Treatment of complicated grief: A randomized controlled trial. *Journal of the American Medical Association, 293*, 2601–2608.

Shear, M. K. & Shair, H. (2005). Attachment loss and complicated grief. *Developmental Psychobiology, 47*, 253–267.

Stroebe, M., & Schut, H. (1999). The dual process model of coping with bereavement: Rationale and description. *Death Studies, 23*, 197–224.

Stroebe, M., Stroebe, W., & Abakoumkin, G. (2005). The broken heart: Suicidal ideation in bereavement. *American Journal of Psychiatry, 162,* 2178–2180.

Stroebe, M. S., Stroebe, W., & Hansson, R. O. (1993). Bereavement research and theory: An introduction to the Handbook. In M. S. Stroebe, W. Stroebe, & R. O. Hansson (Eds.), *Handbook of bereavement: Theory, research and intervention.* New York and Cambridge, England: Cambridge University Press, 3–22.

Stroebe, W., Stroebe, M., Abakoumkin, G., & Schut, H. (1996). The role of loneliness and social support in adjustment to loss: A test of attachment versus stress theory. *Journal of Personality & Social Psychology; 70,* 1241–1249.

Sundin, E. C. & Horowitz, M. J. (2003). Horowitz's Impact of Event scale: Evaluation of 20 years of use. *Psychosomatic Medicine, 65,* 870–876.

Weissman, M. M., Markowitz, J. C., & Klerman, G. L. (2000). *Comprehensive guide to interpersonal psychotherapy.* New York: Basic Books.

Zweben, A. & Zuckoff, A. (2002). Motivational interviewing and treatment adherence. In W. R. Miller & S. Rollnick (Eds.), *Preparing people for change.* New York: Guilford.

10

Evidence-Based Interventions for Parents Following Their Children's Violent Deaths

SHIRLEY A. MURPHY

EVIDENCE-BASED GROUP THERAPY

This chapter is a breathtaking summation of the findings and clinical recommendations from one of the most ambitious studies of violent death bereavement — a community-based, five-year prospective study of parents after the violent death of a child. It is bursting with relevant information, beginning with a scholarly review of intervention studies, followed by a description of a five-year empirical study, including randomized assignment to a short-term group intervention or control group. The findings are refreshingly extensive, beyond the familiar clinical measures of trauma and grief, to include measures of spirituality, meaning, marital satisfaction, and perceived support. The data verify what clinicians have long suspected — that high risk of persistent distress can be predicted in highly traumatized mothers whose child died by homicide, and a short-term intervention is associated with significant symptomatic improvement in highly distressed mothers, but not fathers — and there is a significant degree of spontaneous symptomatic improvement within the first year of bereavement. The findings are so comprehensive, resonating themes introduced from the opening chapters and remaining chapters on intervention, that this chapter is foundational.

The chances of a parent having a child die by violent means have increased substantially over the past several decades (U.S. National Center for Health Statistics, 1992). Accidents, homicides, and suicides are the leading causes of death among young people in the United States. Most violent deaths are classified as accidents. Within the accident category, motor vehicle crashes are the major cause of death. Homicide is second among U.S. causes of death among young people. Deaths by homicide are expected to continue to rise as 40 million children reach adolescence by 2010. Suicide rates tripled among U.S. youth between 1970 and 1990 (U. S. National Center for Health Statistics, 2000). When violent deaths of young people occur, the suddenness, irrevocability, and disbelief that an offspring has died before the parent causes intense personal suffering, and affects reintegration into community life.

This chapter is consistent with the primary purpose of this text; that is, it addresses the question, "What happens to individuals bereaved by violent death after the immediate crisis period?" Over a five-year period, 173 parents bereaved by violent death shared their experiences with us in various formats: interviews, written responses, and in bereavement program sessions.

VIOLENT DEATH AMONG YOUTH AND YOUNG ADULTS AND PARENT BEREAVEMENT

An important developmental task of youth is the definition of self, including one's independence from parents. Many young people perceive themselves as being invulnerable to harm (Dryfoos, 1991). It is in this context that many deaths of youth and young adults occur. All three modes of violent death discussed in this chapter (i.e., accidents, homicides, and suicides) produce both similar and different adjustment tasks for parents bereaved in these ways. These experiences reported by parents have serious implications for their ongoing adaptation and can be overlooked by the clergy, grief counselors, and other treatment providers. The three similarities addressed here are: (1) the interplay between grief and symptoms of posttraumatic stress disorder (PTSD); (2) changes in parents' assumptive worlds; and (3) disruptions in interpersonal relationships and social networks.

Parents are devastated by a child's death. Grief responses include intense sorrow and longing brought about by the child's absence, missing the child and hoping for his or her return, and feelings of guilt, anxiety, anger, and depression (Gilbert, 1997; Klass, 1999; Lord, 1996). The grief response overlaps with the trauma response (PTSD). Many parents bereaved by violent death report symptoms in one or all three PTSD symptom clusters: reexperiencing (images of the death scene); as written avoidance (attempts to rid the self of the reality of the death); and hyperarousal (difficulty sleeping, being easily startled, feeling fearful) (American Psychiatric Association, 1987; Amick-McMullen, Kilpatrick, & Resnick, 1991; Murphy, Braun, et al., 1999; Murphy, Johnson, Chung, & Beaton, 2003; Thompson, Norris, & Rubeck, 1998).

A second common consequence among parents bereaved by violent death, often not addressed by professionals, is the parents' shattered assumptive worlds. The phenomenon "assumptive world," was poignantly described by Janoff-Bulman and Frieze (1983). These trauma experts postulate that most persons generally view the world as benevolent and meaningful and the self as worthy. Trauma brings about an abrupt change in one's worldview: "I have become helpless and weak in a malevolent, meaningless world." This part of the theory explains why parents bereaved by traumatic death are at risk for lowered self-esteem and self-efficacy and express concerns about personal safety. The predominant early emotional responses are fear and anxiety that result from trying to make sense of what has happened. Denial and numbing represent efforts to shut out reality, whereas the opposite — intrusive thoughts and reexperiencing the event — represent efforts to confront reality.

A third common consequence in violent death bereavement is a change in parents' interpersonal relationships and social networks. Janoff-Bulman and Frieze (1983) and Wortman and Lehman (1983) posited that an individual's initial reaction to another's victimization challenges his or her own vulnerability; that is, "this could happen to me." The personalizing of another's plight, particularly when the same event is perceived as possible for them, is apparently so compelling that feelings of threat, vulnerability, helplessness, and anxiety occur. These uncomfortable feelings are dealt with by blame, avoidance, and discounting the victim's (bereaved parent) experiences. Silver and her colleagues (Silver, Wortman, & Crofton, 1990) suggested that the bereaved who can present a "balanced coping portrayal," by acknowledging that they are having a difficult time, while simultaneously convincing others that they are coping well, are more likely to receive needed support than those who cannot present themselves in this way.

BEST PRACTICES FOR THE TREATMENT OF BEREAVEMENT CONSEQUENCES

Currently, there are several approaches to determine evidence-based practices, or more simply, "best practices." The first approach is the generation of definitions. For example, Sackett (1996) wrote that evidence-based practice is the conscientious, explicit, and judicious use of the best evidence gained from systematic research for the purpose of making informed decisions about the care of individual patients.

A second approach to determine best practices is to conduct a critical review of the literature. Allumbaugh and Hoyt (1999) conducted a meta-analysis of 35 studies to address the effectiveness of grief therapy. These authors noted that the average delay between a death and treatment was 27 months. Poor treatment outcomes were attributed to this time lag and other factors. Kato and Mann (1999) published a review of psychological interventions for the bereaved. Thirteen studies met their inclusion criteria. These authors concluded that testing of theory was rare, interventions were methodologically flawed, and treatment effect sizes were small. Most of the studies reviewed by Allumbaugh and Hoyt and Kato and Mann were based on spousal bereavement. However, theses authors provide some indication of the quality of bereavement intervention studies conducted since the early 1980s.

A third approach to determine best practice is to develop criteria and then look for practices that meet the criteria. The Board of Directors of the International Society for Traumatic Stress Studies (ISTSS) appointed a task force to develop best practice treatment criteria specific to PTSD. The task force defined six levels (A through F). Level A evidence is based upon randomized, well-controlled, clinical trials. "Well-controlled" studies include the following: clearly defined target symptoms, reliable and valid measurement tools, manualized, replicable, specific treatment programs, unbiased assignment to treatment, and client adherence to treatment. Levels B through F provide additional, less rigorous criteria (Foa, Keane, & Friedman, 2000). It is not clear from the ISTSS report whether the recommended treatment modalities were tested specifically with bereaved parents. Because of the "state of the science" in regard to the lack of knowledge of the effectiveness of therapies for bereaved parents, this chapter includes a description of an empirical study conducted by the author.

THE PARENT BEREAVEMENT PROJECT

A randomized controlled clinical trial was implemented at study sites in Seattle (WA) and Portland (OR). The National Institutes of Health (NIH) funded the project for five years. Additional small grants were obtained to conduct a five-year follow-up and continue with data analysis for another five years. The purpose of the bereavement program was to reduce bereaved parents' symptoms of mental distress and posttraumatic stress, maintain physical health, improve marital and parental role performance, and promote loss accommodation following the accidental, homicidal, or suicidal deaths of a 12- to 28-year-old child (Murphy, Johnson, Cain, et al., 1998). Approval of recruitment procedures and consent for participation were obtained from the investigator's university and the Oregon State Health Division Institutional Review Board. The initial plan was to follow parents for two years after the intervention.

Study Recruitment and Enrollment Procedures

Study inclusion criteria were: (1) to recruit parents of 12- to 28-year-old children who died violently within the past two to six months. "Parent" was defined for study purposes as married or single mothers and fathers of a biological, step, or adoptive child; (2) parents needed to reside in a three-county area in either western Oregon or Washington to be available to meet with the research team and complete questionnaires; (3) the deceased child was to be unmarried and between the ages of 12 and 28 at the time of death; and (4) the cause of death was limited to accident, homicide, or suicide.

We used several procedures to keep selection bias at a minimum. First, parent contact information was obtained from death certificates of the deceased children so that every bereaved parent we could contact would have an equal chance of being in the study. We did not recruit parents from support groups and treatment providers because treatment seekers are known to differ from nontreatment seekers (Lipsey, 1990). Second, knowing that nonresponders differ from responders (Levy & Derby, 1992), we made every effort to enroll all parents that we could contact (we reached 329 of the 571 for whom we obtained contact information, that is, 58%. Of these, 62% agreed to participate in the study).

Letters were mailed to parents that included a mail-back form with a posted envelope. The letter stated that a follow-up phone call would be made if the form was not returned within a week. The primary reasons given for refusal were work schedules and perceptions that help was not needed. We found no demographic differences between study refusers and study joiners.

Three years were required to recruit a sample of parents large enough to conduct multivariate data analysis. During the three-year period, we enrolled 261 parents (171 mothers and 90 fathers who represented 204 households). The sample included 69 married couples. Most of the remaining 123 persons were single mothers. Fifty-six percent of the parents were randomly assigned to the intervention and 42% were assigned to the control condition. Married couples were assigned to the same treatment condition.

Four groups were conducted simultaneously each September, January, and April with eight to 10 parents per group. The program began two to three weeks after parents were initially contacted. The bereavement program was conducted in small groups, with eight to 10 parents per group.

The Participating Parents

Parents' ages ranged from 32 to 61 years, with 45 years being the average age. The sample was 86% Caucasian, which was consistent with the population in the two Northwest states in the 1990s when the study was undertaken. Study parents' average years of schooling was 13.8 and 65% were employed. Nearly 80% of the parents professed a religious affiliation. Among the married couples in the study, the average number of years married to the current spouse was 18 years. Ninety percent of the study parents were the biological parents of their deceased children; 5% were adoptive parents; and 5% were stepparents. Four percent of the sample consisted of parents of an only child who died. Only a few study parents witnessed their children's deaths.

The Deceased Children of Study Parents

The average age of the deceased child was 20 years old; 65% were males and 35% were females. The most common cause of death was accidents (57.8%) followed by suicide (23.6%). Homicide (9.7%) and causes of death not classified by coroners (8.9%) were less frequent.

The Bereavement Program

The program was offered for 12 consecutive weeks with each weekly session lasting two hours. The sessions were held in conference rooms in community colleges and office buildings. The program had two dimensions, problem-focused support and emotion-focused support (Thoits, 1986; Yalom, 1985). The problem-focused dimension offered a different topic with skill-building experiences during each session. Examples are: Managing the Marital Relationship, and Managing Feelings Toward Others, especially anger, hostility, and revenge. The emotion-focused dimension was a professionally led support group (Murphy, Johnson, Cain, et al., 1998). Pretreatment and posttreatment data were collected in small groups with research staff present. All sessions were tape recorded to monitor consistency of the content offered.

Parents provided evaluations of the program after each session, and the staff participated in debriefings after each session. Parent attendance was high: 94% attended six or more sessions. The problem-focused support component was delivered according to protocols. The longitudinal study design provided the opportunity to measure seasonal effects and major holidays that could confound study results, observe therapist characteristics, and note the effects of different group themes that evolved as a result of differing group constellations.

Several strategies were implemented to reduce attrition, or dropping out, between data collections: (1) $25 stipends (made possible by funding) were issued within a week following each data collection. Parents had the option of having the project send the stipend to a fund of their choice or have payment mailed to them; (2) a project newsletter was sent to parents between data collections to maintain parents' interest in the study and to keep mailing addresses current; (3) a tracking system kept the research team informed of the status of each study participant as he or she moved through the ongoing data collections; and (4) parents were telephoned to determine if letters were received and to remind them of upcoming sessions.

Five years later, 173 parents (115 mothers and 58 fathers, i.e., 67% of the original sample) remained in the study. Statistical tests for attrition bias between early dropouts and those remaining in the study were all nonsignificant.

Intervention Results

Intervention group mothers showed significant improvement on mental distress and PTSD when compared with control group mothers. These benefits were sustained up to 18 months (two years postdeath) after the program ended. Intervention group fathers did not differ statistically from control group fathers on any outcome measured. The lack of apparent benefit for fathers may have been due to the small group sizes for statistical comparisons and known differences between men and women, that is, role socialization; men tend to underreport symptoms on health questionnaires, and some bereaved men have what Martin and Doka (2000) refer to as "dissonant coping", that is, a persistent way of expressing grief that is at odds with the griever's primary internal experience.

Spouses who attended the program together reported significantly more practice of communication and other skills between sessions than parents who attended without spouses.

Parents' Evaluation of the Bereavement Program

After each of the two-hour weekly sessions, parents completed a three-page questionnaire. Items that addressed the relevance and timing of content and clarity of the presentation evaluated the problem-focused dimension. The emotion-focused dimension was evaluated by asking parents to rate group leader qualities and Yalom's (1985) nine therapeutic factors, shown to facilitate change in members participating in small group treatment.

The program was highly endorsed by parents. The relevance of the topics and their timing in bereavement were highly rated. The emotion-focused dimensions rated most highly were cohesion ("helped me feel I belonged") and universality ("helped me feel I'm not alone"). Ratings regarding the usefulness of each of the two program components showed that 63% of the parents rated "both parts equally useful." Seventy-five percent of the mothers and 65% of the fathers completed the open-ended comment section. The following were representative comments: "We came here as strangers and now say things we wouldn't say to anyone else"; "the session tonight helped validate my feelings, actions, and reactions"; "I learned something important tonight about letting others help me"; "talking helps, listening helps even more." Less than 1% of the comments were negative or suggested how things might be done differently (Murphy, Baugher, et al., 1996).

Five years later, the 173 parents (115 mothers and 58 fathers) who remained in the study over time, were asked to think back about their bereavement and tell us what would have been the ideal help at several time periods (i.e. the first six months, the second year, etc.). Parents could choose any of several options being offered: the phone number of another bereaved parent; the phone number of a professional helper; a program similar to the Parent Bereavement Project; or a list of community resources. The most frequent response was "having a program similar to the Parent Bereavement Project."

Part I: Longitudinal Study Findings

The longitudinal findings reported here are based on data collected from the 173 parents who remained in the study for five years and for whom data were available on all variables at 4, 12, 24, and 60 months after their children's deaths. These findings include four of the primary outcome variables (mental distress, PSTD, physical health, and finding meaning); one of two secondary outcome variables (marital satisfaction, not family functioning); and seven intervening variables (parents' coping strategies, self-esteem, social support, job absenteeism and productivity, existential beliefs and religious practices, beliefs of preventability, and acceptance of the children's deaths), and are discussed in relation to how they affected parents' major outcomes. The majority of the study variables were measured by standardized questionnaires. In addition, some items included in the questionnaire packet asked parents to "list" concerns; some items were open-ended (i.e., parents could write as much or as little as they desired).

Gender Difference Findings over Time on Major Outcomes

Mental Distress.

Bereaved mothers' scores on mental distress as measured by the Brief Symptom Inventory (BSI) (Derogatis, 1992) were higher than fathers' scores at all measurement times; however, the two highest BSI subscale scores were the same for both fathers and mothers (cognitive performance deficits and depression). Higher scores signify higher distress. Mothers also scored high on interpersonal sensitivity and anxiety. The steepest decline in scores for mothers was between four and 12 months postloss. Intervention group fathers' scores were similar to those of the control group until the second year, when they increased, then decreased by five years postdeath. In comparison with nonbereaved adults in their same age groups, both study mothers and fathers' mean scores on all BSI subscales were at least *twice as high five years postdeath.* It must be emphasized that scores are group averages. There was a wide range in scores (Murphy, Chung, & Johnson, 2002; Murphy, Johnson, Cain, et al., 1998).

Parents' written and verbal comments provide a "human face" on the numerical scores. Selected comments regarding mental distress include: "I am on an emotional roller coaster: feeling like I am going crazy, have anger, guilt, emptiness, loneliness, numbness, and nausea all at once"; "If misery goes away, the connection will be gone too"; "Your friends want you to be like you were"; "Thoughts are like a glass you've dropped — shattered and scattered"; "I found a stack of clean socks in the freezer."

PTSD

PTSD symptoms were measured by DSM-III criteria (APA, 1987) and differed significantly by gender. Four months postdeath, 60% of the mothers and 40% of the fathers whose children were murdered met diagnostic criteria for PTSD, whereas the percentages were lower for accidental and suicidal deaths; that is, 35% of the mothers and 17% of the fathers met criteria for PTSD diagnosis. Symptoms in the reexperiencing symptom cluster were nearly twice as common as symptoms in the avoidance and hyperarousal clusters. One father's dream illustrates the reexperiencing symptom cluster of PTSD. The father's 20-year-old daughter was killed while crossing a street in a marked pedestrian lane. The dream was that the death had not occurred; his daughter was home asleep. According to the father, the dream was so real, when he awakened, he went to his daughter's room, but she was not there. He sat down on her empty bed and yelled out, "Why am I being tortured like this? She's dead, isn't that enough?!"

There were striking differences between parents who met PTSD criteria and those who did not. Parents who met PTSD criteria reported higher rates *Look* of mental distress, lower self-esteem and self-efficacy, and poor job perfor- mance, and used more repressive coping strategies than parents without PTSD. Five years later, 28% of the mothers and 12.5% of the fathers met PTSD diagnostic criteria. Symptoms reported in the PTSD clusters showed that 61% of the mothers and 55% of the fathers reported reexperiencing symptoms; 48 % of the mothers and 38% of the fathers reported avoidance symptoms; and 47% of the mothers and 33% of the fathers reported hyper- arousal symptoms (Murphy, Braun, Tillery, et al., 1999; Murphy, Johnson, Chung, et al., 2003).

Health Status, Health Behaviors, and Help-Seeking

The majority of mothers rated their physical health status as "good" to "very good" and fathers reported their physical health status as "very good" to "excellent." However, parents who rated their health status low reported higher levels of mental distress and PTSD symptoms. Mothers with poor health compared with mothers in excellent health were 11 times more likely to report concurrent emotional distress. Fathers in poor health compared with fathers in excellent health were 15 times more likely to report emotional distress. Mothers' reports of physician visits and prescribed antidepressant and antianxiety medication were much higher than fathers' Fathers reported being troubled by physicians' comments such as "get on with your life." These statements are part of a standardized health questionnaire.

A positive finding was that over 70% of the mothers and nearly 60% of the fathers practiced two or more health protective behaviors (i.e., weekly exercise, eating a healthy diet, not smoking, and moderate alcohol use). *Look* The practice of healthy behaviors was significantly associated with fewer stress-related illnesses, days absent from work, and nonproductivity at work (Murphy, Lohan, Braun, et al., 1999).

Parents' Processes of Meaning Making

The five-year prospective longitudinal design of the study provided the opportunity to view finding meaning in a child's death as a process that unfolded over time. At 12 months postdeath, only 12% of the study par- ents reported that they had found meaning, but by 60 months postdeath, *Basic hell* 57% felt they were able to make some sense of their children's deaths and were trying to go forward with their own lives. Parents' comments about meaning early in bereavement show the intense emotional and intellectual struggles associated with this process. Two themes in the early process of finding meaning were the parents' perceived unfairness of the deaths and parents' self-questioning of their responsibilities for the deaths: "All the oth- ers survived the accident except my child"; "He was turning his life around. He was clean and sober the night he died"; "Why couldn't it have been just a close call?"; "What role and to what degree did I and his father play in his not wanting to live?"

Between 12 and 60 months postdeath, three themes revealed parents' continued struggles with finding meaning—1 Establishing rituals/memorials: Parents established scholarships and other lasting memorials. On children's birthdays and other "anniversary days," parents lit candles, released balloons, and made gravesite visits. 2 Seeking justice and revenge: "I want him (perpetrator) to stay in prison a long time." "He will be released soon and may come after us." 3 Realistic acceptance of the deceased children as they lived their lives: Many parents were forthcoming about children's high-risk behaviors (i.e., drug use, and chronic problems). One mother told of going to her son's gravesite and said, "S—, you are free now and so am I." Another parent stated, "We finally realized that we could do nothing more for her depression."

Five years after the deaths, parents' themes showed increasing acceptance and changes in their own behaviors. Many parents spoke of reordering priorities, learning of one's strengths in the face of adversity, valuing their child, and beliefs that the child's suffering had ended. Representative comments on these themes were: "Life is to be lived as precious — each day may be your last"; "I was not willing to lose another child to suicide"; "He didn't want to hurt me; he just couldn't live in this world"; "I have gained empathy for other parents struggling with rebellion, drugs, and runaway kids."

Finding meaning was associated with lower mental distress, higher marital satisfaction, and better physical health compared with not being able to find meaning. Significant predictors of finding meaning five years postdeath were the use of religious coping and support group attendance (Murphy, Johnson, & Lohan, 2003a).

Despite these encouraging findings of parents' strength and resilience, nearly half, 43%, of the parents told the research team they could find no meaning in their children's deaths. Parents commented: "There is no meaning in her rape and murder unless it points to dangers for others"; "I have not found meaning in my daughter's death. It was a permanent solution to a temporary problem. I can't fill the hole in my heart that she left"; "I cannot understand it or accept it" (Murphy, Johnson, & Lohan, 2003a).

Self-Esteem and Coping Strategies

Both mothers and fathers reported moderately high self-esteem. Both mothers and fathers used problem-focused and emotion-focused coping strategies in nearly equal numbers with little change over time. Mothers reported more use of religious coping and repressive/disengagement types of coping strategies than did fathers. The coping findings do not support the gender socialization hypothesis — that women use more affective modes of coping whereas men use more problem-oriented strategies.

We tested whether personal resources (self-esteem and financial status), positive coping strategies (emotion- and problem-focused coping combined), or repressive coping (denial, disengagement) had influences on outcomes of mental distress and PTSD symptoms. The results showed that at one and five years postdeath, self-esteem was a significant predictor of mental distress and PTSD. After controlling for self-esteem, the use of active/affective coping strategies predicted less mental distress for fathers but not for mothers. Active/affective coping strategies were not significant predictors of lowered PTSD symptoms for either mothers or fathers. Rather, repressive coping strategies were significant predictors of higher PTSD symptoms for both mothers and fathers at both one and five years postdeath. These complex findings suggest the need for interventions that target both genders with skill training in self-esteem and various coping strategies (Murphy, Johnson, & Lohan, 2003b).

Social Support

We conducted an extensive analysis of parents' social network size and actual support received and the perceived availability of support. Parents who reported having three or more close confidantes reported lower symptoms of mental distress and PTSD, better physical health, and better coping strategies than parents with fewer confidantes. Five years later, perceived social support was a significant predictor of the reduction in PTSD symptoms (Murphy, Lohan, Dimond, & Fan, 1998).

Existential Beliefs and Religious Practices

Spiritual beliefs were the second most commonly reported influence on finding meaning in the child's death. Religious coping was measured by the four-item subscale, Turning to Religion, (TTR) or COPE, the coping instrument used to obtain data on problem, affective, and disengagement coping. The TTR items pertain to individual behaviors, such as, "I pray more than usual"; I put my trust in God." Data were also collected on private and family prayer, church attendance, and pastoral/spiritual counseling. None of these factors were significantly correlated with reductions in symptoms of distress or trauma. However, at the five-year data collection period, we asked parents to think back about the things that helped them the most to manage their bereavement experiences and then list them. The four most helpful items recalled by both mothers and fathers were family members and friends, beliefs/faith/prayer, participation in the parent bereavement study and/or another support group, and passage of time.

Consistent with past studies, bereaved parents in our study were very outspoken about their need to maintain strong emotional and spiritual bonds with their deceased children. Content analysis of parents' responses to an open-ended question, "What challenges are you currently facing that are associated with the death of your child?" also revealed the importance parents placed on maintaining bonds with their deceased children. At four months postdeath 76% of all replies and at 12 months postdeath 52% of all replies to this question contained themes of maintaining bonds with their deceased children. A predominant theme was the fear of forgetting some of the child's characteristics: "What if I can't remember how his voice

Yes

sounded?" "I haven't touched a thing in his room." This finding is inconsistent with loss resolution models that advocate "letting go and moving on."

Part II: Findings Related to the Child's Cause of Death

For these analyses, we grouped parents by their children's causes of death and compared the three groups on four outcomes: mental distress, PTSD, acceptance of death, and marital satisfaction. The effects for *time* comparing the outcomes at 4, 12, 24, and 60 months postdeath were highly significant: all parents grouped by the child's cause of death reported decreases in mental distress symptoms, PTSD, marital satisfaction, and increases in acceptance. Symptom reductions were greatest between four and 12 months postdeath. PTSD scores were the only ones to show a main effect for *group*.

Parents of murdered children showed the highest rates of distress, the lowest marital satisfaction, and the least acceptance of the deaths compared with the other parents grouped by their children's deaths; however, the only statistically significant effect for group was for PTSD.

There was a statistically significant Group × Time interaction effect for acceptance; that is, the differences found for one group are not the same as found in the other two groups. Parents in the homicide group did not show the same levels of acceptance over time as did the accident and suicide parents.

Some examples of intrusive thoughts and images reported by parents are offered to help to explain the high rates of trauma among parents bereaved by violent death. Homicide: "I can't get past how my child must have struggled with his killer." "I fear for my own life." Suicide: "My son shot himself in front of his twin brother." "I found him hanging in the basement." Accident: "Authorities told us she didn't suffer. How do they know that?" "I took her on vacation and didn't bring her back."

Next, we asked parents whether they believed their children's deaths were preventable. Five years postdeath, 65% of accident parents, 70% of suicide parents, and 55% of homicide parents believed the deaths could have been prevented. Attributions of preventability and closeness to the child have been shown to predict prolonged and intense levels of grief (Bugen, 1977; Murphy, Johnson, Wu, et al., 2003).

Summary and Interpretation of the Findings

(1) Gender makes a huge difference in parents' loss accommodation. Mothers' scores on mental distress and PTSD started out higher than fathers; and gradually decreased over time. On the other hand, fathers' scores on these measures were lower than mothers' at four months postdeath, were higher at two years postdeath than at four months postdeath, and decreased sometime between two and five years postdeath. (2) Mothers used many of the same problem-solving coping skills as did fathers, but mothers also used more religious coping and more destructive forms of coping such as denial and disengagement. (3) Parents who found meaning in their child's

death and parents who engaged in health-protective behaviors reported less intense symptoms of mental distress and PTSD than those who did not find meaning or engage in healthy behaviors. (4) Parents differed significantly on four outcomes when grouped by their children's causes of death. Parents whose children were murdered fared worst. (5) All secondary outcome variables and intervening variables had an effect on major outcome variables suggesting that the variables we selected for the test of the loss accommodation model played an important role.

The study met several criteria for Level A "best practices" as identified by the ISTSS task force (Foa et al., 2000). We conducted a randomized, controlled trial; we defined and measured target symptoms using reliable and valid measurement tools; we developed a manual for treatment; we randomized parents to treatment prior to collecting baseline data; and we were successful in keeping parents in treatment. Nonetheless, we urge readers to be aware of several study limitations that might affect the findings. First, as Norris (2002) and others have noted, it is nearly impossible to have collected preevent data from study parents since violent death is a sudden, unexpected event. The lack of predeath data is a concern because national epidemiological data show that about 15% of the U.S. population has or has had a depressive disorder at some point in their lives. Similar data are available in regard to trauma. Thus, we don't know how many parents may have had preexisting conditions or the extent to which the death of a child may have contributed to preexisting conditions (Kaplan & Maldaver, 1993).

A second caution is in regard to sampling. Even though we obtained parent contact data from medical examiners' offices and did not rely on obituaries, ongoing support groups, and so on, we were unable to contact many parents, and some of those contacted chose not to participate in the study. Another sampling concern is the lack of sufficient numbers of members of ethnic minority groups for statistical comparison. This is a problem because of known high rates of suicide among Native Americans and known high rates of homicide among African Americans. We have no data from parents who reside in rural areas.

Third, there was a three-year gap between the last two data collections. Another measurement limitation was that we were unable to use family-functioning data in major analyses because of the small sample size. (Only parents with children living at home completed the family-functioning items as required by measurement tool directions.)

Recommendations for Assessment and Intervention

First, we learned a great deal about bereaved parents' strengths and coping skills that we believe professional helpers and family members will find helpful. Next we use study findings to show how risk for long-term consequences can be assessed. Next we suggest which parents need treatment, how soon after the death treatment should begin, how long it should continue, how to retain parents in treatment, and how various treatment modalities can be "matched" to meet individual, couple, and family needs.

Assessment of Parents' Strengths and Coping Skills

Study parents were devastated by their losses, yet most returned to work in about a month after the death even though they perceived problems with cognitive skills. Parents spoke of "making it one day at a time." Our findings showed that both problem-focused and emotion-focused coping skills are helpful for loss accommodation. Based on this supporting evidence, if mothers in particular are still reporting disengagement/repression/denial beyond the first year, specific treatment is recommended to address this issue.

We were encouraged by the results showing the importance of health protective behaviors. The use of two or more on a regular basis was associated with better health, better job productivity, and symptom reduction. These findings are important because they show that parents can do positive things to help themselves. We recommend the assessment of coping skills and health protective behaviors carefully and suggest "listening" for parents' comments that demonstrate resilience, such as "I am learning about myself and how much strength I have."

Prevention of Long-Term Consequences

Latent growth curve models were used to measure initial symptom levels, the rate of change over time, and significant predictors of change five years later for both mental distress and PTSD. Mental distress and PTSD were highly intercorrelated. For mental distress, significant predictors of change over time were gender, self-esteem, and affective and repressive coping. The analytic models predicted that mothers will be worse off than fathers, because fathers may be reluctant to report symptoms. Breakout sessions by gender are recommended. Counselors and support group leaders need to assess self-esteem and coping strategies and provide skill training as necessary. For PTSD, only parents' gender and social support accounted for symptom reduction over time. These findings again suggest that some parents, particularly mothers, may need interventions specific to PTSD.

The cause of death analyses showed that parents whose children had been murdered reported the highest rates of distress, the least marital satisfaction, and the lowest acceptances of death at all measurement periods, 4, 12, 24, and 60 months postdeath. The cause of death data also showed that at five years postdeath, the majority of parents in all three groups believed their child's death was preventable. These attributions present a treatment challenge. A workbook for trauma survivors written by Rosenbloom and Williams (1999) contains a section in regard to changing beliefs.

Support networks need to be assessed. The availability of social support appears to be a two-way street that merits clinical attention. Withdrawal of support may occur as a result of friends and colleagues not knowing what to do or say *and* by parent behaviors such as ruminating too much in the presence of important others (Janoff-Bulman & Frieze, 1983; Silver, Wortman, & Crofton, 1990).

Determining Which Parents Need Treatment

Our frequency data showed scores on a continuum of distress and trauma symptoms. While we do not advise using some "cutoff" score, future studies might test this in conjunction with outcome data provided by the long-term growth models. In general, women with high symptom distress and PTSD, low self-esteem, who use repressive coping, and whose children died by homicide should be considered at high risk and be offered treatment. Our statistical analysis of the intervention effects showed that mothers made the most progress in symptom reduction by 12 months postdeath. This finding appears to favor early treatment.

Fathers' distress trajectories showed that they were worse off two years postdeath than in early bereavement. This finding suggests that bereaved fathers need to be monitored carefully over time.

Look

Postdeath Timing of Treatment

Ruzeck and Watson (2001) defined early intervention as treatment designed to prevent chronic emotional problems and minimize long-term deterioration in quality of life following trauma exposure. According to Foa et al. (2000), who wrote on behalf of the PTSD Treatment Guidelines Task Force organized by ISTSS, trauma victims with PTSD have a better prognosis if clinical intervention is implemented as early as possible. Our study findings support the ISTSS recommendation. Parents in our pilot study and the NIH study, said, "the earlier the better." Our statistical analysis of data from pilot study parents bereaved three to six months and those bereaved seven to 13 months showed significant differences favoring the early bereavement group. The early treatment recommendation was also supported by the meta-analysis findings of Allumbaugh and Hoyt (1999), who noted the average delay between loss and treatment was over two years with little improvement following treatment. Screening is recommended. A few parents in our NIH study could not manage completing the baseline questionnaires and did not return. Goodman and Weiss (2000) and Yalom (1985) also recommend screening prior to group treatment.

Duration and Intensity of Treatment

Study mothers benefited from weekly two-hour group treatment sessions. However, parents suggested that the program be increased to 16 weeks. Group interventions designed to treat persons with PTSD have ranged in length from 16 weeks to six months with weekly meetings (Goodman & Weiss, 2000).

Matching Treatment Modalities to Client Needs

Indications for Group Treatment

   Group is an environment in which treatment takes place, and not the treatment itself; however, there are direct benefits that group members provide to one another, such as normalization after a traumatic event, identification with others who have experienced the same traumatic event, and using the group as a safe place to express feelings and learn new coping skills (Yalom, 1985). Johnson and Lubin (2000) wrote that the group environment is very relevant for traumatized individuals due to the experience of isolation and lack of support commonly experienced by traumatized individuals. The group serves as a symbolic societal witness to each victim's experience as it is retold and relived in the group process. Group treatment is efficient, effective, liked by parents, and according to Goodman and Weiss (2000), is the treatment of choice for traumatized individuals. Therefore, we recommend the group environment as the primary setting for treatment of individuals bereaved by violent death.

Group Treatment Strategies

   The goals for treatment must be clearly defined. Support groups differ from treatment groups in many ways including lay versus professional leadership and treatment options. Foa et al. (2000) wrote that cognitive–behavioral therapies have been shown to provide very good outcomes for individuals with PTSD. However, these results are based primarily upon treatment of veterans and rape victims with PTSD. It is not clear if any of the ISTSS studies reviewed included samples of bereaved parents. A description of combined psychoeducational and cognitive–behavioral approaches has appeal for bereaved parents. Psychoeducational approaches early in bereavement inform individuals about symptoms, course of trauma, and available treatment. Cognitive–behavioral strategies focus on changing negative behaviors and on learning new skills (Goodman & Weiss, 2000). Writing about a traumatic event has been shown to be helpful (Pennebaker, 1988). Changes in parents' assumptive worlds, social relationships, fears, and feelings specific to the child's cause of death must also be addressed (Janoff-Bulman & Frieze, 1983; Lord, 1996; Rando, 1996).

   Several experts have described group treatment for trauma victims as occurring in phases, that is, initially helping group members to feel less isolated, provide skills, and foster hope for the future. A second phase involves sharing and working through traumatic experiences, that is, the telling and witnessing of each person's narrative and restoring trust in one's assumptive world. Examples of the format for the current study and others can be found in various publications (Johnson & Lubin, 2000; Murphy, Johnson, Cain, et al., 1998).

Treatment Retention

   A commonly reported problem in group treatment is that participants come for a time, and then drop out before the program ends. Low group attrition (dropout) in our study can be attributed to organizational, leader, and group member factors. Organizational factors were an orientation to the program, notebooks provided to parents that included objectives and outlines for each segment of the problem-focused support. Parents valued the two-pronged approach, that is, "didactic" topics and group support facilitated by a clinician. Parents had the opportunity to evaluate each session attended. Group leader factors that may have led to treatment retention were that the treatment was "manualized"; that is, session guidelines assisted clinicians in the didactic component to maintain the same content over the three-year period, group leaders were competent and compassionate, training was provided, and debriefings were held after every group session. The most important group composition factor was the relatively homogeneous nature of the groups; that is, all participants were parents who ranged in age from 32 to 61, and children's causes of death were sudden and violent, the deceased children's ages ranged from 12 to 28 years, and the time since the death of the child was four to five months on average, upon entrance to the study. We consider homogeneity to be a huge factor. We kept the group size to 10 maximum and tried to have a gender mix, which was very difficult for some 12-week sessions because more women than men participated in the study. Similar strategies that address retention are recommended by *Look—Rotation* others (Goodman & Weiss, 2000; Yalom, 1985).

It is recognized that some of these factors cannot be replicated, such as, homogeneity in cases of community support programs. However, providing an orientation and materials and having well-trained group leaders and as much homogeneity as possible are recommended. Parents valued giving us their opinions following each session. Thus, many practices can be incorporated in formal and informal treatment offerings that have been shown to be effective and endorsed by parents.

Other Treatment Modalities

Individual treatment may be needed for medication monitoring and other consequences, such as a history of multiple losses, suicidality, or a preexisting psychiatric disorder. In these cases, group treatment should be delayed until other critical issues are resolved. Couples' therapy is indicated in cases of poor communication, for example, when one spouse blames the other for the child's death, and in situations where the sudden death of a child has exacerbated serious marital conflict present prior to the death (Gilbert, 1997; Rosenblatt, 2000; Schwab, 1992). Family therapy is indicated in situations where parents' grief is so intense that one or both parents cannot be psychologically present for their other children, in situations where a sibling is inadvertently put into the role of the deceased child, in cases where siblings are having multiple bereavement adjustment problems, and in situations where the family was dysfunctional prior to the death (Lohan & Murphy, 2002).

Researchers and clinicians alike must carefully evaluate additional support and treatment options such as Internet support, bereaved parent-to-parent interactions "partnered" for support based on circumstances of death, telephone and crisis hotlines, existing community resources, and self-help approaches.

Our data suggest an important role for the clergy throughout the bereavement process. At the time of death, parents in our study agonized over decisions that needed to be made quickly, and once made, were final (i.e., burial or cremation).

Religious coping was a significant predictor of finding meaning. The clergy can help parents view the finding of meaning as a process that takes time. Another role of the clergy is to help parents resist pressures of "letting go and moving on." We found over 900 entries on the Internet in regard to what the bereaved can do to promote healing. Clearly, the societal expectation is that within a relatively brief period of time, the bereaved will return to their "preloss" levels of functioning. There is sufficient literature to suggest that grief counselors and professionals believe that one of the goals of intervention is to "loosen the ties between the deceased and bereaved." Parents vehemently disagree. As Klass (1999) wrote: "A significant portion of a bereaved parent's spiritual life revolves around developing and learning to live with a continuing bond with a dead child" (p. 5).

The clergy can also be helpful in educating their congregations about the public's tendency to avoid the bereaved, make inappropriate statements to them such as "you have other children," and "this was apparently God's plan for her." One mother in our study got up before her church congregation of 800 persons one Sunday and stated, "Stop shunning us. It hurts!" Unfortunately few parents have the strength to take such an action.

CONCLUDING REMARKS

A growing body of knowledge shows that parents bereaved by the violent death of a child are at risk for multiple short-term and long-term consequences. The results of our longitudinal prospective study showed differences in bereavement responses by parents' gender and the child's cause of death. The findings have important implications for treatment because of the complex interrelationships among multiple risk factors. Despite the need for simultaneous assessment and treatment of grief and trauma, the predominant topic of discussion in support groups and individual treatment is grief. Intense efforts are needed to incorporate best practices into bereavement support and therapies.

REFERENCES

Allumbaugh, D. & Hoyt, W. (1999). Effectiveness of grief therapy: A meta-analysis. *Journal of Counseling Psychology, 46* (3), 370–380.

American Psychiatric Association. (1987). *Diagnostic and statistical manual of mental disorders* (3rd ed., rev.). Washington, D.C.: Author.

Amick-McMullan, A., Kilpatrick, D. G., & Resnick, H. S. (1991). Homicide as a risk factor for PTSD among surviving family members. *Behavior Modification, 15,* 545–559.

Bugen, L. (1977). Human grief: A model for prediction and intervention. *American Journal of Orthopsychiatry, 47,* 197–206.

Derogatis, L.R. (1992). *BSI-Administration, scoring, and procedures manual* (Vol 2). Baltimore: Clinical Psychometric Research.

Dryfoos, J. (1991). Adolescents at risk: A summation of work in the field. Programs and policies. *Journal of Adolescent Health, 12,* 630–637.

Foa, E., Keane, T., & Friedman, M. (2000). Guidelines for treatment of PTSD. *Journal of Traumatic Stress, 13* (4), 539–555.

Gilbert, K. (1997). Couple coping with the death of a child. In C. Figley, B. Bride, & N. Mazza, (Eds.), *Death and trauma: The traumatology of grieving* (pp. 101–122). Washington, D.C.: Taylor & Francis.

Goodman, M. & Weiss, D. (2000). Initiating, screening, and maintaining psychotherapy groups for traumatized patients. In R. Klein & V. Schermer (Eds.), *Group psychotherapy for psychological trauma* (pp. 47–63). New York: Guilford. *Look*

Janoff-Bulman, R. & Frieze, I. (1983). A theoretical perspective for understanding reactions to victimization. *Journal of Social Issues, 39* (2), 1–17.

Johnson, D. & Lubin, H. (2000). Group psychotherapy for the symptoms of posttraumatic stress disorder. In R. Klein & V. Schermer (Eds.), *Group psychotherapy for psychological trauma* (pp. 141–169). New York: Guilford .

Kaplan, K. J. & Maldaver, M. (1993). Parental marital style and completed adolescent suicide. *Omega, 27,* 131–154.

Kato, P. & Mann, T. (1999). A synthesis of psychological interventions for the bereaved. *Clinical Psychology Review, 19* (3), 275–296.

Klass, D. (1999). *The spiritual lives of bereaved parents.* Philadelphia: Taylor & Francis. 12–93.

Levy, L. & Derby, J. (1992). Bereavement support groups: Who joins; who does not; and why. *American Journal of Community Psychology, 20,* 649–663.

Lipsey, M. (1990). *Design sensitivity. Statistical power for experimental research.* Newbury Park, CA: Sage.

Lohan, J. A. & Murphy, S. A. (2002). Family functioning and family typology after an adolescent or young adult child's death. *Journal of Family Nursing, 8* (1), 32–49.

Lord, J. H. (1996). America's number one killer: Vehicular crashes. In K.J. Doka (Ed.), *Living with grief after sudden loss* (pp. 25–39). Bristol, PA: Taylor & Francis.

Martin, R. L. & Doka, K. J. (2000). *Men don't cry ....Women do: Transcending gender stereotypes of grief.* Philadelphia: Taylor & Francis.

Murphy, S. A., Baugher, R., Lohan., J., Scheideman, J., Heerwagen, J., & Johnson, L. C. (1996). Parents' evaluation of a preventive intervention following the sudden, violent deaths of their children. *Death Studies, 20,* 453–468.

Murphy, S. A., Braun, T., Tillery, L., Cain, K. C., Johnson, L. C., & Beaton, R. D. (1999). PTSD among bereaved parents following the violent deaths of their 12 to 28 year-old children: A longitudinal prospective analysis. *Journal of Traumatic Stress, 12* (2), 273–291.

Murphy, S. A., Chung, I. J., & Johnson, L. C. (2002). Patterns of mental distress following the violent death of a child and predictors of change over time. *Research in Nursing & Health, 25,* 25–437.

Murphy, S. A., Johnson, C., Cain, K., Dimond, M., Das Gupta, A., Lohan, J., & Baugher, R. (1998). Broad-spectrum group treatment for parents bereaved by the violent deaths of their 12 to 28 year-old children: A randomized controlled trial. *Death Studies, 22,* 1–27.

Murphy, S. A., Johnson, L. C., Chung, I. J., & Beaton, R. D. (2003). The incidence of PTSD following the violent death of a child and predictors of change over time. *Journal of Traumatic Stress, 16,* 17–26.

Murphy, S. A., Johnson, L. C., & Lohan, J. (2003a). Finding meaning in a child's violent death: A five-year prospective analysis of parents' personal narratives and empirical data. *Death Studies, 27* (5), 381–404.

Murphy, S. A., Johnson, L. C., & Lohan, J. (2003b). The effectiveness of coping resources and strategies used by bereaved parents 1 and 5 years after the violent deaths of their children. *Omega, 47* (1), 25–44.

Murphy, S. A., Johnson, L.C., Wu, L., Fan, J. J., & Lohan, J. (2003). Bereaved parents' outcomes 4 to 60 months after their children's deaths by accident, suicide, or homicide: A comparative study demonstrating differences. *Death Studies, 27,* 39–61.

Murphy, S. A., Lohan, J., Braun, T., Johnson, L. C., Cain, K. C., Baugher, R., Beaton, R. D., & Dimond, M. (1999). Parents' health, health care utilization, and health behaviors following the violent deaths of their 12 to 28 year-old children: A prospective, longitudinal analysis. *Death Studies, 23,* 1–29.

Murphy, S. A., Lohan, J., Dimond, M., & Fan, J. (1998). Network and mutual support for parents bereaved following the violent deaths of their 12 to 28 year-old children: A longitudinal prospective analysis. *The Journal of Personal and Interpersonal Loss, 3*(4). 303–333.

Norris, F. (1992). Epidemiology of trauma: Frequency and impact of different potentially traumatic events on different demographic groups. *Journal of Consulting and Clinical Psychology, 60,* 409–418.

Pennebaker, J. W. (1988). Confiding traumatic experiences and health. In S. Fisher & J. Reason, (Eds.), *Handbook of life stress, cognition, and health* (pp. 671–684). New York: Wiley.

Rando, T. A. (1996). Complications in mourning traumatic death. In K. Doka (Ed.), *Living with grief after sudden loss* (pp. 139–159). Washington, D.C.: Taylor & Francis.

Rosenblatt, P. (2000). *Help your marriage survive the death of a child.* Philadelphia: Temple University Press.

Rosenbloom, D. & Williams, M. B. (1999). *Life after trauma. A workbook for healing.* New York: Guilford.

Ruzek, J. & Watson, P. (2001). Early intervention to prevent PTSD and other trauma-related problems. *PTSD Research Quarterly, 12* (4), 1–7.

Sackett, D. (1996). Evidence-based medicine: What it is and what it isn't. *British Medical Journal, 312,* 71.

Schwab, R. (1992). Effects of a child's death on the marital relationship. *Death Studies, 16,* 141–154.

Silver, R., Wortman, C. B., & Crofton, C. (1990). The role of coping in support provision. In B. R. Sarason, I. G. Sarason, & G. R. Pierce (Eds.), *Social support: An interactional view* (pp. 397–426). Wiley.

Thoits, P. (1986). Social support as coping assistance. *Journal of Consulting and Clinical Psychology, 54,* 416–423.

Thompson, M. P., Norris, F. H., & Ruback, R. B. (1998). Comparative distress levels of inner-city family members of homicide victims. *Journal of Traumatic Stress, 11,* 223–242.

U.S. National Center for Health Statistics. (1992). *Vital statistics of the United States: Vol. 2. Mortality Part A [for the year 1966–1988].* Washington, D.C.: U.S. Government Printing Office.

U.S. National Center for Health Statistics (2000). *Deaths and death rates for the 10 leading causes of death in specified age groups, by race and sex. United States, 1998. Table 8.* Washington, D.C.: U.S. Government Printing Office.

Wortman, C. B. & Lehman, D. R. (1983). Reactions to victims of life crises: Support attempts that fail. In I. G. Sarason & B. R. Sarason (Eds.), *Social support: Theory, research, and applications* (pp. 463–489). The Hague: Martinus.

Yalom, I. (1985). *The theory and practice of group psychotherapy* (3rd ed.). New York: Basic Books.

11

Restorative Retelling After Violent Dying[1]

EDWARD K. RYNEARSON, FANNY
CORREA, JENNIFER FAVELL, CONNIE
SAINDON, AND HOLLY PRIGERSON

Restorative Retelling

In restorative retelling, a short-term group intervention, the narrative of the life and dying of the loved one is the "ground" of intervention and a model of narrative restoration is presented. Tentative clarifications of "restorative" terms, including resilience, reframing, imaginative transcendence, transformation, and dialectic "suffering" introduced in previous chapters, are developed, and illustrative case presentations detail how these restorative capacities are reinforced with intervention. The intervention follows an agenda beginning with education, stress moderation, and reinforcement of resilience, followed by restorative reprocessing of the narrative of the life and dying of the deceased, and finally, conjoined support of the family in preparing for reengagement with living beyond the intervention. A separate time-limited group intervention (criminal death support) for family members during the investigation and trial after homicide is also described, and outcome data is presented from a pilot study of 64 subjects treated for heightened distress following violent death (homicide, suicide, or accident) revealing significant diminishment of distress, low drop-out rate, and absence of clinical complications or casualties. A multisite training project has replicated restorative retelling interventions at national and international sites.

INTRODUCTION

Violent dying from homicide, suicide, or accident accounts for nearly 10% of annual deaths in the United States. Clinical studies document the commonality of a syndrome of combined trauma distress (intrusive thoughts, flashbacks, and dreams of the dying, even though the dying was rarely witnessed) and separation distress (pining and searching for the deceased) in close friends and family members (Rynearson & Geoffrey, 1999). This syndrome usually diminishes within months of the death, but may be associated with a prolonged and dysfunctional bereavement syndrome in a sizable minority of family members and friends (Amick-McMullan, Kilpatrick, Vernon, & Smith, A., 1989; Armour, 2002 a & b; Parkes, 1993). Mothers of children who died violently are at highest risk for prolonged trauma distress (20% remain highly traumatized five years after the death) because of their intense caregiving attachment, no matter the age of the child (Murphy, 1999; Murphy, Johnson, & Lohan, 2002). Young children who witness the violent dying of a family member are also at high risk for prolonged distress, presumably because of their intense dependent attachment upon the deceased and direct exposure to the dying (Eth & Pynoos, 1994; Pruett, 1979).

When the violent dying is deemed a criminal act (homicide or criminal negligence) the media, medical examiner, police, and judicial system begin a mandatory public announcement and inquiry regarding the dying to find and punish whoever was responsible. The public retelling of the violent dying story is very different from the public respect for the family's privacy in retelling a natural death. Once declared criminal, the public and media demand a spotlighted reenactment of the dying that in some cases becomes voyeuristic. Public repetition of the dying reenactment may heighten the distress of friends and family members.

AVAILABLE INTERVENTIONS

Beginning in the 1970s, peer-led support groups offered the first interventions specific for friends and family members bereaved by violent dying. While these groups continue to provide crucial services of advocacy and support, there are no criteria for participation, formal agenda, session format, explicit goals, or limitation on sessions or membership. In the absence of standardization of intervention procedures and eligibility criteria, it is difficult to determine the efficacy of peer-led interventions.

In 1978, one of the authors (EKR) volunteered as a psychiatric consultant in a peer-led support group for family members after homicidal death, and a subsequent report (Rynearson, 1984) described the specific syndromal combination of trauma and separation distress he noted in dysfunctional family members. The association of intense posttraumatic responses with nonaccommodation also demonstrated the limitations and complications of an open-ended, unstructured group format. The drop-out rate for new members was unnecessarily high because intensely distressed subjects were not screened for traumatic comorbidity and could not tolerate immersion in the violent dying stories of the other members. With that recognition, the group leader was urged to assess the level of trauma distress in potential members and provide those intensely traumatized with individual support to avoid their being exposed prematurely to the stories of other family members. This insight served as a screening guideline for the group leader and led to a more detailed appraisal of the psychological imprint of the dying imagery and its reprocessing as a story during treatment (Rynearson & Sinnema 1999).

In 1989, one of the authors (EKR) initiated a community-based support project for family members after violent death that built upon these early clinical observations. Since that time we have treated over 2,000 family members, and have developed a dynamic clinical model, a systematic process for screening for high-risk and specific short-term interventions to deal with the combined distress of trauma and grief associated with prolonged and intense violent dying imagery (Rynearson & Geoffrey, 1999).

The clinical literature on the psychological effects and management of bereavement after violent death has been largely descriptive and anecdotal. However, several more rigorous and promising research studies have been carried out of adolescents and adults grief stricken following violent dying, including outcome studies measuring the effects of time-limited interventions for grief-related dysfunction.

1. Pynoos and collaborators at the National Child Traumatic Stress Network include an extensive list of references on their Web site: www,NCTSN.org describing school-based protocols for screening and measurement of time-limited interventions for children exposed to violent death associated with homicide, disaster, and warfare.

2. Salloum and collaborators established a community-based program for adolescents in a crime-ridden, intraurban setting, and developed a time-limited group intervention for adolescents with bereavement after violent death. Following a decade of a pragmatic, school-based protocol for identification and support of highly distressed youngsters, Salloum and coworkers completed a series of studies documenting its effectiveness (Salloum, 2004; Salloum, Avery, & McClain, 2001; Salloum & Vincent, 1999.

3. There have been reports demonstrating the effectiveness of individual, time-limited intervention with adult subjects presenting with complicated grief (Shear et al., 2001; Shear, Frank, Patrick, & Reynolds, 2005). Though the sample from the most recent study was heterogeneous (subjects presented with complicated grief after natural death and violent dying), those subjects grieved by violent dying were responsive to the author's specific intervention — apparently more effective than interpersonal psychotherapy (IPT) with which it was compared.

THE NARRATIVE DYNAMIC

Fundamental to violent dying is the challenge of retelling its successive events. Since less than 5% of violent deaths are witnessed by family members or loved ones, the teller is in the ironic position of retelling a story of a violent dying in which they played no part. Further, it is the repetitive, imaginary retelling of this dying *story*, lasting for many months, which is associated with dysfunction and need for assistance (Rynearson,1995). Since the dying *story* is paramount in the repetitive, imaginary retelling, revising the story is a primary focus in restoring the patient, and a conceptual model has been developed to clarify the process of reconstructive narration.

The story form is a basic mental paradigm of coherence. Constructing a story around an experience of any kind, including a traumatic experience, brings order and meaning (Neimeyer & Levitt, 2000). The story form provides a beginning, middle, and an ending — with characters who share and mutually resolve needs and conflicts — and the story celebrates and endorses social values at the same time. Apparently, after a violent dying, the mind reflexively relives the dying moments of the person as a story, and because there was a caring relationship, it is intolerable to imagine the victim's terror and helplessness. There is no way that the violent dying of a loved one can end with meaning, only an empty absurdity. This never should have happened. Unwitnessed, the imaginary action of the violent dying story assumes a surreal perspective, fashioned from fragments of police and media reports, exaggerated and distorted by vivid, private fantasy. The imagined story of the victim's dying cannot fully register as "real."

The *reenactment* story of the violent dying is a primary response, and recurs as a repetitive thought, flashback, or nightmare for days or weeks after the death. There are also compensatory or secondary stories whose purpose is to make the dying "unhappen," and they occur in combination rather than alone:

1. Story of remorse: "I am somehow responsible for the dying. I should have prevented it from happening, and I wish that I had died instead."
2. Story of retaliation: "Someone else is responsible for the dying. I am going to find that person and get even."
3. Story of protection: "I can't allow this to happen to anyone else who is close to me. I need them close to me so I know that we are safe."

These repetitive stories fill the mind during the first days and weeks of traumatic grief, but with the support of family and friends and through the finality of the funeral, the memory of the violent dying and its storied reprocessing begin to fade. Most family members and loved ones are able to revise the reenactment imagery by engaging in a spontaneous restorative retelling and meaningful rituals and commemoration of the deceased with family, friends, and community. The story of the life of the victim gains ascendancy and becomes stronger than the story of his or her dying.

If the violent dying was a homicide or accident, the media, police, and the court are also involved in retelling the dying — they promise that they can solve it, and carry out a process of retribution for the deceased and punishment for the perpetrator. Sometimes the public retelling of the dying by the media, police, and courts is inaccurate, insensitive, and misleading, and complicates the private retelling. It is difficult for the friend or family member to finally accommodate to the dying until this public processing of the dying story has been completed.

Trauma and Separation Distress

Our model proposes that trauma distress and separation distress are concurrent responses to the reenactment narrative — trauma distress to violent dying and separation distress to death. While the thoughts, feelings, and behaviors of trauma and separation distress are not specific, they are roughly separable into two syndromes, as presented in Table 11.1.

Clinical dysfunction is associated with repetitive, intrusive, and enervating images and stories as the memories of the deceased, the dying, and the observing self simultaneously converge and merge:

1. Dysfunctional images and stories of the deceased contain their terror and helplessness as they were dying.
2. Dysfunctional images and stories of the *dying* recur as an involuntary witnessing of a disintegratory drama that cannot be controlled.
3. Dysfunctional images and stories of the *self* persist as being remorseful, retaliatory, or the ultimate protector for remaining friends and family members.

Trauma distress takes neuropsychological precedence over separation distress. Since the dysfunctional images and stories are primarily related to the trauma of the dying, supportive strategies to deal with trauma distress are the initial goals of any intervention.

Before dealing with separation distress, someone who is highly traumatized by violent dying needs to be stabilized, and intervention initially focuses on restoring the subject's capacity for maintaining a sense of *safety, separateness, and autonomy* from the dying experience. We call these preverbal capacities *resilience*— and without them the subject will be overwhelmed in the dying

TABLE 11.1
Trauma distress and separation distress

	Trauma distress	**Separation distress**
Thoughts	Reenactment	Reunion
Feelings	Fear	Longing
Behavior	Avoidance	Searching

imagery and stories. Without resilience the observant self risks disintegrating in the same, nameless swirl of terror and helplessness as the deceased. The clinical association of resilience (Bonanno, 1999) with the trajectory of grief has been endorsed in a prospective study of spousal death that establishes a positive association of resilience with transient, nondysfunctional bereavement responses (Bonnano, Wortman, Lehman, & Sonnega, 2002).

A Description of the Interventions

Each of the interventions (criminal death support [CDS], and restorative retelling [RR]) is applied in a small group setting (seven to 10 members). Each group is closed, time-limited (two-hour sessions for 10 consecutive weeks), and follows a written agenda and format (Rynearson & Geoffrey, 1999). Potential members are screened to assess them for comorbidity (disorders of depression, PTSD, substance abuse) and exclusion criteria (active psychosis, active substance abuse, intellectual handicap, severe Axis II disorder).

The agenda and goals of the interventions are directly shared with group participants through discussion and handouts. We clarify for each member of the group that revision of dysfunctional images and stories of the deceased, the dying, and the self will diminish the distress responses of trauma and separation.

CRIMINAL DEATH SUPPORT INTERVENTION (CDS)

Criminal death support is designed to provide clarification and support for family members stressed by the demands of the media, detectives, and the courts during the investigation and trial. It is offered to family members and friends who have lost someone in a violent death and are involved with the criminal justice system. A primary challenge for any family member during the investigation and trial of a violent death is the absence of an active role in the process, and our model views this loss of control as enormously stressful. CDS group offers an intensive resource of advocacy, support, and information to those who are bewildered by the police, the media, and the courts.

Criminal Death Support Group Agenda (10 weekly, two-hour sessions)

Session 1: Introductions
The first session begins with the leaders' presentation of group norms and rules of confidentiality. Each member is then encouraged to briefly tell the other members about the dying that brings him or her to the group.
Each group (Session 1 through 10) ends with exercises of relaxation and guided imagery.

Session 2: What is Grief?
The model of combined trauma and separation distress is presented and the group members are encouraged to present their ways of coping

with these distress responses. The leaders clarify resilient capacities and present group and individual exercises for their reinforcement.

Session 3: Different Ways of Showing Grief
Male members may be more avoidant in showing their grief, while women members may be more despairing, guilty, and overprotective of surviving family members — and this should be accepted rather than challenged. Violent dying may be followed by possessive thoughts of retaliation, self-blame, and retaliation that may or may not be satisfied by the police and the courts.

Session 4: Self-Care
Each group member is finally responsible for caring for his or her own needs. Strategies to improve diet, exercise, calming, and thought diversion are encouraged, and definition of comorbid risk factors are emphasized.

Session 5: The Criminal Justice System
Translation of legal terms begins and preparations for frustrations of the criminal–judicial process are shared. A representative from the office of the police or prosecutor is invited to attend this session.

Session 6: The Impact of the Criminal Justice System on Grief
The system needs to solve and punish the dying while the member's grief also needs to honor and remember the loved one. Members are cautioned that the system cannot and will not answer any of their needs beyond the dying and may disregard or disrespect the memory of the loved one. Strategies for maintaining an emotional distance and healthy skepticism regarding the media, police, and courts are encouraged.

Session 7: Commemoration
In this session each member presents the memory of his or her loved one through pictures, poems, videotapes, or any memorabilia that enlivens the member's presence within the group. This is an occasion for celebrating the vitality and value of the loved one.

Session 8: Family and Friends
Group members invite supportive members of their family or community to join in their insights and progress. This session reinforces continued support within the member's family or community in anticipation of group termination.

Session 9: Exploring Questions of Faith and Spirituality
Living beyond the memory of dying and death requires an ongoing engagement with activities and beliefs that are of value and meaning. A member of the clergy is sometimes included in this session.

Session 10: Closing
A formal group exercise of remembrance for each lost loved one is completed. A final exercise of commemoration for the group and each of its members closes the group.

RESTORATIVE RETELLING INTERVENTION (RR)

During the active phase of investigation and trial of the perpetrator of a violent death, the family member is preoccupied with the enervating demands of the compulsory recounting of the dying and the guilt or innocence of the perpetrator. This prescribed ordeal can last for many months, and sometimes years in some jurisdictions where there is a long wait for a trial date. In our experience, it is difficult for family members to engage in an intervention beyond CDS that requires them to focus on their internalized memories of trauma and grief. It is after the investigation and trial have been completed that they are in a psychological "space and time" to allow processing of the intrapersonal residuals of the violent dying that remain preoccupying and "possessive."

RR is designed to provide an active range of cognitive and emotional strategies for the family members who for months or years after the tragedy cannot keep themselves from the intrusive thoughts and flashbacks of the violent dying . Its purpose is to initiate the process of restoring themselves within the retelling of the violent dying. Because language connects us in sharing and understanding experience, RR reenacts the dying through words and images. For family members and loved ones of the deceased, the recounting of the violent dying story contains more than a recitation of the "facts" and finding a solution for the dying drama: they retell not only the events of the death but their memory of someone they loved who died isolated from their support.

Violent dying thus triggers an internalized narrative dilemma for the loved one who remains "possessed" by images of the self and loved one distorted by violent death — how to continue a vital story of self as alive while acknowledging and retelling the story of a "part of" the self rendered terrorized and helpless by violent death. The dynamic of a restorative retelling proceeds at both levels — the immediate verbal expression of the action and solution of the dying (the recounting) and a secondary retelling to include the vital memory (the remembrance) of the deceased now traumatically transformed by the violence of his or her dying and projected into the life story of the teller.

Retelling is a normative, time-limited response. In the first days and weeks following a violent death, the repetitive recounting of the dying and remembrance of the life of the loved one is preoccupying. A prospective study of family members suggests that after a violent dying, the compulsion to recount and remember spontaneously diminishes in most loved ones within weeks of the dying. Family members restore one another through restorative retellings within and without the family, including close friends, coworkers, and church members at the time of burial and memorial. Of course the narrative of the dying and life of the loved one remains implicit, but is no longer so intense or prominent — it can be summoned or dismissed from awareness.

However, a significant minority of family members, particularly mothers and young children, remains preoccupied with traumatic narratives of recounting that contain themes of remorse, retaliation, and fear of recurrence. Some vulnerable individuals become dysfunctional — "possessed" by these intrusive and repetitive narratives. After several months of feeling overwhelmed and exhausted, an intervention to cope with these traumatized narratives may be considered.

The narrative of the life and dying of the loved one is the "ground" of the RR intervention. For the family member, the words and retelling of the story mediate between the internal mental representation of what the victim suffered and the external "reality" of the dying. RR transforms this intensely private monologue into an intermediary experience. The story of the dying, now spoken, is suspended between the teller and the listener. This "suspension" of the dying story becomes the grounding experience of a developing retelling between teller and listener.

There is an opportunity inherent in this narrative suspension for creative change. It may be that participating in the dialogue of the dying story of a loved one — the unfolding of a narrative that includes the victim's vitality and the teller's unfulfilled thoughts, feelings, and behaviors for the victim (who died suddenly and all alone) — is more corrective than the factual truths contained in recounting.

The clinician can serve a restorative role by encouraging a retelling that aims beyond the simple "exposure" of the recounting. Restorative retelling shapes and shades the chronicle of violent death by recreating a story around it — beyond the historical facts and solution of what happened. Its purpose is to restore meaning through poetic transformation within the narrative and the teller.

This transformation begins by establishing a transcendent perspective connected to, but suspended from, the dying narrative. By including words and metaphors portraying the vitality of the deceased and the teller, the dialogue catalyzes a train of memories and associations that establishes an altered perspective — a transcendence from the incoherent drama of the dying and a reconnection with hope and living. Without the operation of imaginative thinking there is less opportunity for transcendence — the violent dying continues to intrude as a possessive recounting of its "factual" reenactment, including compensatory themes of retaliation and remorse.

The goals of RR do not include detailed inquiry of stressors from past or present, but a limited focus on accommodating to the direct effects of the dying through:

1. Moderation of distress
2. Revision of the internalized relationship with the deceased
3. Reconnection and recommitment to living
4. The clarification of restorative "terms"

Resilience is a preverbal, stabilizing "offense" that maintains the sense of safety, separateness, and survival during overwhelming trauma, either from without or within. Transcendence cannot begin without resilience: there can be no transcendence if the teller disintegrates and disappears in the drama of the killing. Therefore, the first task of intervention is the reinforcement of at least three preverbal capacities (the 3 Ps) before beginning a detailed retelling:

Pacification	Have being	safety	(I exist)
Partition	Territory	space	(I am separate & autonomous)
Perspective	Interpenetration of	time	(I can survive & remember)

Reframing is a disentangling from the dilemma of "living within violent dying," an awareness of the destructive self-distortion of recounting (violent dying disintegrates me). Focusing more on remembrance and less on recounting (restorative reframing) restores a perspective of safety and mastery that governs future action. Restorative reframing allows an active living with what is not always the same, a dynamic vitalism, rather than static, reified living that cannot accept change (the only way I can survive is to change what happened).

Imaginative transcendence is a narrative reframing of immense significance. The "answer" to the narrative dilemma of violent dying is not to be found solely in "reasoning" a factual truth by recounting (I can restore myself by reasoning about the violent dying. I think, therefore I am.), but in searching for an imaginative and "subversive" perspective within the retelling itself (I can restore myself by imagining a vital reconnection. I can imagine, therefore I can be.). Imaginative transcendence establishes the objectivity of "my world" while assuming no more than my part in it; that is, all the questions that I can ask I must ask from the standpoint that is mine. Therefore, imaginative transcendence must bear the marks of my perspective (including the vital attachment with my loved one) which is the perspective of the "possible." Imaginative transcendence finds an "answer" or solution in the premise of the possible instead of certainty. Imaginative transcendence does not require spiritual or religious beliefs of divinity or eternity, though belief systems that include a spiritual "release" with death may provide transcendent support.

Transformation through retelling arrives at a plausible truth among possible truths. It is not enchantment in the sense of a bewitching that transforms things to what they were, but retelling is itself redemptive and transforms the teller. In the imaginative retelling, plausibility is produced and brings to light otherwise hidden and withdrawn explanations. It is fundamentally repeatable and hence permanent.

Dialectical experience (suffering). Finally, restorative retelling cannot and should not promise recovery or closure. The violent dying of a loved one initiates a persistent dialectic process in survivors. The intense confluence of living and violent dying causes permanent changes in the experience of living. Though humans anticipate natural death at a time when their life "has run its course," the expectation of violent death is dreaded and denied. Since any experience worthy of the name contains a theme opposite to our expectation (including violent dying), violent dying carries a fundamental negativity that emerges in the relation between experience and insight. Insight is more than the knowledge of this or that situation. It also involves an escape from something that had deceived us and held us captive (like a "possessive" recounting). Violent dying confounds acceptance, because it never should have happened.

Paradoxically, human reason cannot find reason or reversal in the drama of recounting. The experience of violent dying cannot be a science that provides an ultimate answer or "truth." The truth of experience contains an orientation toward new experience — someone "experienced" is open to new experience — radically undogmatic. The dialectic of experience has its own fulfillment not in definitive knowledge, but in that openness to experience that is encouraged by experience itself. Suffering (the knowledge of the limitation of humanity) realizes the limited nature of all prediction and the uncertainty of all plans. Real experiencing is that in which we become aware of our finiteness, the limits of the power and the self-knowledge of planning reason, the illusion that everything can be reversed (undone), and that there is a always time for everything and that everything somehow returns.

Mystical

RESTORATIVE RETELLING GROUP AGENDA

Purpose: For family members and friends who cannot accommodate to images of the violent dying (reenactment) or images of self (remorse, retaliation, protection) six months following the death. The primary focus of the group interaction is on moderating trauma and separation distress and reinforcing resilience, before the direct engagement of the group in the imagery of violent dying. Agenda (10 weekly, two-hour sessions).

Session 1: Introductions
The leader presents the norms of the group and rules of confidentiality and clarifies the model of restorative retelling before group members begin their retelling. Each member then tells the story that brought her or him to the group.
Each group (Session 1 through 10) ends with exercises of relaxation and guided imagery.

Session 2: Sources of Support
Resilience is defined and resources of resilience (personal, family, work, community) are clarified. Each member's concept of death (which may include spiritual beliefs) is explored. An active reengagement with living through activities of value and reconnection with meaningful beliefs is encouraged.

Session 3: Prevailing Instead of Recovering
Members cannot expect life to be the same after the violent death of someone they loved. Our objective in prevailing, rather than recovering, is to

find a way to live around and through an event that will forever change us. Members are encouraged to talk about these changes.

Session 4: Comorbidity — A Definition of Distress and Disorder
The difference between psychiatric disorders and distress (reenactment, remorse, retaliation, and overprotectiveness) is presented. This is followed by an explanation of restorative retelling and how it moderates distress and possessive thoughts. Since commemoration serves as a basis for restorative retelling, preparation for session 5 is outlined.

Session 5: Commemorative Presentations (4 or 5 members)
Each member has 15 or 20 minutes to commemorate the life of his or her loved one through images, writings, songs, or memorabilia and to revivify his or her caring role with the deceased before the dying.

Session 6: Commemorative Presentations (4 or 5 members)
There is a continuation of commemoration. Preparation for death imagery: group members will prepare a drawing using crayons or colored pens portraying the imaginary drama of the violent dying. This exercise may be completed outside the group, or as a group exercise if it is too threatening for some members.

Session 7: Death Imagery Presentations (4 or 5 members)
Each member has 15 or 20 minutes to present and restoratively retell the imagery of dying. With the guidance of the leaders and other group members they imaginatively reenact their caring role from the commemorative presentation within the dying story.

Session 8: Death Imagery Presentations (4 or 5 members)
Continuation of death imagery

Session 9: Family and Friends
Each member introduces supportive family or members of the community to consolidate changes and reinforce postgroup support in anticipation of group termination.

Session 10: Ceremonial Goodbye
A formal group exercise of remembrance for each loved one is completed. A final commemorative exercise for the group and each member closes the last session.

Case Illustration: Criminal Death Support Group

A victims' assistance worker referred Donna, a 38-year-old woman, from the local district attorney's office. She was unable to contain her anger and anxiety subsequent to the homicidal death of her 18-year-old daughter four months before. She was dreading the impending trial of the man who had been identified as the murderer, and was unable to sleep or quiet her mind of the images of her daughter's rape and murder.

During her assessment she was referred for psychiatric consultation. The consultant concurred with the impression that this woman needed support and advocacy during the trial and prescribed a short-acting tranquilizer (alprazolam 0.5mgm HS) that she could take as needed to ensure the return of a normal sleep cycle at times of increased stress.

She was apprehensive before and during the first group session, but after the seven members were introduced, and recounted their stories of how their loved ones had died, and their shared frustration with the media, police, and the courts, she felt substantial relief and continued as an enthused participant.

The initial group sessions prepared her for the impending trial with information that clarified the dynamics of her trauma, grief, and the commonality of intrusive imagery, and the ways in which the criminal investigation and trial reinforced those responses. She also began to practice exercises of guided imagery and relaxation to positively cope with overwhelming distress. These skills were supplemented with an early session that focused on the importance of self-care. After the first four sessions, she was sleeping soundly without medication and was no longer having flashbacks of the dying imagery on a daily basis.

Subsequent sessions provided accurate information on the legal process and the impending trial that included a representative from the homicide division who attended the group to clarify group members' questions about what to anticipate in the ongoing investigation and eventual trial. Her anger with her perceived helplessness in the criminal/judicial process diminished after this session. She was also reassured by the promise of other group members' availability for support over the phone and attendance at hearings or trial if she requested.

For the first time since the homicide she was able to celebrate the positive memories of her daughter's life with the other group members during a commemorative session where she passed around photos of her daughter and her daughter's watercolors. This was reinforced the next week during a session that included family members, when her husband and younger son expressed support of her progress in group.

During the last session, she tearfully expressed her appreciation to the coleaders and other group members, now confident that she could manage her distress on her own with the understanding that she could contact us at any time that she felt she would need more support.

She sent a message of appreciation in a note announcing the completion of the trial several months later, which she was able to manage with the support of the victims' assistance worker who had originally referred her.

Case Illustration: Restorative Retelling Group

A psychiatric resident who was caring for the patient during a medication study referred Bernice, a 28-year-old secretary. Her depression had not been responsive to a six-month trial of an antidepressant and in further conversations the resident discovered that Bernice had witnessed the murder of her fiancé three years before.

When directly questioned about the violent death, she began crying for the first time. On the evening of his death she watched as three teenage boys robbed, beat, and stabbed him as he was trying to move his car in front of their apartment. She held his hand as he expired in the emergency room after which she numbly collected his personal effects that she later sent off with his ashes to his family who lived in Europe. The murderers were apprehended, but after their arrest she had no further contact with the police, and before their trial she impulsively moved across country "to make a fresh start." While her grief was "frozen," her trauma was not. She continued to have daily flashbacks of his dying and recurring nightmares of watching him in the emergency room as he expired.

During the group, she burst into tears as the group members introduced themselves and tentatively retold the stories of violent dying that brought them to the group, but remained dry eyed as she told her own. She explained that "being an actress" allowed her to smile and avoid what she was feeling, but she was grateful "that I can cry for you."

Her reenactment imagery began to subside during the initial sessions that explained the dynamics of trauma and separation distress and included skill enhancement exercises of guided imagery and relaxation. She was reassured in the recognition that her complicated grief was separable from the clinical disorder of depression and in the assumption that she would be able to prevail over this tragedy by revising her memory of her fiancé's dying to include his living memory that she had all but forgotten.

During the session of commemoration, she talked not only about the tenderness and trust of their attachment, but her agonized decision to abort their child when she discovered that she was pregnant after his death. It was during this session that she first released her sadness, not only for herself and her fiancé, but also for the loss of their child.

During the session of exposure of the death imagery, she drew an image of his hand as it dangled over the cart in the emergency room rather than the image of his beating and stabbing. With our encouragement, she imagined holding his hand and constructed a conversation in which they were able to enact a caring connection with one another as they were separating.

Though there were no available friends or family members to attend the family session, she talked of her realization that she needed a friend — a realization that began to crystallize as she felt closeness to the other group members.

At the time of termination she was no longer dysphoric, and the flashbacks and nightmares had all but disappeared. Though we remain available for assistance in the event of recurring distress, she has not asked for additional help.

OBJECTIVES OF THE PILOT STUDY

With the support of a training grant from the Office for Victims of Crime, manuals for the criminal death support and restorative retelling interventions have been prepared (available from the authors on request Restorative

Retelling Manual www.vdbs.org). The training grant covered expenses for nearly 100 clinicians to attend four separate, five-day trainings to replicate this community-based project and its interventions at 19 sites across the United States.

With trained clinicians in different sites, we began an open trial outcome study in adult subjects who sought and completed time-limited group intervention (either CDS or RR) for distress secondary to violent death at one of two sites (Seattle or San Diego) from 1999 through 2000.

Preparatory to a controlled outcome study, this study was confined to measurements of change in distress before and after an open trial of the intervention to (1) document an association of diminished distress with intervention, and (2) ensure that the intervention was associated with a low rate of complications and drop-out.

Methods

Internal review board approval of the study was obtained at both sites. Participants were contacted by outreach or spontaneously sought assistance for intense distress following the violent death of a close friend or family member. It should be emphasized that a tiny minority of community members seeks psychological assistance, so these participants represent a biased subsample of the community who were highly distressed by the violent death (Rynearson, 1995).

All participants were assessed in a semistructured, individual interview to provide requisite crisis support, before enrollment in one of the group interventions: the CDS group if they were bereaved by a criminal death in the process of investigation or trial, or the RR group if they remained highly distressed after a completed investigation or trial of a criminal death (or by an accidental or suicidal dying with an abbreviated investigation and no trial).

After agreeing to an intervention and signing an informed consent, each participant completed a questionnaire that included a detailed account of the dying, an assessment of the relationship with the deceased, and demographic and historical data on each subject before the violent death. All participants then completed the following standardized measures of distress that have been reliably replicated in grief-related studies (Jacobs, 1999; Murphy, 1998; Stamm, 1999):

The Beck Depression Inventory (BDI), a self-report measure of clinical depression; the Inventory of Traumatic Grief (ITG), a self-report measure of death-related trauma and separation distress; the Revised Impact of Events scale (IES-R), a self-report measure of death-related trauma; and the Drug and Alcohol Screening Test (DAST), a self-report measure of drug and alcohol use.

The Death Imagery Scale, a self-report measure of death-related imagery (reenactment, rescue, revenge, or reunion) was developed by one of the authors (EKR) as a useful indicator of intense imagery, but has not been rigorously tested or verified.

The same measures were repeated at the end of the intervention for comparative analysis.

Statistical Procedures

Means and standard deviations were calculated for the assessed continuous measures (e.g., age, time since loss); frequency distributions were calculated for categorical measures (e.g., violent mode of death — homicide, suicide, accident). T-tests were used to compare prepost means for each psychological distress outcome measure (e.g., testing to reject the null hypothesis of no difference between baseline and follow-up means). Pearson correlation coefficients were used to determine factors significantly associated with the outcome distress measures. A repeated measures analysis of variance then modeled the effects of each factor found to be significantly bivariately associated with an outcome measure. Specifically, these models simultaneously estimated the effects of treatment group, psychiatric treatment history, witnessing the victim die, prior worry about the victim, attachment and dependence on the victim on each outcome summary score, adjusting for the within-subject effects of time (prepost differences).

Results

Table 11.2 presents the demographic data of the 64 subjects as predominantly Caucasian (68.3% White; 18.7% Hispanic; 10.3% African American; 6.9% Asian), female (73%), adults (mean age 42.9 years) who were well educated (63% college graduates), and reported a high frequency of previous mental health treatment (29.6%) and psychiatric diagnosis (25.4) by history before the violent deaths. Nearly all (98%) were related to the deceased (29.6% parent of deceased child, 24.1% child of deceased parent, 14.8% sibling, 7.4% spouse, 13.0% other). The majority of the violent deaths were homicidal (68.3% homicide, 15.9% suicide, 15.9% accident).

The participants began intervention soon after the violent death (median: 6.3 months). The interval between pre- and post-self-report measures was 3.6 months. Nearly two-thirds (65.6%) of the participants were enrolled in the RR intervention because that intervention included subjects after a violent death related to suicide or accident as well as homicide.

Since there were no significant differences in the treatment effects of RR or CDS, Table 11.3 contains the mean scores and statistical analyses comparing the self-report measures before and after the interventions on all 64 participants. The mean scores of the BDI, DIS, ITG, and RIES before intervention were elevated, suggesting a high level of generalized distress. The DAST score was below the cut-off score (< 8.0).

The data show a highly significant ($p < 0.05$ to 0.0001) decrease on all measures of distress coincident with the interventions. The DAST remained low before and after the interventions.

Table 11.4 presents the Pearson correlation coefficients between outcome summary scores and loss characteristics, exposure to the death and relationship to the deceased that were nonsignificant except for those subjects who (1) had actually witnessed the dying (higher pre- and postintervention BDI, DIS, ITG & RIES measures); (2) had previously worried about the deceased (higher pre-intervention DIS and ITG measures); (3) had an emotionally positive relationship with the deceased (higher postintervention RIES measures); and (4) were emotionally attached (higher pre/post ITG) and dependent on the deceased (higher pre/post-BDI, DIS & ITG).

TABLE 11.2
Descriptive Statistics. N = 64

Variable	Mean (SD) or %
Age[a]	42.9 (11.4)
Months From loss[a,d]	median: 6.3
Months between pre & post	3.6 (1.5)
Female	73.4 %
Race	
White	63.8 %
Black	10.3 %
Hispanic	18.7 %
Other	6.9 %
Education[b]	
Junior high school	3.4 %
High school	33.9 %
College	52.5 %
Graduate school	10.2 %
Psychiatric disorder history[c]	25.4 %
Psychiatric treatment history[c]	29.6 %
Relation to deceased	
Spouse	7.4 %
Child	29.6 %
Parent	24.1 %
Sibling	14.8 %
Other relative	13.0 %
Other	1.9 %
Mode of death	
Homicide	68.3 %
Suicide	15.9 %
Accident	15.9 %
Treatment group	
CDS	34.4 %
RR	65.6 %
Location	
San Diego	69.6 %
Seattle	30.4 %

[a] at Preassessment
[b] highest level completed
[c] self-reported
[d] Median months from loss is reported here because there are outliers inflate the mean, making it a misleading estimate of the central tendency of this variable.

Discussion

Participation in an open trial of short-term, group intervention, with highly distressed participants, within the first year of the violent death of a loved one, was correlated with significant improvement on standardized measures of depression (BDI), death imagery (DIS), and trauma and separation distress (ITG & RIES).

Intervention was marked by a high degree of engagement in participation (less than 20% of subjects dropped out of group at either site) and there were no reported complications.

It would be misleading to disregard the spontaneous improvement that these 64 subjects might have realized within the same time interval (3.6 months) without intervention. A comparison of subjects randomly assigned to a different intervention or a nonintervention control group that might validate the effectiveness of CDS and RR awaits study; however, this report's documentation of improvement in highly distressed subjects should not be dismissed. It could be held that a highly distressed cohort would not show such robust improvement in so short a time without intervention.

TABLE 11.3
Outcome summary scores: Pre- and postmeans

Sum variable	Premean (SD)	Postmean (SD)	t or χ^2	P values
BDI[a]	19.4 (11.3)	15.5 (10.5)	-3.45	**
DIS[b]	7.4 (5.2)	5.7 (4.7)	-2.95	**
Reenactment	2.8 (2.0)	2.1 (1.8)	-3.36	**
Rescue	1.5 (1.8)	1.0 (1.5)	-1.65	
Revenge	1.5 (1.8)	1.0 (1.4)	-1.18	
Reunion	2.0 (1.7)	1.7 (1.7)	-1.20	
TG diagnosis[c]	24.6 %	13.1 %	6.00	*
ITG[d]	35.3 (14.0)	29.6 (14.8)	-4.51	****
RIES Totale	38.3 (13.6)	28.7 (16.5)	-5.32	****
Avoidance	15.8 (8.2)	11.1 (8.5)	-4.57	****
Intrusion	22.5 (8.7)	17.6 (9.9)	-4.24	****
DAST[f]	4.0 (4.4)	3.9 (4.7)	-0.19	

[†] *P < 0.10; * P < 0.05; ** P < 0.01; *** P < 0.001; **** P < 0.0001; two-tailed.*
Values of p < 0.05 indicate that there is a significant difference between the Pre and Post means.
[a] *BDI = Beck Depression Inventory, a 22-item scale; summary score ranges from 0 to 66.*
[b] *DIS = Death Imagery Scale is made up of four items (reenactment, rescue, revenge, and reunion), each ranging from 0 to 5; summary score ranges from 0 to 20.*
[c] *Traumatic Grief (TG) diagnosis was calculated using the diagnostic algorithm of the Inventory of Traumatic Grief (ITG).*
[d] *ITG = Inventory of Traumatic Grief, an 18-item scale; summary score ranges from 0 to 72.*
[e] *RIES = Revised Impact of Events Scale, a 15-item scale (summary score ranges from 0 to 75), made up of a 7-item Intrusion subscale (summary score ranges from 0 to 35) and an 8-item Avoidance subscale (summary score ranges from 0 to 40).*
[f] *DAST = Drug/Alcohol Screening Test, a 32-item scale; summary score ranges from 0 to 85.*

TABLE 11.4
Bivariate linear regression models entering loss characteristics, exposure, and relationship to deceased to predict outcome summary scores.

	DIS		BDI		ITG		RIE		DST	
	Pre	Post	Pre	Post	Pre	Post	Pre	Post	Pre	Post
Saw scene of death	n.s.	n.s.	n.s.	n.s.	n.s.	n.s.	n.s.	n.s.	n.s.	n.s.
Saw person injured	n.s.	n.s.	0.32*	n.s.	0.28*	0.29*	n.s.	n.s.	n.s.	n.s.
Tried to help	n.s.	n.s.	n.s.	n.s.	n.s.	n.s.	n.s.	n.s.	n.s.	n.s.
Prevented from helping	n.s.	n.s.	n.s.	n.s.	n.s.	n.s.	n.s.	n.s.	n.s.	n.s.
At scene before victim removed	n.s.	n.s.	n.s.	n.s.	n.s.	n.s.	n.s.	n.s.	n.s.	n.s.
Saw victim die	0.28*	0.24†	0.43**	0.24†	0.39**	0.36*	0.35*	0.35**	n.s.	n.s.
First to discover victim	n.s.	n.s.	n.s.	n.s.	n.s.	n.s.	n.s.	n.s.	n.s.	0.31*
Saw victim taken to hospital	0.25†	n.s.	n.s.	n.s.	n.s.	n.s.	n.s.	n.s.	n.s.	0.35*
Victim said something	0.24†	n.s.	n.s.	n.s.	n.s.	n.s.	n.s.	n.s.	n.s.	n.s.
Learned of loss immediately	n.s.	n.s.	0.25†	n.s.	0.30*	n.s.	0.32*	n.s.	n.s.	n.s.
Attended funeral	n.s.	n.s.	n.s.	n.s.	n.s.	n.s.	n.s.	n.s.	n.s.	n.s.
Participated in loss rituals	n.s.	n.s.	n.s.	n.s.	n.s.	n.s.	n.s.	n.s.	0.29*	0.26†
Experienced other recent loss	n.s.	n.s.	n.s.	n.s.	n.s.	n.s.	n.s.	0.27*	n.s.	n.s.
Reminiscent of other losses	n.s.	n.s.	n.s.	n.s.	n.s.	n.s.	n.s.	n.s.	0.27†	n.s.
Previously worried about victim	0.46***	n.s.	0.25†	n.s.	0.39**	0.27†	0.24†	n.s.	n.s.	n.s.
Believed deceased was at risk	n.s.	0.23†	n.s.	n.s.	n.s.	n.s.	n.s.	n.s.	n.s.	n.s.
Wish deceased prevented event	n.s.	n.s.	n.s.	n.s.	n.s.	n.s.	n.s.	n.s.	n.s.	n.s.
Relationship with deceased:										
Distant — Close	n.s.	n.s.	n.s.	0.24†	n.s.	n.s.	n.s.	n.s.	n.s.	n.s.
Conflictual —Peaceful	n.s.	n.s.	n.s.	n.s.	n.s.	n.s.	n.s.	0.31*	n.s.	n.s.

(Continued)

TABLE 11.4 (*Continued*)

Bivariate linear regression models entering loss characteristics, exposure, and relationship to deceased to predict outcome summary scores.

DIS	BDI		ITG		RIE		DST	
	Pre	**Post**	**Pre**	**Post**	**Pre**	**Post**	**Pre**	**Post**
Difficult — Easy	n.s.	n.s.	n.s.	n.s.	n.s.	n.s.	n.s.	n.s.
Unsupportive — Supportive	n.s.	n.s.	n.s.	0.27†	n.s.	n.s.	n.s.	0.29*
Hostile — Compatible	n.s.	n.s.	n.s.	n.s.	n.s.	n.s.	n.s.	-0.33*
Incompatible — Compatible	n.s.	n.s.	n.s.	n.s.	n.s.	n.s.	n.s.	0.34*
Attached to deceased	n.s.	n.s.	0.37**	0.35**	n.s.	0.33*	n.s.	n.s.
Dependent on deceased	0.30*	0.31*	0.46***	0.36**	n.s.	0.50***	n.s.	0.38**

- *Positive correlation indicates that those who endorsed statement were more likely to have higher sum scores.*
- *n.s. = not significant (p>=0.1)*

Finally, the results of this pilot study reinforce the intuitive recognition of the power of the peer group as a matrix for stress reduction and supportive reexposure for highly distressed family members to violent death in a community-based support service.

REFERENCES

Amick-McMullan, A., Kilpatrick, D., Veronen, L., & Smith, S. (1989). Family survivors of homicide victims: Theoretical perspectives and an exploratory study. *Journal of Traumatic Stress, 2*(1), 21–35.

Armour, M. (2002a) Experiences of covictims of homicide: Implications for research and practice, *Trauma, violence & Abuse, 3*(2): 109–124.

Armour, M. (2002b) Journey of family members of homicide victims: A qualitative study of their posthomicide experience. *American Journal of Orthopsychiatry, 72*(3): 372–382

Bonanno, G. (1999) Factors associated with effective loss accommodation. In C. Figley (Ed.), *Traumatology of grieving* (pp 37–41) Philadelphia: Brunner/Mazel.

Bonanno, G., Wortman, C., Lehman, R., & Sonnega, J. (2002). Resilience to loss and chronic grief: A prospective study from preloss to 18-months postloss. *Journal of Personality and Social Psychology, 83* (5): 1150–1164.

Eth, S. & Pynoos, R. (1994). Children who witness the homicide of a parent. *Psychiatry, 57,* 287–305.

Jacobs, S. (1999). *Traumatic grief: Diagnosis, treatment, and prevention.* Philadelphia: Brunner/Mazel.

Murphy, S. (1998). Broad spectrum group treatment for parents bereaved by the violent deaths of 12- to 28-year-old children: A randomized controlled trial. *Death Studies, 22*(3), 209–235.

Murphy, S. (1999). PTSD among bereaved parents following the violent deaths of their 12- to 28- year old children: A longitudinal prospective analysis, *Journal of Traumatic Stress, 12*(2) 273–291.

Murphy, S., Johnson, L. C., & Lohan, J. (2002). The aftermath of the violent death of a child: An integration of the assessments of parents' mental distress and PTSD during the first 5 years of bereavement. *Journal of Loss and Trauma, 7,* 203–222.

Neimeyer, R. A. & Levitt, H. M. (2000). What's narrative got to do with it? Construction and coherence in accounts of loss. In J. H. Harvey & E. D. Miller (Eds.), *Loss and trauma* (pp. 401–412). Philadelphia: Brunner/Mazel.

Parkes, C. (1993). Psychiatric problems following bereavement by murder or manslaughter. *British Journal of Psychiatry, 162,* 49–54.

Pruett, K., (1979). Home treatment for two infants who witnessed their mother's murder. *American Academy of Child Psychiatry, 79,* 647–657.

Pynoos, R. S. & Nader, K. (1988). Psychological first aid and treatment approach for children exposed to community violence: Research implications. *Journal of Traumatic Stress, 1*(4), 445–473.

Rynearson, E. (1984). Bereavement after homicide: A descriptive study. *American Journal of Psychiatry, 141* (11) 1452–1454.

Rynearson, E. (1995). Bereavement after homicide: A comparison of treatment seekers and refusers. *British Journal of Psychiatry, 166,* 507–510.

Rynearson, E. & Geoffrey, R. (1999). Bereavement after homicide: Its assessment and treatment. In C. R. Figley (Ed.), *Traumatology of grieving* (pp. 109–128). Philadelphia: Brunner/Mazel.

Rynearson, E. & Sinnema, C. (1999). Supportive group therapy for bereavement after homicide. In D. Blake & B. Young (Eds.), *Group treatment for post traumatic stress disorder* (pp. 137–147). Philadelphia: Brunner/Mazel.

Rynearson, E. (2001). *Retelling violent death.* Philadelphia: Brunner-Routledge.

Salloum, A. (2004). Group Work with Adolescent Survivors after Violent Death: A Manual for Practitioners: New York; Routledge,

Salloum, A. & Vincent, N. J. (1999). Community-based groups for inner city adolescent survivors of homicide victims. *Journal of Child and Adolescent Group Therapy, 9* (1), 27–45.

Salloum, A., Avery, L., & McClain, R. P. (2001). Group psychotherapy for adolescent survivors of homicide victims: A pilot study. *Journal of the American Academy of Child and Adolescent Psychiatry, 40,* 1261–1267.

Shear, K., Frank, E., Foa, E., Cherry, C., Reynolds III, C. F., Vander Bilt, J., & Masters, S. (2001). Traumatic grief treatment:A pilot study. *American Journal of Psychiatry, 158,*1506–1508.

Shear, K., Frank, E., Patrick, H., & Reynolds, C. (2005). Treatment of complicated grief: A randomized controlled trial. *Journal of the American Medical Association, 293*(21), 2601–2608

Stamm, H. (1999). Empirical perspectives on contextualizing death and trauma. In C. Figley, (Ed.), *Traumatology of grieving* (pp.23–36). Philadelphia: Brunner/Mazel.

NOTE

1. Supported by Grant No. 98-VF-GX-0009, awarded by the Office for Victims of Crime, and funding from The Dart Center

12

Intervention Continuity in Posttraffic Fatality: From Notifying Families of the Loss to Establishing a Self-Help Group

RUTH MALKINSON AND YAEL GERON

[handwritten annotations]

GROUP THERAPY AFTER ACCIDENTAL DYING

In Israel, where long-term supportive therapy is provided by governmental agencies for bereaved family members after violent dying from warfare or terrorist attack, there is no provision of assistance for loved ones bereaved by fatal auto accidents, despite the fact that dying from a fatal car accident is far more frequent and the most frequent mode of accidental death. Accidental dying is culturally viewed as "a nonheroic, marginalized event leaving families to grieve in solitude," and the authors initiated a community-based support program for these neglected family members. The program provides a spectrum of continuous psychological support beginning with death notification, outreach, and assessment, followed by a pivotal short-term group intervention with optional preparation and transition to a self-help support group. The short-term group intervention model is a pragmatic blending of established narrative and psychodynamic approaches. The provision of staff support to avoid vicarious trauma distress is essential and cogently outlined in this chapter.

VIOLENT TRAUMATIC DEATH

Loss through death as a result of road fatality, the focus of our work, is regarded as a sudden, traumatic, and "irresponsible negligence" death also termed *violent dying* (Rynearson, 2001, p. 21). Sudden death is defined as "a death out of time, out of place and it disrupts the individual and social biography ... for the bereaved individual, sudden death is traumatic not only because it truncates the life of the deceased but also because it damages the self-identity of the survivors.... Research on bereavement has shown that the lack of preparation and the often violent nature of sudden death exacerbates the trauma for the bereaved" (Howarth, 2001, pp. 436–437). Janoff-Bulman's term *shattered assumptions* captures the devastation and earthquakelike feelings experienced by families following a violent and traumatic death (1992). Death in war, terror attacks, or mass disasters, in contrast to expected loss, is identified in the literature as traumatic death to which adaptation is difficult because the shock that follows affects the mourners more severely than an expected death (Malkinson & Bar-Tur, 2005; Malkinson, Rubin, & Witztum, 2000; Prigerson & Jacobs,2001; Prigerson, Bierhals, et al., 1996; Prigerson, Frank, et al., 1995; Rubin, Malkinson and Witztum, 2003).

Loss under traumatic circumstances involves responses characteristic of loss and trauma and results in a combined cluster of traumatic bereavement. Rubin et al. (2003) suggested that loss under traumatic circumstances may be approached as a phenomenon of trauma-interfacing bereavement with special emphasis on the relationship to the deceased. The sudden and unexpected death of a child under traumatic circumstances, which is the topic of this chapter, involves especially complex adaptation (Rubin & Malkinson, 2001; Sanders, 1999) .

LOSS FOLLOWING TRAFFIC ACCIDENTS

To our increasing regret, the number of families suffering a loss in road accidents in Israel has risen considerably in recent years, and these families receive no help whatsoever from central sources. The statistics illustrate the dimensions of the problem: The number of fatalities in road accidents since the establishment of the State of Israel in 1948 through 2004 totals 23,412. There was a fluctuation in the number of fatalities, in the years 2002 to 2004, when there were 525, 451, 480 fatalities, respectively (Israeli Central Bureau of Statistics, 2005).

A survey was conducted on the rights of, and services provided to, bereaved families in Israel who lose a loved one prematurely (Florian, Malkinson, & Kasher, 2000). It was designed to gather information on the public's attitude to these services and yielded the following important findings: In general, the Israeli public regards favorably the economic and mental support given to families bereaved in terrorist and military events. In contrast, the public believes that families that lose a loved one from illness or a road accident do not merit such assistance.

SERVICES PROVIDED TO FAMILIES AFFECTED BY
ROAD ACCIDENT FATALITIES

With the exception of bereavement in military or terrorist action, with their own frameworks of intervention that the law provides, until recently there were no national or public bodies in Israel that provided support to groups that suffered losses in nonsecurity circumstances. It became apparent that among the many families who lost a member in a road accident, the lack of assistance provided to those who lost a child was particularly notable, with the exception of the voluntary organization Yad Haniktafim (in memory of victims of road fatalities). Established as a self-help organization, with the aim of perpetuating the memory of loved ones, more recently Yad Haniktafim began offering professional support to families bereaved as a result of road fatalities, through long-term group therapy based on the existing intervention model provided in Israel to bereaved as result of war or terror attack (Geron, Solomon & Ginsberg, 1997). Following legislation concerning assistance for families of accident casualties, enacted in 2002 (Knesset, the Book of Laws, 2002), the Ministry of Welfare has set up a center to help such families. Its mandate is to establish a framework to provide help to these families from the point when they are notified of the accident. This involves organizing teams with the police and municipal authorities, legal assistance, and in conjunction with Yad Haniktafim, psychological assistance in the form of a hot line and support groups.

MARGINALIZED DEATH AND BEREAVEMENT:
LOSS FOLLOWING TRAFFIC ACCIDENTS

Violent death as a result of traffic accidents is characterized by a greater sense of loneliness and isolation on the part of the bereaved than other forms of loss by violent death (Malkinson & Witztum, 1997). It is a marginalized death in that its circumstances and consequences remain hidden from public awareness, but at the same time it is an event that can hurt and threaten each one of us, in the sense that we are all potential victims. This potential danger increases the level of public anxiety, which unfortunately is followed by collective social avoidance of the bereaved, and by little collective acknowledgment and support. In other words, because it is not within the social and political collective consciousness, both social and psychological support are less available (Abramowitz, 2005). Individual bereavement is therefore experienced in much greater seclusion. Paradoxically, though the rates of casualties as a result of traffic accidents are increasing, their social and psychological impact on the public remain low.

Such an event can also be viewed as a "bad" death, as distinct from a "good" death. The former leaves survivors despairing and helpless in the face of meaningless evil or nothingness. "Unpredictability, violence or intentional harm are commonly attributed to bad death..." (Abramowitz, 2005, p. 55). A good death, "represents a cultural ideal that re-enacts a symbolic victory over death, provides meaning, and allows for the regeneration of life" (Bloch & Parry, 1982). It also involves first and foremost, not sudden, bloody, or unexpected or meaningless dying trajectories. Ideally, it is a death without brutality, nor is it punctuated by anger. A bad death has the opposite effect. Its meaninglessness and suddenness leave survivors desolate and pained in the face of what they believe to have been a preventable death.

Unlike death in war or in terror attacks, a traffic death lacks a collective social and political consciousness, most particularly, as resulting from a "public enemy" (Abramowitz, 2005). In Israel the discrepancy in attitudes between loss in war or terror attack and that following a road fatality accentuate the difference between "good' and "bad' death.

Lack of social recognition and social support has been referred to as "disenfranchised grief" (Doka, 1989): "A grief that persons experience when they incur a loss that is not or cannot be openly acknowledged, publicly mourned or socially supported" (pp. 1–2). According to Doka, some types of death in and of themselves may be "disenfranchised," "mainly because their complexities are not well understood"(Corr, 1998). Fatal traffic accidents in Israel belong to this category of being frequently neglected and regarded as valueless. Doka clearly states that disenfranchised grief is always founded on society's values and attitudes. Neimeyer and Jordan (2002) refer to it as an "empathic failure." In Israeli society, for example, losses as a result of war or terror attacks gained collective support when compared to other types of losses such as road accidents and suicide, neither of which has achieved much social or political attention (Florian et al., 2000).

In Israel, only in recent years has the attitude toward traffic fatalities changed, and one of the most significant steps was the introduction of the 2002 law to support families who lost their dear ones in traffic accidents. Understandably, these elements also affect therapists working with families who lost their loved ones in traffic accidents because of the added pressure not encountered when working with clients who have suffered losses that are collectively better recognized.

THERAPEUTIC INTERVENTION FOLLOWING
THE LOSS OF A CLOSE RELATIVE

Over the years a number of therapeutic interventions have been developed to cope with the loss of a close relative. These include individual, couple, family, or group treatment, and may be conducted either by professionals or by self-help groups led by volunteers who have experienced this type of loss and realize that it enables them to comfort and support others in distress. Moreover, the timing of the intervention can vary from taking place close to the event — in the acute phase of grief in the month following the loss — or well into the grief process or even a year or two later (Geron, Solomon, & Ginsberg, 1997; Murphy et al., 1998; Yalom, 1995; Videka-Sherman & Lieberman, 1985).

FROM SUPPORT GROUPS TO SELF-HELP: THE MODEL OF THERAPEUTIC CONTINUITY IN SUDDEN BEREAVEMENT

The model is designed to offer community-based assistance to bereaved families who have experienced a sudden and traumatic loss and for a variety of contextual reasons, lack public services. Continuity in provision of support to these families underlies the model. Moreover, the model stresses continuity in provision of assistance that begins at the moment of breaking the bad news followed by individually tailored referral to community-based agencies. Individual and family's specific needs are assessed and determined based on a differential assessment. The final phase of the model involves assisting a professionally led group to become a self-help group.

Threaded throughout the model is the element of reaching out, the purpose of which is to offer services to potential clients to help them reduce their sense of powerlessness, and to help them to make use of available resources. Moreover, reaching out in itself expresses the professional obligation to support the well-being both of individuals and the community (Pincus & Minahan, 1973).

Three basic principles that reflect the bereavement process across a specific grief theory underlie the presented model: (1) applying relevant updated theoretical and empirical data; (2) intervention and outcome evaluation; and (3) collaboration between various community-based agencies.

We will elaborate on the continuity model as applied to intervention for parents who lost a child in a traffic fatality. These parents are a population at risk and they were chosen for our project for that reason (See Figure 12.1).

The literature has identified parents' adaptation to loss of a child as a complex one because it comprises loss within a special and very significant framework of relationships; it brings with it abrupt changes in biological, hereditary, and psychological continuity because children are an inate part of their parents' life cycle, and their death severs this continuity (Malkinson & Bar-Tur, 2005; Rubin & Malkinson, 2001). When parents mourn their children there is a break in the natural order in that it is children who expect to mourn their parents' death, not vice versa.

Four parts of the suggested model have been applied so far: (1) breaking the bad news — training medical staff to notify families; (2) short-term group intervention; (3) preparing the group for self-help; (4) getting on the road — the active self help group (See Figure 12.2).

Breaking the Bad News — Training Medical Staff

The training of medical staff took place at the Surasky Medical Center in collaboration with the hospital's social services unit. The hospital project on sudden bereavement included outreach of medical staff by the social services unit followed by a carefully planned approach to delivering news of a death to family and friends, and attending to issues of secondary trauma.

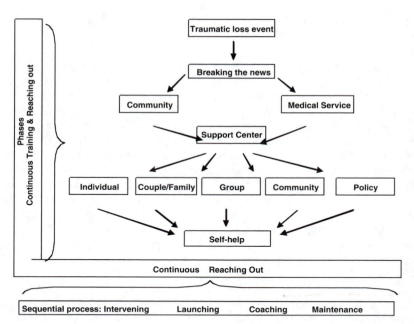

FIGURE 12.1. Model of intervention continuity in sudden traumatic loss: Phases and processes.

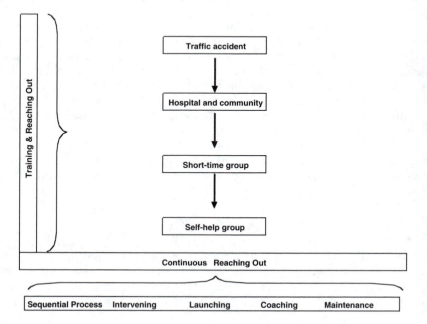

FIGURE 12.2 Model of intervention continuity of traffic accident: Phases and processes.

A workshop was held with medical staff members working in trauma-focused units in order to strengthen their self-efficacy and resilience, and assist them to acquire skills as members of interdisciplinary professional medical teams for dealing with interventions.

The workshops took place in the hospital's wards, and included four sessions, semi-structured dynamic closed group interventions, use of case vignettes, role play, exercising new skills, and homework assignments between sessions (Geron, Keidar, Yagil, Dori, Drori, & Malkinson, 2004).

Short-Term Groups

In general the aims of group intervention with the bereaved are to develop and strengthen group members' informal support network; reduce feelings of isolation and detachment; help the bereaved "to live with the pain"; help them develop problem-solving and social skills; and help them seek information on available resources (Geron et al., 2003; Hopmeyer & Werk, 1994).

Reasons for Joining Support Groups of Bereaved Parents

The most significant reasons motivating parents to join a group for the bereaved were the desire to meet people in a similar situation, a need to belong, and validation of their feelings and reactions following the loss. Additionally, at times they feel uncomfortable among nonmourners, and have acquired a repertoire of responses and behavioral patterns in dealing with mourning (Geron, Ginsburg, & Solomon 2003).

Effectiveness of Group Intervention

Intervention can last from three months to two years, and there are various reports regarding its effectiveness. Some claim (feel) that immediate intervention has the most operative value (Katto and Mann,1999, Litterer-Allumbaugh & Hoyt, 1999), while others hold that therapeutic intervention is best only in cases of complicated grief. It should be stressed that degree of motivation is very significant in terms of outcome; those with the highest motivation for treatment, that is, who have actively sought it, have the best chance of the treatment being successful, compared with those who were referred for treatment but did not actively seek it.

Short-term group intervention, like that of individual therapy, is reported as most effective in reducing the symptoms of distress (Murphy et al., 1998). Some workers claim that through short-term group treatment of loss, an opportunity arises to investigate and examine anew solutions to conflicts linked with intimacy-isolation and dependence-independence (Piper, McCallum, & Azim, 1992). Overall, short-term groups consist of 10 to 15 meetings (Geron, Solomon, & Ginsburg, 1997).

In Israel, the most frequently applied model of group intervention for the bereaved is long term (lasting up to two years). In contrast, the short-term model and that of self-help groups of the bereaved are less well known and their application has therefore been limited to date.

Applying Short-Term Groups as Part of Intervention Continuity

The aims of the short-term group for parents who had lost a child in a traffic accident were as follows: to legitimize bereavement following the accident; assist parents in adapting to the loss through their participation in a short-term, professionally led group intervention; and at the same time to help the group become a self-help group or "a shoulder to shoulder group" as one of the participants suggested.

This short-term group intervention for the bereaved consists of 12 to 15 meetings, and is a known and accepted model applied in many countries. Empirical results show that this model is effective and constructive in reducing signs of distress. It provides the opportunity to choose between short- and long-term groups, and increases the availability of group intervention to more people (Geron et al., 2003; Murphy et al., 1998).

Recruitment

Three resources were available for locating the families: the center for assisting road accident casualties initiated by the Ministry of Welfare in collaboration with Yad Haniktafim, the Sourasky Medical Center located in Tel Aviv, and "a friend brings a friend." This collaboration yielded a number of potential members for the group. These were parents who had lost their child between six months and seven years prior to starting the group but not as a result of military service or a terrorist attack.

Pregroup Screening and Preparation

Individual interviews with the parents were conducted to assess their needs and prepare them for the group meetings. Seven parents — two couples, one bereaved mother who was also a widow (who was also a bereaved mother), and two divorced women constituted the group. The range of time that had elapsed since the loss was six months to seven years.

Activating the Group

A short-term support group led by two professional coleaders and a participant observer was chosen as a form of intervention. There were 12 weekly meetings, each lasting 90 minutes, held at the Bob Shapell School of Social Work. Participants paid a minimal fee to cover refreshments.

Method of Intervention

A half–structured intervention was employed. The focus was on facilitating an adaptive bereavement process by applying Rubin's (1999) two-track model of bereavement and Neimeyer's, (Neimeyer, 2001; Neimeyer, Keese, & Fortners, 2000) theoretical framework of meaning construction regarding the death, and life without the deceased. The style of discussion was dynamic and interactive.

Group Characteristics

An immediate connection between participants was formed which continued after the session ended and included phone calls between sessions. Openness and readiness to be members of the group were apparent from its inception (with the exception of one participant who had lost both her husband and her son six months earlier and was ambivalent throughout the meetings). Willingness to share their stories of the traumatic loss of their children with the group was prominent, and feelings of being fellow sufferers developed right away.

Major Themes

A number of themes were integrated into the group's agenda throughout the meetings, but the focus and scope changed as the group process developed. The major themes discussed were:

Living with continuing pain: Time does not heal the pain of the loss.

Remembering the dead child and struggling to maintain the child's representation: How can the vacuum remain the same, never to be filled again?

Continuing with life following the loss: The feeling that in spite of the difficulties, each parent is fighting to search for ways to continue life for the surviving siblings.

Relationships with spouse, siblings, and the extended family: Feelings of not being understood by others, including family members, when talking about the pain of the loss.

Relationship with the nonbereaved: Struggling to find an appropriate way to talk about the deceased child with other people, to include the child or not when asked how many children do you have.

The group as a safe haven: The unspoken expectation to resume "normal life" is especially hard, and the feeling that only in the group can members discuss their pain, sleepless nights, yearning for the child, and the pain of the "lost future" of their child when their child's friends are getting married and giving birth.

Themes discussed included accepting differences between members while encouraging each person to continue to search for a way to live with the pain of the loss. In contrast to nonbereaved groups, intimacy and coherence were immediate, and as the group progressed differences between members and the styles of mourning became evident.

Reaching Out

In order to ensure continuity between sessions, telephone contact was maintained with group members. Reaching out was also important when the group was making the transition to being a self-help group. This ongoing contact with group members was the leaders' way of reinforcing the importance of keeping in contact between sessions, and in the process increasing group cohesion.

Becoming a Self-Help Group: Giving and Receiving Help

Self-help groups in general are made up of people who share a similar problem which they feel unable to handle on their own; they join together to find a common solution to the problem; all of them are involved with and obligated to the group; they act on the basis of mutual assistance; they help and are being helped (Bar & Sadan, 1989). In connection with bereaved people seeking help, Riches (2001) suggested that "people who join self-help groups prefer befriending to counseling, personal experience to theory and often campaign for reforms associated with their bereavement" (p. 402).

Social support has been identified in the literature as a crucial variable in the process of adaptation to loss through death (Silverman, 2005). It is also a major component in a self-help group and is defined as "having people available on whom the bereaved person can rely" (Sarson, Levine, Basham, & Sarson, 1983, p. 27). It is therefore not surprising that self-support groups are common for bereaved individuals as an outlet to express the distress and the sense of isolation that the death of a loved one commonly elicits in survivors (Riches, 2000; Riches & Dawson, 1996; Reif, Patton, & Gold, 1995).

Research regarding the value of self-help to participants, peer support, and empowerment and its relationship to recovery is only now beginning to receive the attention necessary to objectively verify its value. To date, most of the research studies of self-help and empowerment have found positive benefits related to participation. Supporting the early research findings are testimonials and anecdotal material from a large number of recipients describing self-help as having a positive impact on their lives (Carpinello, Knight, & Jatulis, 1992). Many recipients have found that self-help and empowerment are an invaluable and essential component of their recovery.

In the present model of intervention, continuity in the course of the transition to a self-support group increased members' feelings of empowerment.

Preparing Members for the Self-Help Group

Three meetings for coaching were set up before the change to a self-help group was made. Group members chose to meet at each other's homes. Discussions to help the group set up ways to continue the meetings included ways to choose its peer leader, setting an agenda, frequency, meeting place, and topics to be discussed.

Toward Launching the Self-Help Group and Follow-Up

Three more sessions for follow-up and actual launching of the group were held, with the leaders as observer-participants.

Continuity of intervention requires that the transition from a professionally led group to a self-help group be planned jointly with group members to assist them in actively taking responsibility in leading the group.

The following issues are important:

1. Keep the group united, with all its implications.
2. Determine a clear "setting."

3. Ensure that transition from a professionally led group to a self-help one will be experienced as a phase of continuity and not as a leave taking.
4. Provide the opportunity for an open door for the group's former professional leaders so they can keep in touch with the group in its new manifestation.
5. Preserve commitment to the group and its members.

Getting on the Road

During the transition period the coleaders were present at the meetings, held at a member's home, mainly as a source of indirect support, but without active intervention. One of the group members was responsible for keeping in touch with other group members between meetings. Coleaders' availability continued throughout the transition period. At the same time group members decided to open meetings to additional members and negotiated with Yad Haniktafim's organizers to recruit members from long-term groups that had terminated. As a result, three more couples joined the group and immediately were integrated as fellow sufferers.

Two overlapping elements are central in self-help groups: providing social support to fellow sufferers and receiving it. It is what Riessman (1965) has termed the *helper therapy* principle, and has pointed out that individuals become empowered and help themselves when they help others. In many ways the essence of self-help lies in the North American ethos, which can be applied to other nations to a degree, especially the theme of "reaffirmation of traditions of community, self-reliance, empowerment and democratization of everyday life." (Kurtz, 1997, p. 11).

Returning to our project, the process of intervention continuity, including the training of medical staff and the group, had been evaluated with pre- and post-questionnaires, and pre- and post-interviews. Additionally, a continuing record was kept of the group's activities and participants' personal accounts. The results are being processed and will be published on completion.

THE DUAL IMPACT OF ROAD FATALITIES ON PROFESSIONALS

Compassion fatigue, secondary traumatic stress, and *vicarious traumatization* are terms used to describe the phenomenon. They are defined by Figley (1993, 1995, 1999) as natural behavior and emotions resulting from knowledge about a traumatizing event experienced by a significant other. It is the stress resulting from helping or wanting to help a traumatized or suffering person (Figley, 1995, p. 7).

Secondary Traumatization

In the case of working with the bereaved following traffic accidents the additional stressors include:

Becoming a potential victim of violent death as a result of traffic accident is a horrendous prospect, with a high level of threat that creates a collective meaning construction of fear of the danger. Denial and repression are used as defense mechanisms. The work involves continuous challenges to the professional's defenses and increases the probability for traumatic countertransference. In working with trauma cuntertransference is known to be particularly powerful, complex, and problematic for clinicians suggesting that the intensity of the clients' responses to the trauma often elicit negative countertransference reactions (Arnold, Calhoun, Tedeschi, & Cann, 2005; Calhoun & Tedeschi, 1999; Herman, 1992; Lindy & Wilson, 1994; Widdson & Salisbury, 1990). One of the manifestations of the "approximate threat" of potentially being hurt by a traffic accident among professionals is a form of anticipatory grief, which is defined as "reactions and responses to losses that have not yet occurred and are not currently in progress, that is, to future losses that have not yet moved from expectation to reality" (Corr, 2001, p. 217).

The therapist is confronted directly with feelings of anxiety about possibly being hurt by a similarly adverse event (i.e., the therapist is exposed to the fear "it might happen to me" rather than being able to maintain an attitude of "it won't happen to me"). This threat calls for the development of specific coping mechanisms in order to remain client centered. This process is similar to therapeutic situations where clients and therapists are in the same boat (for elaborations see Geron, Malkinson, & Shamai, 2005). This phenomenon is known as traumatic countertransference that is related to client's traumatic transference (Figley, 2002; Herman, 1992).

Posttraumatic Growth

In line with a number of studies (e.g., Arnold et al., 2005), working with bereaved families who have suffered a loss in traffic accidents is not only strenuous and risky but has also the potential of growth through facilitating clients' posttraumatic growth — described by Neimeyer (2005) as positive changes that result from the struggle with life crises. It seems to us that this description of positive changes also applies to therapists working with bereaved clients who suffered a traumatic loss.

Main findings in studies of positive changes reported some themes characteristic of posttraumatic growth. These include feelings of mission, experiencing the client's posttraumatic growth, a sense of satisfaction from helping clients overcome their trauma, developing empathy for the bereaved clients, growing professionally though acquiring additional intervention, and developing feelings of resilience that increase a sense of self-empowerment (Bradly, Guy, Poelstra, & Brokow, 1999; Kobassa, 1979; Kobassa, Maddis, & Kahn, 1982; Longergam, O'Halloran, & Crane 2004; Pearlman & McCann, 1995; Steed & Downing, 1998).

Studies report that the therapist intervening with clients bereaved as a result of a horrendous event, confront difficulties, as well as feeling challenged by the therapeutic task and mission. Moreover, therapists who are exposed to working under a constant threat of potentially being hurt, should increase their feelings of resilience, self-empowerment, their professional performance, and personal growth. In addition there is a growing sense of acknowledgment that life is precious (Arnold et al., 2005; Calhoun & Tedeschi, 1999). Based on our observations, therapists develop an increased sense of a more realistic and proportionate life philosophy: "In every misfortune there is some good."

CONCLUSIONS AND RECOMMENDATIONS

We have presented a model of intervention continuity for bereaved parents who lost a child to a traffic accident as an example of bereavement that is not acknowledged by society as a whole. Intervention and assistance to these families is a preliminary and necessary stage in their adaptation to a life of bereavement, and is part of a process of enabling them to develop their ability to help and be helped.

Though the suggested model is applicable to all those who have suffered a loss through death, we believe that this model is particularly relevant to the bereaved population-at-risk, such as minorities, and marginalized types of losses (suicide, homicide, and the like), which have not so far received formal, routine assistance. The cultural sensitivity approach is inherent in this model.

The continuity framework in the above model was introduced through two integrated dimensions: phases of bereavement process and phases of intervention process, which are supported both by theoretical-empirical and clinical knowledge. Such an integrated approach enables the provision of updated, appropriate intervention to bereaved people.

A special characteristic of the proposed model lies in its modular potential, which is not necessarily linked to a single interventional framework, but calls for conceptual cooperation between the involved parties. Intervention with bereaved families in a form that is suited to the aforementioned stages of grief will avoid the development of complicated grief.

The suggested model assumes that an optimal collaboration between the relevant services is essential to maximizing the quality of the service delivered to potential clients, and is critical for achieving and planning intervention by professionals. This collaboration is efficient both economically and professionally.

As presented in this model, reaching out was found to be an important component of the various phases and dimensions of the intervention. Loss through death and the bereavement that follows are sensitive issues that increase vulnerability not only of the bereaved but also of the therapists working with them. No less important, then, is the issue of who helps the helper. It is important to develop additional alternatives to help professionals cope with both axes: the stress and the potential growth.

The model proposes empowerment of the self-help factor combined with a professional multidimensional intervention. This joint collaboration can become an additional, meaningful resource for social and political change to families with bereavement that is not acknowledged in the greater society. The continuation of the intervention, with the exception of the acute phase

(the trauma), which is not recommended for group intervention, can be proposed for each and every phase. These can be individuals, couples/families,
and long-term, short–term, or self-help groups.

REFERENCES

Abramowitz, H. (2005). Bad death, the missing and the inability to mourn. In S. Heilman
(Ed.), *Death, bereavement, and mourning* (pp. 53–67). New Brunswick, NJ: Transaction.
Arnold, D., Calhoun, G. L., Tedeschi, R., & Cann, A. (2005). Vicarious posttraumatic growth
in psychotherapy. *Journal of Humanistic Psychology, 45*(2), 239–263.
Bar, N. & Sadan, E. (1989). *KELA — Self help groups.* Jerusalem: Ministry of Welfare. (in
Hebrew)
Bloch, M. & Parry, J. (Eds.). (1982). *Death and the regeneration of life.* Cambridge, UK: Cam-
bridge University Press.
Bradly, J. L., Guy, J. D., Poelstra, P. L., & Brokaw, B. F. (1999). Vicarious traumatization, spiritu-
ality, and the treatment of sexual abuse survivors: A national survey of women psycho-
therapists. *Professional Psychology: Research and Practice, 30,* 386–393.
Calhoun, L. G. & Tedeschi, R. G. (1999). *Facilitating posttraumatic: A clinician's guide.*
Mahwah, NJ: Lawrence Erlbaum.
Central Bureau of Statistics Israel (2005). htpp://www1.cbs.gov.il/shnaton. Retrieved on
August 29, 2005.
Carpinello, S. E., Knight, E. L., & Jatulis, L. L. (1992). A study of the meaning of self-help,
self-help group processes and outcomes. *Proceedings of the 11th Annual Conference on
State Mental Health Agency Services Research and Program Evaluation,* Alexandria, VA:
National Association of State Mental health Program Directors Research Institute.
Corr, C. A. (1998). Enhancing the concept of disenfranchised grief. *Omega, 38*(1), 1–20.
Corr, C. A. (2001). Grief, anticipatory. In G. Howarth & O. Leaman (Eds.), *Encyclopedia of
death and dying* (p. 217). London: Routledge.
Doka, K. J. (1989). Disenfranchised grief. In K. J. Doka (Ed.), *Disenfranchised grief: Recognizing
hidden sorrow* (pp. 3–11). Lexington, MA: Lexington Books.
Figley, C. R. (1993). Compassion stress and family therapist. *Family Therapy News,* 1–8.
Figley, C, R. (1995). *Compassion fatigue: Secondary traumatic stress.* New York: Brunner/Mazel.
Figley, C. R. (1999). Compassion fatigue: Toward a new understanding of the costs of caring.
In B. Hudnall Stanm (Ed.), *Secondary traumatic stress.* Towson, MD: Sidran Press.
Figley, C. R. (2002). Compassion fatigue: Psychotherapists' chronic lack of self-care. *Psycho-
therapy in Practice, 58*(11), 1433–1441.
Florian, V., Kasher, A., & Malkinson, R.(2000). Public and media attitudes towards bereaved
families in Israel: A national survey. *Megamot.* XL (2), pp. 280–297. (Hebrew).
Geron, Y. Ginsberg, K., & Solomon, Z. (2003). Predictors of bereaved parents' satisfaction
with group support. An Israeli Perspective. *Death Studies, 27*(5), pp. 405–426.
Geron, Y., Keidar, R., Yagil, Y., Dori, N., Drory, M., & Malkinson, R. (2004, March 23–25).
The provision of therapeutic continuity following sudden death: The development of a model.
Paper presented at the 21st International Conference on Death and Bereavement. Eilat,
Israel. (in Hebrew).
Geron, Y., Malkinson, R., & Shamai, M. (2005). Families in a war zone: Narratives of "me"
and the "other" in the course of therapy. In J. Kliman (Ed.), *Touched by war zones, near
and far: Oscillations of despair and hope* (pp. 17–25). Washington, D.C.: American Family
Therapy Association.
Geron, Y., Solomon, Z., & Ginsberg, K. (1997). *Evaluation of group intervention for bereaved par-
ents.*A report to the Rehabilitation Department, Ministry of Defense, Israel. (in Hebrew)
Herman, J. L. (1992). *Trauma and recovery.* New York: Basic Books.

Hopmeyer, E. & Werk, A. (1994). A comparative study of bereavement groups. *Death Studies*, *18*, 243–256.

Howarth, G. (2001). Sudden death. In G. Howarth & O. Leaman (Eds.), *Encyclopedia of death and dying* (pp. 436–437). London: Routledge.

Janoff-Bulman, R. (1992). *Shattered assumption: Towards a new psychology of trauma*. New York: Free Press.

Katto, P. M. & Mann, T. (1999).A synthesis of psychological intervention for the bereaved. *Clinical Psychology*, *157*, 373–383.

Knesset, the Book of Laws (2002). The law for victims of traffic accidents (assistance for family member) — Hatashsav — 2002. http://www.Kensset.gov.il/laws/heb. Retrieved October 9, 2005.

Kobassa, S. C. (1979). Stressful life events, personality and health: An inquiry into hardiness. *Journal of Personality and Social Psychology*, *37*(1), 1–11.

Kobassa, S. C., Maddis, R., & Kahn, S. (1982). Hardiness and health: A prospective study. *Journal of Personality and Social Psychology*, *42*, 168–177.

Kurtz, L. F. (1997), *Self-help and support groups*. Thousand Oaks, CA: Sage.

Lindy, J. D., & Wilson, J. P. (1994). Empathic strain and counter-transference roles: Case illustration. In J. P. Wilson & J. D. Lindy (Eds.), *Counter-transference in the treatment of PTSD* (pp. 62–68). New York: Guilford.

Litterer-Allumbaugh, D. & Hoyt, W. T. (1999). Effectiveness of grief therapy: A meta-analysis. *Journal of Counseling Psychology*, *46* (3), 370–380.

Longergam, B. A., O'Halloran, M. S., & Crane, S. C. M. (2004). The development of the trauma therapist: A qualitative study of the child therapist's perspective and experiences. *Brief Treatment and Crisis Intervention*, *4*(4), 353–366.

Malkinson, R. & Bar-Tur, L. (2005). Long term bereavement process of older parents: The three phases of grief. *Omega*, *50*(2), 95–121.

Malkinson, R., Rubin, S., & Witztum, E. (Eds.). (2000). *Traumatic and nontraumatic loss and bereavement: Clinical theory and practice*. Madison, CT: Psychosocial Press.

Malkinson, R. Rubin, S., & Witztum, E. (2005). Terror, trauma and bereavement: Implications for theory and therapy. In Y. Danieli, D. Brom, & J. Sills (Eds.), *The trauma of terrorism: Sharing knowledge and shared care, an international handbook* (pp. 467–477).New York: Haworth Press.

Malkinson, R. & Witztum, E. (1997). Loss following road accidents: A sociological cliche. In *Construction of memory*, Askola Gallery (pp. 172–177). (a publication for an exhibition in Hebrew).

Murphy, S., Johnson, C., Cain, K. C., Das Gupta, A., Dimond, M., Lohan, J., & Baughar, R. (1998). Broad-spectrum group treatment for parents bereaved by violent deaths of their children: A randomized controlled trial. *Death Studies*, *22*(3), 209–235.

Neimeyer, R. A. (2005) Re-storying loss: Fostering growth in the posttraumatic narrative. In L. Calhoun & R. Tedeschi (Eds.), *Handbook of posttraumatic growth: Research and practice* (68–80). Mahwah, NJ: Lawrence Erlbaum.

Neimeyer, R. A. (2001). (Ed.). *Meaning reconstruction and the experience of loss*. Washington, D.C.: American Psychological Association.

Neimeyer, R. A. & Jordan, J. R. (2002). Disenfranchisement as empathic failure: Grief therapy and the co-construction of meaning. In K. J. Doka (Ed.), *Disenfranchised grief* (pp. 95–117). Champaign, Il: Research Press.

Neimeyer, R., Keese, B. V., & Fortner, B. V. (2000). Loss and meaning reconstruction: Propositions and procedures. In R. Malkinson, S. Rubin, & E. Witztum (Eds.), *Traumatic and nontraumatic loss and bereavement: Clinical theory and practice*. (pp. 197–230). Madison, CT: Psychosocial Press.

Pearlman, L.A. & MacCann, P. S. (1995). Vicarious traumatization: An empirical study of the effects of trauma work on trauma therapists. *Professional Psychology: Research and Practice*, *26*, 558–565.

Pincus, A. & Minahan, A. (1973). *Social practice: Model and methods.* Itathca, IL: F.E. Peacock.

Piper, W. E., McCallun, M., & Azim, H. F. A. (1992). *Adaptation to loss through short term group psychotherapy.* New York: Guilford.

Prigerson H. G., Bierhals, A. J., Kasl, S. V., Reynolds III, C. F., Shear, M. K., Newsom, J. T., & Jacobs, S. (1996). Complicated grief as a disorder distinct from bereavement-related depression and anxiety: A replication study. *American Journal of Psychiatry, 153,* 1484–1486.

Prigerson, H. G., & Jacobs, S. C. (2001). Traumatic grief as a distinct disorder: A rationale, consensus criteria, and a preliminary empirical test. In M. S Stroebe, P. R. Hansson, W. Stroebe, & S. Schut (Eds). *Handbook of bereavement research: Consequences, coping, and care* (pp. 613–646). Washington, D.C.: American Psychological Association.

Prigerson, H. G., Frank, E., Kasl, S. V., Reynolds III, C. F., Anderson, B., Zubenko, G. S., et al. (1995). Complicated grief and bereavement-related depression as distinct disorders: Preliminary empirical validation in elderly bereaved spouses. *American Journal of Psychiatry, 152,* 22–30.

Reif, L. V., Patton, M. J., & Gold, P. B. (1995) Bereavement, stress and social support in members of a self-help group. *Journal of Community Psychology. 23*(4),~292–306

→ Riches, G. (2001). Self-help. In G. Howarth & O. Leaman (Eds.), *Encyclopedia of death and dying* (pp. 402–403). London: Routledge.

Riches, G. & Dawson, P. (1996). Communities of feelings. *Mortality, 1*(2), 143–162.

Riessman, F. (1965). The "helper" therapy principle. *Social Work, 10* (27), 27–32.

Rubin, S. (1999). The two-track model of bereavement: Overview, retrospect and prospect. *Death Studies, 23*(8), 681–714.

Rubin, S. S. & Malkinson, R. (2001). Parental response of child loss across the life cycle: Clinical and research perspective. In M. S. Stroebe, W. Stroebe, R. O. Hansson, & S. Schut (Eds.), *Handbook of bereavement* (pp. 219–240). Cambridge, UK: Cambridge University Press.

Rubin, S., Malkinson, R., & Witztum, E. (2000). An overview of the field of loss. In R. Malkinson, S. Rubin, & E. Witztum (Eds.), *Traumatic and nontraumatic loss and bereavement: Clinical theory and practice.* (5–40). Madison, CT: Psychosocial Press.

Rubin, S., Malkinson, R., & Witztum, E. (2003). Trauma and bereavement: Conceptual and clinical issues revolving around relationships. *Death Studies, 27,* 667–690.

Rynearson, E. K. (2001). *Retelling violent death.* New York: Brunner-Routledge.

Sanders, C.M. (1999). *The mourning after: Dealing with adult bereavement* (2nd ed.). New York: Wiley.

Sarson, I. G., Levine, H. M., Basham, R. B., & Sarson, B. R. (1983). Assessing social support: The social support questionnaire. *Journal of Personality and Social Psychology, 44*(1), 127–139.

Shumaker, S. A. & Brownell, A. (1984). Toward a theory of social support: Closing conceptual gaps. *Journal of Social Issues, 40* (4) 11–36.

Silverman, P. R. (2005). *Widow to widow* (2nd ed.). New York: Bruner-Routledge.

Steed, L. G. & Downing, R. (1998). A phenomenological study of vicarious traumatization among psychologists and professional counselors working in the field of sexual abuse/ assault. *The Australian Journal of Disaster and Trauma, 2.* http:\\www.massey.ac.nz/ntrauma/issues/1998-2/steed.htm.

Videka-Sherman, L. & Lieberman, M. (1985). The effect of self-help and psychotherapy intervention on child loss: The limits of recovery. *American Journal of Orthopsychiatry, 55*(1), 70–82.

Widdson, H. A. & Salisbury, H. G.(1990) The delayed stress syndrome: A pathological delayed grief reaction? *Omega, 20,* 293–306.

Yalom, I. D. (1995). *The theory and practice of group psychotherapy.* New York: Basic Books.

13

What about the Very Young Child?

SHARON GANCARZ DAVIES AND ALISON SALLOUM

HOME-BASED THERAPY WITH PRESCHOOL CHILDREN

The emotional complications in very young children who experience violent dying can be very real, but may be disregarded by caregiving adults "because they're too young to understand death." The authors dispel this mistaken assumption and propose an innovative home-based protocol to soften the emotional aftermath of violent death in young children within the matrix of the family system. The description of their intervention begins by citing six clinical principles fundamental for service delivery and sound clinical intervention, and building upon these clinical principles are 12 clinical focuses of inquiry for assessment and restorative intervention. Case illustrations highlight not only the unique needs and expressions of vulnerable children, but personalized strategies for engaging and revising their trauma narratives and interactions with caregiving adult family members. The authors also present a series of highly creative nonverbal techniques of drawing and play to guide the child through an imaginative and restorative narration of the traumatic dying and a hopeful future.

The purpose of this chapter is to describe 12 essential components, of therapeutic intervention with very young children and their families. Before addressing the 12 components, six guiding principles of therapeutic intervention will be offered for children ages six and under who have had someone close die due to violence. These principles are presented as a foundation for service delivery for those who are, or who are planning to serve this vulnerable and often forgotten population.

PRINCIPLES FOR PROVIDING SPECIALIZED INTERVENTION FOR YOUNG CHILDREN

A community program in New Orleans, LA serving children and families after violence and death, developed a specialized infant, toddler, and preschool mental health component to intervene with children ages six and under who had someone close die due to homicide. This community-based program developed six guiding principles as a foundation for service delivery and provision of sound clinical intervention to young children and their families after violent death.

Guiding Principle 1: Specialized infant mental health services, and education about the reactions and needs of young children following a violent death must be offered to families parenting young children and professionals who support families.

Caregivers and mental health professionals who are not trained in infant mental health may not recognize or believe that young children may need mental health intervention after experiencing the violent death of someone close to them. Beliefs, such as the child is too young to grieve, the child will not remember this, or the child will grow out of any developmental delays or problematic behaviors which have emerged after the violent death, are common and may deter caregivers from seeking services for young children. Additionally, mental health professionals may overlook the needs of young children. This omission may be a result of the professional's limited knowledge in the area of infant mental health, or may be a response to a caregiver who only requests services for the young child's older siblings who, through their more advanced verbal capacity or obvious signs of distress, are able to let their caregiver know that they need help. Education of parents and all community members in contact with young children about the needs and reactions of young children after violent death is a critical part of ensuring that the needs of young children following a violent death are identified and addressed.

Guiding Principle 2: Intervention must include both the young child and the caregiver because relationship-focused treatment is the standard of care for infant mental health treatment (Zeanah et al., 1997).

Some caregivers seek treatment for their child but want to limit their own involvement in the treatment process. Parents may have fears of confronting their own pain connected to the violent death, or want to avoid seeing and accepting that their young child has been profoundly affected. In fact, some caregivers seeking treatment for their young child may not be willing, initially, to talk openly and honestly to their child about what has happened. Coates, Schechter, and First (2003), who worked with families after the September 11 attack, noted that many bereaved families were hesitant to talk with their young children about what had happened. For many parents this hesitation is an attempt to protect their children's innocence. Yet, despite the effort to protect the child, some children had developed their own stories from bits and pieces of overheard conversations and from being attuned to their parens't emotional state. These stories, created without direct adult involvement to correct for distortions and to clarify misinformation, can leave children struggling in isolation in a confused state between reality and fantasy.

The caregiver's level of distress, symptomatology, and functioning can have a severe impact on the child's level of distress, symptomatology, and functioning and vice versa (Scheeringa & Zeanah, 2001). Therefore, the caregiver–child relationship must be attended to in treatment, with an emphasis on decreasing the caregiver's symptomatology and increasing the caregiver's capacity to provide responsive parenting. Often young children are referred for counseling as individuals. However, to be effective the clinician is charged with the responsibility to assess and treat the caregiver–child relationship, which includes both persons and the complicated set of thoughts and behaviors that connect them.

A major goal of relationship-based therapy is to establish the parent–child relationship as the source of nurturing and safety that will provide the healing milieu for the child. Parent–child relationships may be in varying stages of readiness to take on that responsibility. The needs of the individuals and the relationship will determine how the clinician structures therapy sessions: working with the caregiver and child in session together, separately, or in some combination of both. However, whether the clinician is working with the child, the caregiver, or the dyad, the clinician is always treating the relationship.

Another major focus in relationship-based therapy is responsive parenting, which is parenting that accurately identifies and meets the emotional and physical needs of the child. Responsive parenting, which includes comforting the child and creating a sense of safety, is the most critical factor in facilitating a young child's ability to cope after a traumatic loss. Responsive parents recognize grief and trauma reactions in the child as related to the traumatic event, as opposed to seeing the changes as misbehavior or evidence of a bad personality. They teach and model coping. Responsive parenting can limit the severity of the child's traumatic reactions and help the child cope with the grief he or she is experiencing.

Guiding Principle 3: It is important to assess the child in the child's environment and with the caregiver.

Home-based assessment and treatment offer several advantages. The clinician can observe firsthand the child's interactions with the caregiver and others such as siblings and extended family. The young child may not have the verbal capacity to describe these relationships. Home visits offer a better understanding of the child and of the strengths and resources available in the environment. Also, when conducting assessments in the home, there may be photographs and belongings of the deceased that can be used by the child and caregiver to express their relationship with the deceased and to share more about the deceased's life. Additionally, home-based assessments offer an avenue for the clinician to provide a rapid assessment of other family members affected by the violent death, to provide education to all family members about common reactions after violent death, and to inform family members about resources for support.

When conducting assessments within the child's environment, clinicians must be knowledgeable about the family's culture, which has a significant influence on how the child, caregiver, and family cope with the violent death. "Culture refers to the traditions, values, customs of child-care and socialization practices and includes rituals and artifacts that symbolize the group's belief system" (Lewis & Ippen, 2004, p. 13). Of course, each family is unique and may not subscribe to all of its cultural group's practices, but clinicians need to understand the funeral rituals, mourning practices, spiritual beliefs, and roles and expectations of bereaved children according to the practices of the cultural group to which the family belongs. Being culturally competent increases the comfort level of the child and family with receiving support since the clinician understands the language, greetings, and customs of the family's culture, and is aware of how interventions may or may not be congruent with that culture.

Guiding Principle 4: Community-based service decreases barriers for caregivers seeking intervention for young children.

After a violent death, caregivers are often faced with numerous adjustments and challenges. Having to ensure that they and their young child attend weekly counseling services at another location is often difficult for some caregivers because their employers may not allow time off, transportation may be difficult and costly, child care for other children may not be available, and they simply may be too tired to meet another demand. We have found that young children are more likely to receive ongoing, consistent intervention when the services are home based. In addition, we have observed that community-based service is especially important for low-income and minority families who are often faced with additional stressors and may not feel comfortable "going to therapy." Community-based services may decrease the stigma associated with seeking and receiving mental health intervention.

Guiding Principle 5: Case management is essential for families in crisis or without adequate resources, and referrals to other types of therapeutic intervention may be needed.

Case management services are a critical part of crisis intervention following violent death and throughout treatment. Clinicians who are aware of community resources are well positioned to help families navigate systems and access the services which can meet their unique needs. Immediately following a violent death, families frequently require information about community resources including: financial assistance, legal assistance, child care, housing, medical care, or investigative information about the death. The death of a family member who contributed to the family income can bring a drastic reduction in the family's financial stability, leaving some families in need of basic resources such as food, clothing, and housing (Rynearson & McCreery, 1993). Although therapeutic interventions may begin at the same time that emergency resources are being mobilized, other families need information and time to stabilize the family before beginning therapy.

Guiding Principle 6: Some families seeking services will want or need only a brief intervention consisting of assessment, education, crisis intervention, or referrals for other resources.

When designing a program to serve young children it is important to recognize that not all families will need long-term treatment. For some families all that may be needed is one to four sessions where the clinician conducts a brief assessment; provides psychoeducation to the family about common developmental traumatic distress and grief reactions; provides a list of resources to meet mental health needs in the future should it be necessary; and raises awareness of the caregiver's and family's coping capacities and resilience to help promote stabilization. This concept of only providing psychoeducation or brief crisis intervention recognizes that many families have and provide healing resources within and only need limited support from clinicians. The clinician may use the limited contact with the caregiver to suggest possible reactions of the child as he or she matures, and to discuss ways that the caregiver can support the child as he or she grows. If the clinician thinks that the caregiver and child may benefit from additional sessions, but thinks that the caregiver's avoidance is interfering with continued intervention, the clinician, in a respectful manner, may address this with the caregiver. The clinician can let the caregiver know that avoidance is a common response to violent death, and that when the caregiver is able and ready, the clinician will work with the family. The clinician should be clear that it will be the caregiver who will set the pace working toward building resilience to counter avoidance and overwhelming feelings.

TWELVE ESSENTIAL COMPONENTS

Mental health intervention may be needed in a situation where the child or caregiver witnessed the violent dying; when the caregiver or child is experiencing grief or traumatic stress that interferes with functioning and child development; when a trial prosecuting the alleged perpetrator of the violent death occurs; or when the child's caregiver has died. The following section discusses 12 components that are critical to providing therapeutic intervention to young children after violent death. Certainly, we recognize that every child and family is unique and has concerns and needs not addressed in this chapter, but these 12 components provide the structure of essential elements to address. The ordering of the sessions along with the time frame will depend on the family's needs. The components are meant to be flexible in order to meet the family's needs, and sensitive to address current challenges that may arise during the course of treatment. For example, if a caregiver is experiencing frustration with the child's behavior of increased aggression, the component on behavioral and developmental challenges may be addressed in the beginning.

Essential Component 1: Connecting with the Caregiver

It may be useful to approach the first session assuming that the family will only need a brief intervention. In other words, in the first session, listen and gather only the necessary facts, explore the caregiver's and child's reactions, provide education about normal responses, and help raise awareness of strengths and coping capacities that can help sustain both the caregiver and child. It is important that families are permitted to request various types of services and that the clinician is prepared to help meet these needs. When the caregiver is clearly seeking only crisis intervention, the clinician focuses on providing education and promoting coping. It is more important to meet the critical needs of the family than to gather information that is not relevant to the urgent needs being presented. If the family continues with therapy, the clinician will widen the scope of the assessment. Some measures that may be useful for assessment (preintervention) and at postintervention to assess effectiveness include the Child Behavior Checklist (completed by the parent, versions for children ages one and half to six) (Achenbach & Edelbrock, 1983); Brief Infant–Toddler Social and Emotional Assessment (BITSEA; completed by parent for a child aged zero to36 months; Briggs-Gowan & Carter, 2001); Traumatic Stress Disorder Semi-Structured Interview (completed by parent with clinician regarding the child; Scheeringa, Zeanah, Myers, & Putnam, 2003); and with children six years old, the clinician may want to do a self-report measure of posttraumatic stress. The clinician may also want to administer standardized measures for depression and posttraumatic stress to the caregiver. As the field of traumatic grief evolves, newer measures of traumatic or complicated grief may be considered as well. Clinicians must be selective about assessment measures as it is imperative to use developmentally appropriate measures and to be conscientious about not overwhelming the caregiver.

It is helpful to meet with the caregiver alone for the first session, allowing a space for the clinician to focus on the caregiver and his or her needs. The caregiver may speak freely about his or her own experience and share details about the violent death that may not have been shared with the child. This time is available for the caregiver to speak freely about the child and their relationship. Also, an adult-only session allows clinician to gather initial information more quickly. Table 13.1 provides a list of categories for assessment to explore with the caregiver.

Case Examples

Three case examples illustrate the varying ways caregivers enter into the therapeutic relationship:

Joining by Learning about Family Separate from the Trauma

Ms. Washington spent several minutes sharing family photographs of her children. The clinician was able to admire the children and ask questions. Following the lead of Ms. Washington, the clinician focused on learning first about the children's personalities and interests. After being introduced in this way to the family, the clinician was able to ask in a more informed way about changes in behavior following the trauma.

Joining by Addressing Urgent Needs

Ms. Stone requested to meet the clinician at the office. She was overwhelmed by a number of life circumstances including homelessness (she was currently living with her sister), excessive media attention, difficulties with her children's schools, difficulties at work, and an ongoing job search. Some of these difficulties were related to and others preceded the traumatic event. The clinician spent the entire first session developing an understanding of the areas overwhelming Ms. Stone. Together the clinician and Ms. Stone identified tasks that needed to be accomplished to resolve each area. They prioritized the areas and tasks. Ms. Stone reported a great sense of relief at the conclusion of the session.

TABLE 13.1
Initial Assessment Categories

Description of child(ren) from caregiver's perspective	Personality, behavior, pretrauma functioning. What most concerns parent at this time? Strengths of parent–child relationship. Strengths of caregiver and child individually.
The child's relationship with the current caregiver, deceased, and/or perpetrator	Meaning of the relationship(s), roles in child's life.
Facts about what happened	Including the details of the child's experience: where was child, who took care of the child, who told child about the death, what were the critical events in the child's experience surrounding the death.
History of violence exposure and previous losses	Domestic violence, past abuse/neglect, other deaths and losses.
Funeral	Who went, what happened, child's reactions, child's questions.
Legal information	Perpetrator known? Apprehended? Trial date set? Who will testify? Interactions with legal personnel?
Past history of treatment and medical history	Inquire about child and caregiver.
Developmental milestones and progress	Developmental delays and temporary trauma reactions.

JOINING BY LEARNING ABOUT TRAUMATIC REACTIONS

Ms. Pierre began by describing the many changes in her children. The clinician actively listened to her description of the children's current behavior. Ms. Pierre was able to describe each child as an individual, with unique reactions to the traumatic event, influenced by the child's age and personality. The clinician then more systematically inquired about reactions of each child using a semistructured interview. The interview served to educate about common reactions while gathering information on each child's current functioning. The clinician inquired about soothing strategies and current efforts to address the changes in behavior. Ms. Pierre was able to identify some effective means to comfort each child.

Essential Component 2: Assessing the Caregiver and Child Relationship

Understanding the parent–child relationship is a critical factor in supporting the family of a young child in meeting the family's therapeutic goals. Knowledge of the history of the parent–child relationship, and the effects of the traumatic loss on the quality of the relationship, is acquired through observation of parent–child interactions, listening to the parent's presentation of both the child and their relationship, and to some extent direct communication from the child.

History of the Parent–Child Relationship

A history of adequate caregiving and secure attachment relationships helps children cope with traumatic loss. A child will painfully grieve the death of a parent with whom they shared a secure attachment bond. However, at the same time that relationship has established a "working model" for the child (an internal template for viewing the self and others), which says "a primary caregiver is a person who can be trusted to be responsive to my needs" (Bretherton & Munholland, 1999). A history of secure attachment with a caregiver can offer protection during a period in which the quality of care by that same caregiver is temporarily disrupted by trauma. Also, this working model can be drawn upon to establish a relationship with another loving caregiver. The new attachment relationship will offer the support the child needs to cope in the wake of the loss.

A functional relationship offers comfort, sets limits, is affectionate, includes more positive than negative interactions, and is responsive to the child's physical and emotional needs. Furthermore, children who shared an insecure relationship with their caregivers are at greater risk for developing psychopathology (Greenberg, 1999). These children may have learned to suppress their urge to seek comfort when distressed and they may have a difficult time accepting comfort. They carry a working model that says "the world is unsafe and people cannot be relied upon to meet my needs."

Effect of the Traumatic Loss on the Quality of the Parent–Child Relationship

A traumatic loss within the family can have a distinct effect on the quality of the parent–child relationship. Traumatic reactions and the resulting behavior changes in the child challenge the parent–child relationship. In many circumstances, especially in the case of young children, caregivers are experiencing the traumatic loss along with the children. A caregiver's own traumatic reactions may temporarily undermine previously responsive parenting. Scheeringa and Zeanah (2001) have identified three patterns of parent–child relationships that can negatively impact children following a trauma: (1) withdrawn/unresponsive/unavailable; (2) overprotective; and (3) reenacting/endangering/frightening behavior. A caregiver who has withdrawn is less able to perceive the child's needs and less equipped to respond to those needs. A caregiver may become overprotective as a result of preoccupation with the fear that the child will be traumatized again or guilt for not protecting the child. Finally, a caregiver's preoccupation with the traumatic event may result in retraumatizing the child by forcing him or her to reexperience the event. A caregiver may excessively question the child or frequently retell details of the death, expose the child to situations, or express content that is insensitive to the child's needs.

Parent's Perception of the Child

The caregiver carries an image of the child and of her or his relationship with the child in her or his mind. This image is the filter through which all interactions with the child are interpreted. Understanding both the filter and the life events in the relationship are helpful when developing an effective treatment plan with the parent. The Working Model of the Child Interview (Zeanah & Benoit, 1995) is a comprehensive tool for developing an understanding of the parent's perception of the child. The interview takes about an hour to complete and includes questions about developmental history, the child's personality, and the parent–child relationship. The parent's perception of the child is also assessed in discussion with the parent about the child. The clinician is interested in knowing: How well does the parent know the child? Does the parent accept the child and hold him or her in positive regard? Does the parent demonstrate empathy and an ability to see the child's perspective?

Parent–Child Interactions

Observations of the parent and child together further inform the clinician's assessment of the parent–child relationship. To begin to assess the relationship clinicians will want to observe and explore some of the following questions: Do the parent and child seem comfortable together? Does the parent convey warmth and affection? Is what the parent told the clinician about the child consistent with what the clinician observes? Does the child respond positively to the parent and does the parent respond to the child's overtures? Does the parent provide effective comforting to the child and does the child seek the parent when he or she is upset? Is the parent responsive to the child's cues and does the child seem relaxed? Does the parent use ages-appropriate discipline and set appropriate limits?

Essential Component 3: Setting Goals and Providing Hope

Discussion of goals begins when the caregiver first discusses her or his expectation of what therapy can offer. Completing an assessment of the trauma and grief reactions with the clinician offers caregivers greater clarity about what changes they would like to see in their child. The clinician will need to identify what parental behaviors would support the child in realizing the changes and offer an understanding of child development and age-appropriate expectations.

Most caregivers bring a sense of cautious hope to therapy. The clinician nurtures the hope that the family can experience relief from the grief and traumatic reactions troubling them. Setting and monitoring goals (short-and long-term goals) with the caregiver allows demonstration of progress. Caregivers become invested in therapeutic activities when they understand the connection between those activities and goals, as well as their role in helping the child achieve the goals. Ongoing discussion of the family's progress leads naturally to termination when the family's goals for treatment have been achieved.

Essential Component 4: Relaxation, Calmness, and Comfort

The caregiver's ability to provide comfort to the child is essential to helping the child after a traumatic loss. A child who is overwhelmed by emotion, who is experiencing intrusive thoughts and is frightened, or who is having nightmares, needs an adult's assistance in calming down. It is important to identify what strategies are effective at providing comfort to this child at this point in time. Often parents require help in identifying strategies, either because old strategies are not working now or because they had never established effective calming strategies with this child.

The clinician can inquire about current comforting strategies by wondering aloud about what helps the child feel better when he or she starts to feel worried, sad, mad, or scared. If the child does not answer or if the child is too young to answer for himself or herself, the question can then be offered to the parent. It is helpful to know what comforts the child, who comforts the child, and how active the parent is in the comforting process. These comforting strategies can be used as transition rituals at the beginning or end of session.

Case Example: The Gardener and the Plant: Parent–Child Relaxation Exercise (See Exercise 13.1)

In the first home visit the clinician sat in the front room with Ms. Pierre and her three children ages five, three and half, and 13 months. The father of the children had been murdered eight months before. The children sat close to their mother on the couch. After a brief discussion about what helps them feel safe, the clinician commented on how well they were using their skills to feel safe right now by snuggling into Mom when a new person was in the house. And how well Mom was helping them! The children visibly relaxed and smiled as Ms. Pierre recognized the compliment by giving them an extra hug. The clinician asked if they would like to pretend to be growing plants that their mother would take care of with a little help from the clinician. The family was guided through "The Gardener and the Plant: Parent–Child Relaxation Exercise" (see exercise 13.1). The two older children clearly enjoyed being seeds growing into plants, while the 13 month old joined Ms. Pierre in patting her siblings on the back.

Exercise 13.1. The child is instructed to curl up on the floor tightly "like a seed." The clinician softly talks about how a seed has everything it needs inside to become a big, healthy plant. The parent is given the role of being the gardener who takes care of the seed. The gardener gently covers the seed with a warm blanket of soil (patting the child's back). The gardener allows the rain to give nourishment to the seed (drumming fingers on the child's back). Sometimes there is a thunderstorm (firmer pats on the back with cupped fingers), then more gentle rain (drumming fingers). The sun shines on the seed (smooth strokes with whole hand from the bottom of the back to the shoulders). The seed begins to grow (child instructed to sit up). A sprout looks all around (roll head in neck circles in each direction). The plant grows a leaf (raises arms above head and locks fingers). The leaf blows in the breeze (stretch arms to each side). The plant grows and grows (child stands). It plants its roots (firm stance legs apart), and reaches to the sky (stretch arms high) (Babeshoff & Dellinger-Bavolek, 1993).

Essential Component 5: Grief, Trauma, and Death Education

Knowledge of the range of typical grief and trauma reactions in adults and young children offers relief to families whose thoughts, physical reactions, and emotions have changed dramatically since the traumatic event. The concept of normal reactions to abnormal circumstances helps parents accept their own experience and those of their children. The caregiver, in partnership with the clinician, will develop an understanding of the thoughts, feelings, and behaviors of the child in the context of developmentally appropriate grief and trauma reactions. The task of the clinician and caregiver is to support the young child in developing an age-appropriate understanding of death, as well as grief and trauma reactions.

Knowledge gained in the assessment process is often comforting to parents. By first giving general information about trauma and then introducing specific posttraumatic stress symptomatalogy and grief reactions in assessment, the clinician normalizes these reactions. Parents often spontaneously comment about the impact of these reactions on their ability to parent. Having learned about and acknowledged their own reactions, the parent is in a good position to learn about the experience of grief and trauma at their child's particular stage of development. Clinicians may want to refer to the modified DSM-IV criteria for posttraumatic stress for young children (see Scheeringa et al., 2003) to use as an educational tool regarding possible traumatic symptoms following violent death. The modified criteria are developmentally sensitive and rely on behavioral observations, as opposed to internal experiences, which in many cases the adult can only assume (Scheeringa et al., 2003).

It is painful for many caregivers to face the reality that their child is suffering. Caregivers may deny that young children can be affected or have unrealistic expectations about how quickly they should "get back to normal." Because most children do not stay sad all day, every day after a death; their desire to play may be misunderstood as indicating that they are fine, or misinterpreted as not caring that the loved one has died. The clinician can play the role of interpreter, helping the caregiver to understand the child's experience and preventing misattributions which can interfere with responsive caregiving.

Example: Let Them Ask Questions (Again and Again)

Ms. Lowell reported that she had told her three-year-old son that his father had died and would not be coming home anymore. Still, the child persisted in looking for his father and asking his mother about him. With the clinician's support she was able to understand his behavior as the result of his current level of development and identify coping strategies to address her reactions to being reminded of the death and the loss they shared.

Example: Death Education

A four-year-old girl's mother died as a result of violence just over one month before beginning treatment. She meticulously played out the part of her mother being hurt, being helped by doctors, dying, being laid out in the church, and then she laid very still for what seemed like a long time not responding to comments or questions. Finally, the clinician asked "What happens next?" And she sat bolt upright and replied "I don't know what happens next!"

An important component of death education is spirituality (for more about spirituality see chapter 4, by Janice Harris Lord). Understanding the family's belief system with regard to the afterlife and spirituality is an important part of joining with the caregiver and supporting the family in conveying the family's belief system to the young children. It is helpful to know what the child has been told and what language was used to share these concepts.

Generally, very young children will perceive death as a temporary state, like sleeping. They are likely to believe that the deceased continues to eat, breathe, and exist. They may believe that they can visit the deceased and that the person will return to life. After the age of five a child may begin to develop an understanding that being dead means the complete end of living and that death is final. Because children's grasp of the concept of death is immature and incomplete it is important to offer a simple and consistent explanation that the child can "grow into." As the following example demonstrates, caregivers need support in explaining the nature of death and permission to use the words dead, death, and dying.

Example: Speaking Openly about Death and Dying

Mr. and Mrs. Cassidy were doting grandparents of four-year-old Lisa, whose mother had been murdered nine months earlier. They proposed telling Lisa for the time being that her mother had gone away, leaving the hope that she may someday return. The clinician listened attentively to their concerns and reflected their desire to protect Lisa, and their wish to give her information in a way that is appropriate for a young child. The clinician shared her experience that waiting for a parent to return was stressful and that it might be confusing and hurtful to Lisa to wonder why her mother was absent. The clinician wondered if it might be more comforting to know that her mother did not want to die and when she was living would have done anything to be with Lisa. Mr. and Mrs. Cassidy confirmed that their daughter had been a devoted mother and only death could have parted her from Lisa. With this new way of thinking about death as the only thing that could separate mother and child they agreed that Lisa should develop an understanding of her mother's death.

Essential Component 6: Feelings and Fears

Primary tasks of treatment include reducing the intensity of overwhelming affects associated with the traumatic experience and experiencing the feelings connected to the loss (Scheeringa & Gaensbauer, 2000). The integration of calming techniques into the caregiver's interactions with the child is an important component of addressing feelings with the child. The clinician can help the caregiver identify traumatic reactions and build empathy for the child's experience. It is often difficult for adults to accept strong emotion from a young child, and often children are told not to feel. For example, caregivers may tell young children, "Don't be mad," "Just give me a smile," or "There is nothing to be afraid of." Children need to learn names for what they feel and receive messages that all of their feelings are okay. They need to develop an understanding of how some of their feelings are connected to the trauma and loss. Clinicians and caregivers will need to assist children in finding appropriate ways to express strong feelings. Adults can help a child by labeling feelings; demonstrating an ability to accept the child who is expressing strong emotion and an ability to keep the child safe; modeling appropriate expression of feelings; giving the child options to express strong emotions through art, play, music, massage, and discussion; and anticipating difficult situations and how to handle them.

One of the most common responses of a young child to a traumatic death is the development of new fears. A fear that emerges directly following the traumatic event should be considered a traumatic reaction, even if the fear is not directly related to elements of the death. Common fears include a fear of the dark and fear of toileting alone. In therapy and home life the clinician and caregiver can emphasize safety. It is helpful to be explicit about how adults keep children safe. Caregivers can support the child by listening to the fear, validating the feeling, and helping the child to feel safe. The caregiver and clinician should help the child to identify the safe people and places in his or her life.

Essential Component 7: Restorative Memories

Parents are the storehouse of the events of their children's early lives. Adults share and nurture memories through family stories, photographs, and important objects. Surviving caregivers of young children are frequently pained by the realization that their children may have few personal memories of the deceased. Collecting, sharing, and saving memories on behalf of the child empowers the caregiver to assume the role of memory keeper and allows the caregiver to appreciate that over time the child can incorporate these shared memories as his or her own.

A strong base of restorative memories allows the family to recall the violent death as only one piece of a rich life which had many chapters; a life which is carried on in the lives of those who love that person. However, in some cases a family member is so overwhelmed that he or she is unable to connect to the restorative memories of the person's life or to share them with the child. These clients may need to begin with strategies to cope with traumatic reactions. A young child's ability to communicate his or her internal experience is limited by developmental capacity. Observations of whether the child can recall pretrauma memories of the person who died, tolerate discussions of the deceased, and look at photographs, will inform the clinician of the child's current ability to participate in the process of building restorative memories. Because young children rely upon their caregivers to support their memories, their opportunities to develop restorative memories are often dependent upon the ability of their caregivers to engage in reminiscence. Therefore, clinicians may need to provide support to caregivers, encouraging them to contribute memories of specific interactions, likes, dislikes, characteristics, and similarities of the deceased to the child. The power of restoration is in the richness of details.

Example: Creating a Memory Book

Ms. Cotter sought counseling for herself and her five children (11 months to 10 years old) following the violent death of her husband. She had informed the clinician that Mr. Cotter's relationship with all of the children had been a warm and active one. Still, in the initial family sessions the children had hesitated to talk about their father, stealing frequent looks at their mother. Ms. Cotter reflected that since the death she had avoided talking about him because her own feelings were overwhelming and she didn't want to sadden the children. The family adopted the goal of creating a memory book with the goals of (1) Demonstrating that it is okay to talk about Daddy; (2) Assisting Ms. Cotter in reducing the intensity of her overwhelming feelings; (3) Recording memories for the young children who may have limited memory of their relationship with Daddy; and (4) Providing an opportunity for older children to document their memories for the future.

Essential Component 8: Reexperiencing and Mastery of the Traumatic Narrative

Children undergo tremendous changes in their developmental abilities within the first six years of life. Perception, memory, emotional understanding and expression, physical abilities, and the development of language impact not only the child's experience of traumatic events but his or her ability to communicate the impact of the violence and loss and ensuing events on the child's thinking, feeling, and behavior. Clinicians are advised to understand the child's developmental capacities at the time of the traumatic event as well as at the time of treatment.

Whenever possible the clinician should gather information about the child's experience of the trauma and related events from the caregiver or others who have knowledge of the death. The clinician should attempt to create an understanding of the event from the child's perspective. The child's narrative may contain information which is distorted or incorrect as a result of his or her developmentally limited perspective. A child may have intense auditory, visual, or emotional images that do not connect into a narrative. Helping a child establish a narrative of the event can facilitate mastery of the memory. Children who experience a traumatic event before developing the capacity for language may retain strong bodily, visual, or auditory memories. These children may be supported in connecting their experience to language which allows communication and further mastery of the event.

Knowledge of the child's perception of the events related to the trauma will inform the clinician's assessment of traumatic reactions. The younger the child, the more dependent the assessment of the young child's trauma reactions will be on behavioral observations as opposed to verbalizations. Young children demonstrate symptoms of reexperiencing in a manner consistent with their developmental stage. Intrusive or distressing images, thoughts, and perceptions may be expressed in play, repetitive behaviors, or verbalizations. Also, children may or may not be able to express the content of distressing dreams.

EXAMPLE: REPETITIVE BEHAVIORS

Monica was a three-year-old who became preoccupied with the color red following the stabbing death of her mother, which she had witnessed. Her daycare teachers reported that she played with red dishes, colored with red crayon, and chose red whenever possible. This pattern was observed at home and in counseling sessions as well. Her grandmother brought an overexposed photograph to the clinician. The photo was a blur of red. Monica identified the photograph as a picture of her mother.

EXAMPLE: REPETITIVE BEHAVIOR AND POSSIBLE FLASHBACK

Martin was 10 months old and in the room when his mother was beaten to death by his father. In the first few months following the death he would frequently make a gagging noise when exposed to images of his mother. Additionally, his grandmother reported two occasions in which he suddenly began grasping and clawing at her for no identifiable reason and seemed to be far away. The grandmother's meaning for these behaviors was that he was imitating the sound he heard his mother make as she was dying, and that he was reliving the horror of that experience as he grasped at her.

Essential Component 9: Family Changes

In the lives of some children, relatively little in daily life changes after the death. Other children find themselves in an entirely new world: new caregiver, new house, new daycare, and new routine. When the child's mother or father dies, the changes that occur are enormous for both the child and the new caregiver. The goal is to find sources of support for the caregiver and assist the caregiver in efforts to minimize the negative impact of changes on the child. A thorough assessment of what is the same and different for both caregiver and child includes the meaning of the changes, and the adjustment process. This allows the family to define areas in which they may want help from the clinician.

Caregivers who had previously not led in the area of discipline or comfort may now have to provide both. Clinicians can support families in maintaining bedtime and daily routines from the child's pretrauma life that can provide comfort and safety. Clinicians should emphasize with caregivers that children benefit from predictability, consistency, and routine.

EXAMPLE: DEFINING GOALS TO ADDRESS FAMILY CHANGES

Ms. Faith had recently assumed care of her four grandchildren (aged two years, 10 months to eight years) following the death of her daughter. With the help of her family she had applied for food stamps and kinship care benefits to aid her support of the children on her limited income. Her husband continued to work but she had been unable to maintain her afternoon/evening job while caring for the children. She had adequate space for the children. The children knew their grandmother well and had lived with their mother in the household at several points in their lives. They adjusted well to the routine of their grandmother's home and enjoyed the benefits of a safer neighborhood. Ms. Faith defined her most difficult adjustment area as needing to be the person who maintained structure and discipline in addition to the fun and comfort role she had been allowed as grandmother. She also expressed feelings of loss regarding not working or having any time to herself. These were incorporated as treatment areas.

Essential Component 10: Behavioral and Developmental Challenges

Young children are constantly growing and changing in their cognitive, physical, emotional, and social capabilities. When the young child has a loved one die violently, the child's developmental trajectory may be derailed and the child's abilities may regress or stagnate. Some common reactions a child might have when he or she has had someone close die violently include aggressive and defiant behavior, separation anxiety, whining, thumb sucking, bed wetting, and speech difficulties. Naturally, understanding the child's pretrauma level of development in all areas will assist the clinician and caregiver in identifying current changes and predicting vulnerabilities. The clinician brings a detailed understanding of typical development and developmental tasks, and the caregiver is the expert in this individual child's development, temperament, and personality. Together the clinician and caregiver can create a plan to support the child through a period of regression or behavior change and aid the child in resuming his or her pretrauma level of functioning.

EXAMPLE: SPEECH DIFFICULTIES

Monique was a two-year, 10-month-old child who had recently witnessed her mother's murder. Immediately following the death she began to stutter, especially if reminded of the trauma. Her grandmother noted the change with concern as Monique was a verbal child who had previously experienced little difficulty communicating. She was relieved to learn that temporary regression was common. She continued to listen to Monique and give her extra time to express her thoughts. The stuttering resolved in the first several weeks of treatment.

Behavior Problems: Aggression and Defiance

It is common for toddlers and preschoolers to demonstrate an increase in irritability, temper tantrums, and aggressive and defiant behavior following a traumatic death. Parents do not always recognize these behaviors as traumatic reactions. Many parents are frustrated with their child for "being bad," a characterization which if left unchallenged can color their understanding of the child's personality and the child's self-image. Education about trauma reactions as discussed above is important. However, most parents need additional support helping the child. To manage aggression and defiance parents need a clear structure of rules and consequences. Scheeringa, Amaya-Jackson, and Cohen (2002) noted that parents frequently report a decrease in discipline of the child following the trauma. Parents express that "the child has already been through enough" or that they just don't have the energy to discipline the child. Consequently, the adult fails to provide the safety of a predictable environment and fails to demonstrate that adults are in control and will keep the child safe, just at the time the child needs safety the most.

The clinician is in a position to support the parent in establishing behavior guidance that is sensitive to the nature of the behavior as a traumatic reaction. However, clear rules which prohibit violence, along with efforts to assist the child in identifying the conflicts underlying the behavior, and alternative means of expressing strong feelings build self-control and mastery of the trauma. Therapeutic sessions with the child can offer the opportunity to explore the conflicts and strong feelings while offering corrective messages and building mastery through metaphors in play.

Essential Component 11: Past and Future Special Events: Anniversaries, Holidays, Birthdays, and Special Events

Over the course of the year following the death of a loved one, families will experience a number of firsts without that person, including holidays, birthdays, date of the person's death, and special events. The negative impact of grief and trauma on family events can be lessened when reactions are anticipated and appropriate support and coping mechanisms are in place. During the discussion of special events, the clinician can assist the caregivers in taking on the perspective of their young child. For example, parents often are surprised that their child recognizes that the anniversary of the death is approaching. However, children may have reminders of the event embedded in their perception of the weather, surrounding holidays, or other temporal cues. In addition, children's reactions to events may differ from those of the adults in the family, and they communicate distress in ways that are distinct according to their developmental stage, temperament, and personality.

EXAMPLE: BIRTHDAYS, HOLIDAYS, AND SPECIAL EVENTS

When Ms. Faith assumed care of her four grandchildren after the violent death of her daughter, she did not want to celebrate Christmas or other holidays, but the children's behavior challenged her wish. On their mother's birthday the children sang "Happy Birthday" during the whole ride to school. The song was a painful reminder to Ms. Faith. As Christmas approached she felt guilty that she was not preparing a proper celebration for them, but struggling with depression, she could not plan. The clinician was able to help Ms. Faith draw upon her family and social supports to provide a Christmas celebration. A Secret Santa program donated gifts, and her former colleagues provided a tree and decorations. Although it was difficult, Ms. Faith was able to celebrate in limited ways with the family. In reflection she expressed gratitude to the children for sharing the value of staying connected and celebrating as part of her own healing.

Essential Component 12: Ending and Celebrating

The final stage of therapy is of critical importance to young children who have lost someone to violent death. The opportunity to participate in a planned goodbye gives the child a chance to have control and rework feelings of powerlessness. Especially important for children still working to develop an understanding of death is the opportunity to contrast death to other absences. Parents can be given permission to maintain some contact with the clinician to emphasize this point. Still, young children often have a difficult time understanding why their contact with the clinician is ending. The process of saying goodbye can reawaken painful feelings of loss. The grieving process is rarely over when counseling ends. Caregivers can continue to support the child's grief process.

Termination is a time to celebrate the strengths that have been identified throughout treatment as well as to celebrate the ongoing parent–child relationship. In addition to celebrating, the clinician, with the caregiver, should identify any ongoing areas of concern and identify signs that would indicate the need for additional therapeutic support in the future.

CONCLUSION

Programs designed to meet the needs of very young children should consider providing community-based services, flexible time-limits, relationship focused intervention, and an array of services. Since young children are often the last to be identified for services, there is a need for outreach efforts, including education about the effects of violent death on young children, and the availability of mental health intervention for this special population. Community members such as extended family, daycare workers and teachers, police, or mental health workers may identify a young child in need of intervention, but we have found that caregivers are more involved in the treatment of the young child when the caregiver is the one who has taken the initiative to seek services for the young child.

The 12 components discussed in this chapter provide the common topics when working with young children after a violent death. With the uniqueness of each family, clinicians may find that particular components are more salient for some families than others. Whether one component is addressed more than others is not as important as strengthening the caregiver's capacity to care for the child and deepening the caregiver's understanding of the child's experiences and needs, while underscoring the importance of the caregiver's ability to comfort the child. Also, young children need to be actively included in the restorative interactions and rituals of the family in a manner that is developmentally appropriate and consistent with the family's culture, as well as to be provided with a caring adult, who can bear witnesses to the child's experiences after the violent death of a loved one.

REFERENCES

Achenbach, T. M. & Edelbrock, C. (1983). *Manual for the child behavior checklist and revised child behavior profile.* Burlington, VT: University of Vermont, Department of Psychiatry.

Babeshoff, K. & Dellinger-Bavolek, J. (1993). *Nurturing Touch: Instroction in the Art of Infant Massage.* Park city, UT: Family Development Resources.

Bretherton, I. & Munholland, K.A. (1999). Internal working models in attachment relationships. In J. Cassidy & P.R. Shaver (Eds), *Handbook of attachment* (pp. 89–114). New York: Guilford.

Briggs-Gowan, M. J. & Carter, A. S. (2001). *Brief infant-toddler social and emotional assessment (BITSEA).* San Antonio, TX: Harcourt Assessment.

Coates, S. W., Schechter, D. S., & First, E. (2003). Brief interventions with traumatized children and families after September 11. In S.W. Coates, J. L. Rosenthal, & D. S. Schechter (Eds.), *September 11: Trauma and human bonds* (pp. 23–50). Hillsdale, NJ: Analytic Press.

Greenberg, M. T. (1999). Attachment and psychopathology in childhood. In J. Cassidy & P. R. Shaver (Eds), *Handbook of attachment* (pp. 469–496). New York: Guilford Press.

Lewis, M. L. & Ippen, C. G. (2004). Rainbows of tears, souls full of hope: Cultural issues related to young children and trauma. In J. D. Osofsky (Ed.), *Young children and trauma: intervention and treatment* (pp. 11–46). New York: Guilford Press.

Lieberman, A. F., Compton, N. C., VanHorn, P., & Ippen, C. G. (2003). *Losing a parent to death in the early years: Guidelines for the treatment of traumatic bereavement in infancy and early childhood.* Washington D.C.: Zero to Three Press.

Rynearson, E. K. & McCreery, J. M. (1993). Bereavement after homicide: A synergism of trauma and grief. *American Journal of Psychiatry, 150,* 258–261.

Scheeringa, M. S., Amaya-Jackson, L., & Cohen, J. (2002). *Preschool PTSD treatment.* New Orleans, LA. Unpublished Manual.

Scheeringa, M. & Gaensbauer T. (2000) Post traumatic stress disorder. In C. H. Zeanah (Ed.), *Handbook of infant mental health* (2nd ed., pp. 369–381). New York, Guilford.

Scheeringa, M. & Zeanah, C. H. (2001). A relational perspective on PTSD in early childhood. *Journal of Traumatic Stress, 14*(4) 799–815.

Scheeringa, M., Zeanah, C. H., Myers, L., & Putnam, F. W. (2003). New findings on alternative criteria for PTSD in preschool children. *Journal of the American Academy of Child & Adolescent Psychiatry, 42* (5),561–570.

Zeanah, C. H. & Benoit, D. (1995). Clinical applications of a parent perception interview. In K. Minde (Ed.), *Infant psychiatry, child psychiatric clinics of North America* (pp.539–554). Philidelphia: W. B. Saunders.

Zeanah, C. H., Boris, N. W., Heller, S., Hinshaw-Fuselier, S., Larrieu, J. A., Lewis, M., Palomino, R., Rovaris, M., & Valliere, J. (1997). Relationship assessment in infant mental health. *Journal of Infant Mental Health , 18,* 182–197.

NOTE

The authors wish to thank the Institute of Mental Hygiene for supporting the infant mental health component of Children's Bureau of New Orleans, Inc.

14

Treating Childhood Traumatic Grief

JUDITH A. COHEN AND ANTHONY P. MANNARINO

COGNITIVE–BEHAVIORAL THERAPY WITH CHILDREN

The authors have established a highly innovative, sequenced trauma and grief-focused intervention for children and parents after violent death. Several open studies of the intervention (applied in a time-limited individual or group protocol) demonstrate diminishment of trauma and grief distress. The model has also been applied with bereaved children following the World Trade Center attack in New York City. The authors' staging of intervention — dealing first with moderation of distress, and then revising of the trauma narrative, and finally a structured involvement with parents at the phase of termination and reengagement with living beyond therapy — echoes the staging recommendations of previous chapters. Their exercises of narrative writing, drawing, and rituals of farewell are most imaginative (as are children!) and undoubtedly have application to bereaved adults. Clinicians working with adults need to be sensitive to the opportunity for working within a more "imaginative" and less "rational" framework after violent dying. Learning and applying these exercises and rituals would be a solid start.

INTRODUCTION

Childhood traumatic grief (CTG) has been described as a condition in which children whose loved ones die under traumatic circumstances develop trauma symptoms which impinge on the children's ability to progress through typical grief processes (Cohen, Mannarino, Greenberg, Padlo, & Shipley, 2002; Layne, Savjak, Saltzman, & Pynoos, 2001). Specifically, these children get "stuck" on the traumatic aspects of their loved one's death in a fashion such that when they start to reminisce, even about happy memories, their memories tend to segue into thoughts about the terrifying manner in which the person died. When this happens, children begin to avoid reminiscing about the loved one, and indeed may avoid any reminders about the deceased because of the propensity of these reminders to stimulate the children's painful trauma memories. Being "stuck" on the traumatic aspects of the loved one's death is the essence of CTG as we currently understand it.

Because children with CTG have become stuck on the traumatic aspects of the death, they are unable to fully experience the grief associated with the death of their loved one. Since reminiscing about the loved one is an essential task of grieving (Wolfelt, 1996; Worden, 1996), and children with CTG avoid reminiscing about the loved one for the reasons described above, these children may be in particular need of therapeutic assistance in resolving their grief. In order to facilitate this process, it may be helpful to assist children in first resolving the traumatic aspects of CTG, and then to introduce them to the tasks of typical grieving. In order to address the needs of these children, we developed cognitive–behavioral therapy for childhood traumatic grief (CBT-CTG). As described in this chapter, the CBT-CTG model is a phased treatment approach which includes both trauma- and grief-focused modules. The CBT-CTG model has been provided in both group and individual settings. It includes parallel child and parent treatment components, as well as several joint child–parent sessions where children and parents meet together to share their trauma and grief experiences.

DEVELOPMENT OF THE CBT-CTG MODEL

The CBT-CTG model was derived from an empirically based treatment for children with posttraumatic stress disorder (PTSD) and other trauma-related symptoms: trauma-focused cognitive–behavioral therapy (TF-CBT; Cohen, Mannarino & Deblinger, 2006). TF-CBT had been tested in several randomized controlled treatment trials for sexually abused and multiply traumatized children (Cohen & Mannarino, 1996, 1998; Cohen, Deblinger, Lippman, & Steer, 1996; Deblinger, Mannarino & Steer, 2004; King et al., 2000) and found to be superior to a variety of other active treatments in improving PTSD symptoms as well as depression, anxiety, and behavior problems in traumatized children. Although we did not have this information when we first developed the CBT-CTG model, our first large multisite study of multiply traumatized children later demonstrated that children who had experienced traumatic loss of loved ones experienced preferential improvement with TF-CBT as well (Cohen, Deblinger, et al., 2004).

Following the crash of USAir Flight 427 outside of Pittsburgh in 1994, we designed a group protocol for children who had lost parents and other loved ones in that disaster, based on using the TF-CBT trauma-focused components with the addition of grief-focused components after children had completed the trauma components (Stubenbort, Donnelly, & Cohen, 2001). After the terrorist attacks of September 11, 2001 and with the formation of the SAMHSA-funded National Child Traumatic Stress Network (http://www.nctsnet.org), we significantly modified our CBT-CTG individual and group protocols in response to comments we received from therapists in New York and Washington, DC in order to make these treatments more acceptable to community therapists. The revised treatment model has since been tested in a 16-session open protocol for Pittsburgh children who lost their loved ones from a variety of causes (Cohen, Mannarino & Knudsen, 2004), and is currently being tested in a randomized controlled trial (RCT) for children who lost their uniformed service parents in the September 11 terrorist attacks on the World Trade Center in New York (Brown, Goodman, Cohen, & Mannarino, 2004). To our knowledge, this is the first RCT for CTG which is specifically measuring improvement in CTG symptoms. Additionally, since community bereavement programs often last for only 10 to 12 sessions, we modified the CBT-CTG model to a 12-session protocol and have conducted a second open trial evaluating its efficacy in this format (Cohen, Mannarino & Staron, in press). These studies are described briefly at the end of this chapter.

ASSESSMENT OF CTG

There are surprisingly few instruments for assessing the impact of bereavement on children, and only two to our knowledge for assessing the impact of CTG to date. The Expanded Grief Inventory (Layne et al., 2001) is a 28-item self-report instrument which evaluates the presence of CTG symptoms in children and adolescents. The Characteristics, Attributions and Responses to Exposure to Death-Youth and Parent Versions (CARED-Y and CARED-P; Brown, Cohen, Amaya-Jackson, Handel, & Layne, 2003) is a 39-item self-report measure which gathers information about peritraumatic aspects of the loved one's death as well as information about the child's premorbid relationship with the deceased and participation in mourning rituals. The psychometric properties of both of these instruments have been documented and, though new to the field, are reasonably well established (Layne et al., 2002; Brown & Goodman, 2005; Brown et al., in press). These instruments are available by request from the authors.

Prior to providing CBT-CTG, it is necessary to ascertain that the child meets the criteria to need treatment for CTG. We have defined this as the child having a certain cut-off score of the CTG subscale of the EGI (at least 30). The treatment thus begins with an initial assessment session, which typically lasts for at least an hour in our clinic setting, and includes individual interviews with parent and child, as well as having both complete standardized instruments. During the interview, the evaluator assesses the child's general emotional and behavioral symptoms as well as those that have arisen following the death of the loved one. The assessment may include the use of a variety of standardized self- and parent-report instruments depending on the child's presentation, but in most clinical settings, the EGI and CARED are the most clinically useful instruments to obtain at baseline, and the EGI is the best to follow during the course of this treatment. Other instruments should be selected based on the individual child's presentation. For example, if the child presented with a preponderance of depressive symptoms, a depression scale might be useful to obtain at different points in treatment in order to monitor the child's symptoms.

THEORETICAL BASIS OF THE CBT-CTG MODEL

As noted earlier, the CBT-CTG model was derived from TF-CBT, a hybrid treatment approach which is primarily based upon cognitive–behavioral, developmental traumatology, and family dynamic principles. At the core of this treatment approach are the following beliefs about the development and treatment of CTG:

1. Children are sensitized to traumatic memories of the death because of the terrifying nature of their personal exposure, their past trauma history, others' emotional reactions, their intrinsic sensitivity, or a combination of the above.
2. Fear, revulsion, or other negative emotions associated with the traumatic nature of the death lead to avoidance of traumatic memories. For example, if a child's sibling died at school, that child may develop school refusal even if he or she attends a different school from the one where the child's sibling had died.
3. Due to generalization, in children with CTG even innocuous memories of the loved one become associated with reminders of the terrifying nature of the death and segue into trauma reminders. This leads to avoidance of any reminders of the loved one. For example, these children might avoid talking about the loved one, avoid going to visit the gravesite, looking at pictures, or reminiscing fondly about the deceased, when other family members begin to do so.
4. Family members, friends, or therapists may inadvertently reinforce the child's ongoing avoidance through their own avoidance or reluctance to talk about the traumatic nature of the death, or death itself. Children rarely have the inherent ability to spontaneously overcome avoidant trauma symptoms without guidance. When confronted with a fearful stimulus like traumatic memories their natural impulse is avoidance.

5. Thus, TF-CBT and CBT-CTG are designed to assist children in mastering trauma memories through first providing stress management skills and then gradually assisting children, with the support of their parents, in telling the story of the traumatic events which they most fear. By learning that they can tolerate these painful memories, children learn to master their fears and move on with their lives instead of being controlled by their fears. Sharing their experiences with their parents also enhances parent–child communication and parental support for the child.

6. In following the above course, the child is able to resolve traumatic memories and begin to experience the grief associated with the loss of the loved one. Once the child is able to begin reminiscing without these memories automatically segueing into traumatic memories, the child is able to negotiate more typical grieving tasks.

7. The CBT-CTG model does not assume that grieving will be "completed" within the time frame of this brief treatment approach, but rather that the child will be facilitated in these tasks within the grief-focused components of the CBT-CTG model. It is not clear at this point how many, or even whether, the grief-focused components of the CBT-CTG model are essential to provide to children after their trauma symptoms have been resolved. This will be the focus of future research.

STRUCTURE OF CBT-CTG

As noted earlier, the CBT-CTG model has been provided in both group and individual settings (Cohen, Mannarino, & Knudsen, 2004; Stubenbort et al., 2002). In this chapter, we will describe how CBT-CTG is provided to children and parents in conjoint individual sessions because this is the more typical fashion in which we have provided it. The group treatment model is available upon request.

TRAUMA-FOCUSED COMPONENTS OF CBT-CTG

The trauma-focused components of CBT-CTG are derived from the TF-CBT model, which is described in greater detail elsewhere (Cohen & Mannarino, 2004; Cohen, Mannarino, & Deblinger, 2006). The core components are summarized by the acronym PRACTICE:

*P*sychoeducation, Parenting skills
*R*elaxation
*A*ffective modulation
*C*ognitive processing,
*T*rauma narrative
*I*n vivo mastery of trauma memories

Conjoint child–parent sessions
Enhancing safety

Each of these components is described briefly below. It is important for therapists to recognize that even though this model is fairly structured, the trauma-focused components are not always rigidly separated from each other, or from the grief-focused components. Rather these components may be revisited at times throughout the course of therapy.

Psychoeducation

The psychoeducation component of the CBT-CTG treatment begins at the first assessment, and continues throughout the course of therapy. The therapist provides information about the impact of trauma, traumatic grief, PTSD, and other comorbid psychiatric conditions the child may have, to both the child and parent. Additionally, the therapist normalizes the child's and parent's reactions as being expected responses to very atypical circumstances (the traumatic, usually premature death of a loved one) and predicts that the child and parent will recover and function normally over the course of time if they receive optimal assistance and support. Parents and children are often reassured to hear that their responses, while upsetting and new to them, are not at all surprising or unexpected to the therapist, and moreover that the therapist anticipates a positive outcome for them.

Parenting Skills

Many parents of traumatically bereaved children react by foregoing typical discipline routines. This may occur for many reasons: parents are overwhelmed by their own grief or trauma reactions; they feel sorry for what the child is "going through" and feel that imposing the usual discipline would be overly harsh at this difficult time; the deceased was the parent responsible for disciplining the child; or the surviving parent never had adequate parenting skills and this lack is especially notable at times when the child is stressed and more apt to show behavioral difficulties. Regardless of the reason, when children are under stress they may be in particular need of the reassurance that daily routines, predictability, and structure can bring. Positive parenting skills can provide positive self-esteem, support, and structure, so the CBT-CTG treatment model provides these to parents and encourages parents to practice these skills at home with children. These include the use of praise, selective attention, time-out, and contingency reinforcement programs for behavioral difficulties. These parenting skills are described in greater detail in the TF-CBT manual (Cohen, Mannarino, & Deblinger, in press) and elsewhere.

Relaxation and Affective Modulation

Before children embark on telling the story of the traumatic death, we believe it is important for them to gain and practice some self-soothing skills. This gives them confidence in their ability to manage their overwhelming fear and other upsetting feelings they are afraid may be aroused upon remembering what occurred when their loved one died (this is what they have been avoiding so strongly). Devoting these early sessions to skill consolidation also allows the child and therapist to strengthen their therapeutic relationship, and for the trust between them to build.

Relaxation and affective modulation components are closely related. We often spend an early session on affective identification games because they are fun and they are easy ice breakers that allow the child and therapist to get to know one another. The goals of these games are to encourage expression of a wide range of feelings and to model acceptance of feelings that children are sometimes hesitant to express (for example, jealousy, anger, boredom, etc). Children and parents are also encouraged to develop and practice individualized relaxation and other affective modulation skills. These may include focused breathing, progressive muscle relaxation, yoga, meditation, or other mind–body techniques; aerobic exercise such as basketball, dance, or running; artistic activities such as knitting, crocheting, painting, or other creative arts activities; journal writing; blowing bubbles (for younger children); listening to music, reading funny stories, and any other appropriate activities that the child or parent finds soothing and relaxing. It is important for the therapist to assist the child and parent in recognizing that different activities may be helpful for soothing different upsetting affective states. The therapist should also encourage the child and parent to practice these activities between sessions.

Cognitive Processing

In the earlier parts of CBT-CTG, cognitive processing does not focus on the traumatic death, but instead assists the child and parent in recognizing connections between thoughts, feelings, and behaviors (see Figure 14.1) in everyday situations. For example, if the child walked into the cafeteria at lunchtime and two children began laughing, what would the child think? If the child says, "I would think they were laughing at me," the therapist can ask how that thought would make the child feel. The child may reply "sad," "mad," or "lonely." Then the therapist can ask, "If you felt sad, what would you do?" The child might say, "I would just leave, I wouldn't feel like eating lunch anymore." The therapist could diagram this in the following way:

Situation:	Walk into cafeteria, two kids laugh.
Thought:	They're laughing at me.
Feeling:	Sad.
Behavior:	Leave cafeteria.

The therapist can then say, "Instead of thinking 'they are laughing at me,' suppose you thought, 'something really funny must've happened in the last period.' How would you feel then?" The child might say, "I would feel curious." The therapist can ask, "If you felt curious, what would you do?" The child might say, "I would go up to them and ask what they were laughing about." The therapist can then diagram this as follows:

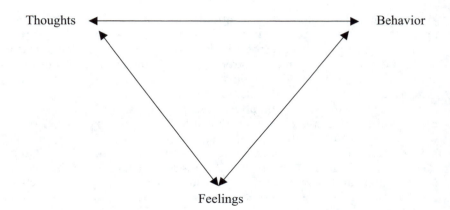

FIGURE 14.1. The Cognitive Triangle.

Situation: Walk into cafeteria, two kids laugh.
New thought: Something funny happened last period.
New feeling: Curious.
New behavior: Ask them what they are laughing about.

The therapist can then ask the child to compare these two scenarios and ask what is different about them. The child will probably recognize that the initial situation was identical; that is, he or she walked into the cafeteria and two kids started to laugh, and what was different was the child's thought about the meaning of the two kids' laughter. The therapist can then introduce the idea of automatic thoughts, and how we all talk to ourselves inside our brains all the time, and these thoughts are not always accurate (correct) or helpful (make us feel good). In order to feel better and not act in ways that are self-destructive, it is important for children and parents to evaluate whether their thoughts are accurate and helpful. As therapy proceeds, cognitive processing will be applied more specifically with regard to cognitive distortions regarding the traumatic events related to the death of the loved one.

Trauma Narrative

Creating a detailed narrative of how the loved one died is probably the component of this treatment model that most differentiates it from other child bereavement treatment approaches. The goals of the trauma narrative include mastering trauma reminders and overcoming PTSD avoidance; identifying cognitive distortions, particularly about responsibility for the death, as children often misunderstand how and why the loved one died, and may inaccurately believe that they could or should have done something to prevent the death; and placing the traumatic death into the larger context of the child's life rather than encouraging the child to focus his or her primary identity as that of someone whose loved one died in a horrific manner. These are discussed in greater detail elsewhere (Cohen, Mannarino, & Deblinger, 2006).

The trauma narrative is developed by gradually encouraging the child to describe more and more details about how the loved one died. This is typically accomplished over several consecutive sessions, and done through repetitive reading of what the child has created in the narrative to that point. For example, at the beginning of each session, if the child is writing a book (the most typical type of trauma narrative), the child would read what he or she has written so far before starting the next "chapter" of the "book." It is often helpful to divide the narrative into discrete sections or "chapters," both to ease the child's way into writing more directly about the traumatic death and to provide a sense of organization and structure to the narrative. For example, the first chapter might describe general things about the child (age, name, appearance, friends, favorite things, family members), the second chapter might describe who the book is about and what their relationship was like before the person died, and the third chapter might be about the day before the death. This prepares the child for describing the actual day of the traumatic death in the fourth chapter. The funeral or other mourning rituals might be the fifth chapter, and what has happened since the funeral might be the final chapter. It is important that the therapist specifically ask that the child include in the narrative what the "worst moment" was and also to include any "hot spots" (trauma reminders) that the child has difficulty with.

In constructing the trauma narrative, it is very important to include not only the details of what occurred, but also to include the child's thoughts, feelings, and bodily sensations during these occurrences. Including these typically requires the child to review the narrative several times, and in doing so, the child is exposed to the traumatic memories of the death several additional times. This allows for additional mastery of trauma reminders. As this process unfolds, the child often recalls additional details of the traumatic death and these can be added to the narrative. It is common for the child's true cognitions to be voiced as the narrative develops as well. If these include cognitive distortions, these should not be challenged immediately, but added to the narrative. Once the narrative has been completed, these cognitions can be addressed, and as more accurate thoughts replace the distortions through cognitive processing, these can be placed in the narrative over time.

In Vivo Mastery of Trauma Reminders

Some children with CTG develop generalized trauma reminders and persistently avoid these reminders to a degree that interferes with their daily functioning. For example, a boy was riding in a car with his father when it was hit by a drunk driver; his father died and this boy is now refusing to ride in any car. For such children, in vivo exposure techniques may be useful to master avoidance of generalized trauma reminders and resume more normal functioning. It is important to differentiate appropriate avoidance of dangerous situations (e.g., a girl who refuses to visit her father who had threatened to kill her mother; mother was eventually killed by a subsequent boyfriend) from avoidance of innocuous situations which have become generalized trauma reminders, such as the boy in the above example who refuses to ride in all cars, not just the one in which his father died.

In vivo exposure techniques are described in greater detail elsewhere but briefly require the child to gradually tolerate increasing periods of time during which he or she is exposed to the feared situation. The parent, child, and therapist must work closely together during this component, have a plan, and stick with it. The rule of thumb in in vivo exposure is that while fear breeds greater fear, mastery breeds greater mastery. This means that at any given decision point the child needs to be encouraged to choose mastery (bravery) over fear because this will breed greater mastery and success over fear in the future for the child. If the child chooses the fearful (avoidant) option over courage, he or she will be opting for greater fear, not only in the present, but in the future. Explaining this to the parent is often a very helpful way of encouraging the parent to encourage mastery in the child. Titration of the in vivo exposure so that it is not overwhelming to the child (or parent) will also help to encourage mastery and assure success.

Conjoint Child-Parent Sessions: Enhancing Safety

The conjoint child–parent sessions are the culmination of the trauma-focused component of CBT-CTG, but it is important to emphasize that in most cases, the parent has been hearing what the child has been doing in therapy all along during the individual sessions with the therapist. In this manner, the therapist has encouraged the parent to reinforce the skills learned in the earlier components of therapy, and to practice these skills at home with the child. For example, if the child had difficulty sleeping at night, the parent would practice relaxation and affective modulation skills. If, for example, the child had upsetting thoughts about the cause of the deceased's death, the parent would reinforce cognitive processing skills. During the sessions in which the child created the trauma narrative, the therapist would typically share the narrative with the parent during the parent's sessions after receiving permission to do so from the child. In our experience, virtually every child readily gives such permission after appropriate reassurance from the therapist that the parent can tolerate the upsetting content of the narrative. Specifically, children's concerns about sharing the narrative almost never relate to what therapists would consider typical therapeutic confidentiality issues but rather revolve around their concerns for upsetting the parent or their concerns that the parent will blame them for not preventing the death. Once these issues have been addressed with the therapist, children are usually not only willing but eager to share their narratives; hesitancy is usually related to fear of witnessing parental distress regarding the contents of the narrative.

The goals of having conjoint child-parent sessions are to enhance the communication between the child and parent, particularly about the traumatic aspects of the death, but also about other issues related to the child and family functioning, and to begin the transfer of the "agency of change" from the therapist to the parent. During the conjoint sessions, the child typically shares the trauma narrative directly with the parent, which may be done by one or both reading the narrative aloud. The therapist and parent then praise the child for this accomplishment. The parent and child are thus able to see the significant gains the child has made from the beginning of therapy to this point in becoming substantially more comfortable and able to describe the details of how the loved one died. The child and parent have likely both become more able to ask questions and discuss aspects of the traumatic death in ways that they could not have done just weeks previously. Since the death may have raised issues related to the child's sense of safety, the conjoint sessions are often used to address how to enhance the child's sense of safety. The child and parent may together brainstorm about how to make the child feel safer and how to implement these suggestions in practical ways. Now that the child and parent have resolved some of the trauma symptoms that initially brought the child to therapy, the focus of treatment turns to the more typical tasks of grief.

GRIEF-FOCUSED COMPONENTS OF CBT-CTG

The grief-focused components of the CBT-CTG model include psychoeducation about grief, death, mourning, and bereavement; grieving the loss (what I miss); ambivalent feelings about the deceased (what I don't miss); preserving positive memories; redefining the relationship and committing to present relationships; making meaning of CTG; joint child–parent sessions; and treatment closure issues. These are similar to grief components used in many bereavement programs and for this reason, only abbreviated descriptions of these components are included here. More detailed information about these components is available in our treatment book (Cohen, Mannarino, & Deblinger, 2006.

GRIEF PSYCHOEDUCATION

Education about "normal" grief may be provided to the child by reading books, playing a variety of board games, or for older adolescents and parents, through direct discussion. The goal of this component is to provide reassurance to the child and parent that even though the child's trauma symptoms have now abated, typical grief reactions may continue for a prolonged period of time. Each person grieves in his or her personal way, and there is no "proper," "right," or "wrong" way to grieve. For younger children, providing basic information about death, the family's religious beliefs about the afterlife (for example, what happens to the body after it is buried, what is cremation, can a person whose body was mutilated go to heaven, etc.) may be important aspects of psychoeducation. It is crucial that the therapist and parent work closely together in this regard, possibly with additional assistance from the family's spiritual or religious community, to provide information that is consistent with the family's religious and cultural beliefs.

GRIEVING THE LOSS: WHAT I MISS

To assist the child in accepting what he or she has lost with the death of the loved one, it may be helpful for the child to make a list, collage, or other concrete representation of what the child misses about the person who died. This typically includes both special and everyday activities the child shared with the deceased person. It is important for children to recognize that not only have they lost things in the past and present with the person who died, but they have also lost the ability to share things in the future, such as graduation, weddings, and births of children. It may be helpful for children to list these things ("What I Will Miss Sharing With My Mom in the Future") and have a parallel list of "Ways I Can Try To Cope."

RESOLVING AMBIVALENT FEELINGS: WHAT I DON'T MISS

When someone has died, particularly under unexpected, horrific, traumatic circumstances, there is a tendency to idealize that person and to overlook or minimize the person's less likable qualities. However, in order for the child to accept the reality of the loss and to reminisce about the totality of the deceased person, it is important for the child and parent to remember not only the good qualities but also the less positive parts of the dead person. For some children and parents, there may have been unresolved issues that now can never be worked out personally with the deceased. Providing a way for the child to work through these issues may be important not only for decreasing CTG symptoms, but also for helping the child to avoid repeating these patterns in future relationships.

In order to assist in this process, the therapist may encourage the child to write a letter to the deceased. The child includes both what he or she does and does not miss — it is important to include both. In order to gain a sense of closure in the relationship (as if the issue had been discussed and resolved between the two people while the deceased had still been alive), it may be helpful to suggest that that child write the letter that she or he imagines the deceased would have written in return if the deceased had had the chance to write back. For younger children, it is important to clarify that although an *imaginary* letter is being written to and from the deceased person, this does not mean that the person is alive in a distant place (where letters are often received from and sent to). Rather, for younger children, the therapist might need to explain that this letter is just something the child is "pretending" to write in order to express feelings.

An alternative method for identifying and addressing ambivalent feelings about the deceased is to make alternative lists, one for things the child misses about the deceased, and one for things the child does not miss:

Things I miss	Things I do not miss
Going to the park	Fights
Playing ball	When he got drunk
Vacations	When he was mean to mom

The therapist can then encourage the child to discuss each of these items in more detail. For many children, it is easier to talk about negative traits when they are "balanced out" by positive ones.

We have found that there is often a "disconnect" between children and parents whereby either the child or parent may have had a more positive relationship with the deceased than the other. It is critically important in this situation that the parent validate and support the relationship that the child had with the deceased, even if it was divergent from the parent's own experience or relationship with the dead person.

PRESERVING POSITIVE MEMORIES

Once the child and parent have resolved avoidant symptoms related to the traumatic nature of the death, an important grief-focused component involves preserving positive memories of the deceased person. The therapist should encourage the child to determine the best way to do this, perhaps with the assistance of the parent, siblings, or extended family members, friends, or members of the broader community. Children may choose to collect pictures, anecdotes, or stories about the deceased, make a collage, memory box, or other collection of mementos which represent their fondest memories of the deceased person. Therapists may assist children who find this component difficult by providing more directive examples of memories that the child may want to recall.

We have found that it is often difficult for parents to preserve positive memories of the deceased loved one, who was typically a spouse, partner, or child (and therefore the parent is often experiencing profound personal grief or even their own traumatic grief). However, it is not unusual for parents who participate in CBT-CTG to begin to face their own memories of the deceased person through trying to assist their child in this component. Many parents thus have reported improved personal PTSD and depressive symptoms through participation in this treatment, even though they were not the direct focus of treatment (Cohen, Mannarino, & Knudsen, 2004).

REDEFINING THE RELATIONSHIP AND COMMITTING TO PRESENT RELATIONSHIPS

One of the primary tasks of grieving for children is to redefine the relationship from one of day-to-day interaction to one of memory (Wolfelt, 1996). The child no longer has the deceased person to interact with as a living, growing, changing person on a daily basis, but only has memories of the deceased person. This may be the most difficult and painful part of therapy for the parent and child because it is a true "letting go" of the deceased.

In order to help children understand the difference between the relationship that used to exist when the person was alive and the relationship that exists now that the person is dead, it may be helpful to use the Balloon Exercise, illustrated below. The Balloon Exercise is a concrete illustration of what the child still has of the relationship, and what must be let go of in the relationship with the deceased. The therapist draws a balloon "filled with helium," which represents all of the things that are gone from the relationship and which the child can never have with the deceased again. The therapist asks the child to write in all of those things which he has to say goodbye to in the relationship, and which will be gone forever. The therapist also draws a second balloon which is "just filled with regular air" and is held in a child's hand in the drawing. In this balloon the therapist asks the child to write in all the things he can still hold onto from the relationship. In this concrete manner, the child is able to see that while some parts of the relationship are gone forever, other things remain. The relationship is not

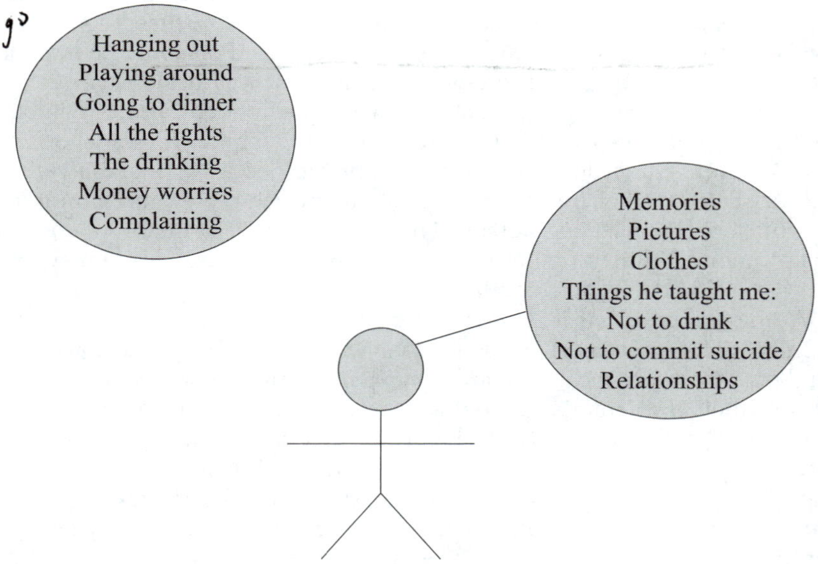

Hanging out
Playing around
Going to dinner
All the fights
The drinking
Money worries
Complaining

Memories
Pictures
Clothes
Things he taught me:
Not to drink
Not to commit suicide
Relationships

FIGURE 14.2. The Balloon Exercise.

over, but it is changed in a permanent way. This change allows the child to commit to present and future relationships without betraying the deceased loved one.

MAKING MEANING OF TRAUMATIC GRIEF

As the end of therapy approaches, it is important for children and parents to consider how they have changed since the person they loved died, what they have learned, and what the traumatic death has taught them about themselves and life. For many families, the traumatic death produced a crisis of faith, leading them to wonder how God could have allowed such a tragic thing to happen in their lives, or whether there even is a God if such a terrible thing could occur. For others, their faith deepened and provided the only comfort through the intense pain of the traumatic loss. Children provide incredibly inspiring messages of strength, hope, and faith in this component of treatment, some of which we share here:

> You are not alone.
> I want other kids to know they will be okay.
> You can be happy again.
> Even though the person isn't here you can still carry them in your heart.
> I found out how strong I am.
> I can still have fun.
> I found out who my true friends are.
> My dad and I got closer.
> It hurts at first but then you remember the good things.
> It's okay to remember.

A number of children and parents have joined groups which memorialize their loved ones in some meaningful way. Examples of this have been parents and youth who have participated in Mothers/Students Against Drunk Drivers, the Flight 427 Air Disaster Support League (formed after the crash of USAir Flight 427 outside Pittsburgh in 1994), the Clothesline Project (formed to memorialize women killed through domestic violence), the American Red Cross, and many other volunteer organizations which assist victims of disaster or violence.

JOINT CHILD–PARENT SESSIONS

Two to three joint child–parent sessions typically occur toward the end of the grief-focused module of CBT-CTG. Goals are to enhance communication between the child and parents, particularly about the death of the loved one, to encourage the child to directly express grief reactions to the parents, and for the parents to appropriately support such expression. As noted above, these sessions are also used to encourage the child and parent to share what the child has done in the preceding grief-focused components, including what the child will and will not miss about the deceased, preserving positive memories, transforming the relationship to one of memory, and committing to present relationships. If the parent and child appear to be divergent with regard to their progress in these areas, the therapist may find it helpful to encourage open communication between them in this regard. For example, helping the child and parent make a specific plan for how to accept and support each other in their own way as they grieve might be the focus of one joint session.

TREATMENT CLOSURE ISSUES

Planning for future trauma, loss, and change reminders (Pynoos, 1992) is another important goal of the grief-focused session that is best done in joint child–parent sessions. The "Three P's" are a useful tool for the child and parent to practice for the future. These include the following: *Predicting* that children and parents will experience future trauma, loss, and change reminders in the future; giving *Permission* to each other to have difficult grief reactions that are different from each other's at times; and *Planning* for how to cope with these reminders in ways that will optimize the child's and family's functioning in the future.

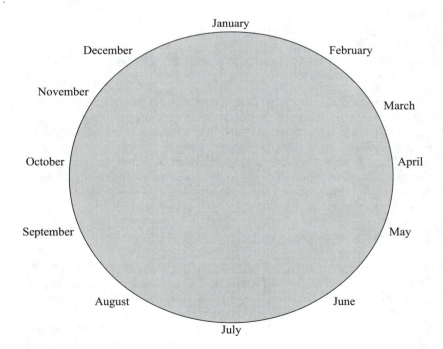

FIGURE 14.3. The Circle of Life.

The Circle of Life is another tool that the therapist can use to assist the child and parent in planning for future trauma, loss, and change reminders. The goal is to identify potential "hot spots," such as, anniversary dates, holidays, or other times of the year that will serve as potential trauma, loss, or change reminders for the family and note these on the Circle of Life. These may include the date of the loved one's death; the loved one's birthday; Father's or Mother's Day (if the loved one was the child's parent); holidays such as Christmas or Thanksgiving; the child's birthday (if this was a day that was typically shared with the loved one); and special events such as the child's first day of school or the first day of baseball season. Since the circle continues without end as illustrated below, the family can see in a concrete way that although these reminders may change from year to year, they will continue to recur every year and the pain may worsen on these dates for many years. This illustrates for the family that grieving is an ongoing process rather than a time-limited event.

Since some children may view the end of treatment as another loss, it is important for the therapist to distinguish planned treatment closure from traumatic death by pointing out that the former is the result of the child's and parent's successful completion of difficult but important work that has resulted in significant gains in skills and psychological growth. The therapist can remind the child of what he previously expressed in the "Making Meaning of Traumatic Grief" component above with regard to how the child has grown, changed, or what has been learned. It is often helpful to let children and parents know that, unlike the person who has died, the therapist will still be available and can be contacted in the future should the need arise.

We typically give children the option of taking their trauma narrative, memory box, collage, and other therapeutic artwork home with them at the end of therapy so that they can have these reminders of the therapist and the time spent in therapy. We have also found it helpful to review with the child and parent the skills they have learned in therapy, and together help them make a "toolbox" for their future use. This typically consists of a set of cards, each of which contains a brief reminder of a separate treatment component or skill that the child and parent learned in therapy and may include the child's own examples from past therapy sessions or new examples that the child, parent, and therapist develop together in the final treatment sessions. In this manner, the family can look back and review one last time what they have gained in therapy and have a concrete way to remember and practice these in the future. This also gives the family the message that the therapist has confidence in the family's ability to continue to implement these components without the therapist in the future, and that the child and parent are ready to move forward independent of therapy.

PRELIMINARY EVIDENCE SUPPORTING THE CBT-CTG MODEL

In two open treatment studies, children receiving CBT-CTG experienced significant improvement in CTG, PTSD, depression, anxiety, and behavior problems. Their participating parents also experienced significant improvement in PTSD in both studies, and in the one in which parents began the study with significant depressive symptoms, these significantly improved as well.

In the first study, children and parents received eight sessions of the CBT-CTG trauma-focused components followed by eight sessions of the CBT-CTG grief-focused components (Cohen, Mannarino, & Knudsen, 2004). Children experienced significant improvement in CTG during both modules, but significant improvement in PTSD symptoms only occurred during the trauma-focused module. This was consistent with our belief that while there are substantial commonalities between PTSD and CTG, there were also distinctions between these conditions; and inclusion of the grief-focused component provided additional benefits in improving CTG difficulties. Parents who participated in this study also experienced significant improvement in their personal PTSD and depressive symptoms.

In the second study, we shortened the CBT-CTG model to 12 sessions in order to more closely match the number of treatment sessions provided to children in many community bereavement programs. A total of seven to eight sessions were trauma-focused and four to five sessions were grief-focused; some of these grief-focused sessions included a few parent–child joint sessions. Children who received this treatment experienced significant improvement in CTG and PTSD as well as in depression, anxiety, and behavior problems. Interestingly, despite the fact that these children received only half as many grief-focused sessions as trauma-focused sessions in this study, their improvement on the EGI was of greater magnitude during the grief-focused module of treatment than during the trauma-focused module. Also of interest in this study was that children experienced improvement in both PTSD and CTG in both modules, with the magnitude of improvement in the expected direction (i.e., greater improvement in PTSD during the trauma-focused module and greater improvement in CTG during the grief-focused module). Parents in this study also experienced significant improvement in their personal PTSD symptoms; they did not have elevated depressive symptoms at pretreatment so these did not significantly improve (Cohen, Mannarino, & Staron, in press). Results from a small randomized controlled treatment trial (RCT) are pending in which CBT-CTG is compared to child-centered therapy for children who lost their uniformed service parents in the September 11, 2001 terrorist attacks in New York City. In the near future, we hope to conduct a larger RCT to examine the efficacy of CBT-CTG.

SUMMARY

CBT-CTG is a sequential trauma- and grief-focused treatment model for children and parents which has been shown in two open studies to successfully decrease children's CTG, PTSD, depression, anxiety, and behavioral problems, and to decrease PTSD symptoms in participating parents. More rigorous trials are needed to compare the efficacy of CBT-CTG to treatments commonly provided to traumatically bereaved children in community settings.

REFERENCES

Bancroft, L. & Silverman, J. G. (2002). *The batterer as parent*. Thousand Oaks, CA: Sage.

Brown, E., Amaya-Jackson, L., Cohen, J. A., Handel, S., Thiel de Bocanegra, H., Zatta, E., Goodman, R. F., & Mannarino, A.P. (2004). Understanding childhood traumatic grief: A multi-site empirical examination of the construct and its correlates. Presented at the 20th Annual Meeting of the International Society for Traumatic Stress Studies, New Orleans, LA, November.

Brown, E., Cohen, J. A., Amaya-Jackson, L., Handel, S. & Layne, C. (2003). Characteristics and responses upon exposure to death (CARED-Youth Report©). National Child Traumatic Stress Network, SAMHSA. (http://www.nctsnet.org)

Brown, E. & Goodman, R. F. (2005). Childhood traumatic grief following September 11, 2001: Construct development and validation. *Journal of Clinical Child and Adolescent Psychology,34* 248–259.

Brown, E., Goodman, R. F., Cohen, J. A., & Mannarino, A. P. (2004). Treatment of childhood traumatic grief: Contributing to a new emerging condition in the wake of community trauma. *Harvard Review of Psychiatry, 12*, 213–216.

Cohen, J. A., Deblinger, E., Mannarino, A. P., & Steer, R. A. (2004). A multisite randomized controlled trial for sexually abused children with PTSD symptoms. *Journal of the American Academy of Child and Adolescent Psychiatry, 43*, 393–402.

Cohen, J. A. & Mannarino, A. P. (1996). A treatment outcome study for sexually abused preschool children: Initial findings. *Journal of the American Academy of Child and Adolescent Psychiatry, 35*, 42–50.

Cohen, J. A. & Mannarino, A. P. (1998). Interventions for sexually abused children: Initial treatment findings. *Child Maltreatment, 3*(1), 17–26.

Cohen, J. A. & Mannarino, A. P. (2004). Treatment of childhood traumatic grief. *Journal of Clinical Child and Adolescent Psychology, 33*, 820–832.

Cohen, J. A., Mannarino, A. P., & Deblinger, E. (2006). *Treating trauma and traumatic grief in children and adolescents*. New York: Guilford.

Cohen, J. A., Mannarino, A. P., Greenberg, T. A., Padlo, S., & Shipley, C. (2002). Childhood traumatic grief: Concepts and controversies. *Trauma, Violence and Abuse, 3*(2), 91–108.

Cohen, J. A., Mannarino, A. P., & Knudsen, K. (2004). Treating childhood traumatic grief: A pilot study. *Journal of the American Academy of Child and Adolescent Psychiatry, 43*, 1225–1233.

Cohen, J. A., Mannarino, A. P., & Staron, V. (2006). A pilot study of modified cognitive–behavioral therapy for childhood traumatic grief (CBT-CTG). *Journal of the American Academy of Child & Adolescent Psychiatry*

Deblinger, E., Lippman, J., & Steer, R. (1996). Sexually abused children suffering posttraumatic stress symptoms: Initial treatment outcome findings. *Child Maltreatment, 1*(4), 310–321.

King, N. J., Tonge, B. J., Mullen, P., Myerson, N., Keyne, D., Rollings, S., Martin, R., & Ollendick, T. H. (2000). Treating sexually abused children with posttraumatic stress symptoms: A randomized clinical trial. *Journal of the American Academy of Child and Adolescent Psychiatry, 39*, 1347–1355.

Layne, C. M, Savjak, N., Saltzman, W. R., & Pynoos, R. S. (2001). *UCLA/BYU Expanded grief inventory*. University of California, Los Angeles: Los Angeles, Unpublished Instrument.

Pynoos, R. S. (1992). Grief and trauma in children and adolescents. Bereavement Care, 11, 2–10.

Stubenbort, K., Donnelly, G. A., & Cohen, J.A. (2001). Cognitive–behavioral group therapy for bereaved adults and children following an air disaster. *Group Dynamics: Theory, Research, and Practice, 5*(4), 261–276.

Wolfelt, A. D. (1996). *Healing the bereaved child: Grief gardening, growth through grief, and other touchstones for caregivers*. Fort Collins, CO: Companion Press.

Worden, J. W. (1996). *Children and grief: When a parent dies*. New York: Guilford.

15

Restorative Retelling with Incarcerated Juveniles

EDWARD K. RYNEARSON, JENNIFER
FAVELL, VICKI BELLUOMINI, RICHARD
GOLD, AND HOLLY PRIGERSON

RESTORATIVE RETELLING WITH INCARCERATED JUVENILES

Violent death bereavement is particularly prevalent in adult and juvenile prisoners, and this is not surprising since the most potent predictors of violent death, drug abuse and use of firearms, may be the norm in incarcerated offenders. Surveys demonstrate at least 50% of prisoners have suffered the loss of a family member or close friend to a violent death, and, though underserved, are vulnerable to its emotional effects. The authors initiated a pilot study of a time-limited group intervention, restorative retelling, in a residential facility for juvenile offenders. The intervention was designed to meet the special needs of juveniles, and more particularly emotionally disturbed offenders, by an insistent focus on the traumatic and grief-related effects of the dying. Pre/post measures of trauma and grief distress were collected and their analysis shows an impressive association of lowered distress following the intervention. Mental health staff in this and other prisons were trained in the intervention and have continued to run restorative retelling groups for adult and juvenile inmates.

BACKGROUND

A growing body of research has documented long-term psychological effects associated with violence exposure in youth (Pynoos & Nader, 1990; Warner & Weist, 1996). The death of a family member or emotionally valued friend from violent death (homicide, suicide, or accident) is a particularly painful, violent stressor. Violent death is commonly followed by prolonged signs of complicated and traumatic grief that are highly dysfunctional and include intrusive, traumatic thoughts of reenactment of the dying (as flashbacks or nightmares), traumatic arousal and behaviors of intense remorse, protectiveness, or retaliation (Rynearson, 1998).

Studies in urban settings report that youth have witnessed homicides at alarmingly high rates (Berman, Berman, Kurtines, Silverman, & Serafini, 1996). Recent reports document that the highest frequency of violence exposure and PTSD occurs within the cohort of incarcerated youth, including a 50% frequency of violent death exposure (Steiner, Garcia, & Matthews, 1997). Violence exposure and perceived lack of safety significantly predict willingness to use physical aggression and gun carrying (Schwab-Stone, Ayers, Kasprow, Voyce, Barone, Shriver, & Weissberg, 1995). Presumably the violent deaths of family members and close friends are associated with behaviors (risk taking, heightened drug abuse, retaliatory behaviors) that may be crime related and associated with arrest and incarceration.

Despite the evidence of the high frequency of exposure to violent dying and its long-term effects on incarcerated youth, there have been few studies that include systematic assessment, measurement, or management. Pynoos & Nader, (1988) first developed protocols for screening and measuring intervention effects with children and adolescents after violent death, and their subsequent work has largely focused on school-based settings after a single, catastrophic event (school shooting) or disaster. Other school-based support programs for intraurban youth after the violent death of a close friend or family member exist in many communities, but these are open-ended group support programs and with one exception (Salloum, 2001) have not included systematic screening or measurement of their effects. Salloum developed a 10-session, closed group, school-based intervention for intraurban youth and demonstrated significant improvement in measures of trauma distress and depression.

THE PURPOSE OF THE CURRENT STUDY

We proposed a pilot study designed to document the frequency of exposure to violent dying within a cohort of incarcerated youth, and to measure the effectiveness of short-term group support for youth who self-selected for intervention. The goals of the study were exploratory — to measure the prevalence of violent dying exposure within a population of incarcerated youth and to measure the associated effects of depression, PTSD, drug and alcohol dependence, and death imagery through reliable, self-report testing before and after a 10-session group intervention.

Though a similar screening and intervention protocol has been applied with adult family and community members, this pilot study with incarcerated youth was preparatory. Before designing and seeking funding for a randomized, controlled study of short-term group intervention, clinical prudence would recommend an open trial of the intervention to ensure that the drop-out rate is acceptably low (< 25%) and that the intervention is relatively free of risk (substantial stress, discomfort, invasion of privacy, or disruptive acting out resulting from the intervention).

STUDY SETTING

Echo Glen is one of eight juvenile detention centers in Washington State, and the only facility with female detainees. It provides correctional services for 208 youth. The majority of detainees (60%) are serving sentences for nonviolent crimes. There is one maximum-security unit, but the majority of youth are in medium-security cottages with a maximum of 16 detainees in each unit. They range in age from 11 to 19 and the same disproportionately high representation of minority races is noted in this facility as in the other juvenile detention centers in the state of Washington.

The detainees are in residence for an average of 14 to 16 months, attend school, and receive a full spectrum of rehabilitation services including psychiatric assessment and multimodal psychotherapies. A high number of detainees (60%–70%) presented with primary psychiatric disorders that required psychiatric management.

This setting was ideal for our project because it contained male and female detainees who would be in residence for a long enough interval to complete a time-limited intervention. It also offered a mental health staff that was enthused about implementing the intervention and training so the intervention could be carried forward when the project was completed.

Preparatory to beginning the intervention, we spent the initial two months orienting the administrative staff and training the clinical staff who would serve as coleaders with us (mental health counselors, school psychologists, unit program managers, and the chaplain who ran a grief support group). We also spent considerable time in the formal review and approval process for the Human Subjects Research Review Committee for Washington State and Virginia Mason Medical Center.

INSTITUTIONAL SCREENING

The identification of youth who had experienced violent death began with the Echo Glen Children's Center mental health treatment coordinator (MHC), who had access to screening information on all detainees. Over 60% of the detainees at Echo Glen had experienced the violent death of a friend or family member.

INDIVIDUAL SCREENING

A program announcement was distributed and posted in each of the cottages to give youth the opportunity to self-refer to the program and for staff to refer potential group participants.

One hundred forty youth were self-referred, referred by staff, or screened as eligible. Next, parents/guardians of these youth were notified of their youths' qualification for participation and were provided with a description of the study. They were given a 10-day period in which to refuse permission for the youths to participate in the project. In total, 49 youth were dropped from further screening for the following reasons:

- paroled to the community
- parents/guardians refused permission to participate
- did not have violent loss
- chose not to participate in the screening interview
- transferred to another facility due to population limits

Ninety-one youth remained eligible and indicated willingness to participate in the screening interview.

We next contacted the youth and arranged for them to attend a small-group informational meeting led by the investigators and Echo Glen staff coleading the groups. At this point, each youth signed an informed consent form, and completed five self-report measures comprising the clinical screening battery.

DESCRIPTION OF SUBJECTS

Forty-four adolescents were self-referred for screening, agreed to participate, and completed the self-report measures. Forty subjects began the intervention. It was decided that the groups would be gender specific (two groups for boys and two groups for girls —10 members in each) to diminish the socialization stress for the participants. Only four of the participants dropped out (usually after the first or second session) because they felt uncomfortable with the group format (a low drop-out rate of 10%). Consistent attendance was not an issue.

Six subjects left prematurely because of unanticipated transfer to another institution. The administrative or judicial mandate for sudden transfer occurs in every correctional facility, and cannot be controlled. Thirty subjects completed the intervention and pre/post measures.

DEMOGRAPHICS OF COMPLETERS

There were several interesting characteristics of the youth who participated in our groups (see Table 15.1): 30.4 months or approximately two and half years had passed since their identified violent losses, suggesting that they were seeking attention for distress that was temporally remote from the death; most attended 9 of the 10 sessions; 66% had a history of psychiatric disorder, with major depression (50%), attention deficit hyperactive disorder (ADHD) (40%), and posttraumatic stress disorder (37%) most prevalent; and more than half of the subjects (53%) were in current psychiatric treatment at Echo Glen. This may have included chemical dependency

TABLE 15.1
Descriptive statistics (N = 30)

Variable	Mean (SD) or %
Age[a, b]	14.9 (1.6)
Female	51.7 %
Months From loss[a]	30.4 (29.5)
Number of sessions attended[c]	9.0 (1.5)
Race	
White	37.9 %
Black	27.6 %
Hispanic	13.8 %
Other	20.7 %
Education[d]	
Elementary school	10.3 %
Junior high school	51.7 %
High school	37.9 %
Psychiatric disorder history[e]	65.5 %
Current psychiatric treatment[e]	53.3 %
Depression[d]	50.0 %
Posttraumatic stress disorder[f]	36.7 %
ADHD[f]	40.0 %
Substance abuse/dependence[f]	43.3 %
Conduct disorder[f]	13.3 %
Anxiety disorder[f]	16.7 %
Multiple recent losses	80.0 %
Relation to deceased	
Parent	7.4 %
Sibling	11.1 %
Other relative	51.9 %
Friend	29.6 %
Mode of death	
Natural (e.g., health-related)	11.1 %
Homicide	48.2 %
Suicide	22.2 %
Accident	18.5 %

[a] *at Preassessment.*
[b] *Age ranged from 12 to 18.*
[c] *Number of group treatment sessions attended; ranged from 4 to 10.*
[d] *highest level completed.*
[e] *self-reported.*
[f] *Baseline DSM-IV diagnosis.*

groups, dialectical behavior therapy groups, grief and loss groups led by the chaplain, or individual sessions. Forty-three percent were identified with substance abuse/dependence in their histories. Eighty percent had multiple losses, with "other relative" being most common, followed by "friend." Forty-eight percent had lost a loved one due to homicide, followed by suicide (22%), and accident (19%) as next most common.

These demographics establish that this cohort of youth presented with a high prevalence of combined psychiatric disorders and major life disruptions — already undergoing a combination of psychopharmacologic and psychological treatment.

DESCRIPTION OF MEASURES AND PRETREATMENT SCORES

Depression

Before the youth began participation in the groups, they were in the moderate-severe depression category as measured by the Beck Depression Inventory (BDI), one of the most widely accepted instruments in clinical psychology and psychiatry for assessing the intensity of depression. The 21 items were self-rated from zero to three in terms of intensity. The maximum total score was 63. Our sample had a premean of 24.

Death Imagery

Two and a half years after their identified violent loss, youth reported they experienced death imagery on a weekly or at least monthly basis.

Traumatic Grief

Based on self-ratings on the Inventory of Traumatic Grief (ITG), 27% of the youth reported thoughts and emotions diagnostic of traumatic grief. Among the core symptoms are pervasive and severe degrees of impairment in daily functioning; preoccupation with thoughts of the deceased; yearning and searching for the deceased; feeling disbelief and stunned by the death; avoidance of reminders of the deceased; auditory and visual hallucinations of the deceased; bitterness and survivor guilt over the death and symptoms of identification with the deceased. Before group, the youth had average scores of 38 of a possible total of 72. When this is compared with median ITG scores of 35 for adult family members six months after a violent death, we concluded they suffered significant levels of traumatic grief distress.

Impact of Events Scale-Revised

This instrument measures the severity of the impact of the loss experienced by an individual and indicates whether someone has symptoms severe enough to suggest a diagnosis of posttraumatic stress disorder. The Impact of Events Scale-Revised is comprised of self-report measures divided into Avoidance and Intrusion subscales. Prior to intervention, the youth had cumulative median scores of 44, which is much higher than scores reported for any other clinical cohort. Again, based on data submitted for publication for adult family members, six months after a violent death, the median avoidance and intrusion scores were 33.

Drug and Alcohol Screen Test

The youth reported median scores of 43 on the Drug/Alcohol Screening Test (DAST). A score of 10 or greater indicates drug and/or alcohol dependence.

Summary of Pregroup Scores

Based on the pregroup scores on all five screening measures, the youth who participated in the groups were seriously disturbed in all areas.

DESCRIPTION OF INTERVENTION

A more detailed description of the intervention with a case presentation is presented in the appendix. A manual of the intervention for incarcerated adults and youth has been prepared and is available upon request, Restorative Retelling in a Correctional Setting, www.vdbs.org.

Briefly described, the intervention followed a short-term (10-session), time-limited (90 minutes per session), closed group format with an agenda of activities and goals for each session. Each member received a written, weekly agenda of the intervention with a notebook in which they were encouraged to record their thoughts and dreams (between sessions) about the violent death that brought them to the group. From the outset, it was emphasized that our primary purpose was to focus on the emotional aftermath of the violent death of their friend or family member, and any thought or feeling that was not connected with that event and that relationship would be discouraged. This was not a group that welcomed complaints about the institution or the social disagreements and differences of the members. We were here "to talk about the dying" and how we could help each other in accommodating to that tragedy.

An initial group exercise focused on developing group norms. Group members shared in developing a written list of behaviors and attitudes that were requisite to establishing and maintaining group cohesion — mutual assurance of confidentiality (no one talked about the group outside of the group) and respect (no one laughed at or interrupted someone else with angry or derisive comments). This list was posted at each meeting as a point of reference if someone disregarded the group norm that had been endorsed.

Structure of the Session

Each session began with a 30-minute "check in" for members to report how his or her memory and perception of the violent dying had changed in the last week. This maintained the group's focus on the goal of the intervention from the outset of each group.

After the "check in" the group leader followed an agenda of clinical topics of traumatic bereavement and strategies for accommodation. The group leader would talk for only five or 10 minutes to clarify these clinical complications and always included sufficient time (an additional 15 or 20 minutes) for group involvement with questions and comments from the group members in developing alternative ways of coping.

After the initial "check in" and clinical clarification and skill enhancement, an hour had passed, and with these kids it is important to offer a break with cookies and refreshments.

During the second hour we presented group exercises combining drawing and poetry to assist the members in externalizing the image of the deceased and their dying through visual imagery and words. These exercises began with a restorative commemoration of the deceased by allowing each member to present whatever would revitalize the presence of the person who died for the rest of us, "Show us through words and pictures what was so special and joyful and important about the person who died." It is important to summon this positive and resilient imagery as a first restorative step.

In later sessions, the second hour focused on drawing and poetry that externalized the image of the violent dying as they imagined that it happened (rarely had the group member actually witnessed the dying).

We hypothesized that accommodation (occurring through the simultaneous externalization and restorative retelling of the revivified memory of the deceased and their violent dying through shared imagery and words) would be enhanced by engaging in this agenda of group exercises and that group members would report less death-related distress at the completion of the intervention.

Results

Multiple regression analysis tested for significance between outcome summary scores and loss characteristics, exposure to death and relationship to the deceased, and demographic characteristics and psychiatric morbidity.

Analyses to determine whether the self-report measures of distress (BDI, DIS, ITG, and IES) declined significantly over time were determined through paired t-tests for significant differences between baseline and termination scores (see Table 15.2).

Depression

Levels of depression decreased significantly. However, scores of 16.8 indicated that while their levels had decreased, these youth reported they continued to be moderately depressed.

Death Imagery

Levels did not decrease significantly, which may have been due to the small sample size. However, change on all four factors related to death imagery did decrease as we predicted.

TABLE 15.2
Outcome summary scores: Pre- and postmeans

Sum variable	Premean (SD)	Postmean (SD)	t or χ2
BDI[a]	24.0 (11.1)	16.8 (10.6)	−3.37**
DIS[b]	10.2 (5.5)	9.0 (6.0)	−1.01
Reenactment	2.6 (2.0)	2.1 (1.8)	−1.21
Rescue	2.4 (2.2)	1.9 (1.9)	−1.05
Revenge	2.2 (2.3)	2.4 (2.2)	0.41
Reunion	3.2 (2.1)	2.7 (1.9)	−1.16
TG diagnosis[c]	26.7 %	10.0 %	3.06[†]
ITG[d]	38.3 (12.1)	31.7 (11.8)	−2.72*
RIES total[e]	44.0 (20.4)	34.2 (13.3)	−2.84**
Avoidance	15.2 (9.0)	12.2 (6.0)	−1.70[†]
Intrusion	17.3 (7.4)	13.3 (6.2)	-3.12**
Hyperarousal	11.5 (6.3)	8.8 (4.4)	−2.48*
DAST[f]	42.7 (18.3)	—	

[†] $P < 0.10$; * $P < 0.05$; ** $P < 0.01$; two-tailed.
Values of $p < 0.05$ indicate that there is a significant difference between the Pre- and Post-means.
[a] *BDI = Beck Depression Inventory, a 22-item scale; summary score ranges from 0 to 66.*
[b] *DIS = Death Imagery Scale is made up of four items (reenactment, rescue, revenge, and reunion), each ranging from 0 to 5; summary score ranges from 0 to 20.*
[c] *Traumatic Grief (TG) diagnosis was calculated using the diagnostic algorithm of the Inventory of Traumatic Grief (ITG).*
[d] *ITG = Inventory of Traumatic Grief, an 18-item scale; summary score ranges from 0 to 72.*
[e] *RIES = Revised Impact of Events Scale, a 15-item scale (summary score ranges from 0 to 75), made up of a 7-item.*
Intrusion subscale (summary score ranges from 0 to 35) and an 8-item Avoidance subscale (summary score ranges from 0 to 40).
[f] *DAST = Drug/Alcohol Screening Test, a 32-item scale; summary score ranges from 0 to 32. Measured at baseline only.*

Traumatic Grief

Postgroup scores indicated a 17% drop in the number of adolescents who met the level diagnostic of traumatic grief. Change in the total ITG score was significantly decreased as well, though it indicated continued high levels.

IMPACT OF EVENTS SCALE-REVISED

Total scores decreased very significantly as did scores on all three subscales. These postgroup levels indicate a high correlation between participation in the groups and a decrease in PTSD signs and symptoms.

The largest effects associated with group participation were the decrease in the Beck Depression Inventory scores, the Impact of Events Scale total score, and the occurrence of intrusive thoughts and imagery on the IES subscale. All changes indicated decreases in the levels of all factors.

Table 15.3 shows the correlations between outcome summary scores and loss characteristics, exposure to the death, and the relationship of group participants to the deceased. These data indicated that witnessing the scene of death and the loved one's injuries, discovering the victim, attending the funeral, previous worry about the victim, and high degrees of attachment and dependence on the victim were most significantly associated with reported high levels of psychological disturbance.

Table 15.4 shows that substance abuse/dependence is the most highly correlated demographic characteristic with depression when measured pre-group and with traumatic grief measured postgroup. Perhaps the very high levels of substance abuse in these youth initially masks the experience of traumatic grief, which became more manifest with our intervention that encouraged exposure to the death imagery — without access to substances.

Table 15.5 indicates that substance abuse/dependence, witnessing the death scene, and dependence on the deceased were most highly correlated with death imagery, depression, and traumatic grief.

Discussion

This preliminary study of an open trial of a focused, time-limited group intervention for incarcerated youth self-referred for treatment of long-term distress following violent death met our limited objectives of:

1. Documentation of its compliance — a low drop-out rate (10%).
2. Documentation of its associated effects — a significant decrease in self-report measures of distress before and after the intervention.
3. Documentation of casualties from the intervention — there were no reports of youth whose distress clinically worsened or acted out concurrent with treatment.
4. Documentation of pragmatic training for resident mental health staff to ensure continuance of the intervention.

Limitations of the study were inherent in our design that lacked random assignment to an intervention group or an untreated control group. In the absence of a control group comparison, our findings of significant pre/post decrease on measures of distress may be associated with change over time. However, considering the high levels of death-related distress and the remote effects (over 30 months since the violent death) it would seem unlikely that such significant decrease would occur spontaneously.

Another limitation of the study was presented by the richness of the therapeutic milieu — over half of the youth were engaged in other modes of treatment that may have had an indirect effect on the rate of compliance, casualty rate, and distress improvement with our group intervention.

A final limitation was presented by the high degree of comorbidity and vulnerability of the subjects themselves — these youth were seriously disturbed and had long-term histories of parental neglect and abuse — so that the high levels of

TABLE 15.3

Pearson correlation coefficients for the associations between outcome summary scores and loss characteristics, exposure to the death, and relationship to the deceased

	DIS		BDI		ITG		RIES		DAST
	Pre	Post	Pre	Post	Pre	Post	Pre	Post	Pre
Saw scene of death	0.50**	0.39*	n.s.	0.37*	0.41*	0.37*	n.s.	0.49**	0.42*
Saw person injured	0.55**	0.40*	n.s.	0.38*	0.34†	0.37†	n.s.	0.51**	0.47**
Tried to help	n.s.	n.s.	n.s.	0.34†	n.s.	-0.34†	n.s.	n.s.	n.s.
Prevented from helping	n.s.	n.s.	n.s.	n.s.	n.s.	n.s.	n.s.	n.s.	n.s.
At scene before victim removed	0.43*	0.47**	n.s.	0.41*	n.s.	0.34†	n.s.	0.63†	n.s.
Saw victim die	0.46*	n.s.	0.35†	n.s.	0.37*	n.s.	n.s.	0.35†	0.38*
First to discover victim	0.47**	n.s.	n.s.	0.54**	n.s.	n.s.	0.31†	n.s.	n.s.
Saw victim taken to hospital	n.s.	n.s.	0.38*	n.s.	0.40*	n.s.	n.s.	n.s.	n.s.
Victim said something	n.s.	0.33†	n.s.	n.s.	n.s.	n.s.	n.s.	n.s.	n.s.
Learned of loss immediately	0.44*	0.46*	n.s.	n.s.	n.s.	n.s.	n.s.	n.s.	n.s.
Attended funeral	n.s.	n.s.	0.34†	n.s.	0.55**	n.s.	0.35†	n.s.	n.s.
Participated in loss rituals	0.34†	n.s.	n.s.	n.s.	0.56†	n.s.	n.s.	n.s.	0.34†
Experienced other recent loss	n.s.	n.s.	n.s.	n.s.	n.s.	n.s.	n.s.	n.s.	n.s.
Reminiscent of other losses	n.s.	n.s.	n.s.	n.s.	n.s.	n.s.	n.s.	n.s.	n.s.
Previously worried about victim	0.36†	n.s.	n.s.	n.s.	0.51**	n.s.	n.s.	n.s.	n.s.
Believed deceased was at risk	n.s.	0.43*	n.s.	n.s.	n.s.	n.s.	n.s.	n.s.	0.39*
Wish deceased prevented event	n.s.	n.s.	n.s.	n.s.	n.s.	n.s.	n.s.	n.s.	n.s.
Relationship with deceased:	n.s.	n.s.	n.s.	n.s.	n.s.	n.s.	n.s.	n.s.	n.s.
Distant — Close[a]	0.38*	n.s.	n.s.	n.s.	n.s.	n.s.	n.s.	n.s.	n.s.
Conflictual — Peaceful[a]	0.43*	n.s.	n.s.	n.s.	n.s.	n.s.	n.s.	n.s.	0.32†
Difficult — Easy[a]	n.s.	n.s.	n.s.	n.s.	n.s.	n.s.	n.s.	n.s.	n.s.
Unsupportive — Supportive[a]	0.46*	n.s.	n.s.	n.s.	0.34†	n.s.	n.s.	n.s.	n.s.

(Continued)

TABLE 15.3 (*Continued*)

Pearson correlation coefficients for the associations between outcome summary scores and loss characteristics, exposure to the death, and relationship to the deceased

	DIS	BDI	ITG	RIES	DAST
Hostile — Compatible[a]	n.s.	n.s.	n.s.	n.s.	n.s.
Incompatible — Compatible[a]	0.47*	n.s.	0.41*	n.s.	n.s.
Attached to deceased	0.47**	0.34†	0.31†	n.s.	0.33†
Dependent on deceased	0.38*	n.s.	0.40*	n.s.	0.32†

† $P < 0.10$; * $P < 0.05$; ** $P < 0.01$; *** $P < 0.001$; two-tailed.

A positive correlation indicates that those who endorse the statement are more likely to have a higher summary score.

n.s. = not significant ($p >= 0.1$)

[a] *A positive correlation indicates that relationships characterized more by the latter word and less by the former word are associated with a higher outcome summary score.*

Note: Several of the above variables were highly correlated with each other. I selected variables to be entered in the adjusted models based on high correlations with outcome variables as well as minimal overlap with other control variables.

TABLE 15.4
Pearson correlation coefficients and F values for the associations between outcome summary scores and demographic characteristics and psychiatric morbidity

	DIS		BDI		ITG		RIES		DAST
	Pre	Post	Pre	Post	Pre	Post	Pre	Post	Pre
Age	n.s.	n.s.	n.s.	n.s.	n.s.	n.s.	n.s.	n.s.	n.s.
Sex	0.46*[a]	n.s.	n.s.	n.s.	n.s.	n.s.	n.s.	n.s.	n.s.
Months from loss	n.s.	n.s.	n.s.	n.s.	−0.31†[b]	n.s.	n.s.	n.s.	n.s.
Num of sessions attended	n.s.	n.s.	n.s.	n.s.	n.s.	n.s.	n.s.	n.s.	n.s.
Race[c]	n.s.	n.s.	n.s.	n.s.	n.s.	n.s.	n.s.	n.s.	n.s.
Education[c]	n.s.	n.s.	n.s.	n.s.	n.s.	n.s.	n.s.	n.s.	n.s.
Psych disorder history	0.44*	n.s.	n.s.	n.s.	n.s.	n.s.	n.s.	n.s.	0.32†
Current psych treatment	n.s.	n.s.	n.s.	n.s.	n.s.	n.s.	n.s.	n.s.	n.s.
Depression	n.s.	0.35†	0.37*	n.s.	n.s.	0.33†	n.s.	n.s.	n.s.
PTSD	n.s.	n.s.	0.36*	n.s.	n.s.	0.34†	n.s.	n.s.	n.s.
ADHD	n.s.	n.s.	n.s.	n.s.	−0.45*	n.s.	n.s.	n.s.	n.s.
Substance abuse/dependence	n.s.	0.45*	0.56**	n.s.	n.s.	0.57***	n.s.	n.s.	0.33†
Conduct disorder	n.s.	n.s.	n.s.	n.s.	n.s.	n.s.	n.s.	n.s.	n.s.
Anxiety disorder	n.s.	n.s.	−0.39*	n.s.	−0.31†	n.s.	n.s.	n.s.	n.s.
Multiple recent losses	n.s.	n.s.	n.s.	n.s.	n.s.	n.s.	n.s.	n.s.	n.s.
Relation to deceased[c]	n.s.	n.s.	n.s.	n.s.	n.s.	n.s.	n.s.	n.s.	n.s.
Mode of death[c]	n.s.	n.s.	n.s.	n.s.	n.s.	n.s.	n.s.	n.s.	n.s.

† $P < 0.10$; * $P < 0.05$; ** $P < 0.01$; *** $P < 0.001$; two-tailed.

A positive correlation indicates that those who endorse the statement are more likely to have a higher summary score.

[a] Men had higher DIS scores at the preassessment than women.

[b] Those who were closer in time to the loss had marginally higher ITG scores at the preassessment.

[c] These categorical variables were entered into unadjusted linear regression models predicting the outcome sum scores. F values are presented in place of Pearson coefficients.

TABLE 15.5
Adjusted linear regression models predicting outcome summary scores[a]

	Outcome summary variables				
	DIS	BDI	ITG	RIES	DAS T[b]
	F	F	F	F	F
Main effects[c]					
Substance abuse/dependence	6.99*	7.82*	8.36*	1.55	0.40
Saw scene of death	16.3***	1.33	3.69†	4.25†	2.01
Attended funeral	3.12†	0.86	2.85	0.80	0.03
Previously worried about victim	0.93	0.05	1.17	0.64	0.62
Dependent on deceased	6.96**	0.44	1.02	1.95	0.46
Time	3.03†	1.63	0.12	3.03†	—
Interactions					
Substance abuse/dep∗time	0.01	0.52	6.51*[d]	0.05	—
Saw scene of death∗time	0.65	0.38	0.00	0.55	—
Attended funeral∗time	0.20	0.04	3.53†[e]	1.85	—
Previously worried∗time	0.15	0.82	3.06†[f]	0.13	—
Dependent on deceased∗time	2.00	1.03	3.18*	0.69	—

† $P < 0.10$; * $P < 0.05$; ** $P < 0.01$; *** $P < 0.001$; *two-tailed*.
[a] *For each outcome summary score, a repeated measures analysis of variance was performed, simultaneously, entering each of the five variables listed under main effects and adjusting for the within-subject effects of time (pre-post differences).*
[b] *The DAST was administered at baseline only so there are no time effects for this variable.*
[c] *All significant main effects except time represent positive correlations with the summary scores. The time effect indicates that summary score means decline between the pre- and postassessments.*
[d] *Those diagnosed with Substance Abuse/Dependence increase their ITG score significantly between pre- and post-assessments, while others decrease their ITG score.*
[e] *Those who attended the funeral had higher baseline ITG scores on average than nonattenders, but these scores had decreased by the postassessment, while nonattenders increased their ITG scores between assessments.*
[f] *Those who had been frightened that something might happen to the victim at times before the death had a higher mean ITG score at baseline but decreased by the post-assessment.*

self-report distress were not specifically related to the solitary stress of the violent death, but also to their highly stressful developmental histories and their limited resilience.

The lack of institutional engagement with the families of the youth missed a crucial opportunity for beginning to intervene with the family dynamics before release. It is very difficult to maintain continued contact with these youth. They are from every corner of Washington State, and the only way to remain distantly engaged with them is through their probation counselors. We have been unable to systematically monitor these youth after their release to document the longer-term impact of our intervention and its contribution to their long-term rehabilitation.

APPENDIX: STRUCTURE AND FORMAT FOR RESTORATIVE RETELLING (RR) WITH INCARCERATED YOUTHS AND ADULTS

Session Structure

- Sessions last 90 minutes and begin and end on time.
- Coleaders refer to the written agenda at the beginning of each session to announce the topic of the session and remind members how many sessions remain.
- Each session begins with a brief "check in" for each member. It is important for the more avoidant or introverted members to report their status so they can be included in the interaction. The members are told to focus on how their experience of the violent death has changed since the last session because that is our primary concern and that is what we need to "check."
- One of the coleaders then presents a simple clarification of one or several of the principles of RR. During the first four sessions these brief "lessons" provide a more coherent framework for the members' understanding of: (1) resilience, (2) restorative retelling, (3) restorative reconnection, and (4) a place for yourself in retelling. Each of these presentations lasts five or 10 minutes with another 10 or 15 minutes of discussion and alternatives for skill enhancement and mastery of the principle.
- Next, the group engages in exercises of poetry writing and drawing to more fully express and experience resources of resilience and to begin preparing material for their presentations of the commemorative and dying image of the deceased.
- Finally, one of the coleaders may lead the group in stress reduction and guided imagery exercises for five minutes to close the session.

The sessions follow a rough time schedule for each session and a predictable, succession:

Sessions 1–4

15 minutes	"Check in"
20 minutes	Lecture and skill enhancement
50 minutes	Art and poetry exercises
5 minutes	Relaxation exercises (optional)

Sessions 5–8

15 minutes	"Check in"
70 minutes	Commemoration and violent dying retelling art and poetry exercises if time permits
5 minutes	Relaxation exercises (optional)

Sessions 9–10

   15 minutes   "Check in"
   75 minutes   Reinforcing support and resilience after release

Farewell Exercise

The initial "check in" promotes an inclusive opportunity for each member to focus on the weekly changes in the thoughts and feelings associated with the violent death experience.

The "lessons" during the first four sessions are for the clarification and progressive reinforcement of skills to prepare for the imaginal exercises (reexposure):

Session 1. Resilience (self-stabilization)
Session 2. Restorative retelling (living "story" > dying "story")
Session 3. Restorative reconnection (imaginary reunion and conversation with deceased)
Session 4. A place for yourself in the retelling (finding a role for the teller)

The poetry and drawing exercises promote an external expression of the commemorative and dying experience.

The imaginal exercises of commemoration and violent dying during sessions 5, 6, 7, and 8 allow a restorative retelling.

The last two sessions focus on identifying and consolidating the changes promoted by RR (and reinforcing their utility after release), with the final session celebrating the group termination over a farewell meal.

REFERENCES

Berman S. L., Kurtines W. M., Silverman W. K., Serafini L. T. (1996). The impact of exposure to crime and violence on urban youth. *American Orthopsychiatric Association, 66*(3) 329–336.
Pynoos, R. S. & Nader, K. (1988). Psychological first aid and treatment approach to children exposed to community violence: Research implications. *Journal of Traumatic Stress, 1*(4) 445–473.
Pynoos, R. S. & Nader, K. (1990) Children's exposure to violence and traumatic death. *Psychiatric Annals, 20* (6) 334–344.
Rynearson, E. K.& Geoffrey, R. (1999). Bereavement after homicide: Its assessment and treatment. In Charles R. Figley (Ed.), *Traumatology of grieving* (pp. 109–128). Philadelphia: Brunner/Mazel.
Salloum, A. & Vincent, N. J. (1999). Community-based groups for inner-city adolescent survivors of homicide victims. *Journal of Child and Adolescent Group Therapy, 9* (1), 27–45.
Salloum, A. (2001). Community-based Groups for inner-city adolescent survivors of homicide victims. Journal of Child and Adolescent Group Therapy. Vol. 9 No.1, pp. 27–45
Schwab-Stone, M. E., Ayers T. S., Kasprow W., Voyce, C., Barone, C., Shriver, T., & Weissberg, R.P. (1995). No safe haven: A study of violence exposure in an urban community. *Journal of the American Academy of Child and Adolescent Psychiatry, 34*(10), 1343–1352.

Steiner, H., Garcia, I. G., & Matthews, Z. (1997). Post traumatic stress disorder in incarcerated juvenile delinquents. *Journal of the American Academy of Child and Adolescent Psychiatry, 36*(3), 357–365.

Warner, B. S, & Weist, M.D. (1996). Urban youth as witnesses to violence: Beginning assessment and treatment efforts. *Journal of Youth and Adolescence, 25*(3), 361–377.

NOTE

This chapter was sponsored by Project on Death in America, Open Society Institute, 20000152.

Part III

Community Outreach and Intervention After Disaster and Warfare

16

Mass Violent Death and Military Communities: Domains of Response in Military Operations, Disaster, and Terrorism

DAVID M. BENEDEK AND ROBERT J. URSANO

THE MILITARY COMMUNITY

The authors describe the cohesion of the military community, enjoined in a common action and purpose, where violent dying is dreaded, but realistically anticipated. Presumably there has been an organized response to violent death within the military for thousands of years, with preparations for the psychosocial support of the bereaved families of soldiers following their deaths from hazardous duty or warfare. The military has implemented effective responses to military disasters (military plane crashes) and terror attacks (e.g. the 9/11 Pentagon attack) which appear to be better organized than those of governmental and nongovernmental agencies for short-term and intermediate support. Presumably the authoritarian structure allows a more rapid, coherent mobilization and delegation of service and providers. With its authoritarian structure, bereavement support flows from the top to the bottom, beginning with death notification, a military funeral with high honors, and an appointed officer to maintain contact and arrange referral to mental health services for as long as the family maintain's residence on the base. However, there is no continued outreach or long-term support for surviving primary (spouse, children) or extended family members (parents, grandparents, siblings).

INTRODUCTION

Like their civilian counterparts, military personnel and their families must confront situations involving violent death due to domestic violence, interpersonal crime, or individual tragedy. However, the military community is also at increased risk for exposure to violent death resulting from combat, training accidents, or other military operations, and for exposure to mass violent death. Military families stationed at high-risk locations face an additional risk of mass violent death created by natural disaster or acts of terrorism. Regardless of the cause, violent deaths in the military profoundly affect not only bereaved family and friends but the close-knit military work and military family communities (which may span many time zones around the world). Active duty and civilian support workers and leaders in the area where the death or deaths occur, and military leaders and workers at remote locations tasked with responsibility in the overall response to such events are also affected. Multiple domains of impact are similarly created when the military participates in civilian disaster response — even when the military does not lose a single member as a direct result of the tragedy.

ENVIRONMENTAL RISK FACTORS FOR MILITARY MEMBERS AND THEIR FAMILIES

Ancient societies conceived of disasters such as floods or earthquakes as acts of the gods. However, the distinction between natural disasters (e.g., earthquakes) and catastrophe resulting from the acts of man (e.g., explosions or plane crashes) is increasingly difficult to make. When death and destruction from an earthquake occur because of poorly constructed housing in urban areas there is a man-made component in an otherwise "natural" disaster. Man-made disasters such as plane crashes may result from "natural" forces such as severe weather but they may also result from intentional acts, as in the case of terrorist attacks. In recent decades the U.S. military has responded to military and civilian air disasters of both types.

War has been defined as a political act involving violence to achieve national objectives or protect natural interests. Clearly war may result in mass violent death, but the U.S. military (and others around the world) have also become involved in humanitarian relief, government stabilization, and peacekeeping missions (operations other than war) in which participants may be exposed to mass death (e.g., from detonation of landmines, the discovery of mass grave sites, or the reemergence of hostilities). Although military family members do not deploy to war zones or on peacekeeping missions with their soldier-relatives they may accompany active duty members to relatively remote and high-risk locations such as Saudi

Arabia, Turkey, Korea, or locations in Africa where the United States maintains either a stabilizing presence or positions itself for subsequent rapid deployment. There, as in war zones, military personnel (and their families) may be exposed to attacks or disaster — and subsequently to the dead, the injured, and the grotesque. They may confront impending or immediate threat to life, the sudden and unanticipated loss of friends and loved ones, and physical injury associated with disability and pain. Today, even work at stateside military facilities (e.g., the Pentagon) places military members at increased risk for attack. Military members and their families are also at risk for the emotional sequelae of exposure to violent death in the aftermath of attack. Like firefighters, police officers, or paramedics, the occupational requirements and operational environments of military personnel increase the risk of such exposure. But more so than the families of civilian first-responders, military family members — by virtue of living in close proximity to active duty worksites — are also at increased risk of exposure to violent death as a result of military operations and exercises.

DEFINING THE MILITARY COMMUNITY

Beyond risk, there are other challenges of military life created by remote duty locations and frequent moves. Military members and their immediate families are often unable to establish deep roots in a civilian community. Building close ties in a community requires a period time in one location not afforded by military tour lengths nor encouraged by the usual requirement for multiple changes in location to assure career advancement.

Military bases provide housing and the work location for assigned personnel and their families. They also provide much of the necessary infrastructure (e.g., medical treatment facilities, schools, clothing and grocery stores, beauty salons, facilities for religious worship, auto shops, recreational fields, parks, and gymnasia) associated with community life. Spouses and older children of active duty members are often employed in these on-base facilities, other employees are military retirees, and other (nonmilitary) locals may seek employment on base because they wish to associate with or assist those who serve in the military. This convenient infrastructure may be safety imperative in some locations but it does little to promote the development on nonmilitary support networks. Military members are also frequently assigned to locations geographically separated from parents, other close relatives, or (nonmilitary) friends. Military leaders have long recognized the potential for social isolation for those on military assignment, and so have developed a rich network of military community programs, support groups, and morale, welfare, and recreation (MWR) programs designed to enhance social connectedness between military members (and their dependent families) on military bases in the United States and abroad.

The challenges associated with developing off-post support and relationships, the convenience of on-post facilities, and the programs in place specifically designed to foster on-post community spirit and connections combine to create a very strong sense of community on military bases. The shared sense of values (e.g., service to country, personal sacrifice) that prompt commitment to the military lifestyle also contributes. On base, families living in close proximity have a common understanding of the work demands (unusual hours, separation from loved ones, hazardous duty, etc.), and this too contributes to the community identity.

It would be misleading, however, to think of the military community as entirely "walled off" from the town or city in which it may be situated. Local civilians often work or offer volunteer services on base, and nearby civilian business establishments rely heavily on military clientele. Military family members (and some "moonlighting" active duty members) obtain employment in these establishments. A more all-encompassing description of the military community might be those active duty members and their families living on or near a base, the civilian employees and volunteers on base, and the local businesses and families that rely in one way or the other on the military for their livelihood, share an understanding of the sacrifices of military life, or an appreciation for military values. In a sense the military community may be regarded as "a part of, yet apart from" the surrounding civilian community. Although separate in many ways from the greater civilian population that surrounds them, the sense of common values, common needs, and interdependency creates a social bond — a sense of family — that may be a unique quality of military life. As a result of the dependency of one military unit on another one (often based at a geographically separate location) for logistical or operational support, ties may develop between military units far removed from one another. It is this extended "family" defined more by mutual understanding and shared values than by bloodline or marital relationships that must confront together the losses of violent death due to military operations. As will be illustrated in the examples below, interventions in the aftermath of mass violent death within this military community must first seek to identify all the affected community members, then understand the extent to which the loss (or losses) may affect each, and finally bring to bear the many resources of the extended community in an effort to provide comfort and sustained support to mitigate the distress, distress reactions, or disorders that may follow.

LOOK

RESPONSE TO MASS VIOLENT DEATH IN A MILITARY COMMUNITY:
THE GANDER AIR DISASTER

Community disaster models have either focused on individuals within a community and aggregated individual reactions to form a community response, or viewed the community as a social unit that must be considered as an entity. Past models have also restricted their perspective to the disaster site and the immediate postimpact phase. The Gander military air disaster illustrated the limitations of such models in capturing the duration and potential spread of the effects of mass violent loss on military communities. The disaster also informed future military responses to events resulting in mass violent death.

On December 12, 1985, the U.S. Army's 101st Airborne Division, based at Fort Campbell, Kentucky began its return home after six months of U.N. peacekeeping duty in the Sinai desert. The unit was to fly home on a small assortment of military and chartered aircraft. On that day one chartered airplane carrying eight aircrew and 248 soldiers crashed and exploded on impact shortly after a refueling stop in Gander, Newfoundland, killing all on board. As word of the crash reached the home base and the flight manifest was confirmed, families of the 101st Airborne Division were notified to assemble in the gymnasium for an announcement. At Gander, Department of Defense personnel worked with Canadian officials to recover the equipment, bodies, and personal possessions of the deceased. These were then transported to Dover Air Force Base, Delaware where an extensive mortuary and body identification process continued for two months. This effort involved more than 1,000 professional and volunteer participants. Of the dead, approximately one-third were married and had lived at Fort Campbell, Kentucky. Thirty-six children lost their fathers. This sudden and violent death, on the eve of a homecoming celebration, devastated the tightly knit military community on the base, with those most significantly affected including next of kin, military leaders, and surviving members of the unit (e.g., those who arrived home on other flights). A small research team documented the experiences of affected individuals after the crash and identified distress reactions and behaviors extending far beyond the boundaries of Fort Campbell. Gander crash site workers, mortuary personnel at Dover, Delaware, and other organizations were profoundly affected by their experiences. Additional families and friends of the victims were located in other civilian communities across the nation and other military communities around the world. (Wright and Bartone, 1994)

The research team also found that military leaders, who were critical to the process of uniting their respective communities and focusing the response efforts, were also affected by their experience, and were frequently neglected by health care providers. With considerable attention focused on the bereaved, the impact on groups such body handlers at the mortuary, security officers at the crash site, and officers and clergy assigned to assist bereaved families, was often overlooked. A later study found that over half the Army body recovery workers showed symptoms of PTSD three to four weeks after the crash. The study highlighted significant emotional distress and effects on persons at Gander, Dover, and Fort Campbell who did not personally know the decedents. Finally, interviews with casualty assistance officers in Washington, DC, involved in coordinating responses at all sites, were also affected considerably. The subpopulations defined by geographical location and relationship to the disaster itself are depicted in Figure 16.1.

The Gander crash investigation helped to illustrate the breadth and complexity of affected communities in the aftermath of military violent death. It also identified elements of the population response, at both the leadership and service provision levels, which have been incorporated into subsequent military responses to mass violent death. In a follow-up

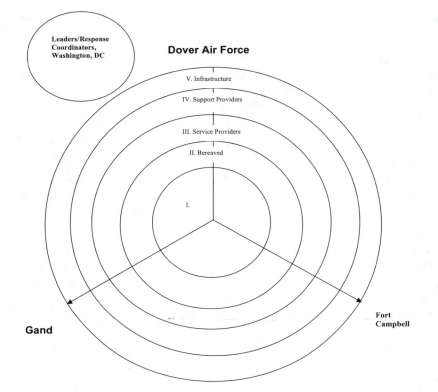

FIGURE 16.1. Gander Plane Crash Disaster Community Model. Adapted from Wright, K.M. and Bartone, P.T. (1994) "Community responses to disaster: the Gander plane crash," in Ursano R.J., McCaughey B.G., and Fullerton C.S., eds., Individual and Community Responses to Trauma and Disaster: The Structure of Human Chaos, New York: Cambridge University Press, 1994.

to the initial report, Ingraham (1987a, 1987b) emphasized the importance of key community leaders assuming leadership roles in the grieving process through the establishment of public rituals and group processes to comfort and insure the welfare of immediate survivors and next of kin. In the immediate aftermath of the plane crash, the brigade commander at Fort Campbell assumed such a "grief leadership" role as he assembled the families and informed them of what had happened. In his announcement he focused on the importance of not being alone and was able to connect empathically with those who had lost friends and family. He demonstrated his own capacity to express grief in his announcements, and in so doing, encouraged other soldiers and family members to do the same. He also assured families that information would be passed along as soon as it was available and took steps to insure that this occurred. The U. S. president and the first lady also attended the memorial service that occurred in the week following the tragedy, spoke privately to family members of the deceased and local leadership, and publicly emphasized the president's role as representing the nation's grief. The ceremony was attended by the greater Fort Campbell community as well as the adjacent townspeople. Several months later, the division commander directed a one minute sounding of the post sirens followed by a two minute silent tribute to all 248 victims as the last body was buried several months later.

Beyond leadership-directed memorials and rituals, the Gander disaster was notable for the emergence of the family assistance center, an ad hoc colocation of casualty assistance officers, chaplains, mortuary affairs personnel, Red Cross volunteers, Army relief services volunteers, judge advocate general's office representatives, and military mental health personnel who established a collective resource and referral center at a central location with Fort Campbell that was established without prior planning or precedent in the immediate aftermath of the disaster. Services ranging from legal guidance to stress management, and individual grief counseling and mental health assessments were made available to grieving family members. As the tragedy unfolded, the site provided an opportunity for exhausted response staff and other community members to reflect on their own experience and obtain support as well. The family support center provided a foundation upon which interdisciplinary support could initially be obtained in such a way that supportive and therapeutic relationships established there were sustained after the center closed its doors. (Wright and Bartone, 1994)

The Gander military air disaster was unprecedented in magnitude for military-related violent death during noncombat operations. Systematic evaluation and analysis of affected individuals and groups provided considerable insight into the nature and complexity of various domains of the military community in the aftermath of violent death. Lessons learned here regarding identification of affected subpopulations, the importance of leadership actions, and public ceremonies and rituals have shaped further military responses to violent loss. The importance of military leadership role-modeling shared grief, focusing on the importance of timely sharing of information, and identifying resources for additional support to the most profoundly affected individuals, have been incorporated into battlefield models of combat stress control and mental health intervention in the aftermath of traumatic loss. While evidenced-based treatment for mental disorders and syndromes in the aftermath of traumatic loss (e.g., depression, acute stress disorder, posttraumatic stress disorder, and complicated grief) have advanced considerably since 1985, important lessons were learned at Gander. These lessons included recognition of the importance of outreach in case identification; the critical roles of key leadership (and the health risks attendant with leadership roles); and the necessity of balancing population-based and individual interventions. Indeed, the lessons provided by the Gander experience were more operationally applied in the development and implementation of Operation Solace — the military mental health response to the September 11, 2001 terrorist attack on the Pentagon.

OPERATION SOLACE: THE MILITARY MENTAL HEALTH RESPONSE
TO THE SEPTEMBER 11 PENTAGON ATTACK

The September 11 attack on the Pentagon created a sudden and dramatic requirement for a focused medical response to casualties. Immediately after the crash, body recovery and identification efforts commenced, but so too did efforts to rescue, provide lifesaving first aid, and medically evacuate and treat victims at the scene injured by the explosion, fire, and partial building collapse. Like the Gander disaster, the Pentagon attack established new military communities forced to confront violent death. At the Pentagon, however, recovery operations commenced in an environment of heightened anticipation of further attack, and accompanied urgent preparation for the military response that was to become the beginning of the global war on terror.

In the early phases of recovery operations, military medical leaders drew on experience from previous disasters, from experience with terrorist attacks in the United States (e.g., the bombing of the Murrah Federal Building in Oklahoma City), and on existing knowledge of behavioral health symptoms in the aftermath of traumatic exposure gleaned from experience with soldiers from the first Gulf War (McCarroll, et. al., 2001). At the direction of the Army Surgeon General, Army behavioral health consultants in psychiatry, psychology, and social work immediately assembled in Washington, DC to establish an organized plan to address the behavioral health needs of survivors and their families and the military communities of the Pentagon and other rescue and recovery unit communities. This plan identified resources to provide for the behavioral health needs of involved communities, addressed health care delivery issues, and provided mechanisms for necessary health surveillance.

The team of consultants recognized the possibility that many persons physically injured or exposed to the death or injury of others might either desire counseling or benefit from treatment as a result of symptoms resulting from their losses or related experiences in the aftermath of the attack. They recognized the likelihood of the emergence of traditional psychiatric disorders such as acute stress disorder, posttraumatic stress disorder, and depression as recovery efforts continued and the need for sustained availability of resources after recovery efforts concluded (Ursano and McCarroll, 1990; Ursano et. al., 1995). The team also identified the potential for the emergence of grief-related distress or complicated grief, and challenges posed by the experience of massive shared grief in a community suddenly forced to prepare for war (see Table 16.1). Finally, the consultants recognized the strong relationship between traumatic exposure and medically unexplained physical symptoms. The emergence of "mysterious" postwar syndromes (such as the Gulf War syndrome) (Strauss, 1999; Engel and Katon, 1999) and the well-documented findings of increased somatic complaints and disability in survivors of the Murrah building bombing (North et. al., 1999) were of considerable concern to the consultants because these syndromes shake public confidence in the government's ability to protect its citizenry and in so doing serve the goals of terrorism. Thus, the plan they

TABLE 16.1
Mental health outcomes in the aftermath of mass violent death

Mental Disorders

     Acute stress disorder
     Posttraumatic stress disorder
     Generalized anxiety disorder
     Panic disorder
     Major depressive disorder
     Brief psychotic episode
     Adjustment disorders
     Complicated grief
     Normal bereavement
     Alcohol abuse
     Substance abuse

Distress

     Anger and irritability
     Fear
     Restlessness
     Concentration and attention difficulties
     Intrusive thoughts or images
     Sadness
     Insomnia (with or without nightmares)
     Somatic complaints:
             Headaches, gastrointestinal distress, musculoskeletal pain
     Diminished interest in activities

Distress-related behavior

     Increased alcohol or tobacco use
     Avoidance of workplace/responsibilities
     Avoidance of travel
     Social withdrawal

implemented — subsequently known as Operation Solace — sought to minimize the occurrence and severity of known psychiatric disorders, to prevent the emergence of a "postattack" syndrome of otherwise unexplained somatic symptoms, and to encourage collective and individual mourning in the face of increased operational tempo.

As the community of need was ultimately defined in the Gander experience, Operation Solace planners first risk-stratified potentially impacted military communities from highest to lowest as follows: injured or physically impacted; family member of someone killed or injured; work colleague of someone killed or injured; emergency responder (military or civilian); other Pentagon employees/visitors during and after the attack; and the national capital region population at large. Levels of intervention for all risk groups were identified as: community-based, workplace-based, primary care, or specialty mental health clinic-based. Although there might be a proportionally decreased need for specialty-based intervention as

risk stratification decreased (e.g., among the outer rings of concentric circles defining the community), Gander and other disasters had shown that
although proximity and degree of exposure to trauma were predictive of
symptomatology, those factors alone could not account for the variability of
traumatic stress responses across populations exposed to a given traumatic
event. Operation Solace sought to optimize the identification of persons
requiring each level of care, by concentrating resources necessary to identify
and assess vulnerable persons in the central circles, while still providing outreach resources across all domains of response.

The fundamental manner in which Operation Solace attempted to overcome barriers to care access was by approaching affected community members in the workplace and engaging them as they entered the primary care
system for any type of medical care. The most important component of both
the immediate and sustained mental health response to the violent death
created by the attack was the "forward deployment" of behavioral health professionals to provide outreach services to offices within the Pentagon and to
surrounding civilian offices (some of which became temporary work facilities
for surviving military personnel displaced by the destruction of their offices
in the attacks). The professionals (including psychiatrists, psychologists,
social workers, mental health nurses, and technicians from all branches of the
military service) were organized into multidisciplinary teams that fanned out
through the Pentagon and surrounding buildings in close coordination with
military chaplains. These interventions, defined as "preclinical," allowed for
the team members to engage affected military communities in their work environments in an informal and supportive manner, without requiring the collection of identifying data or opening medical records. The approach assured
maximal access while minimizing premature "medicalization" of appropriate
distress reactions or grief. At the request of key leaders, the team conducted
informational briefings regarding stress response and management, the use of
home and workplace support networks, discussing the tragedy with children,
and the availability of individualized evaluation and treatment resources put
into place after the attack. Team members provided guidance to workplace
supervisors, division or section leaders, and senior military and civilian leadership on principles of "grief leadership" (see Table 16.2). Key leaders actively
participated in the briefings and they often role-modeled and spoke about
the importance of sharing grief and acting as mutual supports that had been
found helpful by investigators after Gander.

A "public health approach" served as the organizing principle, directing preclinical team movement and concentrating resources. This approach
focused efforts on correct identification of high-risk groups and implementation of secondary and tertiary prevention strategies targeting the
most vulnerable populations. Preclinical outreach visits were implemented
using a "concentric circle" strategy with earliest and highest level of support afforded to those people who had offices within the destroyed wedge
of the Pentagon (and those who were displaced from that part of the building), then people located in neighboring wedges, followed by first-responder

TABLE 16.2
Grief leadership actions after mass violent death

Leader actions	Community effects
Public announcements and appearances	Provide useful, accurate information; reestablish a sense of order/control
Press briefings	Reassure families, others; dispel rumors
Calm demeanor	Provide model behavior
Establishes controls, policies	Provide framework for organizing volunteer efforts efficiently
Organizes memorial services	Demonstrate respect for dead and care for families
Attends funerals, grieves	"Give permission" for others to grieve
Announces/endorses assistance programs	Show concern, establish climate of healing, community support
Provides guidance without excessive policy/rules	Communicate trust in others' abilities; foster cooperation, initiative
Describes loss in positive terms: (e.g. heroic sacrifice, an opportunity to learn), recognizes contributions of survivors and helpers	Redirect community energy into rebuilding efforts
Outlines goals for future	Reorient to future objectives; facilitate preparedness for future challenges/losses

Adapted from: Wright, K. M. & Bartone, P. T. (1994). Community responses to disaster: The Gander plane crash. In R. J. Ursano, B. G. McCaughey, & C. S. Fullerton (Eds.), *Individual and community responses to trauma and disaster: The structure of human chaos.* New York: Cambridge University Press.

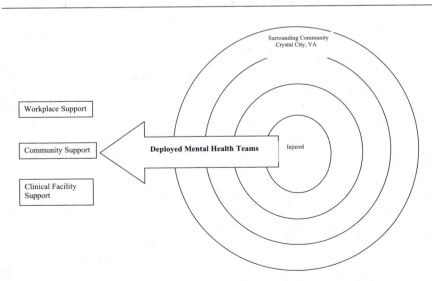

FIGURE 16.2. Public Health Approach to September 11th Pentagon Attack.

TABLE 16.3
Distress reactions and disorders: Vulnerable populations

Leaders

  Work place supervisors
  Religious leaders
  Persons directing and coordinating disaster management

First responders

  Law enforcement personnel
  Firefighters
  Police
  Red Cross/other relief volunteers

Highly exposed

  Close eyewitnesses
  Physically injured
  Uninjured survivors

Bereaved

  Family members
  Close friends

Others

  Children
  Elderly
  Physically disabled
  Persons with chronic physical/mental illness
  Those with previous traumatic exposure

and body handler communities, and those who occupied offices near the Pentagon at the time of the attack (see Figure 16.2). Members of local military units who deployed to provide initial medical response and support to recovery efforts at the Twin Towers were also identified as a result of this outreach, and were afforded similar visits upon their return (see Table 16.3). High levels of specialty staff resources were maintained throughout the holiday season (December and January) and tapered progressively as referrals based from outreach diminished. (Orman et al., 2001)

As with Gander, a family support center was established in the days following the attack. Here again, legal assistance, casualty affairs assistance, Red Cross, military relief services, and adult and child mental health counseling were made readily available to surviving family members of crash victims. There is no military base housing at the Pentagon, so this group traveled from various distances to the Pentagon (alone or with other family members) as the tragedy unfolded. Temporary lodging, daycare, and child schooling services augmented the resources of this center, based on the unique needs of the community it serviced. The family support center, like the preclinical outreach teams, served as a referral source for additional individualized counseling as these needs were identified. Such treatment was provided at the 10 primary care clinics (including the health care clinic at the Pentagon itself, which was staffed with additional mental health specialists after the attack) across the national capital region, and coordinated at remote locations on a case-by-case basis (Orman et al., 2002; Grieger and Lyszcarz, 2002; Grieger et al., 2003).

As the preclinical visits and family assistance center identified individuals requiring more immediate, higher levels of intervention (and referred these to available resources) these sources also developed a voluntary registry of persons considered at higher risk for subsequent difficulties (e.g., child, spouse, close friend, supervisor, or subordinate of someone killed in the attack, physical injury, prior psychiatric illness). Case managers within the initial multidisciplinary teams subsequently hired during the operation followed up with these individuals as the weeks and months after the initial operation to ensure that emerging difficulties were identified, evaluated, and treated as necessary. The extent to which these measures were effective must be measured over time. However, Operation Solace received considerable praise from military leaders and was acknowledged by numerous outspoken survivors and family members. To date, no "post-Pentagon" syndrome of unexplained medical symptoms has emerged.

APPLYING MODELS OF MILITARY RESPONSE TO PUBLIC HEALTH INTERVENTION STRATEGIES

The Gander air disaster and the September 11 terrorist attack on the Pentagon serve as historical illustrations of the components of the military response to mass violent death in accidental and deliberate disasters. The Gander crash involved domains of group and individual response for the family and close friends of the crash victims and others exposed to the trauma of mass violent death (first responders, body handlers, and military and community leaders) across various military communities in Newfoundland, Fort Campbell, Kentucky, Dover, Delaware, and Washington, DC. While the Pentagon is a Department of Defense facility, it is not situated on a traditional military base. Nearly one-half of the Pentagon's 24,000 plus employees are civilians. There is no military family housing colocated with the Pentagon, and the building itself sits at the edge of a civilian business and shopping district (Crystal City, Virginia). Despite restricted access to the building itself, Washington DC's underground mass public transportation system has a public stop located directly below the complex. In many ways, this symbol of American military strength epitomizes the concept of the military as "apart from but a part of" the local community.

The military response to mass violent death after the September 11 terrorist attack on the Pentagon also illustrates the manner in which the military model of domains of response across affected communities might be applied to civilian communities. Since the planes crashed into the Pentagon, the population most immediately affected included family members and close friends of those who perished from the explosion of the plane and those office workers in the "wedge" of the Pentagon who were either injured themselves or witnessed the destruction and death around them as they escaped the building. Other affected communities included first responders, professional colleagues or friends, and other workers in neighboring buildings.

But what if the plane had crashed into a civilian office high-rise in Crystal City, Virginia? In a "civilian" disaster within corporate or business settings, the application of public health approaches to identifying affected groups and those in need of mental health intervention is equally appropriate. Unanticipated death, as might result from the deployment of weapons of mass destruction (and occurred to some degree after the anthrax attacks of 2001), would also require a public health model for quantifying need, and allocating intervention and outreach resources. The degree to which the U.S. military might spearhead the medical and mental health response to these attacks is speculative, but the high number of military personnel living and working in the area would necessitate a military component to the response. In such a case the military approach would have likely been very similar. Multidisciplinary teams would be assembled and would fan out in concentric circles from the epicenter of the crash to identify subgroups that lost family members or coworkers. Teams would have engaged members of these communities at the workplace in a supportive, nonintrusive manner, offering educational briefings, consulting with leaders, and encouraging them to demonstrate the appropriateness of shared grief through rituals. The teams would provide informal individual counseling (and appropriate referral) through periodic site visits and the establishment of a family assistance center. Efforts would concentrate resources first in areas where the largest groups of vulnerable or affected populations were identified but have remained responsive to the potential needs of lower risk-stratified groups through established appropriate networks to available primary and specialty care clinics. Resources would be tapered over time as utilization diminished — but would be increased during anniversary or holiday periods. The same civilian first-responder groups that responded to the Pentagon attack would have responded to a disaster centered on a high-rise office building in Crystal City, and so these groups would have been similarly identified and approached for needs assessment.

Uniformed military personnel mix comfortably with civilian businesspeople and shoppers in the region surrounding the Pentagon, so the use of military teams and a military-staffed family assistance center might have been viewed with suspicion by some, but many others would presumably have been receptive to such services — particularly given the perception of the U.S. military as responsible for services to the nation in times of emergency. In other communities, the degree of military presence before an event might diminish the extent to which the military would be called upon to respond in the aftermath of a disaster resulting in mass violent death. Local government, in consultation with FEMA may or may not deem military assistance necessary. With appropriate planning, civilian resources could sufficiently identify affected communities and bring to bear the domains of individual, workplace, primary, and specialty care across affected communities exposed to mass violent death. Military members and their families remain vulnerable to such experiences as a result of occupational and environmental risk factors unique to military life. Thus, the lessons learned from military experience with these catastrophes should inform future civilian public health interventions in the aftermath of mass violent death. Study of the extent to which specific intervention or combination (e.g., cognitive–behavioral therapy, other exposure-based therapies, pharmacotherapy, or psychological first aid) utilized in public health approaches will actually prevent the development of PTSD and complicated grief, or mitigate depression or other distress reactions, is only in its infancy. Even as best practices become clarified on the basis of further study, optimal promulgation will rely on thoughtful identification of the numerous potential communities and an understanding of the range of distress responses that individuals within these communities may develop.

REFERENCES

Engel, C. C. & Katon, W. J. (1999). Population and need-based prevention of unexplained symptoms.in the community." In Jollenbeck, J. M., Russell, P. K., and Guze, S. B. (Eds.) *Institute of medicine. Strategies to protect the health of deployed U.S. forces: Medical surveillance, record keeping, and risk reduction.* Washington, D.C.: National Academy Press, 31–40.

Greiger, T. A. & Lyszarz, J. L. (2002). Psychiatric responses by the U.S. Navy to the Pentagon attack. *Military Medicine, 167* (Suppl. 9), 24–25.

Grieger, T. A., Fullerton, C. S., & Ursano, R. J. (2003). Posttraumatic stress disorder, alcohol use, and perceived safety after the terrorist attack on the Pentagon. *Psychiatric Services, 54,* 1380–1382.

Ingraham, L. H. (1987a). Grief leadership. In *The human response to the Gander military air disaster: A summary report* (pp. 10–12). Division of Neuropsychiatry Report No. 88-12. Washington, D.C.: Walter Reed Army Institute of Research,

Ingraham, L. H. (1987b). Conclusions. In *The human response to the Gander military air disaster: A summary report* (pp. 37–39). Division of Neuropsychiatry Report No. 88-12. Washington D.C.: The Walter Reed Army Institute of Research.

McCaroll, J. E., Ursano, R. J., Fullerton, C. S., et al. (2001). Effects of exposure to death in a war: Mortuary on posttraumatic stress disorder symptoms of intrusion and avoidance. *Journal of Nervous and Mental Disease, 189,* 44–48.

North, C. S., Nixon, S. J., Shariat, S., et al. (1999). Psychiatric disorders among survivors of the Oklahoma City Bombing. *Journal of the American Medical Association, 282,* 755–762.

Orman. D. T., Robichaux, R. J., Crandell, E. O., et al. (2002). Operation solace: Overview of the mental health intervention following the September 11, 2001 Pentagon Attack. *Military Medicine, 167* (Suppl. 4), 47.

Strauss, S. E.(1999). Bridging the gulf in war syndromes. *Lancet, 353,* 162–163.

Ursano, R., Fullerton, C., Kao, T., et al. (1995). Longitudinal assessment of posttraumatic stress disorder and depression after exposure to traumatic death. *Journal of Nervous and Mental Disease, 183,* 36–42.

Ursano, R. J. & McCarroll, J. E. (1990). The nature of the traumatic stressor: Handling dead bodies. *Journal of Nervous and Mental Disease, 178,* 396–398.

Wright, K. M. & Bartone, P. T. (1994). Community responses to disaster: The Gander plane crash. In R. J. Ursano, B. G. McCaughey, & C. S. Fullerton (Eds.), *Individual and community responses to trauma and disaster: The structure of human chaos* (pp. 267–284). New York: Cambridge University Press.

17

Community Outreach Following a Terrorist Act: Violent Death and the Oklahoma City Experience

JAMES R. ALLEN, PHEBE TUCKER, AND BETTY PFEFFERBAUM

Oklahoma City Bombing

The terrorist bombing in Oklahoma City in 1995 occurred in a community that was small and cohesive enough to allow consolidated community-based projects of emotional support for bereaved family members of the 168 adults and children who were killed and for others who were affected. The authors' involvement in the immediate, intermediate, and long-term emotional residual has produced rich insights. Their clinical observations and data collection suggest guiding principles for clinical assessment and intervention, but it is their sociocultural observations of the long-term effects of traumatic grief and restoration within the community that is equally revealing and novel. The importance of communal retelling is emphasized by an in-depth description of restoration within and between Oklahoma City community members and agencies — beyond the clinical confines of diagnosis and prognosis. The authors close the chapter with a list of 17 "lessons learned," that is as refreshing as it is comprehensive.

The first wave of hot gas was later estimated to have traveled at 7,000 miles an hour. In less than a second it dissipated, to be replaced by a vacuum which created a pressure wave that moved outward and upward, lifting the building and causing floors and beams to weaken and collapse. Then, gravity took over and nine stories of the Alfred P. Murrah Federal Building pancaked.

In a matter of seconds on April 19, 1995, downtown Oklahoma City changed. The bombing was the worst act of terrorism that had been committed on U.S. soil up to that time: the largest mass murder (168); the largest crime scene (800 building structures and almost 50 square blocks); the largest criminal assault (853 injured); and the most costly crime (estimated $625 million in property damage).

Oklahoma City is relatively small, its population stable. More than a third (38.5%) of the community knew someone killed (Smith, Christiansen, Vincent, & Hann, 1999) and most of those affected did not move away. Although the Murrah Building housed 17 different federal agencies, the city's infrastructure was not destroyed. Consequently, Oklahoma City presents a unique opportunity to examine the intermediate (10-year) effects of a single occurrence of terrorism and violent death.

Immediate outreach in response to a crisis has generally been conceptualized in terms of the reaching out by professionals to those in need. The 10-year follow-up of the Oklahoma City bombing, however, reveals a second phase: community groups forming, usually spontaneously, to reach out to others.

Nevertheless, there are several problems in drawing conclusions from the Oklahoma City experience, beginning with problems in definition. First, disasters are sometimes defined by the events themselves and sometimes by their consequences, whether these be physical, psychological, or social. At least temporarily, they overwhelm psychological and physical integrity, However, they also have later long-term effects, for they change perceptions, beliefs, and lifestyles. Unlike other causes of violent death, a terrorist attack aims at influencing the behavior of people other than the victims. Consequently, it takes on additional political and emotional colorings.

Second, there are problems in defining community. Communities are conceptualized as groups with a sense of a common identity and destiny, and complex sets of bonds and interactions; that is, they have both psychological and practical boundaries. They usually have geographical boundaries too, within which social organization provides people with what they need for everyday life. This was true of Oklahoma City. However, because of the widespread, indeed international response, the Oklahoma City bombing also became a national event.

Temporarily at least, a disaster alters the ways in which individuals relate, their social organization, and the availability and utilization of resources. In an extreme case, a disaster may even threaten a community's existence. Property destruction by the bombing, however, was limited to a region in downtown Oklahoma City. A memorial now stands at the site.

Third, there are the problems of defining outreach. A proactive posture is necessary to reach people who need help but may not seek it themselves. There are many reasons for this. Even in nondisaster situations, reluctance to use formal assistance may reflect an emphasis on independence, carrying one's own weight, and avoiding the stigma of using "public welfare." To complain sets an individual apart from those who are undamaged. Thus, seeking help overtly may undermine both a person's sense of self-control and self-esteem, and his or her social reputation. Others have described a trauma membrane, a comfort zone within which survivors of trauma comfort each other and often reject outside help (Lindy, Grace, & Green, 1981). Certainly, in our work with Oklahoma City children and their families we found that some avoided formal assistance in order to protect themselves and to ward off unwanted feelings (Whittlesey et al., 1999). Avoidance is one of the three key symptoms of posttraumatic stress disorder, but it is also a coping mechanism, and it is difficult to accept, let alone look for help, while avoiding unpleasant feelings and reminders, or trying to deny either the effects of an event, its significance, or that anything can be done. In addition, not seeking or accepting help fits with being a certain kind of angry victim in a drama triangle of victims, rescuers, and persecutors.

Because of some people's reluctance to seek help, it has been suggested that clinicians should deliver services in unconventional settings including shelters, schools, work sites, and other gathering places of victims of a disaster. Two important goals in this early phase are: (1) fostering natural healing processes and maximizing the ability of people to draw on mechanisms for healing within their communities, and (2) decreasing the resistance to treatment of those needing more intensive interventions.

WHAT AND BY WHOM?

Immediately after the explosion, four fire department companies were on site. One hundred and fifty police officers were there within 15 minutes. Medical personnel quickly became first-line responders as well. One nurse responder was killed. Later, the Oklahoma County Medical Association was awarded the American Medical Association's Medal of Valor for its efforts. This was the fourth time it has been awarded and the only time it has been awarded to a group.

Mental health professionals may regard emotional support as important when high-stress situations overwhelm people's internal resources, but it was not regarded as such by many of the victims. For them, the immediate "real" issues were to identify and bury the dead, obtain medical care, and grieve losses. Intent on helping the most seriously affected, many traditional mental health professionals tended to discount the importance of outreach, and regarded it as superficial and a waste of money. The victims, however, often did not access the services they offered, arrived late, or cancelled appointments (Call & Pfefferbaum, 1999). Indeed, Call and Pfefferbaum concluded that it might have been better to have had more outreach, especially during the first six months, even if for a shorter period of time than was offered in Oklahoma.

As time passed, individual and community needs changed and unmet needs and duplication of services became apparent. A committee was established in Oklahoma City to address these needs. It continued to function for more than three years. However, the evaluation of unmet needs was complicated by avoidance and the fact that some needs became apparent only after the committee had finished its work.

In May 1995, the Oklahoma Department of Mental Health and Substance Abuse Services sponsored five half-day workshops to obtain community input into the development of specific mental health goals for disaster recovery. This appears unique in the literature on disaster recovery.

TO, FOR, OR WITH WHOM?

It is impossible to be a helper without someone to help, and among mental health workers there was much debriefing of one another and squabbling over turf. Even worse, at times a few of the people who came for help were not seen as "proper victims," but rather just the "ordinary" homeless, mentally ill, or drug addicted. One would-be helper who had come from a nearby city was horrified when her first "patient" turned out to be a runaway youth who wanted 75 cents to buy a condom — and the loan of her car! Like some others, she felt exploited.

INITIAL RESPONSES, INCLUDING OUTREACH

After a Red Cross command center had assisted in initial efforts to rescue people, take care of the injured, and provide confirmation of deaths and survivals, it became apparent that other basic needs such as housing and transportation had to be met before higher-level ones — a demonstration of Maslow's hierarchy (1954). However, the most appropriate timetable to accomplish this varied significantly between different groups. For example, the bodies of the last victims were not removed from the ruins for three weeks. This allowed members of their families to maintain, for several days, hope of finding them alive.

The Oklahoma Department of Mental Health and Substance Abuse Services became the lead organization in crafting the mental health response. Project Heartland, funded by the Federal Emergency Management Agency (FEMA), opened May 15, 1995. It was the first community mental health program in the United States designed to intervene in the short to medium term with survivors of a major terrorist event. Its goals were to provide outreach, education, support groups, and crisis counseling to individuals affected by the bombing. The project had three phases: From May to October 1995, emphasis was on outreach, crisis counseling, support, consultation, and education.

The second phase, from September to December 1996, emphasized contract services to target populations. A third phase addressed the McVeigh trial, January 1997 to February 1998.

In the first few months, trauma-related training was provided to a variety of natural caregivers, such as ministers. The media publicized the availability of services, described typical reactions to disaster, and encouraged discussions with friends. The local psychiatric association manned a telephone bank. As for the generalizability of these efforts, however, it should be remembered that the Oklahoma City infrastructure was left intact, and people were reacting to a single isolated event.

During its first two years, Project Heartland and its eight subcontracted partner organizations screened and evaluated 242 people, supplied emergency services and crisis intervention to 11,629, counseling and therapy to 3,997, and outreach to 106,440 (Call & Pfefferbaum, 1999). Outreach workers visited every home and business within a mile of the blast, as well as the homes of survivors, victims' families, and rescue workers. Two intensive retreats were held for the people directly affected by the bomb. Apartment dwellers were assisted in returning to their homes in the downtown area. Announcements and news about programs, relevant events, and materials about traumatic bereavement were sent to survivors and to families of the dead.

Gradually, however, these efforts as well as social support and public interest diminished, favors were exhausted, and savings and insurance payments used up. This was unfortunate because some psychological distress did not emerge until later.

Approximately 40,000 students were enrolled in the Oklahoma City public schools at the time of the explosion. Six schools were situated within five miles of the bomb site. One of them sustained structural damage. Allen, Dlugokinski, Cohen, and Walker (1999) developed what they called the "Listen to Children Interview" used in the schools to provide an opportunity for children to discuss their stories in a group setting, to facilitate sharing, to listen to the coping strategies of other children, and to expand their options of response. The interview process begins at the cognitive level, grounding the children in the facts of the event, then explores their emotional responses at the time of the disaster, validates the individual, provides ideas for ways to cope with difficult feelings and situations, and finally concludes with education regarding coping, thus bringing the children back into cognitive processing before they leave the group.

Close to 50,000 contact hours were provided by Project Heartland to more than 5,000 students, parents, and school personnel through individual counseling, support groups, training, and other services. Outreach activities to 109,423 included door-to-door visits and mailings. Fifty-seven pupils were evaluated and referred, 2,491 received counseling, largely by students in professional training programs, and 2,519 received emergency services and crisis intervention (Pfefferbaum, Nixon, et al., 1999). However, very few children were actually referred by the school-based counselors to the programs established to provide bomb-related services. Sometimes, it was the child who actively avoided treatment because of painful memories or revenge fantasies, to protect parents or other relatives, or to avoid being seen as "crazy" by peers. Sometimes, it was the parents who avoided, either to protect the child or to protect themselves. Not infrequently, a conspiracy of silence developed supporting this avoidance, at times including school counselors who either did not recognize pathology or were hesitant to ask for help (Whittlesey et al., 1999). It is a matter of concern that only 15% of middle and high school students with high posttraumatic symptoms scores sought counseling (Pfefferbaum, Call and Sconzo, et al., 2003).

PSYCHOLOGICAL REACTIONS

The initial psychological interventions that most people seemed to need included an opportunity to tell and retell what happened and their reactions to it, and receive encouragement to resume familiar everyday activities. They needed a way to structure their time, something to do. They needed to be validated, to feel that they were seen and heard, that they had done what they could, and had made some kind of impact. They needed to feel safe, for their sense of a secure base and trust had been shaken. Indeed, Tucker, Dickson, Pfefferbaum, McDonald, and Allen (1997) reported that anxiety and distress at the behavior of others at the time of the bombing were major predictors of the later problems of 86 adults who sought treatment during the first six months after the bombing. These authors suggested that distress at the behavior of others may be evidence of diminished interpersonal trust and terrorism's ability to erode social harmony.

A number of people were too readily diagnosed as suffering from PTSD after superficial screening, just because they had been connected with the bombing. There were also problems arising from the use of the terms *victim* and *survivor*. These are terms with implicit and sometimes unfortunate implications and prognoses. Unfortunately too, the media pushed pop psychology ideas of "healing" and "closure," although most people seemed to have hoped for the latter rather than really expected it. The idea of closure, a surgical metaphor, sometimes encouraged pathogenic and unrealistic expectations and unnecessary grief for the people who did not meet some preordained and usually rather rigid timetable. This was especially noteworthy after the implosion of the Murrah Building on May 23, 1995, after McVeigh's sentencing, and after his execution in 1997. Each of these events was heralded as the date for "closure." In retrospect, for most people, mass death might better be considered an event to be endured rather than a trauma to be healed.

In the first few weeks after the bombing, there was a 25% decrease in school attendance (Wong, 2001), but this gradually returned to normal. Seven weeks later, approximately 15% of the respondents to a survey of 3,218 local middle and high school students reported that they still did not feel safe at all (Pfefferbaum, Nixon, Krug, et al., 1999). These worries persisted, with about 34% of elementary school children reporting concerns about family members 10 months later (Gurwich, Pfefferbaum, & Leftwich, 2002). For up to one year, one-fifth of the children had trouble calming down in the face of reminders of the event (Gurwich, Sitterle, Young, & Pfefferbaum, 2002).

Approximately five months after the bombing, 19% of the 1,696 local mental health professionals in private practice who had received a survey reported an approximate 8% increase in new patients with bomb-related needs. Oklahoma City community mental health centers reported an 8.2% increase in patients during May, with return to normal demands for treatment by August (Tucker, Boehler, Dickson, Lensgraf, & Jones, 1999).

Using the Diagnostic Interview Schedule/Disaster Supplement, a methodologically rigorous study of 182 direct victims selected from a confidential registry of 255 eligible survivors six months after the bombing, found that 45% suffered a postdisaster psychiatric disorder and that 34.3% had post-traumatic stress disorder (North, Nixon, et al., 1999). Predictors included female sex, disaster exposure, and predisaster psychiatric diagnosis. The onset of PTSD was swift, with 76% reporting that it began the first day. The relatively uncommon avoidance and numbing symptoms virtually assured the diagnosis of PTSD. Indeed, 94% who met avoidance and numbing criteria also met full criteria for PTSD diagnoses. However, in the majority of nonpsychiatrically ill persons, the nearly universal symptoms of hyperarousal and intrusive reexperiencing could have been addressed by nonmedical interventions and support. That is, most individuals were quite resilient, but a significant number were not. The degree of occupational and social impairment associated with PTSD appeared to be mediated in large part by psychiatric comorbidity, most commonly depression. No new cases of substance abuse were observed.

Some people first presented for treatment after the second anniversary of the event, and this phenomenon recurred after later anniversaries, the 9/11 attack, and the invasion of Iraq. During the first few years, there was an exacerbation of mental health problems in those with prior psychiatric diagnoses (Tucker, Pfefferbaum, Vincent, Boehler, & Nixon, 1998). An ongoing clinical trial of the use of two antipsychotics to treat schizophrenia was affected transiently by the bombing. Participants' symptoms increased for a few months but then returned to prebombing levels without requiring medication adjustment (Tucker, 2003).

One and a half to three years after the bombing, a telephone study of the long-term health outcomes of 494 persons, 92% of whom had been physically injured, revealed that 79% rated their general health status as good to excellent (Shariat, Mallonee, Kruger, Farmer, & North, 1999). One fourth, however, reported they had been newly diagnosed with anxiety or depression. One third reported that preexisting medical conditions, including depression (26%) had worsened. The most frequently reported posttraumatic symptoms were "being jumpy" or experiencing "recurring distressful thoughts of the bombing." The most frequently utilized health service was psychological counseling (63%). Rates of posttraumatic symptoms were found to increase as the severity of injury increased. Although 90% stated they had not changed their social habits, 13% reported engaging in fewer leisure activities, and 15% made fewer visits to family and friends.

RESCUE WORKERS

Despite debriefing, the Oklahoma City police chief reported the number of divorces among local police officers and firefighters had risen by 20% to 25% as of midyear 1998 (C. Jones, 1998). It is unknown how many had a prior history of mental illness or had sought mental health treatment (Tucker, Boehler, et al., 1999).

Two years later, on the other hand, the prevalence of posttraumatic stress and depressive symptomatology of 51 body handlers who were willing to respond to a survey was relatively low. Those most in need of treatment had sought it (14% of those surveyed). Of the four with the most posttraumatic symptoms, all reported "jumpiness" at one year. Three reported new medical problems, and 10% reported increased alcohol use in the first two years (Tucker et al., 2002). The low incidence of problems might be attributed to debriefings, the community recognition they received, or to the protective effects of assuming a professional role.

Thirty-four months after the bombing, North, Tivis, McMillen, Pfefferbaum, Spitznagel, et al. (2002) used the Diagnostic Interview Schedule to assess the psychopathology of male firefighters retrospectively both before and after the bombing. Findings from this volunteer sample (representing less than one quarter of the firefighters involved), were compared with those of male primary survivors. The prevalence of posttraumatic stress disorder was significantly lower in the rescue workers (13%) than in the sample of primary survivors (23%), which was assessed approximately six months after the event. Generally, the firefighters reported little functional impairment, positive social adjustment, and high job satisfaction (North, Tivis, McMillen, Pfefferbaum, Cox, et al., 2002). PTSD in the firefighters, when present, however, was associated with reduced job satisfaction and functional impairment, giving diagnostic validity to the diagnosis. Preexisting psychopathology, it was noted, strongly predicted general postdisaster psychopathology. The resilience seen in these firefighters, the authors concluded, may be related to their preparedness, experience, career selection, the fewer injuries they suffered, and to postdisaster mental health interventions.

VICTIMIZATION, REAL AND IMAGINED, ENTITLEMENT, AND RIVALRIES

Overnight, some of the survivors' and victims' family members became media celebrities. This had a mixed effect. Their particular sense of wounded innocence and specialness, combined with the outpouring of support from around the world, encouraged a sense of entitlement. As one woman complained, "Why do they think they own me? They only paid for my car and my house." Some became quite angry when checks and packages addressed to them personally were delivered to the Red Cross, which was overseeing the donations and the insurance settlements on which they were dependent. On the other hand, total strangers came to Oklahoma City to find the graves of the dead children and otherwise behaved in ways suggestive of an intimacy that did not exist. One woman was stalked. One mother even had to take legal action to prevent her dead child's picture from being marketed on a T-shirt (Allen & Allen, 1998b).

Within the bond of sensed uniqueness that developed among the mothers and grandmothers of the dead children, rivalries soon emerged. This was often secondary to media attention. For example, the mother of one child whose body made the covers of nationally circulated magazines told a reporter: "I've taken a lot of grief from other parents because my baby is getting more attention than their children" (Allen, J. R., et al., 1999). Some of the parents of dead children found themselves angry at the parents of living children. At times, this led to formerly close-knit families no longer holding family gatherings.

Rage and Resentment

Anger may be part of the grief process. However, a major additional factor in Oklahoma City was a sense of being exploited. Too frequently, this was an accurate perception, whether the exploitation was for public relations, political, or economic reasons. Worse still, those who had become national celebrities, and who had developed an identity as such, and whose stories and opinions the media had sought repeatedly, were later ignored, yesterday's news.

Rage directed specifically at helpers and caregivers, however, also had many other causes: the fact that one aspect of a person's social support system cannot replace another, feeling misunderstood or not understood at all, and helpers not being sufficiently sensitive to the pace or style of an individual's particular mourning. The rather simplistic models of stages of grief supplied by the media suggested a series of discrete emotional responses which follow in a predictable order. This did not happen. Such models also did not address the symptoms of avoidance, intrusiveness, and sympathetic arousal that may follow trauma and actively interfere with grieving.

In such an atmosphere it might have been predicted that people would be suspicious of being actively deceived. This was the experience of many, including some federal employees, for example, who concluded that their input as to the location of the new federal building — including information given in a special trip to Washington — was ignored, and that the alternative work sites and opportunities they thought they had been promised did not materialize in a timely manner.

Narratives of Understanding and Their Role in Determining
Appropriate Outreach and Other Responses

We make sense of events by putting them into narratives, and narratives lead easily to questions of cause (Allen & Allen, 1998a). As the philosopher Nietzsche (1889/1968) once noted, "If we possess our why of life, we can put up with almost any how" (p. 23). Meaning is important in mastering a sense of helplessness and in overcoming a sense of vulnerability, and people need to rebuild a sense of purpose when their assumptive world has been shattered. Meanings also sustain and are sustained by the cultural fabric which binds individuals into community. Unfortunately, under threat people may lose the ability to conceptualize themselves and others as thinking and feeling entities and the skill to act on this, leading to rigid or magical thinking, splitting, and projection (Holmes, 1996).

The narratives coconstructed after the Oklahoma bombing shaped media activity, political rhetoric, and community response (Allen & Allen, 1999). Almost immediately, competing narratives were elaborated about just what the bombing meant for America and for the individuals affected. Each of these identified certain types of responses, including outreach, as more or less appropriate.

The media immediately began to speak of a loss of a state of innocence — forgetting the losses, betrayals, and aggressiveness that have characterized our history. True, for many people the bombing did destroy any sense of a secure base and did shatter assumptions that middle America was immune from violence.

At first, it was assumed that the bombing was the work of Middle Eastern terrorists. Then, it was discovered that the perpetrator was an American with strong roots in that traditional initiation into American masculinity, the army, and that he had even won medals for Gulf War service. Worse yet, it was feared that he might be the harbinger of a new domestic threat: post-Vietnam American militias with grievances, legitimate or not, against the federal government.

Perhaps, one of the most helpful narratives was articulated by Vice President Gore who spoke of resilience and family in his televised address on the first anniversary of the bombing, reminding Oklahomans of how they had faced other crises, such as the dust bowl and the Depression. Ironically, in Waco, Texas, another group was also meeting that day. The survivors of the Branch Davidians gathered and remembered that they too had once been a family (Allen, 1999)!

Another helpful narrative was enunciated by Attorney General Reno at the Inaugural Symposium of the Oklahoma Memorial Institute on October 25, 1998. Referring to the church service held on the Sunday after the bombing, she observed that the people of Oklahoma City had showed that they would not give in to terrorism and that they would continue to function and solve problems within the rule of law. Indeed, promulgating the idea that terrorism does not work has become a driving force in the work of the Oklahoma City Memorial. However, this idea also has led to distress. For example, it was decided to build a new federal building adjacent to the bombing site. In the minds of decision-makers, this decision may have demonstrated a refusal to give in to terrorism. It has, however, meant that survivors have had to walk daily past the graves of their former colleagues to a building with a wall whose gaping space reminds them of its damaged predecessor. Considering what white men have done to the Kiowa Indians, claims that this space represents a Kiowa dance ground can hardly be expected to be comforting.

Narratives of Guilt and Innocent Victimhood

Memories alone do not sustain our sense of personhood. We are our stories, the accounts of what has happened to us, and what we hope will happen. For stories, we need a protagonist, someone who does things or to whom things are done. In this context, the question "why" and ideas of "before" and "after" are never far off. The resulting stories tend to gravitate toward two poles and to sort out around the axis of competence, pride, or guilt on one hand and victimization on the other: "I did this" or "This happened to me (through no fault of my own)." Such themes then tend to organize our memories and justify our present activities. (Fenwick, 2005)

On the south wall of the old Journal Record Building next door to the Murrah Building, and now the National Memorial Museum, for example, a rescue worker painted a slogan that has been left untouched, and is much quoted. It transforms a God of creation into a God of vengeance:

4-19-95

We seek the truth.
We seek justice.
The courts require it,
the victims cry for it,
and God demands it.

The capacity to acknowledge and accept one's suffering as real, even if unjustified, is important. A sense of pathos results from coming to terms with one's relative helplessness. However, this differs from the pitifulness that comes to operate as subtle (or not so subtle) interpersonal coercion. Both responses occurred.

Ironically, some first responders suffered guilt even as they were celebrated as heroes. They felt that no matter what they had accomplished they still had failed because so many died. In 1999, the Memorial Foundation Families and Survivors group added the rescuers to its title: "Families, Survivors, and Rescue Workers."

Religious Narratives

Almost immediately, there were formal and informal prayers in churches and anywhere people met. This was soon followed by widely televised memorial services. These ceremonies gave people something to do when they did not know what to do. For some, religious leaders and religious ceremonies addressing the historical lineage of human suffering or man's capacity for regeneration or forgiveness were powerful sources of endurance and purpose. Among other people, a vision of a vast cosmic struggle, the forces of good contending against forces of evil, and a subtext of the need to right the balance of good and evil in the world, became popular, although, as Pagels has noted (1996), the Christian gospels are not essentially Manichaean. The Christian tradition, she notes, derives much of its power from the conviction that Christ has already won although the believer may be besieged by evil forces. Nevertheless, one survivor who worked in the Murrah Building, Caren Cook, seems to have spoken for many when she stated: "Many lives of precious people were sacrificed to show the world that grace and love overcome evil." In keeping with this sentiment, she created a memory box entitled "An Explosion of Grace" to honor her dead coworkers (A Celebration of the Spirit, 1996). In his statement to the Capitol press corps at 5:30 a.m. on April 19, President Clinton aligned himself with the forces of good: "The bombing in Oklahoma City … was an act of cowardice and it was evil. The United States will not tolerate it." Later in his eulogy at the memorial service, he said, "As St. Paul admonished us 'Let us not be overcome by evil, but overcome evil with good.'"

In the days following the attack, the battle of good versus evil was a major theme of the Oklahoma City Memorial. Ten years later, however, it had been replaced by an emphasis on hope, on remembrance of the dead, and on promulgation of the idea that terrorism does not work. The sole visible reference to a battle of good versus evil today is on a bronze plaque on the fence outside. In contrast, on the tenth anniversary, a National Week of Hope was proclaimed and a "Reflections on Hope Award" was given to two Afghan women who had founded the Voice of Afghan Women Radio. However, in his address at the memorial Vice President Cheney returned to the Manichaean theme. "Goodness overcame evil that day," he said. He then added, "we want to remember not a single act of malice, but also 10,000 acts of kindness" (Raymond, 2005).

Facing the hopelessness of one's situation may be so unbearable that it is easier to assume that it was one's badness that caused it. This is a decision commonly made by abused children, but this is also a belief that came to haunt some Oklahomans who believe in a God that is both all powerful and totally just. There is also a strong local belief that if people are good, God will take care of them and protect them from harm. When the bombing occurred, it was as if they had a contract with God and He broke it! A therapist might regard this as a rather crooked, one-way, and imaginary child–parent transaction, but these people experienced the bombing as a shattering of their whole belief system, a crisis of faith made worse by the 19 young children who were killed.

A variety of other religious narratives also developed, sometimes of a redemptive nature, sometimes of an apocalyptical one. This is not surprising in a state where much of the population defines itself as born-again

Christian. Almost immediately a book appeared which reported a series of local miracles, including the sighting of a cloud of angels (R. Jones, 1995).

Narratives of "Before" and "After"

A narrative which gained great popularity among media, editorial writers, and survivors was that survivors, the city, and the country would be negatively changed forever (Allen & Allen, 1998b). At once obvious and simplistic, when combined with the media's ubiquitous lists of PTSD symptoms and dramatic expostulations of America's loss of innocence, it provided some people with a guidebook on what to expect. It justified expectations of and demands for compensation. It minimized the possibility of resilience. Although the bombing was indeed a marker event, this narrative ignored the important fact that people had lives before the bombing and after it. One can hardly blame the bombing for preexisting problems — but this was commonly done. One woman, for example, who at middle age had still been highly dependent financially on her mother who was killed, now became dependent on various social agencies, and became enraged when they did not pay for all her needs. Marriages and families weak in cohesion before the bombing were at a disadvantage in dealing with new stressors. A local joke among some police officers became "the bombing made me do it!"

Trauma can, in reality, lead to problems in the regulation of affective states such as anxiety, anger, and sexuality, and problems in social attachment, which may manifest in excessive dependence or isolation (Allen, Pfefferbaum, Speed, & Hammond, 2005). Such changes could make people vulnerable to engaging in a variety of pathological attempts at self-regulation, including alcoholism, chemical abuse, and domestic abuse (Bachrach, 1999). Alterations in the neurobiological processes involved in stimulus discrimination, attention and concentration, dissociation and socialization, as well as shattered trust and hope, a sense of urgency, and a foreshortened sense of future can result, but so can other outcomes.

POLITICS AND CIVIL LIBERTIES

The Oklahoma City bombing has given rise to considerable debate over civil liberties, and has led to political activity and changes in laws. In part, this was probably exacerbated by the troubling fact that McVeigh saw himself acting as a soldier, fighting against government oppression and intrusion. Before September 11, it should be remembered, the most dangerous terrorist groups in the United States were radical Christians such as those who bombed abortion clinics, the kind of groups to which McVeigh reportedly had ties. Not all Christians were terrorists, but most terrorists claimed to be Christians! Local right-wing talk radio had fed antigovernment threats, leading to fear and a sense of vulnerability. One of these talk show hosts notoriously had even been giving advice on how best to shoot government agents!

Soon after the bombing, a section of Pennsylvania Avenue near the White House was closed, over $600 million was spent to improve security in federal buildings, and President Clinton asked Congress to pass his Omnibus Counterterrorism Act. The latter, ironically, was designed to deal with foreign terrorists but it followed a TWA crash originally believed to be due to terrorist activity as well as the Oklahoma City bombing. In 1998, the federal government reported having spent $82,506,558 to investigate the bombing and prosecute its case (Clay, 2005).

TRANSFORMATION OF THE EVENT: FROM MASS MURDER TO PATRIOTIC SACRIFICE

There soon was talk of the bombing site as "sacred ground." A country and western music video, "You Can't Break America's Heart" (Red River), was released. These phenomena heralded a movement toward transforming this event of mass murder into one of patriotic sacrifice. In an article entitled "After the Bombing," the *Christian Science Monitor* stated that "all Americans have a responsibility to those killed in war to ensure their sacrifice was not in vain." (1995, p. 20). Later, a group of Oklahoma survivors and family members campaigned to be compensated in the same manner as the victims and families of 9/11 — and took their lack of success as an insult.

CYCLES OF LOSS AND GAIN

Loss and gain occurred together. Loss of workmates and places of employment sometimes paradoxically increased people's sense of personal mastery, even to an exhilarating degree, for having survived at all or having brought others to safety. Living in a shelter while one's apartment was repaired resulted in increased family closeness, gratitude, and bonding — or in increased family conflict, although from attachment theory, we might expect that threatening situations will increase behaviors to maintain proximity to attachment figures for security and reassurance, at least in the immediate and short term.

People seem to weigh loss more highly than gain. Cycles of gain did occur, but they generally seemed to do so much more slowly than cycles of loss. Trust, for example, is broken quickly, but creating a trusting relationship can take years. The bombing destroyed businesses and homes in a few seconds, but, despite the influx of much money, it has taken some people a long time to recreate their businesses. Some have not yet been able to do this.

Community Groups Reach Out: A Second Wave of Outreach

Over time a number of activities emerged wherein people have organized to help themselves and to reach out to others. These activities have involved subgroups of the Oklahoma City community in a variety of efforts: memorialization, bearing witness, formation of victims' rights groups, political action, befriending others, and education and prevention. Each of these became a source of validation, approval, social recognition, integration, a sense of mastery, and an opportunity to change passivity into activity.

Memorialization

Today, the Oklahoma City National Memorial Foundation is an affiliate of the National Parks. It is a new model of public–private partnership. The outdoor symbolic memorial consists of three structures: a reflecting pool, the Field of 168 Empty Chairs, and The Gates of Time, one marking 9:01 a.m., "The time of innocence" and the other marking 9:03 a.m., "When we were changed forever."

In 2001, the Oklahoma City National Memorial Center officially opened. Today, it contains a museum, executive space, archival space, and office space for the Oklahoma National Memorial Institute for Prevention of Terrorism. The memorial mission statement reads:

> We come here to remember those who were killed, those who survived, and those changed forever. May all who leave here know the impact of violence. May the memorial offer comfort, strength, peace, hope, and security.

The Fence: A Spontaneous Shrine

The wire fence that was constructed around what was left of the Murrah Building quickly became a site of public mourning, and was transformed by diverse motives into an emotionally charged space where all who visited were free to share their feelings and their interpretations. People continue to do so today, coming from all over the country to leave flowers, teddy bears, poems, and birthday greetings for the dead.

The Oklahoma Arts Institute and the Role of Art

Six months after the bombing, the Oklahoma Arts Institute, Quartz Mountain, the Oklahoma School of the Arts for talented high school students, extended an open invitation to the survivors and families of bombing victims to meet together with professional artists at their retreat in southwestern Oklahoma. One hundred and twenty people showed up. Together, they explored the healing properties of art — dance, painting, poetry, short stories, basket weaving, song, and the making of memory boxes. The goal was not therapy per se but to help participants, working together, to transform their experiences and give them significance as they shared stories of those they had lost. The weekend provided a time and space to meet with other survivors, to connect with the health in themselves, to begin to transform what had happened to them into a larger story, to use their own resources and those of the community, and to integrate back into it.

Similar processes were evident in the lives of some preschoolers. Not a few mothers of child survivors noted the value of their children putting together a memory book of photographs of their former school and friends, and their meeting with other nursery school mates who had survived. One three-year-old who had previously been in the daycare center that was blown up, but had moved to another nursery just a few weeks before the bombing, repeatedly made buildings of sand, labeled them "my school" and then stomped down the front half. After meeting with former schoolmates at a Barney's (a large purple TV cartoon dinosaur) party, he settled down, and stopped his repetitive play, and his nightmares subsided. It seems that having seen others who were still alive in a safe setting, and with a predictable routine, he could move on (Allen, Pfefferbaum, et al., 2005).

Befriending

In addition to the well-known flight, fright, and freeze reactions to a threat, there is another common reaction: a determination to offer acts of kindness and caring. This is especially striking in the context of acts which threaten to obliterate our confidence in the power of human kindness (Williams, 1996). Some 12,000 helpers rushed to Oklahoma City right after the bombing, and were greeted in turn by an outpouring of gratitude and support that became known as "the Oklahoma Standard." People pitched in to help and there was no violence or looting.

The kindness of others was later reciprocated. Spontaneously, subgroups of survivors and other people from Oklahoma City went to New York City to help in the wake of 9/11. The arrival there of Oklahoma City fire trucks was a signal event. Other survivors visited the victims of the embassy bombing in Nairobi. On the third anniversary of the bombing, representatives of a survivors group visited the disaster area of Lake Nyos in Cameroon where 1,700 people had been asphyxiated by volcanic gas, and later entertained a delegation from that area. Such activities created a new world of relationships for those involved, a spiritual kinship that functions as a source of community.

Linking Objects and Preserving the Status Quo: Murrah Remnants and Untouched Bedrooms

Paradoxically, relations with the dead stop and don't stop. Memory can continue as an internalized private attachment bringing comfort and stability. Some people, however, seemed to have had an overdetermined need to remember and reconnect. To have withdrawn from their persistent attachment would seem to have left them feeling abandoned.

Physical objects can link people to a past event or to those who are dead. The remnants of the Murrah Building have served as such a linking object, both in the fragments individuals treasure privately, and in the public use of its granite. At one point, mothers and grandmothers of the dead children were given a brooch or bracelet picturing their dead child. These objects chained some of them to the past. The process continues, in a somewhat debased form perhaps, in the T-shirts and coffee mug souvenirs for sale in the Oklahoma City Memorial gift shop.

Linking Past and Future: The Survivor Tree as a Cultural Symbol

A 90-year-old American elm, which had withstood an epidemic of Dutch elm disease, was the only living thing left at the site after the bombing. The tree became a symbol of resilience and endurance, and its postbombing seedlings were given to families of the survivors as a symbol of life. Clones have been made to replace the original when it dies. When President Clinton planted an offspring in the White House lawn, people across the country began to plant trees. On the tenth anniversary of the bombing, he was to say, "You can't forget the past with a tree — it's in the roots. And if you lose the roots, you lose the tree. But the nature of the tree is always to reach for tomorrow with the branches and to always find regenerative power from season to season" (McNutt, 2005, p. 9A).

The Trials

Perhaps the most vigorous effort of survivors and victims' families was expended on the McVeigh trial. In a nationally televised speech on April 20, 1995, the day after the bombing, President Clinton promised that the perpetrators would be found and that justice would be swift, certain, and sure. Ultimately, this led in time to McVeigh's trial in Denver in 1997, his execution in 2001, and Terry Nichols' second trial in Oklahoma in 2004.

These trials precipitated local and national debate over how McVeigh should be judged, and debates about the death penalty and the meaning of justice, vengeance, forgiveness, reconciliation, and the sacredness of life.

Influencing Legislation

A group of bombing victims and their families successfully lobbied the state legislature and Congress for legislation which would speed up appellate processes in death penalty cases. In 1996, state and federal laws were streamlined, resulting in a high number of executions during the next few years. As part of the sweeping antiterrorism legislation, President Clinton signed the Effective Death Penalty Act of 1995; that is, habeas corpus reform. Survivors and family members successfully lobbied Congress to allow closed circuit television of McVeigh's trial. Belief that watching the execution of McVeigh would bring closure reportedly played a role in Attorney General Ashcroft's decision to allow this. In short, because the survivors and victims' families were privileged, their plight and their vigorous political efforts led to cultural and legislative changes not just locally, but nationally.

LONG-TERM PHYSIOLOGICAL AND PSYCHOLOGICAL EFFECTS

Seven years after the bombing, survivors and victims' family members were found to have increased heart rates and blood pressure while talking about the event (Tucker, Pfefferbaum, North, et al., 2004).

What is striking about the impact of trauma on character is that a previously well-functioning individual can experience an overall sharp deterioration in functioning. The American Psychiatric Association (DSM-IV-TR; 2000) has suggested certain criteria for disorders of extreme stress not otherwise specified (DESNOS) and clustered these symptoms into five categories. *The International Statistical Classification of Disease* (ICD-10) has a separate category to accommodate personality changes after catastrophic experience (F620) which includes: (1) permanent hostility and mistrust; (2) social withdrawal; (3) feelings of emptiness and hopelessness; (4) increased dependency and problems with modulation of aggression; (5) hypervigilance and irritability; and (6) feelings of aberration (World Health Organization, 1992).

The Murrah bombing did have a seismic effect on the emotional functioning and worldviews of many, shattering basic and unexamined assumptions (Linenthal, 2001). This certainly was tragic, but for some it has been not without a positive side. Fischer (2005), for example, has found evidence of positive changes in some of those who met criteria for PTSD who did not avoid reflecting on the meaning of the event for their lives. This was more likely to occur in direct survivors of the bombing itself as opposed to those less directly affected, and more likely to occur in women. Among them, she, like Tedeschi and Calhoun (1996) and others in other situations, has found a changed view of self, of relationships with others, and in philosophy of life. These changes include: an appreciation of personal strength in adversity, increased self-reliance, appreciation of vulnerability leading to better self-care, increased appreciation of one's own existence, increased compassion, a reordering of priorities, new purpose, and a greater awareness of the paradoxical quality of life.

A study five years after the event found that birth rates had increased in the counties closest to the explosion, starting 10 months after the bombing (Rodgers, St. John, & Coleman, in press). A study four years after the bombing found that divorce rates had fallen from what would have been predicted in the majority (>60%) of the 77 counties of Oklahoma during each of these four years, and most noticeably in the general Oklahoma City area, with the effect dampening over time. There was also a decline in divorce rates in other key metropolitan areas in the state — more so than in closer rural areas. This, the authors suggest, may be due to social and economic integration of Oklahoma cities through urbanization (Nakonezny, Reddick, & Rodgers, 2004; Rodgers et al., 2005).

LESSONS LEARNED

When we review our experience in Oklahoma City and especially the role of outreach in the 10 years following the Murrah bombing, a number of issues come into prominence.

1.   Immediately after the bombing, people's perceived need was for what they considered "real help," that is, help with resources. The most pressing

of these were for notification of deaths or survival, and the structuring of services. The provision of such services needs to be coordinated, and the required effort may be vast. In Oklahoma City, for example, the Unified Command Post was responsible for coordinating 114 agencies.

2.   The diagnosis of PTSD was sometimes misapplied to describe the emotions and reactions of people with no direct experience of the bombing itself or its victims, and who did not experience a sense of horror or helplessness. That is, problems that elsewhere have been conceptualized as human problems were sometimes unnecessarily pathologized and medicalized with diagnoses that, in the minds of many, have a built-in prognosis. Some reactions to violent death and disaster are essentially normal reactions to an abnormal event. Reexperiencing and hyperarousal were common, but by themselves were generally not associated with later psychopathology or impairment in functioning. A research-informed model of triage incorporating reliable risk factors clearly is needed.

3.   Initial mental health outreach and other interventions need to be coordinated and standardized. In Oklahoma City it took some time for interventions to be coordinated under the aegis of the Department of Mental Health and Substance Abuse. Before this could be done, there was little standardization or individualization. Rather, psychological help sometimes consisted of the work of a variety of people offering what they knew how to do. Even today, for example, it is unclear what was done under the rubric of "crisis intervention" or "debriefing." Consequently, it is difficult to know if any particular intervention was or was not useful. Plans for disaster preparedness should include ways to immediately coordinate, standardize, and evaluate care.

4.   Since the majority of children did not seem to need intensive clinical intervention, schools could be a primary service site for those with mild to moderate reactions. Mental health services could be incorporated into ongoing school curricula and large numbers of children could be screened and served with the stigma of mental health services reduced.

5.   What constitutes a disaster or a crisis and the most appropriate ways to deal with it, including outreach, are defined within a community. They are manifestations of communal constructions of meaning.

6.   Therefore, attention needs to be given to the coconstruction of narratives, metaphors, and symbols. These are important intervening variables in the reactions of both individuals and communities, and some may be quite pathogenic. While popular with the media and politicians, stories of "lives changed forever," "loss of innocence," and the like lay foundations for negative self-predictions and expectations that were then enacted. Others, such as narratives of resilience and possible growth can be helpful.

7.   The metaphor of "closure" and the concept of "forgiveness" were pathogenic for many people in Oklahoma City. More useful seems the idea of prevailing (Rynearson, 2001) and acceptance of what is. Acceptance is something one does for oneself. It involves accepting injury as part of who we are but not all we are. Acceptance does not imply forgiveness with its

religious overtones or its implications of completion and the cessation of animosity.

8. Cultural symbols are important for our psychological well-being. Although commonly unacknowledged as such, they are an important part of our psychological support system and sense of continuity. Objects such as the survivor tree and activities such as church and memorial services took on this function and served as sources of support, secure base, and identity stabilization.

9. Understandings of "normal" grief and reactions to trauma can become problematic when they are used as a benchmark against which people judge themselves or are judged a failure because they haven't "got over it yet," or if they are used as a rather rigid criterion for the need for outreach or other services.

10. There are general differences in how people deal with grief as opposed to traumatic grief, and significant individual differences within each of these. Consequently, no one program, model, or outreach activity fits for all. Consequently, it would be helpful for outreach workers to frame intragroup and intergroup differences in a way that turns potential adversity into a sense of common humanity.

11. Our stories have victims, rescuers, persecutors, and bystanders. These roles can change easily, one into another. They also are cocreated: one cannot be a victim without a persecutor or rescuer and vice versa. Some people got stuck in the bystander role and remembered the trauma only as a helpless witness. Others took a persecutor role and became preoccupied with retaliation or turned their persecution against themselves and felt guilty. Then, switching to a rescuer role, they overprotected others or themselves.

12. Our therapeutic practices including outreach — like our culture — are saturated with an emphasis on problems, deficits, and pathology. This fits with and is supported by a paradigmatic mode of thinking and the diagnostic enterprises at the heart of our current reimbursement systems. However, it is also possible to help people from a perspective based on a more narrative approach, especially one which utilizes their strengths, and emphasizes resilience and efficacy. Not all people who have faced pain and horror are incapacitated. Strengths too can be forged in the smithy of misfortune. The differences may be summarized as follows:

Narrative Strengths Perspective	Paradigmatic Pathology Perspective
Focus on possibility and the future. Life experiences treated as resources. Hopes treated as goals. Emphasis on strengths and possibilities. Resources seen as in the client. Help conceptualized in terms of enhancing efficacy and getting on with one's life.	Focus on pathology, deficits, and the past. Life experiences treated as data for expert diagnosis. Goals embodied in the treatment plan. Emphasis on symptoms and pathology. Resources seen as in the expert. Help conceptualized as reducing symptoms and pathology.

This chart is meant only to invite consideration. Used concretely, such a dichotomization invites legitimate objections that such an approach ignores real problems. However, it does point out how our traditional treatment and research efforts can be limiting.

13. In Oklahoma we saw a general movement from initial shock and dealing with pressing adversities to efforts to make sense of the event and then, based on the meanings that were coconstructed, to efforts to do something active. We witnessed a gradual shift from the need for outreach and help from others to self-help and the development of systems of outreach to others. In best case scenarios, this has led to living engaged and meaningful lives that are not directed at reversing or preserving the past.

14. Coming to terms with violent death is not a one-time event, but rather a process of creation and maintenance of meaning. It is in such areas that posttraumatic growth has been most visible. People reordered priorities, found new purpose, and demonstrated vitality and self-reliance.

15. This was also an area wherein mental health outreach could be useful, for some people's active avoidance or understandings interfered with their full acknowledgment of death and their sorrow, and prevented their growth. The elaboration of scenarios of blame and revenge are examples. Whether the blame was directed internally or externally, these scenarios usually involved holding on to the status quo, or trying to reverse what had already irreversibly occurred.

16. While there is no way to compensate for violent death, there may be ways to transcend it, "Ways out when there seems no way out." In Oklahoma City this has occurred through art, bearing witness, seeking justice, political action, helping others as in New York, Nairobi, and Cameroon, and through education and prevention as now found in the goals of the Oklahoma City Memorial. This represents the social transformation of trauma.

17. In Oklahoma City, burgeoning social networks after the bombing renewed civic engagement by and among various groups, and became a kind of sociological superglue that has reinvigorated the city in the 10 years since the bombing. On the other hand, some survivors neglected major parts of their individual social networks — intimates, confidantes, friends, acquaintances, or colleagues in productive activity. This led to a loss of an individual sense of coherence. In the resulting absence of fuller and more diversified social support, some developed a hostile dependency on a few helping agencies. These are dangers mental health outreach might well help prevent.

SUMMARY

At the tenth anniversary of the bombing, it is apparent that we mental health workers have good reason to be humble as well as proud. As there has been for the survivors and families of victims, there have been and are possibilities for our own posttraumatic growth: greater compassion, greater appreciation of the paradoxical quality of life (and our interventions), a changed sense of priorities, and changed assumptions — including perhaps some altered perspectives on how we might best support community outreach.

The best outcomes for both individuals and for community subgroups seem to involve increased mentalizing, the reflective quality noted by Fonagy and others (Fonagy, Steele, et al., 1994) as associated with secure attachment, a secure base, and a key factor in fostering psychological resilience. It is the ability to conceptualize both self and others as motivated by internal states, that is, as thinking and feeling, and the skill to act in accordance with this. It is important to note that it was just such a sense of a secure base, a sense of safety, which the Oklahoma City bombing disrupted. Unfortunately, as Holmes has noted (1996), in times of anxiety and fear mentalizing abilities and skills are severely threatened, leading to splitting into good and bad, externalization of the bad, rigidity, magical thinking, and the espousal of leaders with a simple message — including perhaps simple messages of how to do outreach and deal with grief and trauma.

REFERENCES

After the bombing. (1995, April 25). *Christian Science Monitor, 87*(104), p. 20.

Allen, J. R. (2005). After the bombing: Public scenarios and the construction of meaning. In J. R. Allen & B. A. Allen (Eds.), *Therapeutic journey: Practice and life* (pp. 110–117). Oakland, CA: TA Press. (Original work published 1999)

Allen, J. R. & Allen, B. A. (1998a). Redecision therapy: Through a narrative lens. In M. Hoyt (Ed.), *The handbook of constructive therapies* (pp. 31–45). San Francisco: Jossey-Bass.

Allen, J. R. & Allen, B. A. (1998b). Transactional analysis notes from Oklahoma City: After the bombing. *Transactional Analysis Journal, 28*(3), 202–209.

Allen, J. R., Pfefferbaum, B., Speed, L., & Hammond, D. (2005). Stressors, trauma, and development. In J. R. Allen, & B. A. Allen (Eds.), *Therapeutic journey: Practice and life* (pp. 196–237). Oakland, CA: TA Press.

Allen, J. R., Whittlesey, S., Pfefferbaum, B., & Ondersma, M. (1999). Community and coping of mothers and grandmothers of children killed in a human-caused disaster. *Psychiatric Annals, 29*(2), 85–91.

Allen, S. F., Dlugokinski, E. L., Cohen, L. A., & Walker, J. L. (1999). Assessing the impact of a traumatic community event on children and assisting with their healing. *Psychiatric Annals, 29*(2), 93–98.

American Psychiatric Association (2000). *Diagnostic and Statistical Manual of Mental Disorders: IV-TR*. Washington, D.C.: Author.

Bacharach, P. (1999, January 13). After the fall: Rescue workers have become the latest victims of the Federal Building bombing. *Oklahoma Gazette*, pp. 26–30.

Call, J. A. & Pfefferbaum, B. (1999). Lessons from the first two years of Project Heartland, Oklahoma's mental health response to the 1995 bombing. *Psychiatric Services, 50*(7), 953–955.

Clay, N. (2005, July 30), Nichols' defense costs $ 6.3 million in taxpayer funds. *The Oklahoman*, p. 15A.

Conspiracy: In the throes of a paranoid nation (1995, June 22). *Oklahoma Gazette*.

Fenwick, B. (2005, January 19). Cold case. *Oklahoma Gazette*, p. 24.

Fischer, P. (2005, February 3). *Beyond resilience: Fostering posttraumatic growth in survivors of trauma*. Presented at Department of Psychiatry and Behavioral Sciences Teaching Conference, University of Oklahoma Health Sciences Center, Oklahoma City, OK.

Fonagy, P., Steele, M., Steele, H., Higgit, A., et al. (1994). The Emanual Miller Memorial Lecture 1992: The theory and practice of resilience. *Journal of Child Psychology and Psychiatry, 35*(2), 231–257.

Gurwitch, R. H., Pfefferbaum, B., & Leftwich, M. J. T. (2002). The impact of terrorism on children: Considerations for a new era. *Journal of Trauma Practice, 1*(3–4), 101–124.

Gurwitch, R. H., Sitterle, K. A., Young, B. H., & Pfefferbaum, B. (2002). The aftermath of terrorism. In A. M. La Greca, W. K. Silverman, E. Vernberg, & M. Roberts (Eds.), *Helping children cope with disasters and terrorism.* Washington, D.C.: American Psychological Association.

Holmes, J. (1996). *Attachment, intimacy, autonomy: Using attachment theory in adult psychotherapy.* Northvale, NJ: Jason Aronson.

Jones, C. (1998, August 4). The blasts' fallout: Rescuers, survivors, still nursing emotional wounds. *USA Today*, p. 1A.

Jones, R. (1995). *Where was God at 9:02 a.m.?* Nashville, TN: Thomas Nelson.

Lechat, M. F. (1990). The public health dimensions of disasters. *International Journal of Mental Health, 19*(1), 70–79.

Lindy, J. D., Grace, M. C., & Green, B. L. (1981). Survivors: Outreach to a reluctant population. *American Journal of Orthopsychiatry, 51*(3), 468–478.

Linenthal, E. T. (2001). *The unfinished bombing: Oklahoma City in American memory.* New York: Oxford University Press.

Maslow, A. H. (1954). *Motivation and personality.* New York: Harper.

McNutt, M. (2005, April 20). Dignitaries join survivors, others for ceremony. *The Oklahoman*, p. 21.

Nakonezny, P. A., Reddick, R., & Rodgers, J. L. (2004). Did divorces decline after the Oklahoma City bombing? *Journal of Marriage & Family, 66*(1), 90–100.

Nietzsche, F. W. (1968). *Twilight of the idols; And the anti-Christ* (R. J. Hollingdale, Trans.). Harmondsworth, UK: Penguin. (Original work published 1889)

North, C. S., Nixon, S. J., Shariat, S., Mallonee, S., McMillen, J. C., Spitznagel, E. L., & Smith, E. M. (1999). Psychiatric disorders among survivors of the Oklahoma City bombing. *Journal of the American Medical Association, 282*(8), 755–762.

North, C. S., Tivis, L., McMillen, J. C., Pfefferbaum, B., Cox, J., Spitznagel, E. L., Bunch, K., Schorr, J., & Smith, E. M. (2002). Coping, functioning, and adjustment of rescue workers after the Oklahoma City bombing. *Journal of Traumatic Stress, 15*(3), 171–175.

North, C. S., Tivis, L., McMillen, J. C., Pfefferbaum, B., Spitznagel, E. L., Cox, J., Nixon, S., Bunch, K. P., & Smith, E. M. (2002). Psychiatric disorders in rescue workers after the Oklahoma City bombing. *American Journal of Psychiatry, 159*(5), 857–859.

Pagels, E. H. (1988). *Adam, Eve, and the Serpent.* New York: Random House.

Pfefferbaum, B., Call, J. A., & Sconzo, G. M. (1999). Mental health services for children in the first two years after the 1995 Oklahoma City terrorist bombing. *Psychiatric Services, 50*(7), 956–958.

Pfefferbaum, B., Nixon, S. J., Krug, R. S., Tivis, R. D., Moore, V. L., Brown, J. M., Pynoos, R. S., Foy, D., & Gurwitch, R. H. (1999). Clinical needs assessment of middle and high school students following the 1995 Oklahoma City bombing. *American Journal of Psychiatry, 156*(7), 1069–1074.

Raymond, K. (2005, April 20). April 19, 1995: 10 years later. Oklahoma City changed us all. *The Oklahoman.*

Rodgers, J. L., St. John, C., & Coleman. R. (in press). Did fertility go up after the Oklahoma City bombing? Analysis of births in metro-political counties in Oklahoma 1990–1999. *Demography.*

Rynearson, E. K. (2001). *Retelling violent death.* Philadelphia, PA: Brunner-Routledge.

Shariat, S., Mallonee, S., Kruger, E., Farmer, K., & North, C. (1999). A prospective study of long-term health outcomes among Oklahoma City bombing survivors. *Journal of the Oklahoma State Medical Association, 92*(4), 178–186.

Smith, D. W., Christiansen, E. H., Vincent, R., & Hann, N. E. (1999). Population effects of the bombing of Oklahoma City. *Journal of the Oklahoma State Medical Association, 92*(4), 193–198.

Tedeschi, R. G. & Calhoun, L. G. (1996). The posttraumatic growth inventory: Measuring the positive legacy of trauma. *Journal of Traumatic Stress, 9*(3), 455–472.

Tucker, P. (2003, July). *Terrorism: Lessons learned from Oklahoma City*. Presented at the Nebraska Mental Health Conference, Omaha, Nebraska.

Tucker, P., Boehler, S. D., Dickson, W., Lensgraf, S. J., & Jones, D. (1999). Mental health response to the Oklahoma City bombing. *Journal of the Oklahoma State Medical Association, 92*(4), 168–171.

Tucker, P., Dickson, W., Pfefferbaum, B., McDonald, N. B., & Allen, G. (1997). Traumatic reactions as predictors of posttraumatic stress six months after the Oklahoma City bombing. *Psychiatric Services, 48*(9), 1191–1194.

Tucker, P., Pfefferbaum, B, Doughty, D. E., Jones, D. E., Jordan, F. B., & Nixon, S. J. (2002). Body handlers after terrorism in Oklahoma City: Predictors of posttraumatic stress and other symptoms. *American Journal of Orthopsychiatry, 72*(4), 469–475.

Tucker, P., Pfefferbaum, B., Nixon, S. J., & Foy, D. W. (1999). Trauma and recovery among adults highly exposed to a community disaster. *Psychiatric Annals, 29*(2), 78–83.

Tucker, P., Pfefferbaum, B., North, C. S., Kent, A., Wyatt, D. B., Hossain, A., & Burgin, C. (2004, June.). *Long-term autonomic reactivity in Oklahoma City's direct victims of terrorism*. Paper presented at the Royal College of Psychiatrists, Harrogate, UK.

Tucker, P., Pfefferbaum, B., Vincent, R., Boehler, S. D., & Nixon, S. J. (1998). Oklahoma City: Disaster challenges mental health and medical administrators. *The Journal of Behavioral Health Services & Research, 25*(1), 93–99.

Whittlesey, S. W., Allen, J. R., Bell, B. D, Lindsey, E. D, Speed, L. F., Lucas, A. F., Ware, M. M., Allen, S. F., & Pfefferbaum, B. (1999). Avoidance in trauma: Conscious and unconscious defense, pathology, and health. *Psychiatry, 62*(4), 303–312.

Williams, G. (1996, April 4). Oklahoma's charities and the bomb. *Chronicle of Philanthropy,* 34.

Wong, M. (2001). School crisis recovery. In M. Wong, J. Kelly, & R. D. Stephens (Eds.), *Jane's school safety handbook*. Alexandria, VA: Jane's Information Group.

World Health Organization; WHO Collaborating Centres for Classification of Diseases (1992–1994). *International statistical classification of diseases and related health problems* (pp. 136–138, 10th rev. ed.), Geneva, Switzerland: Author.

18

Healing After September 11: Short-Term Group Intervention with 9/11 Families

PRIYA J. SHAHANI AND HEATHER M. TRISH

9/11 TERRORIST ATTACK

The terrorist attack on the World Trade Center in New York City in 2001 occurred in a community so large and diverse that it was difficult to centralize a community-based project of emotional support. The authors of this chapter, staff clinicians from an established and respected victims' assistance agency in New York City (Safe Horizon), were instrumental in initiating an outreach and intervention program of support for the family members of those killed in the attack. They describe an extensive, four-year outreach program and detailed clinical observations after completing 14 time-limited, restorative retelling groups for over 90 family members. There are multiple case illustrations describing the importance of assuming an attitude of clinical flexibility and creativity with heterogeneous groups of traumatically bereaved family members challenged not only by violent death but complicated by the enormity of the destructive spectacle — intense media coverage, fragmented or vaporized bodies, victims compensation fund decisions, local and national political response, ongoing terrorist threats and rebuilding the WTC site.

INTRODUCTION

At 8:46 a.m. on September 11, 2001 a hijacked Boeing 767 plane crashed into the North Tower of the World Trade Center in New York City. Then at 9:03 a.m a second hijacked Boeing 767 aircraft hit the South Tower. Both buildings were engulfed in flames and collapsed in just hours. Two additional planes were hijacked that morning. One crashed into the Pentagon in Washington, DC. The other plane, headed toward an unknown target widely believed to be the White House or the United States Capitol, crashed in an open field in Pennsylvania. America had been attacked by operatives from Osama Bin Laden's al Qaeda network. By using commercial airplanes as weapons, the 19 Islamic terrorists killed close to 3,000 people and physically injured almost 9,000.

Prior to September 11, 2001, two prominent domestic acts of terrorism had taken place in the United States: the bombing of the World Trade Center in New York City on February 26, 1993 killing six people, and the bombing of the Alfred P. Murrah Federal Building in Oklahoma City, Oklahoma on April 19, 1995, which resulted in 168 deaths. International examples of terrorism with high levels of fatalities include the 2004 hostage taking at a school in Beslan, Russia, which killed 366 people, the midair bombing of Air India flight 182 in 1985 killing all 331 people on board, and the truck bombings of U.S. embassies in Nairobi, Kenya, and Dar es Salaam, Tanzania in 1998 killing 303 (Johnstons Archive, n.d.). None, however, came close to the number of lives lost on September 11, 2001.

The 9/11 Family Assistance Center was developed by city government to serve as the central location where those affected by the disaster could access critical services and information. The center was based on the often-used Federal Emergency Management Agency (FEMA) Disaster Recovery Center (DRC) model. Prior to 9/11, no facility as comprehensive had ever been created in the United States to service disaster victims. The Family Assistance Center had representatives from more than 60 nonprofit, governmental, and private organizations from the federal, state, and local levels. Safe Horizon, a nonprofit agency that has serviced victims of crime and abuse for over 25 years, was one of the agencies represented at the Family Assistance Center. Together, these organizations provided financial benefits, crisis counseling, spiritual care, legal assistance, immigration advice, DNA collection, missing persons' information, childcare, and more. At the height of activity, over 600 people per day came to the Family Assistance Center seeking services.

In order to provide the best quality of service to a large volume of clients, a coordinated intake process was created among several of the key agencies. This coordinated effort included a landmark agreement between nonprofit organizations to share client information in order to streamline the application process for clients seeking assistance in what was becoming a very complex array of benefits. As this network of agencies continued to serve the multitude of clients, a new nonprofit organization began to form. In December 2001, the 9/11 United Services Group (USG) was established by major social service agencies to act as the coordinating entity for the organizations providing assistance. A hallmark of the work done by USG during its existence was the creation of the Service Coordination network, which provided concrete assistance to clients through over 200 uniformly trained service coordinators from over 40 agencies. Clients wishing to be assigned a service coordinator could make this request by calling the September 11, 24-hour support hotline, operated by Safe Horizon. In January 2002, the Family Assistance Center relocated to a midtown Manhattan office building. Safe Horizon became the managing entity of the day-to-day operations of the Family Assistance Center, and along with several other key agencies, Safe Horizon continued to provide service coordination and began to develop much needed mental health programs.

Studies by the National Center for Post Traumatic Stress Disorder show that victims of terrorism can suffer psychological repercussions for years after the traumatic event. Symptoms can include hyperarousal, avoidance, intrusive reexperiencing, emotional numbing, dissociation, anxiety, and depression (National Center for Post Traumatic Stress Disorder, n.d.). In response to the growing need for mental health services for the thousands who were psychologically impacted by the events of 9/11, dozens of New York City agencies created counseling programs to address the diverse needs of those affected. Safe Horizon developed counseling programs at the Family Assistance Center and at four other preexisting Safe Horizon sites in New York City. Master's level clinicians were hired to provide mental health services and outreach to family members, the injured, displaced residents, evacuees, rescue and recovery workers, displaced workers, witnesses to the attacks, and impacted children. Surviving family members, in particular, were confronted with incomparable hardships in the aftermath of the deadliest terrorist attack in United States history.

Losing a loved one to a violent death can lead to long-term distress resulting from the violent, intentional, and unexpected nature of the death. In situations of traumatic grief, memories of the deceased often segue into disturbing traumatic images of the loved one's death. Surviving family members often become consumed by these intrusive and graphic images, which, over time can impact daily functioning. As family members work to avoid these disturbing images, they may also avoid positive memories of their loved ones and are unable to participate in the natural grieving process. Instead of mourning the loss, family members are often left unable to process the death or even believe that it is real. Losing someone to a traumatic death, therefore, requires a specialized form of intervention that provides treatment for both the trauma and the loss. What follows is a description of how Safe Horizon utilized short-term community-based support groups to address the mental health needs of individuals who lost loved ones on September 11, 2001.

GROUP EFFECTIVENESS

Group treatment has proven to be an effective modality to address the mental health needs of family members affected by 9/11 for a number of reasons: First, participation in groups helped to decrease the sense of isolation that many experienced after 9/11. The public nature of the event and the constant media attention caused many family members to withdraw in an attempt to mourn their loss privately, away from the public spotlight. As a result, these individuals were disconnected from other 9/11-affected families who were going through a similar experience. Compounding the isolation, many struggled interpersonally after 9/11, finding it difficult to rely on their previous support systems. It was common for survivors in the same family to grieve in such different ways that supporting one another in this process was challenging. Seeking support through friends or others who did not lose someone on 9/11 was also difficult because many family members felt that only those who had experienced a similar loss could understand them. Group treatment was effective in providing members with a place to address their shared experience of losing a loved one in a global tragedy which took place only miles from where they sat for group each week. Participants were able to connect with other family members, share similar concerns, see how others were coping, and support one another.

Many members reported relief at hearing others in the group voice experiences similar to their own. Over time, because of pressure by family and friends to "move on," the group evolved into one of the only places where participants felt comfortable talking about their loss. Group validated and normalized the fact that participants still felt affected years after the tragedy and provided the comforting space that many needed and were unable to get elsewhere. Finally, support groups were a place where members could share their innermost thoughts about their loved ones' deaths while comparing facts, time lines, and other information to piece together an often spotty story line of their loved ones' last moments. By sharing and by listening to others, members came to see that others experienced similar fears and that they were not alone in the horror they lived with daily. In this safe and confidential space, away from the media coverage and public interest that pervaded the outside world, members were able to experience the power of a collective retelling of the events of September 11.

The group model that was implemented was derived from the "Restorative Retelling" group-counseling model developed by Edward Rynearson, MD. Dr. Rynearson had a professional working relationship with Safe Horizon for several years prior to September 11, 2001. Since 1998, he had been training the staff of the Safe Horizon Families of Homicide Victims program in the application of his group model. Following the events of September 11, he volunteered to train and supervise the Safe Horizon counselors who counseled the groups.

GROUP STRUCTURE

Safe Horizon began offering family groups, based on this restorative retelling model in January of 2002. The following sections outline the structure of the group including outreach, screening and assessment, attendance, and the group model overview.

Outreach

Over the course of three years, Safe Horizon conducted a total of 14 time-limited support groups for individuals who had lost loved ones on September 11. Approximately 90 individuals received family group services, with an average of six members per group. Initially, many referrals came through word of mouth since Safe Horizon was one of the agencies in the forefront of the 9/11 response effort. A number of referrals also came from service coordinators who encouraged their clients to seek mental health treatment. The steady stream of referrals began to decline in the second year after 9/11; however, based on the number of lives lost, it was believed that there were still thousands of impacted family members in need of assistance. In response, Safe Horizon conducted a large-scale outreach effort. Outreach letters were developed informing family members of the various support services available. Names and addresses were obtained from Safe Horizon's comprehensive database of 9/11 affected family members. Letters were regularly sent to families throughout New York City and parts of New Jersey for several years after the tragedy.

Alternative forms of outreach were also implemented to reach other relatives of the deceased. Safe Horizon counseling information was distributed via resources that 9/11 family members would contact, including 9/11-related websites, the medical examiner's office, 9/11 programs and agencies, and the Family Room, a room overlooking the World Trade Center site where only family members were permitted. In addition, program representatives attended 9/11-related meetings and events to distribute information on support services. Referrals also continued from other social service agencies, the Safe Horizon September 11 Support Hotline, the New York Mental Health Association's referral hotline, word of mouth, and client referrals. The steady flow of responses to the letters, in conjunction with these other types of outreach, allowed Safe Horizon to continue running groups for four years after the tragedy.

Screening and Assessment

Composition of family groups included anyone who had lost a family member during the attacks of 9/11, regardless of the relationship to the deceased. Groups consisted of a mix of parents, grandparents, siblings, spouses, fiancés, long-term cohabitating and same sex partners, adult children, and in-laws. The screening process for group membership consisted of an initial phone assessment followed by a face-to-face session between the potential group member and facilitators. The intake session, approximately one hour in length, was used to obtain a biopsychosocial history and to assess individuals for group appropriateness. If a potential member was in treatment with another mental health provider, a phone consultation was a crucial element of the screening process.

Attendance

Attendance was consistent. Members appeared to look forward to group sessions and expressed a wish to be there both for themselves and for others. Facilitators emphasized the important role members played in supporting each other simply through their presence in the group from week to week. An essential component of the healing included not only accepting guidance and support but also providing it to others. Members in the family groups appeared to benefit from this ability to positively impact others. Their ability to attend group consistently and follow through with their commitment to one another in the midst of tragedy was a true indication of how resilient the 9/11 family members were.

9/11 Group Treatment Model

The group followed a structured model outlining a clear agenda for each session. Initially, 10 sessions were offered in a group cycle, similar to that of Dr. Rynearson's model. After completing three 10-week family groups, the length of the group cycle was extended to 14 weeks in response to client and facilitator feedback. It was felt that a disaster on this scale had repercussions for family members that required a longer-term treatment intervention. Despite the changes, the focus on restoration through stress moderation, reconstructive exposure, and reengagement (the central themes of Dr. Rynearson's model) were maintained.

The order of the sessions in the group model was purposeful in that each session built upon the previous ones. The first three sessions focused on building trust among members and moderating stress. Group discussions focused on grieving and coping styles, identifying internal and external strengths, and on education around traumatic response. The fourth session was dedicated to commemorating the lives of those lost on 9/11, where members were asked to bring in photos and share the story of their loved ones' lives. Sessions 5 through 9 addressed the trauma around the death. This portion of the group began with a discussion of the meaning of death and then moved into the "death imagery presentations," which facilitators referred to simply as "retellings." Retellings were an opportunity for members to verbalize the imagery they held of how they believed their loved ones had died. The last stage of the group, sessions 10 through 14, focused on separation distress and support systems. Members were given the opportunity to share memories, talk about what they missed, and identify ways that they stayed connected to their loved ones after their death. In this final phase of the group, members were encouraged to recognize their existing support systems and valued relationships. In order to help reconnect them to their present life, members were asked to bring a support person to one of the final sessions. The group cycle ended with a discussion of moving forward and saying goodbye.

All of the groups were facilitated by two master's level clinicians and were scheduled to meet once a week for an hour and a half. Each session of the family group began with a brief "check in" and ended with a brief "check out." At "check in" participants were asked to share any feelings or thoughts connected to their loss that may have surfaced since the last group session. It was quite common for members to also use this time to share general news about their lives. This became a time for members to provide updates and reconnect to one another after a week apart. During "check out," facilitators asked participants to share how they were feeling in the here and now. "Check out" brought closure to each session and oriented members to the present. "Check out" was particularly important because it provided facilitators with an opportunity to gauge the impact of the session on each member and determine whether individual follow-up and support was required. Following "check out," relaxation or breathing exercises were conducted. These exercises were meant to ground group members at the end of a session and provide them with a tool to manage stress.

CLINICAL INTERVENTIONS WITH 9/11 FAMILY MEMBERS

Clinical interventions included connecting to living memories, and creating and verbalizing the dying narrative. The facilitator's role in the retelling process and benefits of retelling will also be discussed.

Connecting to Living Memories

One of the crucial interventions in the group model for 9/11-affected family members was to commemorate the life of the deceased through sharing photos and reminiscing on the life of the loved one. This was a particularly important group intervention prior to the death imagery presentations because in recovering and sharing memories, members were able to reconnect to the lives of their loved ones, which for many had become overshadowed by thoughts of the death. Many participants expressed anxiety going into this session because they had been avoiding photos or other reminders of their loved ones because of the pain associated with these memories. Others felt that it might be too overwhelming to look at photos of the other group members' loved ones and listen to their stories.

After completion of this commemoration session, however, members often expressed that reflecting on the life of their loved ones was helpful. One participant shared the relief he experienced after being given the opportunity to talk about his mother "more tonight than I had since she died." The session helped move some members into another stage of their healing. For instance, a woman who had lost her son reported that she had not looked at any of his photos since he died because she feared losing control of her emotions. She confronted her avoidance in the commemoration session and reported one week later that she has since been looking at more photos of her son. Many of the members came to realize that they were so preoccupied with images of their loved ones' deaths that they had not been focusing on the lives their loved ones had lived. This session allowed members to get back in touch with the loving memories and helped to prepare members for the more difficult part of the group, sharing the story of their loved ones' deaths.

Creating the Dying Narrative

The media coverage of 9/11 was unprecedented in that mass violent dying had never before been captured on film in such detail and broadcast live as the events unfolded. In the days after the event, each time grieving family members saw images replayed of the towers being hit, burning, and collapsing to the ground, they were reminded of the horrific way in which their loved ones were killed. The cause of death for the majority of 9/11 victims was never determined, so many family members were left feeling overwhelmed by the unknown. One of the most common and distressing concerns for family members was whether their loved ones died immediately or lived for hours or even days after the initial attack. Questions about these last moments consumed the thoughts of many who wanted to know if their loved ones died alone and in pain. Did they know they were going to die and if so, were they afraid or able to find some peace in the last moments? Others were consumed with thoughts around the cause of death. Did they burn, jump from the towers, suffocate from the smoke, or were they crushed when the buildings collapsed?

As in most violent deaths, highly distressed 9/11 family members searched for answers to these questions by creating a narrative in their mind of how they imagined their loved one died. This story, most often disturbing and overwhelming, was then replayed over and over. Whereas for a majority of survivors from other traumatic events this obsession with recounting and ruminating over the dying subsides in days or weeks, 9/11 was unique in that the public nature of the event and the media's replay kept the death imagery in the forefront of the minds of grieving individuals. Family members who witnessed the events in person often had an even greater difficulty working through the traumatic aspect of the death because their direct exposure to the attacks increased their risk of developing post traumatic stress disorder. One member stated that she "hated herself" for watching the events unfold because she then could not get the images out of her mind.

The death narrative developed out of the individual family member's personal experience on 9/11 combined with whatever information he or she learned over time about their loved ones' death. In many cases, the narrative changed over time based on new information disclosed from stories told by survivors of the event, the media, the findings of the 9/11 commission, 9/11-related documentaries, or even after listening to other family members retell their story in group. For instance, someone who knew that their loved one worked on the 103rd floor of the World Trade Center might have initially created a story around the belief that the loved one died from smoke inhalation. After watching the televised replay of bodies falling from high floors of the towers, this individual's story could have changed dramatically to a scenario in which their loved one jumped to their death.

Verbalizing the Dying Narrative

Many grieving 9/11 family members were consumed by thoughts of their loved ones' deaths, yet, most had never verbalized the graphic and distressing imagery that they carried in their minds. The thought of talking about this was often terrifying and anxiety provoking. Many exhibited resistance to the idea of retelling and questioned facilitators as to whether verbalizing their story was "safe." Many stated that they wanted to focus on the future, seeing no reason to go back to that day. One member stated that she had never thought about how her mother died, nor did she want to think about it. Avoidance, inherent to the emotional aftermath of trauma, can be an adaptive response if used in the short term. If used over time as the primary means of coping, however, it can interfere with healing and recovery. Research with various traumatized populations has indicated that individuals who try to cope with their trauma by avoiding feelings and thoughts about it have a tendency to develop more severe psychological symptoms (National Center for Post Traumatic Stress Disorder, n.d.). The retelling process in the 9/11 family groups was challenging the avoidance that many had been working hard to maintain.

Following is a case example of Richard, who expressed on multiple occasions that the thoughts of his brother's death were exactly what he had been avoiding since 9/11 because contemplating the possible death scenarios was too overwhelming. As was observed in Richard's case, a highly distressing dying scenario led to more intense and frequent intrusive imagery, flashbacks, and other trauma-related symptoms.

Richard is a 24-year-old Jewish male who lost his younger brother Thomas on 9/11. His service coordinator, who felt that his anxiety and depression had been increasing during the time she was working with him, referred him to a family group. At the group prescreening appointment, he appeared to be more consumed by separation distress, the longing for his brother, than with trauma distress. He reported that in the months after 9/11 he experienced overwhelming depression in response to the loss of his brother, who was his closest friend. Because he had been avoiding thoughts around Thomas' death, Richard's anxiety levels increased as the retelling sessions approached. He was willing to retell his story, but needed a great deal of assurance from facilitators that it would be "safe" to do so. As the last member of the group to retell, Richard shared three different scenarios about how he believed his brother had died. He imagined that either Thomas had jumped, was "vaporized," or was blown out of the building, falling almost 100 stories to be buried alive for days under the rubble. Richard reported that thinking about Thomas lying helplessly under the rubble was the most overwhelming part of the story.

Following the retelling portion of the group cycle, Richard became preoccupied with the thoughts of his brother's death and as a result, had a difficult time identifying any positive memories of Thomas. Richard became particularly concerned about the way in which he mourned in the days after 9/11. He reported that it was his religion's custom to mourn for a specific period of time after a death and since Richard was not sure *when* Thomas had died, he was worried that he may not have fulfilled the religious obligations necessary for his brother's soul to be at rest. Despite his struggles,

Richard expressed that he looked forward to group every week and felt a strong connection to the group members. After completing group, Richard decided to join the next cycle of the 9/11 family group so that he could have the continued weekly support he felt he needed.

The second group that Richard joined had fewer members and was more intimate. Richard went through the retelling process with less resistance the second time, sharing with group members that although his first retelling had been difficult, it had helped him to confront his fears around the dying memory. In his second retelling, Richard's personal narrative of his brother's death changed in that he now reported only two death scenarios. He was no longer preoccupied with the possibility of his brother jumping. He appeared to be less frightened by the story the second time and chose to share with the group members the missing person's poster he had distributed in the days immediately after 9/11. He stated that sharing the poster was a "big deal" for him because any such reminders of the days immediately after 9/11 were the most painful since it was in those days that he believed Thomas was still alive buried in the rubble. After completing the second group cycle, Richard reported a decrease in symptoms. He was less anxious, less depressed, no longer was consumed by the death, was able to work again, and finally married, something that he was putting off because of his sadness and guilt that Thomas would not be there.

Facilitator Role in the Retelling Process

To address the anxiety and prepare members for the retelling sessions, facilitators helped to create a safe space for members to share their stories and encouraged members to express their feelings around the process. Facilitators validated and normalized members' fears and explained the rationale and process for retelling. It was explained that establishing a restorative story could help members counterbalance their tragic stories with more peaceful memories of the dying. The facilitator's role during the retelling was to help the group member become an active participant in the story by asking them to fantasize what they would have wanted to say or do for their loved ones as they were dying. The purpose was to help group members incorporate themselves into their stories so that they were not left feeling helpless after telling them. Being participants helped members to reframe the story so that each person felt more in control.

Benefits of Retelling

All group participants were encouraged to go through the retelling process but were not obligated to do so in order to continue in the group. Most of the group members who initially stated that they did not want to retell their stories ultimately did actively engage in this process after hearing others. One member stated that after listening to the group members retell their stories, she felt strong enough to talk about her daughter's death. As painful as the retelling sessions were, most members expressed feeling relief after going through the process. One member stated that retelling the death helped her to stop running from her pain and allowed her to finally go through the grieving process. Another member shared that the retelling offered her "some sort of release," perhaps, she speculated, as a result of the collective retelling. Yet another member reported that after she retold the story of her husband's death, she felt like a "dam opened up and a lot of the anger came out." She felt that the process helped to launch her into a new phase where she was better able to face her fears, was more in control, and no longer felt that sadness would consume her. The following is Mary's story, which illustrates some of the potential benefits of the retelling process.

Mary, a single female in her 40s, lost her younger sister, Anna, on September 11. Mary reported that she and her sister had a tumultuous relationship; there were periods in their relationship in which they had not spoken for years at a time. Mary felt grateful for their reconciliation just prior to September 11, where they had begun to repair their relationship and support one another. Because of their prior strained relationship Mary felt particularly affected by her sister's death, feeling robbed of the possibility of a better relationship in their future. Mary's family had never been close, which Mary felt had hindered her ability to process her grief because she felt unable to have emotional conversations about her sister with any of her family members.

Mary had been searching for a 9/11 family support group for the first year after Anna's death. She joined the Safe Horizon family group just prior to the first anniversary of September 11, a self-imposed time line in which Mary hoped to begin feeling less anxious and depressed. At the initial group prescreening appointment, she reported experiencing intrusive imagery, nightmares, and disturbing thoughts about how her sister might have died. During her retelling, Mary emotionally recounted her fears about her sister's dying. Because Anna's body was one of the very few bodies recovered intact, Mary believed that her sister might have jumped out of the window, which for Mary was a more distressing scenario than to believe Anna was consumed by the fire or crushed in the building collapse. Mary stated that she believed her sister would have been terrified as she realized she was going to die and imagined Anna lying on the floor in the smoke filled room struggling to breathe. Mary sobbed as she recounted the horror her sister must have felt in those last moments. Mary was able to speak openly about her traumatic imagery in a group where members acutely understood and were supportive and accepting.

The week following Mary's retelling, she reported a significant decrease in her intrusive imagery and expressed great relief at these changes. For the first time since 9/11, Mary had nontrauma related dreams of Anna and fewer nightmares. Mary attributed this transformation specifically to the process of retelling, never having verbalized the details of her sister's death in this way before. After the group cycle ended, Mary reported that she did not require any after care because she felt she had gotten what she needed out of the group experience. In a follow-up contact one year later, Mary reported that she continued to feel better and was doing well.

MOVING FORWARD

Family support groups served several therapeutic functions for members beyond the retelling experience. The support of others, the safety within the group, the validation and normalization of the members' very unique yet collective experience, and the flexibility of the group facilitators, combined together to create a healing environment. Throughout the group process, members were encouraged to utilize internal and external resources that could facilitate their healing process. Sessions dedicated to discussing personal strengths, coping, and support systems helped members to identify what remained in their lives, in spite of their loss. Many of the group members denied their inherent ability to cope with their loss despite the fact that members had taken a positive step by seeking out and joining the 9/11 family group. Many found it difficult to recognize or acknowledge the many ways in which they were in fact coping. There was resistance to identifying activities or people that made them feel good, with members saying "nothing helps."

Members often spoke of feeling guilty if they felt better. It appeared as if members would lose the connection to their loved ones if they let go of their grief. These members continued to lament their loss full-time, holding on tightly to their grief. Facilitators, in an effort to combat this tendency to refuse recognition of coping skills, worked diligently to help members identify things that helped. Rituals, like visiting graves or memorial sites, lighting candles in remembrance of loved ones and creating or attending charity memorial events, were some of the ways family members were able to make themselves feel better while still acknowledging their loss. Maintaining structure by working, attending the family group, participating in individual therapy, and taking care of loved ones were coping strategies that members employed without even realizing the benefit it provided. Reminding members of their inherent resilience was an important aspect of the facilitators' work because grieving family members did not know how to see themselves as having the capacity to restore themselves in the midst of tragedy.

In the final stage of the group, helping members reconnect with their present lives allowed them to recognize their ability to survive and move forward. A family and friends night was one of the last sessions of the group model, and members were asked to bring to group a supportive person. This session was dedicated to members sharing how this person was helpful to them and guests identifying the changes they have observed in the group member over time. The session often strengthened and reinforced the individual relationships, encouraging members to continue engaging and seeking support with valued people in their lives.

CHALLENGES UNIQUE TO 9/11 GROUPS

Those who lost loved ones on September 11 faced an unprecedented set of challenges. Because the country had never experienced a tragedy on this scale before, there were a number of unanticipated and distressing issues that surfaced for family members in the aftermath of 9/11. Some of these included struggling with the public nature of the attacks, grieving in the midst of daily 9/11 reminders, coping with a long-term recovery effort, managing a complicated and controversial financial compensation process, and struggling with an unspoken hierarchy of pain allowed to each family member dependent on his or her relationship to the deceased. Family members were also coping with personal reactions towards the U.S.-led wars in Afghanistan and Iraq, confronting their belief systems toward "Arabs and Muslims," 9/11 anniversary reactions, the rebuilding of the disaster site, and the creation of a 9/11 memorial, to name a few. Because these topics often came up in group sessions, facilitators had to be flexible and make time for such discussions despite the structured format of the model. Literature on previous traumatic events such as the Oklahoma City bombing and accounts from war stricken nations were helpful in preparing clinicians for some of these difficult and often controversial issues that came up in group sessions. Ultimately, however, because so many unique topics emerged after 9/11, facilitators had to rely on their own instinct, clinical experience, and supervision to effectively address the many challenges that surfaced daily in their work, some of which will be discussed further.

Comparison of Grief

Loved ones with varying relationships to the deceased reached out for support. Oftentimes, loved ones seeking support services would request a relationship-specific group in the initial phone screening, such as a "widows' group" or a "parents' group." These potential group members reported feeling that they would be better understood in a group where all members shared the same relationship to the loss. Facilitators felt strongly that potential members could benefit from a group with a diversity of relationships to the deceased and encouraged interaction between family members. This benefit was apparent with Eric, a 30-year-old newlywed man who had lost his wife. He had been so consumed with his own loss that he had not thought about the grief experienced by his in-laws until meeting Julia, a 58-year-old woman who had lost her son. Eric had been struggling to get along with his wife's family and the presence of Julia in this group helped him to seek unbiased opinions about how to address issues with his mother- and father-in-law while gaining a deeper perspective into the grief of a parent who had lost child. As a result, Eric's relationship with his in-laws moved in a more positive direction once he began the group.

The diversity within these groups did, at times, result in members comparing "whose pain was greater." There were instances in which participants compared their loss and placed value on the relationship to the deceased; valuing and respecting some members' experience, while minimizing the feelings of pain and loss experienced by others. In one group cycle a mother expressed her grief and the pain of losing her child, stating, "You don't know what it's like to have my child die before me." In contrast, a man who lost his brother came to group feeling that his pain was not as valid as the other members because someone outside of group had commented to him that, "You're just the brother." Similar issues arose around placing value on the life that was taken, for example, whether the person was a businessman/ woman, busboy, firefighter, or building maintenance person. In one case, a group member expressed anger because she felt that the police and firefighters received more recognition than others who died and displayed a lack of sensitivity toward another member who had lost his brother, a police officer. Comparisons and judgments of whose pain was worse were discouraged and clinicians encouraged members to focus on the commonalities among group members. Clinicians continuously affirmed that each person's grief was equally real and painful.

The Public Nature of the Attack and 9/11 Triggers

The attack on the World Trade Center was a very public incident and therefore became the central focus of most political and world discussions. The events of that day were watched on television around the globe and the images were replayed for months after. Years after the tragedy, "9/11" continues to be referenced regularly on television and radio, in newspapers and magazines, and on the Internet. All of this has made it almost impossible for family members to escape being reminded of that horrific day. In addition, for those living in the New York City area in the months after 9/11, it was often difficult to navigate around the physical reminders of their loss: a downtown area that was heavily guarded by armed military and civilian police forces, piles of steel and rubble where two of the tallest towers in the world once stood, tourists flocking in from all over the world to get a glimpse of "Ground Zero," and vendors throughout the city streets selling 9/11 memorabilia.

Then there were the ongoing terror threats and world events that triggered the same panic, fear, and anxiety that individuals experienced on 9/11. There was the crash of the space shuttle Columbia on February 1, 2003, the train bombings in Spain on March 11, 2004, and the tsunami disaster in the Indian Ocean on December 26, 2004, and Hurricane Katrina on the U.S. Gulf Coast on August 29, 2005, all throwing 9/11 survivors into painful reminiscences about what it was like to lose a loved one in a sudden and violent manner. In addition, the findings of the 9/11 Commission and the U.S.-led wars in Afghanistan and Iraq pushed family members in a variety of directions in considering whether their 9/11 losses were being avenged or being used as justifications for more unwarranted deaths. So whether it was due to the media, the war, ongoing terror threats, disasters around the globe, or proximity to the disaster site, there were many reminders for family members of their very painful and public loss.

Financial Compensation

The financial compensation offered to the families of those killed on 9/11 created yet another set of challenges for family members. Finances and paperwork were two regularly discussed topics in early September 11 family support groups. In the months after the tragedy, there was an enormous amount of money donated by private citizens and public organizations from around the world to the victims of September 11. In addition to the donations, the U.S. government created the September 11 Victim Compensation Fund (VCF) which provided compensation for economic and noneconomic loss to victims of the attacks and their surviving family members. The fund provided a no-fault alternative to litigation and could have only one claimant per victim. Family members were required to go through a lengthy application and verification process if choosing to apply for the VCF or any other charitable funds.

In addition to cumbersome paperwork, family members were required to submit documentation in support of their applications, such as forms of personal identification, proof of relationship to the deceased, and a death certificate for their loved one. The application process had to be repeated in varying forms for compensation from each organization and charity. This forced families to maintain focus, organization, and presence of mind at a time when many were still feeling overwhelmed by their loss. This process was often experienced as retraumatizing for family members who felt barely able to function as it was. Families were often left frustrated and angry, and as a result, many did not apply for any financial assistance at all. On the other hand, some family members found that focusing on the paperwork requirements and putting together application materials was a welcome distraction from their intense feelings of grief.

The Victim Compensation Fund and other charitable funds were considered to be controversial because family members were being financially compensated for their loss on September 11, whereas families of the victims from previous disasters had not had the same generosity awarded to them. The VCF placed a monetary figure on the victim's life in order to establish the amount to be awarded to the claimant. For many family members, the money they were to receive felt like an exchange for their loved ones' lives, essentially "blood money." This often brought up feelings of guilt and anger, making it difficult for some family members to accept or spend the money. Disputes within some families arose as a result of the monetary issues, often placing one family member against another in their claim as dependents or as next of kin. The public knowledge of the financial compensation often led to resentment and judgments toward families by the public, which was yet another hurdle faced by family members. Family groups provided an environment of confidentiality and safety where members could talk about the struggles they faced and the questions they had with regard to the VCF, charity fund applications, and other paperwork required of family members who were dealing with the financial compensation resulting from their loved ones' deaths.

Long-Term Recovery and Identification Process

The rescue and recovery efforts at Ground Zero began immediately after the attacks on September 11 and concluded eight and a half months later on May 30, 2002. Family members were asked to submit DNA samples of their loved ones (toothbrushes, hair brushes, etc.) to the medical examiner's office for comparison with samples of the remains. Of the nearly 2,800 lives that were lost at the World Trade Center site, only 1,594 individuals were identified through their physical remains. The medical examiners office received a total of 19,964 human remains, out of which 10,834 were identified (Office of Chief Medical Examiner, The City of New York, 2005). This identification process continued until February of 2005, at which time the medical examiner's office felt that it had exhausted all DNA technology available to it. The process may resume in the future if new technology emerges.

Particularly during the first year post-9/11, the topic of body parts was one that often came up in family groups. This was a subject that was rarely discussed outside of group, as participants felt they could only talk about this highly sensitive issue in a safe and confidential space with other 9/11 family members. Discussions often revolved around what it meant to have received either a full body, body parts, or no body at all. The many who did not receive any remains were often left haunted by what had happened to their loved ones' bodies. Most held the belief that their loved ones "vaporized," and for many the thought of their loved ones instantly dying brought a sense of relief even if that meant they had no remains. Others felt that they needed a body in order to feel some sense of finality or to have a burial and subsequently a place to grieve. For some, no remains led to fantasies that their loved ones might still be alive.

The reactions of the very small percentage of family members whose loved ones' bodies were recovered intact ranged from relief at having their loved ones returned to them whole, bewilderment as to how a body could have remained intact under the collapse, to increased distress because for many, an intact body meant that their loved ones could have been one of the many who jumped from the towers that morning. For most family members this was the worst-case scenario because it led to the belief that their loved ones' last moments must have been extremely distressing

Those who received remains in the form of body parts were often notified of additional identifications multiple times during the long-term identification process. Some of the body parts that were recovered were so small that family members questioned what to do with a "shard of bone." They were also faced with what to do with the additional remains after a burial had already occurred. Those that chose to bury body parts as they were received often buried the first pieces deeper than in a normal burial, allowing for several containers to be buried on top of one another in the same plot. For many, new identifications caused old feelings of grief to resurface and were often accompanied by increased feelings of depression. As a result, many opted not to be informed by the medical examiner as additional body parts were identified. Others lived in a heightened state of anxiety, not knowing when or if they would receive the dreaded phone call from the medical examiner with news of identified remains.

In a number of cases, many who were contacted did not share information about the identified body parts with other family members to protect them from the painful news. Often, the group became the only place where family members would share this information with others. In one case, a group member had received an additional body part of her brother almost three years after the tragedy and chose not to share this information with her elderly mother. The member expressed gratitude to the group for giving her a place to share this information and receive the support she felt she could not receive anywhere else. Another member reported feeling "shaken up" by the recent body part identification of his daughter. The group members joined in their support of this member and at the close of the session the member stated that the experience of sharing and talking openly about his daughter's remains was very helpful.

The following case example illustrates one member's struggle with the identification of his son's body and how the group process helped him to address this.

Charlie lost his son, Paul, a 22-year-old firefighter for the New York City Fire Department. Charlie had been unaware of the attacks on the World Trade Center until hours after the towers had collapsed. Once he was told that Paul had reported for work that day and that he was now missing, he said that his knees gave out and his younger son had to put him in bed. For the next few weeks, he rarely moved from his bed and was glued to the television where he watched the 9/11 news coverage nonstop. When Charlie first chose to participate in a family group a year and a half after September 11, he was experiencing anxiety, deep sadness, loss of appetite, withdrawal from friends and family, an inability to work, and difficulties concentrating and making decisions. He was experiencing deep guilt and regret about not discouraging Paul from working as a firefighter, something he felt would have prevented his death. Charlie reported having fantasies of his own death, believing this would allow him to be reunited with his son. He had become extremely religious since 9/11, finding comfort in surrendering his questions about his son's death and suffering to God. It was reassuring for Charlie to believe that justice would be done to those who had perpetrated his son's death.

As the retelling sessions approached, Charlie told the group that he had never spoken about his son's death with anyone before. His story focused on the days after 9/11, after Paul's body was recovered. Charlie was profoundly disturbed that his son's body was recovered intact except for a missing leg, ruminating on what had happened to cause this. Charlie told the group that for a long time after Paul's body had been recovered, his own leg hurt in the same place that his son's leg had been severed. The week before he was to recount this story to the group, he reported that his leg had begun to hurt once again in that same spot. Charlie, a funeral director by trade, chose to be the one to clean and dress his son's body for the burial, something he wanted to do as his way of saying goodbye. After the burial, he learned from the person who recovered Paul's body that his leg was severed by a steel beam that had fallen on top of him. When the body was found, the leg had fallen into a smoldering pit of fire and could not be reached. Charlie reported hope that his son's leg would be recovered so that he could bury his leg and reunite it with the rest of his body. Charlie shared with the group that this was a particular concern for him because he desperately wanted his son to be whole again, for his body to exit the world as it had entered the world at birth.

Group members reported being horrified by Charlie's graphic story of dressing his own son's body for burial because it led many to contemplate how they might have reacted if they had experienced the same situation with their loved ones. Despite their shock, group members were supportive, listening intently, offering glasses of water and tissues during his retelling, commenting on Charlie's strength, and expressing their sympathy. After retelling his story, Charlie reported that his leg no longer hurt. By the end of the group cycle, he reported that for the first time he felt relieved and more relaxed. It seemed possible that Charlie's leg pain was connected to the pain of losing his son, demonstrating that a piece of him was now also missing. Charlie went on to join another cycle of group in order to continue his process of accepting his loss and healing himself. The valuable reparative work Charlie was able to do in the group and his retelling in particular, allowed him to begin to function more fully in his life. Charlie reported less paralyzing sadness, was more active and communicative, and reconnected with friends and family.

Vicarious Trauma

Clinicians working with the 9/11 impacted populations were asked each day to bear witness to the grief and horror experienced by each group member. Counselors were expected to maintain their professionalism as they envisioned in their minds the violent deaths of each group member's loved one. After the retelling sessions, hearts were often heavy and minds were preoccupied with horrific images. Over time many clinicians reported a refusal to watch the news, read the newspaper, or have anything to do with 9/11 when outside of the office. Unlike other trauma work, reminders of 9/11 were everywhere: in the newspaper, on television, in books, on the Internet, in subway ads, and in discussions of both a public and private nature.

To add to the challenge of providing 9/11 related mental health services, clinicians had their own personal experiences on 9/11. Some were downtown that morning, some had family members working in or near the World Trade Center, some were caught in the evacuation out of Manhattan, and some knew people who died that day. All experienced a great loss as New Yorkers, as Americans, as human beings. So it was crucial for individual clinicians to be aware of their own responses to the stories they heard, to the ongoing terror alerts, and their own safety concerns while living or working in New York City post-9/11.

To address the high potential for vicarious trauma and burnout, each group had two facilitators who were expected to debrief immediately after each group session. Each clinician also attended individual and group supervision, group processing meetings, and self-care meetings. Clinicians used these forums for support, guidance, and to help one another better understand their own feelings and reactions to what they were hearing day in and day out. In addition, Safe Horizon planned several afternoon self-care retreats, on-site massages, professionally run group processing sessions, and made other healthy and nurturing activities available to staff. Individual self-care routines outside of the office were encouraged as well, so that individual clinicians would feel able to continue providing these valuable and needed services.

AFTER GROUP ENDS: ONGOING CARE FOR 9/11 FAMILY MEMBERS

The termination phase for each group cycle raised anxiety levels for many participants who did not want the group to end. For many, group had been their primary support. Many participants feared that they might regress without the ongoing support of the group. Some bargained for more sessions while others, who may have had consistent attendance throughout the group, did not show for the last session. To address the requests from many family members for ongoing support once the weekly group ended, Safe Horizon established a number of options for aftercare. Options included repeat of the weekly group, referrals for individual counseling, participation in a monthly group, or no further services for those who stated that their needs had been met. A monthly group was formed for group members who wished to stay connected and felt they would benefit from ongoing support services. The monthly group, facilitated by the same counselor every month, was open to anyone who had completed the weekly group cycle. Membership in the monthly group changed over time and new people came in and dropped out as their needs changed.

Family group members, already struggling with issues around loss, were encouraged by facilitators to use the termination phase of the group to explore their feelings around endings and saying goodbye. For some the end of group was a relief, while for others, it was a trigger for the loss they experienced on 9/11. Facilitators also encouraged members to use the termination phase for feedback about the group process as a whole. One member stated that she did not feel as bad as she had before the group, while another member shared that being in group helped him speak about his loss to friends and acquaintances. Another participant stated that he learned to be more verbal about 9/11 outside of group as a result of the group experience and was relieved to be able to now express painful thoughts and emotions to close family and friends. He shared that before group the only 9/11 dialogues he had were in his head and that the group was able to give a voice to his thoughts. Another member reported that the grief process made her grow and that she appreciated having the group to facilitate this process. Members also gave one another feedback on the changes and the progress they witnessed in each other through the course of the group cycle. One participant told a fellow group member that he now smiled more and did not appear as sad as when he first entered the group. In another group, several members made the same comment to one member, stating that they noticed a dramatic positive change in her since the beginning of the group. To honor the end of the group cycle, some members brought gifts for the whole group such as memorabilia of their loved ones which included 9/11 related T-shirts, photos, and newspaper articles about their loved ones, while others brought inspirational items to help group members continue to move forward after the end of the group. Many built lasting relationships, which allowed them to continue to support one another after the group ended.

SUMMARY

The benefits of providing a community-based intervention for family members of 9/11 victims were evident immediately following the collapse of the World Trade Center towers and continued several years posttragedy. As victims of a large-scale public tragedy perpetrated by terrorists, participants used the Safe Horizon family groups to overcome their natural inclination to isolate. Many built relationships with one another that continued to be supportive long after group had ended. By conducting a family support group that allowed for ongoing flexibility in the model, members were able to address timely issues like terrorism, media coverage, body parts, finances, ongoing terror threats, and rebuilding at the World Trade Center site. Group provided a place to normalize reactions and emphasize coping skills in the first year when family members were experiencing more trauma-related symptoms of shock, anxiety, and numbness, were suffering from flashbacks and nightmares, having fantasies of rescuing loved ones, and feeling guilt over not being able to protect those who died.

In the second year, when symptoms of trauma were decreasing and members were experiencing increased depression, isolation, and anger, and realizing the finality of their loss, group provided a space where members could adjust to their changing lives. And in the third year, when groups tended to be comprised of caretakers who were just beginning to acknowledge their own needs, the family group became a crucial means of ongoing support when many other 9/11 programs were being discontinued. Members were able to address all of these issues in group while simultaneously moderating their levels of traumatic distress, reconstructing a personal narrative of how their loved ones died through the process of retelling, acknowledging positive resilience, and reconnecting with people and activities in order to move forward in their lives. Important aspects of the success of the Safe Horizon family groups were their ability to provide support at varying stages of member grief, to adjust to the needs of members over time, and ensure a safe and confidential space where grief could be shared and the process of healing could begin.

ACKNOWLEDGMENTS

Thank you to Christy Gibney Carey for her invaluable leadership at the Family Assistance Center and for providing the historical perspective of Safe Horizon's 9/11 program in this chapter. Thank you to Nadine Karaskevicus for her eagerness in documenting some of the successes of the 9/11 groups. And a very special thank you to Michele Vigeant for her years of clinical guidance and hours of hard work editing this chapter. All of their contributions are greatly appreciated and honor not only the victims of 9/11 but also the family members who attended Safe Horizon's family groups.

REFERENCES

Federal Bureau of Investigation. (n.d.). *28 code of federal regulations section 0.85*. Retrieved from Federal Bureau of Investigation's website January 24, 2005: http://www.fbi.gov/publications/terror/terror2000_2001.htm

Johnston's Archive. (n.d.). Worst terrorist strikes — U.S. and worldwide, compiled by William Robert Johnston. Retrieved March 13, 2005, http://www.johnstonsarchive.net/terrorism/wrjp255i.html

National Center for Post Traumatic Stress Disorder. (n.d.). Department of Veteran Affairs. What are the traumatic stress effects of terrorism? A National PTSD Center Fact Sheet by Jessica Hamblen, Ph.D. and Laurie B. Slone, Ph.D. Retrieved April 28, 2005, http://www.ncptsd.org/facts/disasters/fs_terrorism.html

Office of Chief Medical Examiner, the City of New York. (2005, August 19). *Office of chief medical examiner: World trade center operational statistics*. New York: Author.

Rynearson, E. K. (2001). *Retelling violent death*. Philadelphia: Brunner-Routledge.

19

Group Therapy for Palestinian Family Members After Violent Death

KHADER RASRAS, SUAD MITWALLI, AND MAHMUD SEHWAIL

THE ISRAELI OCCUPATION

Touring trauma clinics in Israel and Palestine, the editor visited a trauma center in Ramallah where the staff had already completed a time-limited group intervention for family members suffering traumatic grief related to the Intifada and the Israel incursion and occupation. A time-limited group intervention was selected for clinical and pragmatic reasons — with military occupation family members physically and emotionally isolated from one another, and because of frequent curfews and arrested movements with checkpoints, it was difficult for family members to attend the clinic with any predictability. Scheduling an entire group for an appointment promised an opportunity for socialization and more consistent attendance. The intervention for the closed group of women lasted for 21 sessions with a low drop-out rate and no casualties. Case illustrations demonstrate the cultural variations of grief when violent dying is viewed as heroic martyrdom, and the specific therapeutic strategies designed to meet the dominant religious and cultural beliefs. A description of the agenda also highlights the advisability of group support with an intervention carried out in the social context of persistent trauma and incursion where the entire community identifies itself as oppressively traumatized, and where group cohesion plays a prominent supportive role.

BACKGROUND

The Treatment and Rehabilitation Center for Victims of Torture (TRC) began its service in 1999 as a nongovernmental agency funded by international donations providing free mental health service to the 120,000 citizens of Ramallah and surrounding West Bank communities. Since its inception, a multidisciplinary team has been assembled (clinical staff currently consists of one psychiatrist, one psychiatric resident, seven psychologists, and nine social workers).

Services can be roughly divided into the following categories:

- Outreach and crisis intervention programs
- Family counseling/individual and group therapy
- Mental health and human rights training
- Media and public awareness program

TRC was initially designed to serve victims of torture and organized violence associated with the Israeli occupation. However, since the second Intifada began in 2000, the agency has been overwhelmed by the clinical needs of the 135 Ramallah families who lost family members to Israeli military attacks. It became progressively more difficult to establish contact with these highly distressed clients since the Israeli Occupying Forces divided the West Bank into prisonlike segments through a series of checkpoints, closures, and curfews. Before the Intifada, staff provided service at TRC's main office in Ramallah, but the temporal and spatial obstacles of occupation rendered it necessary for multidisciplinary teams to evaluate and support community members in their homes. Since 2000, the outreach program is now the fundamental venue for providing service — 43 of 125 clients received outreach services in 2000, 349 of 490 clients in 2001, 557 of 663 in 2002, and 419 of 474 in 2003.

After frequent visitations, staff recognized the specialized needs of recently bereaved family members and established a more comprehensive service. Outreach workers realized that there were inherent cultural factors that complicated accommodation to intense trauma and grief following violent death that might be modified with a group-based intervention.

Palestinian culture "ordains" someone killed by the Israeli occupiers as a martyr whose soul is destined to a favored space in heaven. This spiritual transformation complicates mourning by discouraging the exaggerated expression of sadness. To further complicate accommodation of trauma and grief, during the first year of bereavement Palestinian traditions discourage bereaved family members from expressing happiness aloud or celebrating personal anniversaries or showing signs of joy on social occasions. In addition, women whose husbands died violently live under social restrictions that limit interaction (parties, excursions) with anyone outside the immediate family. Widows are objects of severe criticism if they violate these norms of communication or interaction; however, despite these sociocultural restrictions, Palestinian women experienced responses fundamental to trauma and separation as a result of the violent death of their loved ones.

It was decided that a group intervention might offer a more supportive, empathic, and interactive context for distressed and culturally suppressed family members to create a setting open to communicating residual trauma and grief distress. Group therapy might also reduce another source of persistent social unrest — the unpredictable and high-risk nature of day-to-day Palestinian safety with the Israeli occupation and insurgency and its daily reminder of violent death and the possibility of its recurrence in surviving family members (Sehwail &Rasras, 2002). Group therapy could offer a sheltered and protective setting where family members could express their ongoing fears of this recurrence.

The authors researched descriptive and empirical reports documenting the applicability and effectiveness of time-limited individual therapy after complicated grief, and group therapy for family members after violent death for adults (Rynearson & Sinnema, 1999) and children (Saloum, Avery, & McClain, 2001). These reports documented the effectiveness of time-limited individual therapy and group therapy in reducing distress and the sense of emotional isolation and stigma commonly noted in family members following a violent death. Group therapy also provided insight and opportunity to share problems and care for one another — a mutual engagement and caregiving. The authors anticipated that the group interaction would instill a sense of "universality" between members and reduce their culturally reinforced isolation.

CHARACTERISTICS OF THE PARTICIPANTS

The group participants (14 bereaved women — 10 mothers and four widows) agreed to attend a closed, time-limited (20 sessions) group therapy after outreach assessment established enduring and dysfunctional symptoms of trauma and grief persisting for four to 12 months after the violent death. The women were adults (median age 40, range 26 to 50). Ten of the participants were from the city of Ramallah while the remaining four were from refugee camps, in the same districts. Nine of the group members (eight mothers and one widow) were bereaved by the violent death of a noncombatant, while five (two mothers and three widows) were bereaved by a combatant death.

Participants underwent psychiatric consultation prior to treatment that substantiated a presumptive diagnosis of complicated grief in all 14 subjects, and comorbid major depressive disorder in four subjects, two of whom agreed to a course of antidepressant medication while attending the group. None of the other participants were on psychotropic medications during the course of the time-limited group therapy. All 14 participants completed the time-limited group intervention.

DESCRIPTION OF THE INTERVENTION

A therapist and a cotherapist hosted each of the weekly sessions, which lasted 90 minutes, followed by 30 minutes of relaxation exercises. Since each participant was overwhelmed by an imaginary replay of the final moments of her family member's violent dying, occurring with such intensity and frequency that it interfered with her concentration, the initial goal of the intervention was to diminish the trauma distress associated with this imagery. Each participant was similarly preoccupied with the self-imposed obsession that she should have prevented the dying , that she had somehow failed the deceased in allowing the dying to occur, so the intervention also focused on diminishing these obsessions.

Supportive therapy with a cognitive–behavioral focus was utilized to help the group members understand the nature of their thoughts, behaviors, emotions, psychosomatic complaints, and irrational thoughts, focusing on their recurring thoughts of the dying and remorse.

Group members requested that the home visits by TRC's field worker be continued. To announce the group therapy program, media interviews (TV and radio) were offered to the participants to give them an opportunity to publicly address their traumatic experiences. This served as a "testimonial" reinforcement to restore the patient's awareness.

Since a sizable number of children accompanied the group participants to sessions, it was decided to gather the children in a separate room where they could have specific play therapy and leisure activities with another TRC psychologist.

FIRST PHASE (SESSIONS 1–7)

Initially the group concentrated on revealing the extenuating circumstances of the violent deaths — a brief recounting of the dying, how they received the news, and how they reacted. The atmosphere of these sessions was highly emotional. The women were of a great support to each other. Many mothers expressed guilt. One mother revealed her pent-up guilt subsequent to her son's death. She had scolded him the day before he was killed, and said many things that she didn't mean. She believed his death was directly related to her angry behavior. The group members could empathize with her remorse and helped her realize the irrationality of her obsession.

Common to group members was the expression of anger at surviving and fury at the deceased for leaving them alone, vulnerable, and burdened with responsibilities they felt unable to cope with. Several members were stifled in their mourning because they were forbidden from seeing the bodies of their loved ones before burial — because the death occurred during a curfew or the body was maimed or disfigured. Everyone in the group recognized that remembering your loved one as healthy and alive was more restorative than remembering a marred corpse. Group members were able to share pictures of their beloved lost ones to share vital and nurturing memories and cry openly.

Group members began discussing physical problems, mostly psychosomatic in nature. They also mentioned having poor appetite, disrupted sleep, and an inclination to solitude, exhaustion, headaches, joint, muscle, and back pain.

SECOND PHASE (SESSIONS 8–14)

These sessions focused on sociocultural issues that interfered with their personal restoration from trauma and grief. The group modified the cultural proscription of mourning behaviors that reinforced feelings of despair and isolation. A cleric attended the group to soften some of the restrictive cultural assumptions related to grief.

Group members became more aware of the patterns of mourning and grief within their primary and extended families, and were able to be more tolerant and supportive of the differences and uniqueness of the responses of others.

At the close of this phase, members began mutually searching for private and public alternatives in accommodating to trauma and grief. This culminated in a procession of visits to group members' homes at the end of each session to prepare and share a meal while continuing to socialize.

THIRD PHASE (SESSIONS 15–20)

The third phase of group therapy inaugurated a significant improvement in trauma and grief distress. The topics of conversation shifted from the effects of the violent deaths and began focusing on the routines of daily life. The participants began considering plans for the future beyond this tragic event. For example, the women admitted to a decrease in their visits to the burial site of their lost loved ones, decided to donate or distribute the clothes of the deceased after hording them, revised the colors of their own clothing from the dismal black that was customary during the first phases of loss, and were committed to activities that would make their families happy. Physical and emotional complaints decreased; however, emotional pain was still often clear in the participants' facial expressions and gestures.

The American invasion of Iraq occurred during this phase of treatment and the participants supported one another in their mutual fear of recurrence — that Palestine might somehow become involved in an escalation of warfare with heightened risk of violent death of another family member.

Five of the group members went to Mecca during the group therapy intervention; the other group members who had gone the year before discussed how this religious ritual helped them in accommodating to the violent death.

An additional gathering of the group (session 21) was added as an "open day" for group members to bring along their families and especially their children. The day began at 10 a.m. and ended at 1:30 p.m. and was hosted by the coleaders and a group of professionals from RTC who supervised art and play activities for the children and their mothers. The children had their faces painted with bright colors, joined group movement exercises, dance, and group songs.

The main goal of the last session was to give the mothers a chance to interact with their children in mutual activities designed so the children could play with their mothers and see their mothers simply enjoying the role of motherhood. The activities showed the children that their mothers were not only grieving for the lost family member, but were capable of giving their children love, attention, and concern. The complementary activities clarified for the children that their presence and sharing was restorative for their mothers. The day not only served as a recreational open day, but also as the last session of group therapy and a graduation ceremony.

NARRATIVE CASE PRESENTATIONS

To clarify the uniqueness of the events of the violent dying in a Palestinian community under persistent incursion and occupation, we include the following narrative case presentations:

Case 1

Firyal, a 41-year-old mother and housewife, lived in Ramallah with her husband and six children. In April 2002, the Israeli Occupying Force (IOF) raided the apartment complex where Firyal's family resided. The men in the complex were herded onto the roof or into one room of one of the apartments. Firyal's 18-year-old son, Murad, was arrested despite Firyal's pleading with the IOF. Murad had recently suffered a head injury and was recovering from a neurosurgical procedure. Sixteen hours later after the men were released from collective detention, Murad didn't reappear. Neighbors reported that he hadn't remained on the roof where he had been initially detained. Instead, he was beaten and tortured so severely that he had to be taken to hospital where he died the same day.

Doctors who worked on Murad at the hospital documented that he had multiple bruises from being beaten and died from multiple gunshot wounds. Because he died during an Israeli-imposed curfew, Firyal was denied access to the body and was unable to view his remains or attend his burial. There were so many combat-related deaths that day that it was impossible to bury the large number of corpses brought to the hospital so the remains were buried in a collective grave during the curfew.

Later, the curfew was broken and Firyal was contacted by TRC and supportive therapy began through the outreach program. She was in a state of total denial — experiencing auditory and visual hallucinations of her dead son's voice. She claimed to see his face in the moon, especially a full moon, and had long conversations with him. She maintained herself in this private, idealized fantasy of restitution, managing to hide her feelings from the rest of her immediate family. Firyal was diagnosed with acute stress reaction manifested by avoidance, fatigue, extreme sadness, nervousness, aggression, and inability to express joy. She now realized the negative impact of continuing to live in the apartment complex where her son was tortured, admitting that she was still able to see his blood, and imagined she could hear his cries. Because of her severe distress, the family was further disoriented and strained by Firyal's decision to uproot them from their home and move to a new location.

Phase 1

Firyal joined TRC's group therapy program where other group members empathically listened as she began putting words to her private fantasies of restitution, which rapidly diminished. At first she requested some media documentation of her son's dying. At the time of his death, his life and death were not given the respect they deserved from the media, nor did the family go through the burial rituals because he was buried at the hospital. She didn't see him and wasn't even able to bid him farewell. She wrote a letter of farewell to her son in which she explicitly described her feelings and a second letter describing the details of his death (how he was arrested, tortured, and killed), and asked TRC how she could publish it. TRC released these letters to the local newspaper and broadcast them on the radio. Members of group therapy also received copies of these letters.

During this time she spoke of her "bad luck" and compared the sadness she was bearing to the weight of a huge burden pressing on her. She released her suppressed sadness during this time, followed by intense feelings of retaliation, and she tried to monopolize the conversations during group therapy. She also spoke of her children's suffering and related dreams that they had of their dead brother. During this first phase she spent a lot of time at her son's grave.

Phase 2

She now expressed anger at her children who wouldn't allow her to express her sadness openly. Her children wanted her to go to her room to cry. She wanted to go on a pilgrimage to Mecca, but this would mean that her children would be left alone during the big Muslim holiday. TRC suggested that she should go on the pilgrimage with four other group members who were going. In order to memorialize her dead son, she decided to take the letter describing his dying to Mecca (and TRC photocopied some 100 copies) that she distributed by hand to other pilgrims.

TRC visited her children during her absence. Staff and group members reinforced that the children should rejoice during the holidays and not wallow in sorrow, and organized a "fun day" for her children during the holiday.

Phase 3

After her return from Mecca, she felt considerable relief and transformation — that God had helped her overcome her grief. She believed that she had to carry on with her life and began concentrating on nurturing remaining family members, particularly her son who was old enough to marry and was searching for a bride. At this time the war in Iraq began and the West Bank was put under great stress. She became preoccupied with her son's safety — that he would be arrested and put to death. She began avenging her son's anticipated death with murderous thoughts of Ariel Sharon and expressed anger and fury at the political situation in general. She complained that while she was trying to be happy, she felt the same heavy burden was now inside her and prevented her from rejoicing freely.

Slowly, she realized that she was again neglecting her children and husband and vowed to try to give them more attention. Over the remaining weeks of group she was surprised and encouraged by all the frustrations she was able to bear and began discussing her earlier life, her marriage, extended family, and her husband's family, and began wearing colors other than black.

Case 2

Summar is a 37-year-old mother of five who lost her husband on July 5, 2001. She married at the early age of 18, and mourned not only the loss of her spouse but the strong, happy relationship they shared. She was deeply in love with and committed to her husband. He shouldered the family's responsibilities while Summar devoted her time to the family and maternal duties. Their financial situation was relatively stable, and the family was content. At the time of her husband's death, her eldest child was 17 and her youngest child was four.

In the summer of 2001, Summar's husband was playing soccer with friends in the park near their home. She had asked him not to go because the political situation was so unstable. An Israeli tank passing the soccer field began shooting randomly and killed him. She heard the shots fired by a tank and immediately thought it was related to her husband. Once her suspicions were confirmed, she decompensated with severe anxiety and dysphoria.

Summar was treated with high doses of antianxiety medication during her husband's funeral and burial and was not alert when she bid his body farewell. She became isolated, and preoccupied with vivid fantasies of restitution that her husband was still alive (she was able to see, hear, and communicate with him), and lost interest in caring for her children. Her four-year-old daughter, who was used to bedtime stories and special pampering, suffered greatly.

She was unable to function as head of her family and unable to deal with her new and overwhelming responsibilities. She lost control of her teenage children. The eldest boy refused to be disciplined by her and their relationship became very tense. He accused her of trying to replace the powerful role of his father. At the time, Summar was benefiting from TRC's outreach program, but her eldest daughter had a problem with her mother seeing a therapist. The girl was afraid that her mother and the entire family would be labeled. The negativity about her therapy from her two oldest children only increased her hopeless state.

Phase 1

Summar initially expressed her disbelief in the death of her husband. She was clearly in denial, but eventually began exploring ways she could cope with her new responsibilities. Summar talked more directly about her husband and his death that she blamed on the lack of care he received at the hospital. She wanted to return to the hospital and go through his files because when he died she was drugged and could not remember any of the details of those hours and days. During sessions she often suffered from headaches and panic attacks, and would often tell the group that she suffered from these attacks because of something that she couldn't discuss. Though she persistently wept and mourned, other group members encouraged Summar to talk with her husband's friends, especially those who were working out with him when he was killed. She did so, and their stories helped in summoning a clearer story of his dying.

Phase 2

In later sessions she developed a more coherent narrative of her husband's living as well as his dying, and wept as she mourned more openly about his loss. She was so drugged at the time of his death that she couldn't say "goodbye," and felt isolated and received no support from his family. She admitted to having hallucinations, of hearing her husband's voice, and seeing him coming home. She was worried that the group would think she was crazy at first, but decided to tell them so that they would understand why she had panic attacks. The group reassured and supported her and recounted their similar hallucinatory experiences of restitution.

Phase 3

During the holiday, she didn't want her children to wear new clothes or celebrate the holiday in any way. The group told her that she should prepare for the holidays joyfully, if only for the sake of her four-year-old daughter. At this time, her older daughter also had a birthday and she didn't want to celebrate. Again the group encouraged her to make a cake and have a simple party. She was encouraged to carry on with happy occasions and celebrations. At this time she started concerning herself with her family. She told the group that she began telling her young daughter bedtime stories and she cooked their favorite meals.

She began wearing brighter clothing and talked about her life before the trauma, her marriage and how vital and energetic she had been. She noticed that her children's moods became happier as she felt less distress and now concentrated on the responsibilities of raising her children. At the end of the group therapy activity, she asked to continue at TRC with individual therapy, which she continued for about four months.

Case 3

Fatma, a 43-year-old woman and mother of five children, all under the age of 18, was traumatically bereaved following the death of her husband.

Her husband was a high-ranking member of the Palestinian security force and was killed in a shootout with the Israeli Occupying Force.

Her emotional dependence on her husband was intense because she had been separated from her extended family when they had moved to Ramalla 10 years before. She was so socially dependent on her husband and children that she hadn't developed a strong social circle since her move to Ramallah.

Shortly before his death he had abandoned Fatma and his family and married a younger woman. While this was devastating for Fatma, she remained emotionally and economically dependent upon him, and they were on good terms when he died. Their relationship remained strong and he continued to function as a dependable father and provider.

After his death, Fatma suffered from the lack of any form of social support because all of her relatives were abroad and she had invested little time in making new friends. TRC intervened with outreach visits and found that her trauma was exacerbated by a weak supportive system and that she was overwhelmed by her maternal responsibilities. She couldn't control her children because they were used to their father's discipline.

Phase 1

During the initial phase of group therapy, Fatma exhibited extreme sadness, was silent most of the time, and not cooperative or interactive with the other group members. She persistently complained that she was unable to handle the daily demands of her children, and she remained angry with her husband's second wife.

Phase 2

After expressing her despondency to the group, who patiently tolerated her verbalization of hopelessness, she talked more openly about her ambivalent feelings toward her husband, not only of sadness and grief over his death, but anger toward his abandonment of her for another woman. As she became more trusting of the group members' support, she started to exchange visits with them outside of the group therapy sessions. She stated that she felt more empathic tolerance and understanding from the group members than from her relatives or other adults in her support system.

She began making an active effort within her home to revise the sad atmosphere by scheduling and celebrating holidays and birthdays and allowing her children to play outside the home and encouraged them to be more carefree.

Phase 3

During the last phase of group, she had the capacity to deal more calmly with her children's problems and actively assumed the missing father's role at home. She also could more openly share her own grief with her children. Finally, she changed from her widow's weeds (black clothes) to colorful clothes, and became more cheerful and cooperative with the group members by making jokes and laughing in addition to talking about daily concerns and conflicts. We all noted a return of her optimism about herself and her future.

At the closing of the last session, she said, "I deserve to be happy and live my own life."

SUMMARY

Fourteen bereaved family members completed a closed, time-limited group therapy. All of the participants were women who had lost their loved ones during the second Israeli invasion of the West Bank. All of the participants presented with symptoms of complicated grief and PTSD. Ten of the group members initially attended brief individual counseling sessions at the Treatment and Rehabilitation Center for Victims of Torture (TRC) on a regular basis while the remainder were irregular clients at TRC.

The first group session began on December 14, 2002 and continued until June 16, 2003. A therapist and cotherapist led 21 sessions of cognitive behavioral therapy. The 21 sessions were roughly divided into three cognitive phases: the first phase (sessions 1–7) focused on moderating intense trauma distress by encouraging a supportive, shared loosening of denial, and avoidance of the traumatic dying imagery through an open acknowledgment and retelling of the event of loss. The second phase (sessions 8–14) focused on promoting a renewed awareness of the cognitive and emotional bonds with the deceased by relating memories, personal characteristics, symbolic meanings, and identification of their missed role. The third phase (sessions 15–20) focused on helping group members to redefine their roles within their family and community through resuming the duties of everyday life and enhancing their sense of self-efficacy. Group members were actively taught self-regulatory techniques to promote self-care while resuming their caregiving role with others in their immediate environment. As termination approached, a full repertoire of cognitive and behavioral techniques of self-regulation was emphasized to promote ongoing self-monitoring and evaluation.

This trial of time-limited group therapy at our agency was judged successful by the group members, who showed a high degree of support for one another as they mutually enacted an emotional release of their traumatic bereavement. They were able to articulate intense grief and trauma distress by retelling death related stories, despite intense denial and avoidance, and group members remained highly compliant in engaging in the cognitive, emotional, and behavioral tasks of the time-limited group with a low rate of drop-out (10%). All members subjectively reported a significant reduction of grief and trauma symptoms, and the group continued mutual supportive interaction through social gatherings in the homes of participants following termination of therapy.

APPENDIX: GROUP AGENDA

Session 1

The first session was introductory, covering an agreement on the schedule and rules of the group, clarification of roles (clear designation of time for speaking), discussion of issues that might hinder participation, and solutions. The group also discussed media issues, such as television and newspaper coverage.

Session 2

Each participant explained how her son or husband was killed (martyred).

Session 3

This was a continuation of the second session in which the group discussed their experiences in more detail, including their initial reaction to the news of the dying.

Session 4

The discussion began with the news of a child who had been killed (martyred) in Ramallah the day before, and how the group members were adjusting to the incident. One of the mothers' sons was a friend of the martyr, and she discussed how the dying affected her son. This discussion then moved to their previous experiences related to the funeral and mourning period of their loved ones.

Session 5

That day there was bombing and violence in Ramallah, and the group members shared their immediate responses of fear for their families and their fury at Sharon, a discussion that resonated with the fear and rage experienced when their family members had been killed months before.

Sessions 6 and 7

Both sessions were related to the annual Muslim pilgrimage to Mecca, as several of the group members received approval to travel and go on the pilgrimage. The members who had been to Mecca the year before discussed the experience and expectations with those who planned to go. At the end of the discussion, the group asked for a session facilitated by a religious figure to discuss the procedures involved in the pilgrimage. TRC decided to invite a large group of bereaved families to participate in the session facilitated by a religious figure. Group members agreed to discontinue the group for approximately one month during the pilgrimage.

Session 8

Participants brought in pictures of their lost sons/husbands and asked to display these pictures in the group therapy room. Then they discussed the upcoming religious holiday. The women agreed to visit the families of the group participants who were to go on the pilgrimage to provide support while their mothers were away at pilgrimage.

One of the group members mentioned that she had children who, while watching television, would cry and become emotionally upset every time they saw a strong father figure. Another group member expressed her refusal to have a birthday party for her daughter because she (the mother) was too overwhelmed with grief. Both problems were discussed with the group and suggestions and advice were given.

Session 9

Participants discussed the upcoming religious holiday. Some members were determined to remain in their grief, while others expressed interest in participating in the joyous holiday. All participants agreed to introduce some level of joy into the family home for the sake of the children.

One-Month Break — Mecca Pilgrimage

Sessions 10 and 11

Participants returned from the pilgrimage and discussed their experiences. Participants then discussed the lack of social support outside of the group. Widows felt very constricted and pressured by social expectations and regulations. Mothers who had lost a child felt that organizations and society were only concerned with finances and that no one offered emotional support. Participants expressed that their experience after violent death was unique, and their loss could not be compared to any other loss. Coincidentally, this session took place around the time of Mother's Day, making the situation all the more difficult.

Session 12

Participants discussed their fear resulting from news of the beginning of the invasion of Iraq. Group members were worried how the war would affect them, fearing that they might lose another loved one, and concerned as to how the political situation in Palestine might be indirectly affected.

Session 13

This session came at a time when many of the participants were commemorating the one-year anniversary of their loss, and discussion was related to how this anniversary should be managed. The tone of the group was very sad, and they discussed their visits to the cemetery.

The pictures of their lost loved ones that participants had hung on the wall had been covered with a white sheet (this was previously agreed upon so that the pictures would not become the focus of concentration during the sessions), and as the commemoration of their dying approached, the members decided to remove this sheet so that the pictures could be openly viewed at all times.

Sessions 14 and 15

Now that the pictures of the dead family members surrounded them, the group members acknowledged the ongoing conversations that they maintained with their loved ones despite their deaths. They also encouraged one another to be open with remaining family members about commemorative memories of the deceased.

Session 16

Participants discussed physical and emotional problems, their relationships with their children, and how they could be more sensitive to the emotional needs of their children.

Session 17, 18, and 19

Participants discussed their daily problems and the skills used to overcome their frustrations. They made some changes at home and returned to a routine, such as cooking and cleaning, and discussed the small things they did for their children to help them overcome the trauma. During these sessions, the members decided to change their usual sitting places to make their feelings/mood better. They felt that their former seats were designated for sadness, and by moving they were no longer in the "sad" chair/role.

Session 20

Participants began visiting each other socially outside of group, noting that these visits maintained the very supportive interactions of the group. The session ended in discussing the good memories and times that they now remembered sharing with their deceased loved ones. They reported that their physical pain was improved, and their relationships with their family members were more pleasurable.

Session 21

Open Day

REFERENCES

Rynearson, E. K. & Sinnema, C. (1999). Supportive group therapy for bereavement after homicide. In D. Blake & B. Young (Eds.), *Group treatment for post traumatic stress disorder* (pp. 137–147). Philadelphia: Brunner/Mazel.
Salloum, A., Avery, L., & McClain, R. P. (2001). Group psychotherapy for adolescent survivors of homicide victims: A pilot study. *Journal of the American Academy of Child and Adolescent Psychiatry, 40,* 1261–1267.
Sehwail M. & Rasras K. (2002). Group therapy for victims of torture and organized violence. *Quarterly Journal on Rehabilitation of torture, 12*(2), 432–439.

Closing Thoughts

EDWARD K. RYNEARSON

Repeating the themes of theory and practice contained in the preceding chapters risks redundancy by repeating the theoretical insights and clinical strategies that cascade from one chapter to the next. However, it is noteworthy that this repetition is not derived from reference to "gold standard" investigations. There are no tested measures of violent death bereavement, diagnostic criteria for violent death grief, or verified treatments to be widely cited and applied. While the study of violent death bereavement is increasingly robust, it is correspondingly diverse and drawn from a variety of sociocultural contexts and bereaved family members as a result of differing kinds of violent death (disaster, homicide, suicide, accident, or warfare).

Despite this diversity, the authors arrive at comparable principles of theory and practice. This is all the more remarkable since our professional training as clergy, social worker, psychologist, or psychiatrist lacked training on managing the long-term emotional effects of violent death.

The opening chapters on *Restorative and Clinical Essentials* establish that theory of violent death bereavement flows from a mixture of familiar conceptual models generated from trauma or grief theoreticians, followed by subsequent chapters in this section introducing restorative insights more specific to the combination of violent dying and bereavement after violent dying — that resilience reinforcement, family support, and reestablishment of meaning through spiritual, narrative, and performative restoration, reframes the family members' memories of the violent dying and their loved one — and an understanding of neurobiology and the prudent use of medication(s), while not specific to violent dying bereavement, needs to be considered as an important accompaniment to therapy.

The middle chapters on *Restorative and Clinical Interventions* recognize that the clinical prognosis of violent dying bereavement is good. Within a year most family members remain resilient and spontaneously accommodate to trauma and grief distress, and a minority (<10%) seek clinical support after violent death. Resilience is the normative response and resilience is sufficiently reinforced by surviving family, friends, spiritual beliefs and practices, and community agencies. Mothers and young children of the deceased may remain vulnerable to heightened trauma and grief distress after violent death — a vulnerability that might be addressed through community outreach for assessment, case identification, and intervention. Outreach and supportive "first aid" to reinforce resilience are indicated during the initial days and weeks of bereavement, but it is rare for formal assessment and intervention to be initiated until six months have passed — and mothers are the family members who most frequently seek clinical assistance including intervention. The authors all cite the use of time-limited group and individual interventions for children and adults who remain highly distressed and dysfunctional four to six months following the violent death. Regardless of the number of sessions, procedures, or techniques, intervention includes an agenda of similar clinical objectives: (1) the moderation of distress; (2) the imaginal exposure of the violent dying narrative; and (3) the reestablishment of meaning and purpose.

Though these three intervention objectives may be sequenced in a different order or presented simultaneously and repeated, their presence appears to be fundamental to intervention.

The closing chapters on *Community Outreach and Intervention after Disaster and Warfare* describe the planning, organization, and long-term dynamics of community-based support following an event of violent death with mass casualties. A community-based service attempts an integration of community support personnel and agencies and follows a public health model in its design and implementation. The resources to be enlisted include first responders, hospitals, medical examiners, and family assistance for starters, followed by enlistment of schools, religious organizations, media, mental health personnel, victims' assistance agencies — and the list can grow much longer in larger communities with existent disaster plans and agencies, not to mention state and federal players if mandated by the governor and president.

If substantial funding for mental health care materializes there is a counterproductive wave of agency and institutional territoriality and demands for exclusivity in providing service. It is a wonder that a community service can be summoned with requisite flexibility and creativity from so many players.

The authors detail the organizational lessons they have learned in planning and developing programs of community support and highlight the important role that community-based events serve by engaging members of the community in cohesive activities of:

1. mental health service planning,
2. community memorial services for the deceased,
3. ceremonial celebration and affirmation of survival,
4. commemorative ceremonies each year after the disaster,

5. community involvement in legal trial and retribution, and
6. community planning for restoring the site of the disaster.

These closing chapters also present time-limited, individual, and group interventions closely corresponding to the intervention agendas and objectives cited in the previous section of the book.

OBJECTIVES OF FUTURE STUDY

Violent death bereavement deserves specific inquiry. While there is not enough evidence to designate violent death bereavement as categorically distinct from complicated grief or PTSD, there are clinical phenomena and dynamics more specifically associated with violent dying that might be included in a more parsimonious conceptual model that would guide more specific interventions.

The DSM categorical model with formal criteria of objective signs and symptoms cannot capture the dynamics of the momentary, tortuous reprocessing of memories of violent dying admixed with memories of the relationship with the deceased. The processing of the memory of a loved one and his or her violent dying is categorically different from the memory of the violence of an assault or rape: an assault or rape may create overwhelming trauma, but a loved one was not killed. Clinical theory needs to be inclusive of the private and subjective memory registration of both the violent dying and the relationship with the deceased:

1. The memory register of the violent dying is qualitatively different from the memory register of the relationship and is "retold" in several predictable narrative forms:

Reenactment, Retaliation, Retribution, Recurrence

The store of memories associated with the violent dying is surreal (95% of violent deaths occur as a solitary event without the presence of family members), based on police and media reports, and can become preoccupying through the identificatory replay of iconic horror and helplessness. Violent dying is a human act, associated with human intention or negligence. Suicidal, homicidal, accidental, or terrorist "killing" is followed by a socially proscribed inquiry to investigate and determine who was "responsible," because this is a dying that should not have happened. The intense inquest by the media, medical examiner, the police, and sometimes by the courts socially reinforces the personal demand for investigation, and retribution if investigation determines that the deceased was the "victim" of a crime. Natural dying is rarely followed by such a narrative inquiry, and it is not normative for grief following natural dying to include persistent narrations of reenactment, retaliation, retribution, or dread of recurrent violent dying.

2. The memory register of the relationship with the deceased, based upon real time and space, is separable from that of the violent dying and is "retold" in specific, predictable narrative forms:

Remorse, Rescue, Reunion, Relinquish

The store of memories associated with the relationship with the deceased is vitalizing because it was within the living experience of the family member; however, violent dying prevented the opportunity for nurturing interchange. There was no time or space for the family member to be at the side of the deceased, actively trying to prevent the dying, or providing comfort — and finally saying goodbye — as death could no longer be averted. The retellings of guilt over failures to prevent the dying, the intense need to maintain an active reunion with the memory of the deceased, and an inability to accept the finality of the death are commonly associated with violent death. These "retellings" are also common to complicated grief in family members, after natural death, who had opportunity to nurture and support during the dying, but in complicated grief it is the family member herself or himself who feels disintegrated and helpless without the relationship. Complicated grief is more specifically associated with the relational needs of an emotionally vulnerable family member than it is with natural or violent death.

Future theorizing and modeling about violent death bereavement might address these subjective narrative themes of violent dying and the relationship with the deceased by developing standardized procedures and reliable measurement of persistent narrative representations. The significance of the variety of narrative representations might be objectively established by studying bereaved subjects after natural and violent dying to compare their measured frequency, pattern, and change over time. Knowing which one or combination of representations was associated with high risk of persistent distress would not only clarify case identification, but guide in the designing and testing of intervention(s) more specific to revision of the distressing narration (i.e., restorative intervention for revising the persistent narration of reenactment requires specific techniques and focus, different from those for the revision of narration of remorse).

Further, this consideration of narrative representations would "reframe" the perspective of assessment and intervention for the clinician beyond the narrow confines of DSM criteria and pathology. The task of narrative reconstruction might then become as important as arriving at a psychiatric diagnosis. Joining in the narrative of the bereaved family member places the clinician in a role that encourages resilience and serves as catalyst for retelling the story from a different perspective, and that is how restoration begins.

Reframing and Restoration

As a clinician I have joined in thousands of retellings with thousands of distraught family members in narratives that are memorable, unique, and sometimes transformative — when we have been able to fashion a restorative narrative in our work together.

Occasionally some narratives are so luminous and immediate in their restorative purpose that they are poetic in their first telling. I was not anticipating the powerful immediacy of such a story, but I might have. I was on a training tour of trauma clinics in Israel and Palestine teaching the recognition and management of violent death bereavement. I wanted to not only train clinicians, but develop a collaborative training network to foster a professional connection between clinicians that transcended the war.

In this part of the world the narrative of violent dying has become instrumental in dividing Palestinians and Israelis. Violent dying narration has assumed a cultural and political purpose, distorting the act of violent dying into a narrative of deterrence, retribution, potency, and even martyrdom. While touring clinics I heard many Israeli and Palestinian retellings, but regardless of whether the loved one died in a suicidal bomb blast in a crowded café in Jerusalem, or was machine gunned from a hovering helicopter in Gaza City, each carried the familiar narrative themes of violent death. Bereaved families, Palestinian or Israeli, were struggling with the retellings of reenactment, retaliation, retribution, and the dread of recurrence, combined with sorrowful longings for reunion and interrupted caregiving.

While isolated from one another by militancy and hardening boundaries, the Palestinian and Israeli family members were joined by an overarching shadow of violent death bereavement.

Let me retell the story that I heard only once, but in that single retelling provided a humanistic connection with the mutuality of their suffering.

Jabaliya, Gaza, February 21, 2005

With the late morning sun at our backs we hiked to a ridge top overlooking the field. In the welcome coolness of a light breeze and the smell of the freshly worked soil from the valley floor, we looked down over the rows of green strawberry plants stretching below us. Descending and then ascending toward the next ridgeline a half-mile from where we stood, the symmetry of the rows abruptly ended at the base of the next ridge that bordered an Israeli settlement. Because the settlement was beyond the ridge, all we could see was its foreboding perimeter — a "no-man's" land of plowed field, a brown smear across its face, a high fenced barrier across its spine and a guarded observation tower at its highest point.

The Palestinian family who farmed this field, mother, father, and 14 children, lived in a tiny cinderblock house on the outskirts of Jabaliya, a city in North Gaza. When there was no answer at their door we walked to the field where they would be working. Ibrahim, a Palestinian psychologist from the local trauma clinic, was counseling the family with weekly visits and had prepared them for my appearance. The father greeted us and then left to gather family members from the field at a work shed where they ate and rested. Two daughters brought chairs, insisted that we sit, and returned with trays — one with glasses of hot Turkish coffee and another with freshly washed strawberries. The mother appeared with her five-year-old son who helped steady her. She sat on a rug her husband spread at the base of a tree and leaned back against the trunk explaining to Ibrahim that she was still fatigued and unable to work the fields since the deaths of her children six weeks before.

The night of their deaths, Palestinian terrorists attacked the Israeli settlement with rockets and mortar from the far edge of the family's strawberry field. Within minutes an Israeli tank drove to the base of the observation tower and opened fire with rockets, cannon, and machine gun straight across the field and into the village. The terrorists escaped, but five of the family's children were killed when a rocket fired from the tank made a direct hit on the wall beside their house where they huddled for protection.

The mother needed to talk, and needed to talk to me, her eyes fixed on mine through the retelling, interrupted only by Ibrahim's translation. She reenacted the dying of her children in detail so I would witness a recounting, not only through her words, but drawing me into the space where this had happened, where she pointed — the edge of the field, the base of the tower where the tank was parked, even struggling to her feet to point to the wall where the children had been killed.

The father insisted that Ibrahim and I examine rocket fragments gathered from the death site — mute remnants verifying that this had really happened. Four of the children had died immediately. They buried two, but two of the bodies were so disintegrated that there was nothing left to bury. Weeks after the deaths, they were still finding body parts of children scattered across the field. The fifth child, badly disfigured and burned, was transferred to a trauma hospital in Israel where he died. The Israelis would not allow her to visit him and now she waited for his body to be returned to Jabaliya so he could be buried beside his two brothers. Ibrahim interrupted to ask how the family was adjusting. The father said that they were beginning to cry because they were accepting the finality of the deaths, "that they are gone forever." One of the daughters said they were having recurring nightmares of the attack, and the five-year-old son was wetting his bed and refused to separate from his parents, "but he's getting better."

I asked to see pictures of the children when they were alive. The photographs passed between us and included a large poster produced by the local newspaper showing the smiling faces of the five children with their names and confirmation of their martyrdom.

As Ibrahim and I rose to say goodbye the mother insisted we stay because she had something else to tell me. She spoke at some length, again staring intently at me, but this time with feeling, her eyes brimming with tears, and as she finished they streamed down her face.

> She wants you to know that she does not want revenge for what happened....
> She wants the killing to stop....
> She says that all of us are farmers, not soldiers. The Israeli people are not soldiers either....

Our terrorists and their soldiers are the ones who are fighting, but it is the leaders who won't stop it. Arafat, Sharon, and your President Bush are the men who continue this killing....

We have had enough. We need this to stop....

She hopes that Abbas and Sharon and Bush will make peace....

She wants the deaths of her five children to be the last deaths in this awful war...."

As Ibrahim and I walked back to the car he reminded me that Palestinians have a long tradition of dealing with wars, despotic leaders, and violent death. Despite the thousands of years of trauma and grief that reverberated over these hills and fields, like other Palestinians this family stubbornly remained.

To me, the mother's message went beyond that shared capacity for stoicism and persistence, and beyond the familiar demands for retaliation and retribution. Her retelling contained an empowering combination of narrative and performative meaning, expressive of horror, rage, and despair counterbalanced by empathy and hope. "Reaching out" to Israeli families transformed the death of her children into an affirmation of the future as vital, ending her retelling with a "golden cord" of its own. Like Theseus, lost in the labyrinth of violent death, she transcended her senseless tragedy by committing herself and us to retelling a story that led us toward a life of mutual caring and respect.

It was her tears of vulnerability as a mother that opened her to connecting with the suffering of every family, Palestinian and Israeli. She wanted her retelling and my witnessing to serve an enlivening connection through and beyond her tragedy — that the deaths of her children might promise the beginning of a respectful reconciliation with Israeli families suffering the deaths of their children — to stop the killing.

Index

A

Accidental death, 49, 211, 217–219. *See* also Traffic fatalities
Act of nature, death from, 49
Action-grounded meaning making, 101–121
   characteristics of, 106
   in clinical practice, 117–118
   hypocrisy, declarations exposing, 107–108
   literature review, 102–105
   psychological implications, 116–117
   purpose, sense of, 113–115
   self-determination, declarations of, 108–110
   truth declarations, 107–112
Adaptation. *See* Resilience
Adolescents
   research studies, 197
   restorative retelling, 275–291
Affect dysregulation, 123–142
   affect dysregulation, 131–132
   amygdala, 126–127
   anxiety, 132–133
   autonomics, 129–130
   countertransference, psychopharmacologic, 135–136
   depersonalization, 130–131
   in grief, 136–137
   hippocampus, 127–129
   hypoarousal, 130–131
   medications for, 131–132
   neuroanatomy, 126–129
   psychotropic agents, 133–134
   sensitivity of nervous system, 129–130
   short term memory, 127–129
   side effects of, 137–139
   stress, effect on emotion processing, 128–129
   suicide, 134
   target symptom, identification of, 136–137
   transference, psychopharmacologic, 134
   trauma, defined, 125–126
Aggression, with preschool children, 250–251
Amygdala, 126–127
Anger, 22
Anxiety, medications for, 132–133
Art, role of, 325–326
Autonomics, medications for, 129–130

B

Balloon exercise, cognitive behavioral therapy for childhood traumatic grief, 268
BDI. *See* Beck Depression Inventory
Beck Depression Inventory, 212
Before/after, narratives of, 323
Behavioral challenges, with preschool children, 250
Biobehavioral model, complicated grief, 158–161
Buddhism, 72

C

Case studies, 87–89, 148–149, 162–166, 170–173, 239–240, 243–244, 362–366
CBI. *See* Core Bereavement Items

CBT-CTG. See Cognitive-behavioral
    therapy for childhood
    traumatic grief
Changes in lives, dealing with, 23–25
Children, 179, 197, 211, 234, 236–237
    caregiver-child relationship,
        240–242
    cause of death, 186
    cognitive-behavioral therapy, 255
    conjoint child-parent sessions, 260
    home based therapy, 233
    interventions for parents, 175–194
    joint child-parent sessions,
        269–270
    parent-child relaxation exercise,
        243–244
    parent's perception of, 242
    preschool, 233–253
    safety issues, 52–54, 260, 264–265
    specialized intervention for,
        234–238
    traumatic grief of, 255–273
    very young, 233–253
Christianity, 74
Chronic grief, 20–21
Circle of life, cognitive behavioral
    therapy for childhood traumatic
    grief, 270
Civil liberties, 323–324
Civilians, death in combat, 50, 357–370
Clinical theories, 3–29
    anger, 22
    care, 19–23
    chronic grief, 20–21
    cognitive behavior therapy, 19
    community responses, 13
    complicated grief, 20–21
    Core Bereavement Items, 17
    costs of recovery, 19
    departing from deceased, 11–12
    engagement, 17–19
    elements of, 18
    grief, 7–23
    grief counseling, 20
    The Grief Experience
        Inventory, 17
    Grief Screening Scale, 17
    identity, 21–23

information/communication,
    12–13
Inventory of Complicated Grief, 17
liaison worker, 14–15
long-term issues, 23–25
    changes in lives, dealing with,
        23–25
    circles of individuals
        affected, 24
    justice, 24–25
    meaning, 24–25
    memorialization, 24
    nature of safer world, 25
    resolution, 24–25
malevolence, 23
memory, 22–23
normal bereavement, 5
notification of death, 10
offers of intervention, 19
outreach, 19
pathological grief, 5–6
phenomenology of
    bereavement, 7
physical survival, 9–10
psychological survival, 9–10
resilience in bereaved, 8–9
response resources, 13
role, 21–23
social issues, 21–23
support for bereavement, 14–15
Texas Revised Inventory
    of Grief, 17
therapeutic assessment, 15–17
touching, 19
transition, 15
transmission, 23
traumatic bereavement, 20
traumatic bereavements, 6–7
victim identification, 10–11
viewing, after multiple
    deaths, 12
violence, 23
vulnerability in bereaved, 8–9
Cognitive-behavioral therapy for
    childhood traumatic grief, 19,
    255–273
    affective modulation, 260–261
    ambivalent feelings, 266–267

assessment of, 257–258
balloon exercise, 268
circle of life, 270
cognitive processing, 261–262
cognitive triangle, 262
development of model, 256–257
evidence supporting, 271–272
grief-focused components, 265
grief psychoeducation, 265–266
joint child-parent sessions,
269–270
making meaning of traumatic
grief, 269
parenting skills, 260
positive memories, preserving,
267
psychoeducation, 260
redefining relationship, 268–269
relaxation, 260–261
safety issues, 264–265
structure, 259
theoretical basis, 258–259
trauma-focused components,
259–265
trauma narrative, 262–263
trauma reminders, in vivo mastery
of, 263–264
treatment closure, 270–271
Cognitive triangle, cognitive
behavioral therapy for childhood
traumatic grief, 262
Combat
civilian deaths, 50, 357–370
military deaths, 49
Commemorations, 201
Community responses, 13
Complicated grief, 20–21, 157–174
A# evidence-based individual
therapy, 157
biobehavioral model, 158–161
case studies, 162–166, 170–173
clinical features, 161–162
middle phase, 166–169
treatment, 166–173
Conjoint child-parent sessions, 260,
264–265
Coping, pragmatic, 39–40
Coping skills, 184–185, 188

Core Bereavement Items, 17
Costs of recovery, 19
Countertransference,
psychopharmacologic, 135–136
Counting method, 145–155
applications, 153
case studies, 148–149
Criminal justice system, 201
impact on grief, 201

D

Death education, with preschool
children, 244–246
Defiance, with preschool children,
250–251
Departing from deceased, 11–12
Depersonalization, medications for,
130–131
Disorganization of personal narrative,
92–93
Disrespect issues, 48–50
Disruption patterns, 36
Dissociation of personal narrative,
94–95
Dominance, narrative, 93–94
Driving, after road fatality trauma, 227
Drug/Alcohol Screening Test, 212

E

Emplotment in personal narrative, 90
Engagement, 17–19
elements of, 18
Environmental risk factors, military
communities, 296–297
Evidence-based individual therapy, 157
Evidence-based parental intervention,
175–194
bereavement consequences
treatment, 177–178
bereavement program, 180
child's cause of death, 186
coping skills, 184–185, 188

deceased children of study
    parents, 179
duration of treatment, 189–190
enrollment procedures, 178–179
evaluation by parents, 181
existential beliefs, 185–186
gender difference, 182–186
group treatment, 190
health status, 183
intervention results, 180–181
long-term consequences,
    prevention of, 188–189
longitudinal study findings, 181–182
meaning making, 183–184
mental distress, 182
modalities, 190–191
parent bereavement project, 178–192
parents' strengths, 188
participating parents, 179
PTSD symptoms, 182–183
retention, 190–191
self-esteem, 184–185
social support, 185
spiritual practices, 185–186
study recruitment, 178–179
timing of treatment, 189
Existential beliefs, 185–186

F

Faith, 65–84, 185–186, 201
    Buddhism, 72
    Christianity, 74
    dying rituals, 70–74
    graph, 80
    Hinduism, 71–72
    in immediate aftermath, 68–70
    Islam, 73–74
    Judaism, 72–73
    mental health practice, 74–75
    in moderating stress, 75–78
    multifaith death, 70–74
    Native American spirituality, 70–71
    for reconnection, 81–82
    restorative retelling, 78–81
    stress, 75–78

Family resilience, 47–63
    act of nature, death from, 49
    after intrafamily murder, 60–62
    alliance, family, 51–62
    assessment, 52
    belief systems, 55
    disrespect, 48–50
    dying of innocent civilians in
        combat, 50
    homicide, 49
    human act of commission,
        accidental death from, 49
    literature review, 50–51
    military dying of personnel in
        combat, 49
    mutual respect, 54
    nurturing behaviors, 55
    practice guidelines, 51–55
    problem-solving strategies, 55
    reinforcement, 56–60
    retaliation, 48–50
    retribution, 48–50
    sense of safety, for children, 52–54
    signs of, 54–56
    suicide, 49
    terrorism, 49
Financial compensation, September
    11th attack, 348–349
Flashbacks, with preschool children,
    249
Future studies, objectives of, 373–377

G

Gander air disaster, 298–301
Gaza, 375–377. *See also* Palestinian
    families
Gender difference, 182–186
Grief
    biobehavioral model, 158–161
    in children, 233–253, 255–273
    chronic, 20–21
    clinical theories, 7–23
    cognitive-behavioral therapy for
        children, 265
    comparison of, 347–348

complicated, 20–21, 157–174, 303
counting method, 145–155
criminal justice system impact, 201
defined, 200–201
education regarding, 244–246
evidence-based interventions, 175–194
family resilience, 47–63
The Grief Experience Inventory, 17
Grief Screening Scale, 17
imagery, 145–155
incarcerated juveniles, 275–291
Inventory of Complicated Grief, 17
Inventory of Traumatic Grief, 212, 283
leadership actions, 305
meaning through, 101–121, 269
medications, 123–142
medications for, 136–137
military communities, 295–309
narrative integration, 85–100
Oklahoma City bombing, 311–334
Palestinian families, 357–370
pathological, 5–6
posttraffic fatality, 217–232
psychoeducation, 265–266
psychopharmacologic interventions, 136–137
resilience, 31–46
restorative retelling, 195–216
September 11th, 335–355
spiritual practices, 65–84
Texas Revised Inventory of Grief, 17
traumatic, 212, 283
ways of showing, 201
Grief counseling, 20
The Grief Experience Inventory, 17
Grief Screening Scale, 17
Group treatment, 190

H

Hinduism, 71–72
Hippocampus, 127–129

Home based therapy, preschool children, 233–253
Homicide, 49, 60–62, 211, 324
Hypoarousal, medications for, 130–131
Hypocrisy, declarations exposing, 107–108

I

ICG. *See* Inventory of Complicated Grief
Identity, 21–23
Imagery, 145–155
    applications of, 153
    case studies, 148–149
Incarcerated juveniles, restorative retelling with, 275–291
    alcohol screen test, 281
    death imagery, 280, 282
    demographics, 278–280
    depression, 280, 282
    drug screen test, 281
    format, 289–290
    Impact of Events Scale-Revised, 280–281
    impact of events scale-revised, 283
    individual screening, 278
    institutional screening, 277
    intervention, 281
    outcome, 283
    Pearson correlations, 285–287
    pregroup scores, 281
    pretreatment scores, 280–281
    sample sessions, 289
    session structure, 281–282
    structure, 289–290
    subjects, 278
    traumatic grief, 280, 283
Information/communication, 12–13
Innocent victimhood, narratives of, 321
Integration of narrative, 85–100
    case studies, 87–89
    disorganization of narrative, 92–93
    dissociation, narrative, 94–95

dominance, narrative, 93–94
emplotment, 90
methods of assistance, 95–97
narrative disruption, forms of,
    92–95
thematic deconstruction, 91–92
violent loss experience, 89–92
Intrafamily murder, 60–62
Inventory of Complicated Grief, 17
Islam, 73–74
Israeli occupation, intervention with
    Palestinian families, 357–370
    case studies, 362–366
    first phase, 360
    group agenda, 367–370
    narrative case presentations,
        362–366
    participants, 359
    sample sessions, 367–370
    second phase, 361
    third phase, 361–362

J

Jabaliya, 375–377. See also Palestinian
    families
Joint child-parent sessions, 269–270
Judaism, 72–73
Justice, 24–25
Juveniles
    research studies, 197
    restorative retelling, 275–291

L

Legislation, 327
Liaison worker, 14–15
Long-term issues, 23–25
    changes in lives, dealing with,
        23–25
    circles of individuals affected, 24
    justice, 24–25
    meaning, 24–25
    memorialization, 24

nature of safer world, 25
    resolution, 24–25
Long-term recovery, September 11th
    attack, 349–352
Loss, clinical theories, 3–29

M

Malevolence, 23
Marginalized death/bereavement, in
    road fatalities, 219
Meaning, issues in, 24–25
Meaning making, 101–121, 183–184
    action-grounded, 106–107
    characteristics of, 106
    in clinical practice, 117–118
    hypocrisy, declarations exposing,
        107–108
    literature review, 102–105
    psychological implications,
        116–117
    purpose, sense of, 113–115
    self-determination, declarations
        of, 108–110
    truth declarations, 107–112
Medical staff training, for road fatality
    trauma, 221
Medications, 123–142
    affect dysregulation, 131–132
    amygdala, 126–127
    anxiety, 132–133
    autonomics, 129–130
    countertransference,
        psychopharmacologic, 135–136
    depersonalization, 130–131
    in grief, 136–137
    hippocampus, 127–129
    hypoarousal, 130–131
    neuroanatomy, 126–129
    psychotropic agents, 133–134
    sensitivity of nervous system,
        129–130
    short term memory, 127–129
    side effects of, 137–139
    stress, effect on emotion
        processing, 128–129

suicide, 134
target symptom, identification of,
    136–137
transference,
    psychopharmacologic, 134
trauma, defined, 125–126
Memorialization, 24
Memory, 22–23
    short term, medications for,
    127–129
Memory book, with preschool
    children, 247
Military, 49, 295–309
Military communities, 295–309
    art, role of, 325–326
    before/after, narratives of, 323
    befriending, 326
    civil liberties, 323–324
    community groups, 324–325
    defining, 297–298
    distress reactions, 306
    environmental risk factors for,
    296–297
    Gander air disaster, 298–301
    grief leadership actions, 305
    guilt, narratives of, 321
    innocent victimhood, narratives
    of, 321
    legislation, 327
    memorialization, 325
    mental health outcomes, 303
    military response
    models, 307–309
    Oklahoma Arts Institute,
    325–326
    Oklahoma City Bombing, 311
    Operation Solace, 302
    outreach, 314
    patriotic sacrifice, 324
    physiological/psychological
    effects, 327–328
    politics, 323–324
    psychological reactions, 316–318
    rage, 319
    religious narratives, 321–323
    rescue workers, 318
    shrines, 325
    survivor tree, 327

    trials, 327
    understanding, narratives of,
    320–321
    victimization, 318–323
Military dying of personnel
    in combat, 49
Military response models, 307–309
Multifaith death, 70–74
Murder, 49, 60–62, 211, 324
Murrah Building bombing,
    Oklahoma City, 311–334
Mutual respect, within family, 54

N

Narrative disruption, forms
    of, 92–95
Narrative integration, 85–100
    case studies, 87–89
    disorganization of narrative,
    92–93
    dissociation, narrative, 94–95
    dominance, narrative, 93–94
    emplotment, 90
    methods of assistance, 95–97
    narrative disruption, forms of,
    92–95
    thematic deconstruction, 91–92
    violent loss experience, 89–92
National Child Traumatic Stress
    Network, 197
Native American spirituality, 70–71
Nature of safer world, 25
Neuroanatomy, 126–129
Neurobiology, 123–142
    affect dysregulation, 131–132
    amygdala, 126–127
    anxiety, 132–133
    autonomics, 129–130
    countertransference,
    psychopharmacologic, 135–136
    depersonalization, 130–131
    in grief, 136–137
    hippocampus, 127–129
    hypoarousal, 130–131
    neuroanatomy, 126–129

psychotropic agents, 133–134
sensitivity of nervous system,
    129–130
short term memory, 127–129
side effects of, 137–139
stress, effect on emotion
    processing, 128–129
suicide, 134
target symptom, identification of,
    136–137
transference,
    psychopharmacologic, 134
trauma, defined, 125–126
Normal bereavement, 5
Notification of death, 10, 217–232
Num of sessions attended, 287
Nurturing behaviors, within
    family, 55

O

Offers of intervention, 19
Oklahoma Arts Institute, 325–326
    role of art, 325–326
Oklahoma City bombing, 311
    community outreach, 311–334
    role of art, 325–326
Operation Solace, military community,
    302
Outreach, 19

P

Palestinian families, intervention
    with, 357–370
    case studies, 362–366
    first phase, 360
    group agenda, 367–370
    narrative case presentations,
        362–366
    participants, 359
    sample sessions, 367–370
    second phase, 361
    third phase, 361–362

Parent bereavement project, 178–192
    bereavement program, 180
    child's cause of death, 186
    coping skills, 184–185, 188
    deceased children of study
        parents, 179
    duration of treatment, 189–190
    enrollment procedures, 178–179
    evaluation by parents, 181
    existential beliefs, 185–186
    gender difference, 182–186
    group treatment, 190
    health status, 183
    intervention results, 180–181
    long-term consequences,
        prevention of, 188–189
    longitudinal study findings,
        181–182
    meaning making, 183–184
    mental distress, 182
    modalities, 190–191
    parents' strengths, 188
    participating parents, 179
    PTSD symptoms, 182–183
    retention, 190–191
    self-esteem, 184–185
    social support, 185
    spiritual practices, 185–186
    study recruitment, 178–179
    timing of treatment, 189
Pathological grief, 5–6
Patriotic sacrifice, 324
Phenomenology of bereavement, 7
Physical survival, 9–10
Pragmatic coping, 39–40
Preschool children
    aggression, 250–251
    assessment categories, 240
    behavioral challenges, 250
    calm, 243–244
    caregiver/child relationship, 240–242
    case studies, 239–240, 243–244
    connecting with caregiver,
        238–240
    death education, 244–246
    defiance, 250–251
    family changes, 249–250
    fears, 246

flashback, 249
goal setting, 242–243
history of parent-child
  relationship, 241
home based therapy with,
  233–253
memory book, 247
parent-child relationship,
  241–242
parent's perception of child, 242
referrals, 237
relaxation, 243–244
repetitive behaviors, 248
restorative memories, 247
speaking openly about death,
  245–246
special events, 251–252
specialized intervention for,
  234–238
speech difficulties, 250
traumatic narrative, 248–249
Psychoeducation, cognitive behavioral
  therapy for childhood traumatic
  grief, 260
Psychological survival, 9–10
Psychopharmacology, 123–142
  affect dysregulation, 131–132
  amygdala, 126–127
  anxiety, 132–133
  autonomics, 129–130
  countertransference, 135–136
  depersonalization, 130–131
  in grief, 136–137
  hippocampus, 127–129
  hypoarousal, 130–131
  neuroanatomy, 126–129
  psychotropic agents, 133–134
  sensitivity of nervous system,
    129–130
  short term memory, 127–129
  side effects of, 137–139
  stress, effect on emotion
    processing, 128–129
  suicide, 134
  target symptom, identification of,
    136–137
  transference, 134
  trauma, defined, 125–126

Psychotropic agents, 133–134. See also
  Medications
Purpose, sense of, 113–115

R

Range of individuals affected, 24
Recovery, resilience, distinguished,
  33–35
Referrals, with preschool children, 237
Relaxation, with preschool children,
  243–244
Repetitive behaviors, with preschool
  children, 248
Resilience, 8–9, 31–46
  after September 11th terrorist
    attack, 40–42
  disruption patterns, 36
  factors leading to, 38–40
  family, 47–63
  flexible adaptation, 38–39
  pragmatic coping, 39–40
  recovery, distinguished, 33–35
Resolution, 24–25
Response resources, 13
Restorative memories, preschool
  children, 247
Restorative retelling, 78–81, 195–216
  adolescents, 197
  agenda, 205–208
  criminal death support group,
    200–202, 206–207, 211
    agenda, 200–201
  described, 200
  dynamics of, 198–200
  group support, 207–208
  incarcerated juveniles, 275–291
  protection story, 198
  reenactment story, 198
  remorse story, 198
  retaliation story, 198
  separation distress, 199–200
Retaliation, 48–50
Retribution, 48–50
Revised Impact of Events Scale, 212
Rituals for dying, 70–74

Road fatalities, 217–232
    driving, 227
    family services, 219
    impact on professionals, 227–229
    intervention continuity model, 222
    joining support groups, 223
    marginalized death/bereavement,
        219
    medical staff training, 221
    posttraumatic growth, 228–229
    secondary traumatization,
        227–228
    self-help group, 226
        activating group, 224
        effectiveness, 223–227
        follow-up, 226–227
        group characteristics, 225
        intervention method, 224
        launching, 226–227
        pregroup screening, 224
        preparing members for, 226
        reaching out, 225
        recruitment, 224
        themes, 225
    short-term groups, 223–224
    therapeutic continuity model,
        221–227
    therapeutic intervention, 220
Role, 21–23

S

Safety issues, for children, 52–54, 260,
    264–265
Sample sessions, 289, 367–370
Self-care, 201
Self-determination, declarations of,
    108–110
Self-esteem, 184–185
Sense of safety, for children, 52–54
Sensitivity of nervous system, 129–130
September 11th terrorist attacks, 335
    clinical interventions, 341–346
    dying narrative, 342–344
    effectiveness, 337–338
    financial compensation, 348–349

group intervention
    assessment, 339
    challenges, 346–353
    clinical intervention, 341–346
group structure, 338–341
group treatment model, 340–341
identification process, 349–352
long-term recovery, 349–352
memories, connecting to, 341
military mental health
    response, 302
ongoing care, 353–354
ongoing care for group members,
    353–354
outreach, 339
public health approach, 305
public nature of attack, 348
resilience after, 40–42
retelling process, 344
screening, 339
short-term group, 335–355
treatment model, 340–341
unique challenges, 346–353
vicarious trauma, 352–353
Short term memory, medications for,
    127–129
Shrines, 325
Side effects of medications, 137–139
Signs of resilience, 54–56
Social issues, 21–23
Speaking openly about death, with
    preschool children, 245–246
Speech difficulties, with preschool
    children, 250
Spiritual practices, 65–84, 185–186, 201
    Buddhism, 72
    Christianity, 74
    dying rituals, 70–74
    graph, 80
    Hinduism, 71–72
    in immediate aftermath, 68–70
    Islam, 73–74
    Judaism, 72–73
    mental health practice, 74–75
    in moderating stress, 75–78
    multifaith death, 70–74
    Native American spirituality,
        70–71

for reconnection, 81–82
restorative retelling, 78–81
stress, 75–78
Stress
effect on emotion processing, 128–129
spiritual practices, 75–78
Structure of session, 281–282
Suicide, 49, 134, 211
Support for bereavement, 14–15
Survivor tree, 327

T

Target symptom, identification of, 136–137
Terrorist attacks. *See* Oklahoma City bombing; Palestinian families; September 11th terrorist attack
Texas Revised Inventory of Grief, 17
Thematic deconstruction, personal narrative, 91–92
Therapeutic assessment, 15–17
Touching, 19
Traffic fatalities, 217–232
driving, 227
family services, 219
impact on professionals, 227–229
intervention continuity model, 222
joining support groups, 223
marginalized death/bereavement, 219
medical staff training, 221
posttraumatic growth, 228–229
secondary traumatization, 227–228
self-help group, 226
activating group, 224

effectiveness, 223–227
follow-up, 226–227
group characteristics, 225
intervention method, 224
launching, 226–227
pregroup screening, 224
preparing members for, 226
reaching out, 225
recruitment, 224
themes, 225
short-term groups, 223–224
therapeutic continuity model, 221–227
therapeutic intervention, 220
Transference, psychopharmacologic, 134
Transition, 15
Transmission, 23
Trauma, defined, 125–126
Traumatic stress reactions, 7
Trials, 327
TRIG. *See* Texas Revised Inventory of Grief
Truth declarations, 107–112

U

UCLA PTSD Index for DSM-IV. *See* Grief Screening Scale

V

Victim identification, 10–11
Viewing, after multiple deaths, 12
Violence, 23
Vulnerability in bereaved, 8–9